MW00915726

BECOME A MOVIE DIRECTOR AND/OR MOVIE PRODUCER

A Step-by-Step Handbook & Course In

Directing, and Producing Movies,
and in Financing, Making and Selling
Independent, Low Budget, Micro-Budget,
And No-Budget Movies

By Edward Hunt

ACKNOWLEDGMENTS

A very special thanks to my sister and her husband who helped me when I needed help.

Thanks to Skip Press for his editorial skill and for helping to make this book what it is.

I would also like to thank anyone who ever helped me in any way during the process of making the dozens of movies I've made and worked on over the years, and in doing the research that turned into this book.

TABLE OF CONTENTS

Preface

What's In This Book

Part One: Directing Movies

Part Two: Background and Brief History of Independent Low Budget Movies

Part Three: Making Independent Movies And Being A Movie Producer

v

The purpose of this book is to aid or help people who want to become movie directors or movie producers, or people who are in the process of becoming movie director or producers. This book should also be of use to those who want to be better movie directors or movie producers, and people who are working on, or making low budget independent movies, and are doing such jobs as assistant director, second assistant director, production manager, line producer, co-producer, associate producer, or even production assistant.

I have directed and/or produced and/or written at least ten professional feature length, professionally distributed movies. On some of these films I was the director, the writer or co–writer, and one of the producers. Nine of these movies received distribution in theaters before being distributed in the home video, TV, and foreign markets. One of my movies, *Starship Invasions*, which starred Christopher Lee and Robert Vaughn, was produced independently and was distributed theatrically by Warner Bros. and was sold to and shown on NBC in prime time, and also shown repeatedly in TV syndication. Two of my movies, *Plague* and *UFOs Are Real*, received significant awards. *UFOs Are Real* was shown repeatedly on the Fox network in a prime time Sunday evening slot that *The X-Files* later occupied for many years. I've been told that my film *The Brain* (in addition to being in the horror section of most video stores in North America at one time or another) has become a "cult classic" in Canada where it is repeatedly shown on a horror movie cable TV channel. Most of my movies have received worldwide distribution in several media.

I've made professionally distributed movies on budgets as small as $23,000, shot in 35mm color, as well as on a budget of almost $1,000,000. I've shot professionally distributed movies on shooting schedules of 12 and 13 days, and on schedules as long as 70 days. I have also directed several more movies, long and short, with much smaller budgets and shorter shooting schedules that the movies that are on my resume. I have negotiated distribution personally for some of my movies and I have signed their distribution contracts myself.

I have done such filmmaking jobs as:

> 1st assistant director
> 2nd unit director
> Editor
> Sound FX recordist
> Sound FX editor
> Dialogue and music editor
> Negative cutter
> Boom person
> Trailer and promo editor
> Still photographer
> Model maker
> Animation sculptor
> Set dresser
> Art department production assistant

Film booker
Camera operator
Cinematographer
Camera assistant
Gaffer
Consultant
Producer
Co-producer
Screenwriter

In other words, I am very experienced in all phases of low budget independent movie production. I have seen many people achieve the opportunity to make a movie on a low or limited budget. Very many of them fumbled or squandered opportunities; some squandered them very badly. Often, the disasters that resulted were unnecessary, and usually could have been prevented by basic proper preparation. Toward that end, consider this quote from the ancient Chinese philosopher, Confucius:

> *The outcome of all contests is determined by previous preparation. Without such preparation, failure is assured.*

I have a copy of that quote on the front page of my director's notebook, and I read it every morning of pre-production and production.

One of the major purposes of this book is to present some of the things that I learned the hard way, and offer some advice about those types of situations so that people who read this book and learn from it need not also learn these "lessons" *the hard, expensive, and embarrassing way that most filmmakers do*.

Very few people would think that they were qualified to fly an airplane simply because they'd ridden in one as a passenger many times. Very few would consider themselves qualified to perform surgery without a serious course of *study* and *practice*. Very few people would consider themselves qualified to drive a motor vehicle in heavy traffic or on a freeway without a serious amount of study and practice. Over very many years, however, I have not noticed any shortage of people who think that they can write and/or direct or produce movies without *proper preparation*, which includes study and practice. Many of these people think that they can direct a movie simply because they, acting only as a viewer seeking to be entertained, not as a serious student avidly studying and analyzing, have casually watched many movies. Many of these people have never even watched one movie several times and studied it. Many of them never engaged in any serious program of study and practice before attempting to direct a movie. In every case that I observed, this unpreparedness ended in bad, very bad, or horrific (and even tragic) results.

Some people think they will be good directors simply because they have strong opinions and prejudices about which movies were good and which were not, or because they can criticize successful movies and dismiss these successful movies because they did not match the would–be director's personal tastes. They felt that they were automatically more qualified to direct than any director they criticized. In each instance, these people I encountered found out the hard way that being able to criticize a pilot's "bumpy landing" does not automatically make one more able to fly a plane than a professional pilot. Usually, such a realization in the film arena was learned in a very costly, embarrassing, and emotionally and financially painful way. Simply having a lot of opinions and prejudices about movies, and having seen a lot of movies, is not a substitute for *study* and *practice* and *knowing what you are doing*. When a would-be director is on the set stumbling and fumbling around, trying to direct a movie, and blaming others constantly to cover the obvious fact that they are not qualified or prepared to direct a movie, it is rare that such a person will recognize what is destroying their efforts is *lack of preparation*.

This seems so obvious it does not seem necessary to state it, but it is necessary because any person who has not gone through a process of study and practice of some sort, whether self-taught, or in a formal academic setting, or by working in related fields like acting, writing, or camera operation, or being a professional movie critic writing published reviews and movie analyses, or making short movies only should *not* expect to be able to direct a feature film when they have not taken any steps to *learn* how to direct a movie. They would not expect to be able to drive a car, fly a plane, practice medicine or surgery, or law without learning how to do these activities. The process of becoming a professional is exactly the same when learning to make movies.

Sadly, there seems to never bee a shortage of unqualified, unprepared lemming-like would-be director and producers ready, willing, and anxious to charge off a cliff trying to make a movie, even if they have no real knowledge of how movies are actually made. There is no sane reason to believe that such want-to-bes have the knowledge of how to make a professional movie of any commercial or artistic value.

Far more people around the world are performing surgery, practicing law or medicine, flying planes, or driving motor vehicles than are successfully directing, producing, or writing movies. There is a lot to learn about these activities. Directing, producing, and writing movies are *not* easy professions to enter or in which to succeed. Some very smart, very talented, very hard-working, very determined, very disciplined, very experienced, and very well-trained people make up the main body of people succeeding in these professions and certainly comprise the upper layers of these professions. Competition is tough in the movie business!

Anyone who walks onto a movie set and thinks that he or she can direct a movie without serious study and practice is like someone who hops into the cockpit of an airplane and tries to fly it without proper preparation. They will virtually always get the same result as an untrained pilot trying to fly a plane. People are not born knowing how to direct a movie. One way or another, they either learn how to do it, or they don't. The legendary literary giant Goethe (the author of *Faust*) said: "He who does not know the mechanical side of a craft cannot judge it." I would embellish that quote a bit and say that he or she who does not know and understand the mechanical side of movie directing may never get a chance to show what they could do with the artistic side of directing. They may just sink into an ugly quicksand of self-induced confusion or be so self-entrapped and harassed, overwhelmed, frustrated, and mechanically inept that artistic expression in the form of a well-made movie is impossible or out of reach for them.

Here is a relevant quote from an "old-time" veteran director: "It helps a lot it you know what the hell you're doin'." Facts are facts, and facts matter. Reality is what reality is. Non-reality no matter how much it's propounded does not work. Writing the word "director" on a camera slate next to a person's name, or on a staff and crew list next to someone's name or saying they are the movie's director does *not* automatically make that person, *in reality*, a *real, functioning, qualified, effective movie director*.

There are five basic levels of preparation a person usually should accomplish before they are really prepared to walk onto a movie set and direct a scene, much less a full movie. For a person to be qualified to direct a scene or a movie, a director needs to be *generally qualified* and prepared. This means that *generally* they know what the director's job is, and how to do it. This sets up several areas of necessary knowledge for making a movie.

First, a director's level of preparation can include a lot of specific levels of preparation and knowledge that can be acquired in various planned or unplanned ways, either by intense study involving very focused learning or they can be absorbed in more ambient ways, such as by being an actor for many years watching and working with many directors and camera operators. These aspects of being prepared to direct a movie are covered in this book, and in the "Learn It Yourself Course" in the back of this book.

Secondly, a director needs to be prepared to direct the *type* of movie that they are attempting to direct. Directing various genres can require special study or experience and preparation. Someone who is prepared to direct comedy may *not* also necessarily be prepared to direct horror or serious drama. Someone who can direct horror or action may not necessarily be prepared to direct comedy. Individual movie genres usually have specific conventions, and specific types of *commercial content* that matter intensely within that movie's genre.

Remember this: *Different movie genres to some degree often have different audiences.*

The director needs to know how to engage, use and satisfy the specific "desires to see" of the actual audiences that patronize the genre of the movie the director is making. Thus, a director needs to be *genre-prepared*. Directors need to be expert in the genre of the movie that they are attempting to make.

Tertiarily, a director needs to be prepared to direct *the movie they are directing*. They need to be very familiar with the movie's script, its characters, its themes, and the opportunities in the script to create emotion in an audience or viewer, and the movie's opportunities to build audience interest in an emotional involvement with the movie's characters and story, and with the movie's opportunities to provide the viewer or audience with genre-appropriate, viewer-pleasing and satisfying commercial content! A director needs to be the expert on the script they are directing and the movie that they are making. In some instances and circumstances, the director may even be responsible for "fixing" the script or its weaknesses or defects, or rewriting the script, or for shooting scenes, sequences or shots that are not in the script.

Fourth, a director needs to be very prepared to direct the actual scenes and shots that they are shooting. This may involve storyboards and shot lists.

Fifth, a director needs to be prepared to understand the audience for the movie that they are directing. They need an awareness of that audience, and what that audience *wants to see* and why they would pay money to see a movie. The director needs to respect that audience and understand that he or she is actually *working for that audience.*

Alfred Hitchcock said that some directors direct the actors and some direct the camera, but really good directors direct the audience's attention. I've witnessed people who had the opportunity to direct a movie who walk onto the set totally unprepared to direct a movie on *all* of the levels of preparation mentioned above. Others were unprepared in a serious way on one or more of these levels. This always caused bad results. Some times, it caused tragic, ugly, unnecessarily, wasteful, disastrous, awful, painful, or worthless results.

There is an American slang saying about the vital importance of preparation similar to the previously mentioned statement from Confucius. It goes: "Proper preparation prevents piss poor performance." This book offers people a chance to properly prepare to director or produce a movie. Unprepared directors or partially prepared directors rarely create good or valuable movies. They almost always cause atrocities that do not receive professional distribution or deserve it. Thus, the vast majority of independent, low budget, micro-budget or no budget movies that have been made or will be made will *never* receive any significant real commercial distribution, and they will not deserved any real distribution.

What is even more sobering to contemplate is that a very large percentage of these indie movies are doomed to *never* receive any real distribution before their script is completely written! Long before their scenes are written or shot, the majority of indie movies being made are doomed to receive no real distribution by a defect or mistake, or omission that is so basic that it undermines these movies even before the camera's roll. In this book, I will discuss this basic defect, mistake, or omission that cripples so many indie movies. I will also offer a method to protect against this sort of doom. I will discuss this basic defect, mistake, or omission in great detail and offer a very clear, simple to follow path to avoid being a victim of this malady.

This book offers a lot of clear, practical, useful advice and a clearly marked path to become a movie director and/or producer, and specific guidance in how to make an independent movie that at least has a chance of being sold and becoming successful in the world marketplace. It covers everything in detail: how to run a set, how to get a script to a star, how to budget a movie, how to make a distribution deal, and how to get your movie financed.

Most of all, this book really tells you how to *not* let the difficult struggle that it takes to make a low budget or micro-budget indie movie turn into your own personal one-way express ticket to filmmaker hell! Many first-time directors are also last-time directors. Don't let that happen to you. The "Learn It Yourself" movie-making directing and producing course near the back of this book can go a long way toward helping the reader to avoid the ugly and often unnecessary fate of being a first-time/last-time director. Welcome to your solution.

WHAT'S IN THIS BOOK

This book is intended for people who are *serious* about becoming movie directors and/or producers. It is for people who are willing to work very, very hard and are willing to diligently study and think seriously and learn in order to achieve those goals. *None* of this book has been "dumbed down" to appeal to a wide audience of people who forever will be "want-to-bes." This is not a book for dilettantes, dummies, idiots, or a broad general public who simply want to dip their toes in the ocean of the movie business. Certain places in this book are very detailed, repetitive, and even technical because they parallel the actual tasks of directing and making movies, and are why I think the book can be so useful for *people who are actually going to make movies*. These people that will actually make low budget indie movies are the people for whom this book is written. It is for people who want to navigate successfully across the ocean of the movie business, not just for people who want to timidly test the biz's exciting but treacherous and tumultuous waters.

It requires attention, willingness to study, and a desire to learn to get through this book, but it will not short change those who are serious and willing to work hard to achieve their goals. This book is organized in ten sections. The Introduction, which I hope you've read, and the Preface that you are now reading is its first section.

The second section is <u>Part One: Directing Movies</u>. It is intended to be of use to directors regardless of the size of the budget of the movie. It contains, among other things, some useful "tricks of the trade" and workable methods of doing key parts of the director's job.

The next section is <u>Part Two: Background and Brief History of Independent Low Budget Movies</u>.

This is followed by <u>Part Three: Making and Producing Independent Movies</u>. It contains a lot of detailed, practical, and useful advice, with "how to" suggestions and "Do's" and "Don'ts" related to independent, low budget, and micro-budget movie production. It outlines a detailed step-by-step workable process and method of making indie movies.

<u>Part Four: About Budgeting and Financing</u> is logically followed by <u>Part Five: Selling Independent Movies</u>. Both those sections are based on my own personal experiences doing these actions. Part Five has a very different and much more reality-based approach to this vital subject than any other book that touches upon this subject.

<u>Part Six</u> is a short essay on the vitally important role of the professional storyteller in a culture, while <u>Part Seven</u> is a Learn It Yourself course to becoming a movie director or producer. It is clearly laid out to help an aspiring filmmaker acquire the experience, skills, and knowledge necessary to be able to get a movie made.

<u>Part Eight</u> is a guide to various pathways to getting into the movie business and to becoming a professional director or producer. <u>Part Nine</u> of this book is entitled "Aim Higher" and offers practical advice on making better films.

At the end of the book there is a section covering awards, recognition, and some production material from one of my movies, *The Brain*.

What this book cannot supply is: talent, charisma, discipline, a willingness to work very hard and long hours, tenacity, stamina, patience, wisdom, knowledge of human nature, knowledge of movies, innate leadership potential, artistic sensibility, or a charming or influential personality. All of those qualities are valuable to a director, and while this book cannot imbue you with those qualities, it can help a would-be director properly prepare and make the most of the gifts and abilities and artistic talents, insights, and skills he or she possesses or can acquire.

The outcome of all contests is determined by previous preparation, without such preparation, failure is assured. Preparation cannot guarantee success but lack of preparation can almost guarantee failure.

In the last 1950s and 1960s, the legendary moviemaker, director, and screenwriter Jean Luc Godard said that movies will not be truly an art form until the costs of making a movie approximate the costs of pencil and paper, or paints and canvas. That day has not yet completely arrived, but it may not be that far in the future. It is much closer than it was fifty years ago when Godard made that statement. Very recently, a movie entitled *Paranormal Activity* was reportedly made for $15,000 and was picked up by Paramount Pictures for distribution in U.S. theaters. It grossed over $151,000,000 worldwide and was #1 at the box office two weeks in a row in its initial U.S. theatrical release. $15,000 in 2009 money was a lot closer to the costs of pencil and paper or paints and canvas in the 1950s, compared to the costs of making a movie at that time.

Robert Rodriguez's movie *El Mariachi* was shot in 16mm color for $8,000. The movie *Clerks* was shot in 16mm by Kevin Smith and friends for $35,000. Many years before, *Night of the Living Dead* by George Romero was made for $114,000. Spike Lee's *She's Gotta Have It* was made for $100,000. And then there's video. Not long before I wrote this book, a movie made on video by a film school graduate for $12,500 was shown at the Sundance Film Festival.

The lowest budget film that I know of that received a commercial distribution was *A Polish Vampire in Burbank*. Shot in 8mm color and transferred to video by Mark Pirro, it was very profitably distributed in the home video and cable TV markets. The movie's cost was $2,500. Interestingly enough, the limiting factor in the film was not that it was shot in 8mm or its low budget or production values, or even the quality of the acting. It had an "OK" script for a low budget horror comedy and was well enough made, but it was not *a breakout movie* like others mentioned above because the script quality did not match those other movies.

In 2008, *Once*, a movie musical shot in Ireland for $100,000, won the Best Song Oscar and ended up with worldwide distribution. Its success was reminiscent of Roger Corman's classic *Little Shop of Horrors* (1960), which was reportedly shot in two days. Corman movies were almost always shot on a very small budget.

All the movies mentioned here except *Once* were shot on film, and virtually all of them could be made more cheaply if they had been shot on video, which is increasingly taking over with indie filmmakers. In an interview on the re-release of *Pulp Fiction*, Quentin Tarantino said that if he had not directed a movie and wanted to become a director he would shoot on video. Robert Rodriguez has some very interesting and compelling things to say about the merits of shooting on video in his commentary on *Once Upon A Time In Mexico* and on other commentaries about his movies. I strongly recommend viewing all of Rodriguez's comments on that DVD. Studying commentaries like that are part of the necessary education of any beginning or even contemporary director, and are prerequisite to accurately considering the merits of shooting on video versus shooting on film.

The legendary filmmaker Roger Corman reportedly said that whether you have a huge crew, lots of equipment, and a multi-million dollar budget and are shooting on a studio backlot, or if you are holding the camera yourself in a back alley with almost no budget, *it all comes down to an actor or actors in front of a lens*. I would expand that statement to say that it also comes down to a director and a script. It's amazing what directors operating on tiny budgets have accomplished in indie movies. Have you seen all the movies I've mentioned here? How about *Coffee and Cigarettes, Dancer in the Dark, Breaking the Waves, Night of the Living Dead, Kentucky Fried Movie, Texas Chainsaw Massacre, Hollywood Blvd., Faces, Targets, Breathless, Los Olvidados, The Blair Witch Project, Simon in the Desert, Halloween, Easy Rider, The Evil Dead, Memento, Roger And Me*, or *Sex, Lies and Videotape*? The directors of all those movies had a good or excellent script and did their jobs as directors superbly, despite limited (and in some cases, very limited) resources. These movies had good or excellent scripts that were turned into movies that captivated significant segments of the movie going public. Those directors developed their vision into shots and sounds that connected with people deeply.

It is also remarkable and interesting to me to note that in many cases, enormous resources including some of the biggest movie stars can be of *very little use* and can deliver very little satisfaction to moviegoers when these resources are not combined with a good or excellent concept, script or story, particularly when combined with a director that cannot turn a script or story into a vision that connects with audiences.

Legendary director Fritz Lang (*Metropolis* and other classics) said: "In the script it's written, and on the screen it's a picture, motion picture it's called."

That's the director's job, to take something that's written and make it into a motion picture. Sometimes the director operates with enormous resources and support and a clear mandate to *make their movie*. Sometimes the director operates with limited or tiny resources and no real support. The quality and value of the final movie is usually determined mostly by the quality of what was written by the screenwriter, or screenwriter/director, and how well or how poorly the director does his or her job of turning what was written into a motion picture, not necessarily by how many resources were available to the director, or the production.

Decades ago, many people who now choose to become filmmakers would have been novelists, playwrights, painters, short story writers, sculptors, stage directors, poets, architects, and other artistic professions. People can still be all those things, but there has never been a better time to become a movie director and/or producer. Many art critics have commented on how movies have become the "pre-eminent" or most important art form of our time because of the cultural dominance of film and TV. As a social force and art form. This is only likely to increase as the

21st century proceeds. Filmmaking can be one of the most exciting and fulfilling forms of artistic expression possible. This is particularly true for a writer/director. One way to become a movie director is to make and/or direct a "break-out" independent movie. This route is how Sam Raimi, Robert Rodriguez, Quentin Tarantino, Stanley Kubrick, Kevin Smith, Wes Craven, George Romero, John Landis, Jean Luc Godard, Francois Truffaut, Peter Bogdonavich, Luis Bunuel, and many other great directors launched their careers.

There's a joke about God showing up at a Hollywood party. Someone asks God what it's like to be God. He replies, "Oh, it's OK. I have a job I enjoy, and have a lot of fun being God, but what I really want to do is direct."

God in this joke isn't alone. Your competitors are out there, and many of them are very smart. Many of them are studying making movies very seriously, and began their quest toward being a director or producer at a very early age. Many of them (possibly you, too) have already made short movies. Well, whatever your situation, good luck! I say that because people largely make their own luck. As the poet Emily Dickinson said: "Luck is not chance, it's toil; fortune's expensive smile is earned."

I hope this book helps you make some luck.

PART ONE

DIRECTING MOVIES

CHAPTER ONE:
TWO VERY DIFFERENT DEFINITIONS
OF THE MOVIE DIRECTOR'S JOB

Here are two very different definitions of the movie director's job:

1. The minimal or essential or necessary director's job is to tell the actors where to stand, whether to move or not, and where to move or not, and to coach the actors' performance and tell the cinematographer where to put the camera (roughly or exactly) and whether the camera will move or not, and the type of shot, close-up, medium, long shot, etc. The director might also discuss the exact framing of the shot. The minimal director then rehearses the actors, decides when to begin filming or videotaping, and says "Action" or "Cut" and "Print" at the appropriate time. That is a pretty basic bottom line definition and description of the job of what I call "Minimal Director." Some directors even out-source some parts of this Minimal Director's job to the cinematographer, or actors, or others.

2. The second definition of a movie director's job is that the director creates a world on a screen. This director's job is to, by whatever means necessary, make that director's world, that exists only on a screen, so real, interesting, entertaining, and compelling that the movie viewer becomes so interested and captivated by that world that the viewer mentally enters that world and cares so much about that world and the characters who populate it that the viewer, for the duration of the movie, no longer thinks about his or her own real life. A movie made by this type of director causes an audience to mentally dwell in and become emotionally involved with that director's creative world and its story. This "director created world" is ruled by the director's views of life, money, love, good, and evil. This second definition of the movie director's job is what I call the "author of the movie" definition of the director's job. This "author of the movie" definition of the director's job literally involves the director in thousands of decisions that make a movie what it is. Some of these decisions can be as major and as drastic as radical changes in the script, or adding to the movie new locations that were not in the script, or shifts in the movie's tone, or literally creating scenes that were not in the script from storyboards, or rewriting and reworking dialog with the actors in rehearsals or on set. John Ford, the legendary director of many of the most classic Western movies ever made, would often discard the dialogue written in scripts that studios gave him and he'd ask the actors "Isn't that the worst piece of crap you ever read? How would you say that in your own words?" And to another actor, "How would you respond in your own words?" He would rework the dialogue so that it felt *real* and *natural* to the actors and would be real and natural on the movie screen when it was shot and shown to movie audiences. On other movies, like *Stagecoach*, Ford worked with a writer he respected, Dudley Nichols, and they outlined the script together. Ford bought the story upon which the movie was based; he would have Nichols on the set and if anything in the script needed fixing or changing, he and Nichols would do it together on the set.

Here's a story that illustrates the power of the "author of the movie" director. John Ford was reportedly a few pages behind schedule, and the studio brass sent a flunky down to the set to harass Ford about being behind schedule. When the flunky harassed Ford, the director looked at the flunky like he was some sort of rodent, and looked through the script and found a few pages that he didn't admire that much. He tore them out of the script, handed them to the flunky, and said, "Give these to your bosses and tell them *now* I'm on schedule!"

The equally legendary movie director and producer Howard Hawks made a point of deliberately not shooting dialogue as it was written in the movie's script. He would bring out a long yellow legal pad and ask the actors to rework each line of dialogue, as they would say it in their own words. The dialogue that would be shot was the dialogue handwritten on the legal pad, *not* the dialogue in the script that a screenwriter wrote. I saw Hawks' comment in an interview that he didn't know whether the dialogue they came up with on the set was really better than the dialogue in the script or it just seemed that way because it was new and fresh. Movie critics seem to know. Repeatedly, Hawks' movies were complimented and admired by critics for their brisk, snappy, realistic dialogue.

You can look a long time in John Ford's and Howard Hawks' movies and you won't find a single dialogue scene that does not *work*! That is *not* because the writers who wrote the scripts that they shot never wrote a bad dialogue scene or a dialogue scene that did not work. Ford, Hawks, and many other directors did not take any writing credit for rewriting or changing or outlining scripts. They just correctly considered it part of their job as directors. Ford and Hawks were definitely "authors" of their movies and they obeyed the two central golden axioms that apply to that type of director who enjoys that kind of mandate. These axioms are:

1. No matter what's been written or what conditions or excuses exist, the good director always puts something good on the screen.

2. A good director makes a good movie!

"Author of the movie" directors have a lot of power, and a lot of responsibility. If their movie is bad or does not please the public They are held responsible and blamed. They can't point the finger of blame at the writer. They committed to shoot the script and they had the power to change it. If the movie is good, and it works and audiences love it, they get a lot of credit. Some times they even get credit that actually should have gone to writers, but that is a double-edged sword that I will discuss in detail in another book.

Some times, when a minimal director is hired, they are told to shoot every word in the script exactly as written. Occasionally that kind of language is even in their directing contract, or is enforced on them by a producer who has the power to fire them. Some times, a script is just so damned good or written by a writer of such prestige or power that the script does not need or get any changes and the director just feels that on this movie it is the director's job to shoot the script exactly as written. "Perfect scripts" are rare, but they do occasionally exist.

Alfred Hitchcock is one of the strongest and most intense "author of the movie" directors ever. Hitchcock and his wife often wrote a detailed treatment laying out the proposed structure of a script before they turned the story over to a screenwriter to write the script. Hitchcock and/or his wife rarely took screen credit for this writing. Mostly they did not. If the screenwriting did not meet with Hitchcock's approval, he and his wife would make extensive and detailed notes for a rewrite and commission another screenwriter to rewrite the script in line with their rewritten notes. Hitchcock directed the writing of many of his movies. *Vertigo* (widely considered his ultimate masterpiece and one of his most personal movies) was written exactly by this method. Hitchcock directed the development of the *Vertigo* story, based on a novel, and he also directed the writing of the several drafts of its scripts. An "author of the movie" director often has major involvement in the creation of the movie's script, either by writing it or co-writing it himself or herself or rewriting the script when it becomes a shooting script, or by guiding and directing the writing of the script, or even originating the movie's story, concept, or acting as a de facto story editor. Directors that I characterize as "minimal" or "essential" typically shoot a script that is written by someone else and typically they shoot it exactly, or almost exactly, or largely as written. Participation in the creation and perfection of a movie's script is usually something that separates an "author of the movie" director from a minimal or near minimal director. It is, however, usually not the only important difference between these two types of directors or directing circumstances.

Hitchcock exemplified the "author of the movie" director, not just in his serious involvement with the creation and perfection of the movie's scripts. He would call for the exact millimeter of the lens that he'd want on the camera for each shot, and for the exact framing of each shot. He'd tell the editor during the final states of editing to remove a single frame or few frames from various edits. He supervised the editing to the frame, and the camera to the exact millimeter of the lens. Many minimal directors never even discuss or care what millimeter of a lens the cinematographer uses, and might not even show up in the editing room, let alone guide the editor to improve specific edits.

The question of "What does a director actually do?" is at the heart of this chapter. The real answer to that question is that different directors on different movies do and some times don't do different things.

What a director does on a movie depends upon or is influenced by, to a large degree, what the director wants to do, is able to do, is allowed to do, or has to do to get the movie made, or to make a good movie. Let's take a look at the legendary movie director Stanley Kubrick's early career. When Kubrick was very young, he became a successful still photographer. He entered the arena of moviemaking by making three short films in the early 1950s before he was 25 years old. When he was 25 he made his first feature film, *Fear And Desire*, which was produced independently with money borrowed from a lettuce grower in Orange County, California, in 35mm black and white, in 1953. Kubrick did virtually every major artistic job on this first feature. He operated the camera, was the cinematographer, writer, editor, sound editor, production manager, casting person, de fact art director, as well as director and producer. He was, without question, the author of that movie. Kubrick's next movie was *The Killer's Kiss*, also made independently two years later, and again it was made from Kubrick's own script. He was that movie's author, its director of photography, and editor. On Kubrick's third feature film, *The Killing*, he surrounded himself with professionals. The movie was based on a novel, *Clean Break*, by Lionel White and additional dialogue was added by Jim Thompson. Kubrick's director of photography was the great Lucien Ballard, who shot *The Wild Bunch, The Ballad of Cable Hogue*, and many other fine films. Kubrick partnered with James B. Harris to produce his third film. *The Killing* is Kubrick's first really good movie. His fourth film, made when he was 29 in 1957, is *Paths of Glory*, which is an absolute masterpiece. Many feel it is Kubrick's best. It starred Kirk Douglas, who was also the movie's producer. Kubrick was the co–screenwriter, again with Jim Thompson. It is one of the best, if not the best, anti-war movies ever made, and features what is probably Kirk Douglas' best performance in any movie, ranking with the most superb screen performances of all-time. Kubrick is clearly the movie's author. His personal and unique genius and point of view on life, war, authority, politics, good and evil, and his particularly acidic, ironic but unpleasant truthful insight is clearly on view throughout the movie, and is imbedded in the movie's spectacularly and superbly realized details. *Paths of Glory* is a work of virtually perfect moviemaking and genius. Its ending is one of the very best, most powerful and meaningful scenes that exists in any movie. Over 50 years after it was made, *Paths of Glory* does not seem the least bit dated. If anything, it may still be a bit ahead of its time. Its dialogue and acting are as real and natural as any modern movie. It is as relevant as the latest report from the Afghanistan war. *Paths of Glory* is an "art movie" that is not the least bit arty. It is simply a great piece of true and major art.

The movie's distributor did not understand the film, however, probably because it was so ahead of its time. The 1950s were *not* an anti-war decade. The film was distributed as though it was a routine post World War II "guts and glory" war movie. Its reception was lukewarm. Its cost was not large. It was shot mostly in eastern Europe, which Kubrick made look exactly like World War I France. Only much later, when Kubrick's undeniable masterworks like *Dr. Strangelove*, *Lolita*, and *2001: A Space Odyssey* were winning worldwide audiences and his cinematic genius was obvious, and as the Vietnam war made audiences more understanding of anti-war movies, did *Paths of Glory* get shown in revival theaters where it was recognized by audiences of significant size as the masterpiece it is. Before that, only a few critics and film historians had noticed it. When it was shown to largely young audiences during the Vietnam war, it hit with the impact of a lightning bolt. Its original release did not elevate Kubrick to the status of star director, or even a studio director. Although unrecognized, Kubrick, based on *Paths of Glory*, was one of the very best movie directors in the world at the time of making that film. Kirk Douglas recognized Kubrick's talent and genius and three years later hired him to direct the big budget studio extravaganza *Spartacus*. On Kubrick's first four movies he was those movies' absolute author. Two of Kubrick's early movies were indisputably good; *The Killing* and *Paths of Glory*, but Douglas did not want *Spartacus* to be another "art movie masterpiece." He wanted it to be a major studio mass audience-pleasing blockbuster, financially spectacular, mainstream movie. Kubrick said that Douglas listen to him on *Spartacus* but that Kubrick was only one of many people that star and producer Douglas listened to. Kubrick is *not* the author of *Spartacus*, and he eventually disowned it as not his movie. He even made a sarcastic putdown joke about it in *Lolita*. Kubrick was very qualified and able to be an "author of the movie" director on *Spartacus* and he wanted to be that, but he was not allowed to be the movie's author. The actual author of *Spartacus* was Kirk Douglas and its screenwriter, Dalton Trumbo. Kubrick found his experience on *Spartacus* to be so unpleasant that from that point on in his career he ensured that he would be the author of the movies that he directed. He was producer or co-producer and co–screenwriter on almost all his other movies including *Dr. Strangelove, Lolita, 2001: A Space Odyssey, A Clockwork Orange*, and *Full Metal Jacket*.

Kubrick turned down a chance to direct *One-Eyed Jacks*, a Western that starred Marlon Brando, because he felt he would not be the movie's author. When everyone who works on a movie, including the screenwriter (who in reality is working for the director) labors to put the director's vision on the screen, that director is likely – but not always – the author of the movie, and is likely operating as an "author of the movie" director. If, on the other hand, the director is really working for the producer or screenwriter to put the producer's or screenwriter's vision on the screen, then the director is typically *not* the movie's author, and it typically not operating as an "author of the movie" director.

The dichotomy of the two types of director could be placed on a scale from one to ten, with the minimal or essential director in his or her rawest most minimal form at one on that scale, and the "author of the movie" director in his or her most encompassing and contributing form at ten on that scale. Here are a few quick examples to provide some elaboration. Directors like Kevin Smith, Quentin Tarantino, Robert Rodriguez, Lars Von Trier, Stanley Kubrick, Federico Fellini, Ingmar Bergman, David Zucker, David Mamet, Alfred Hitchcock, Howard Hawks, D.W. Griffith, W.F. Marnau, Akira Kurosawa, Orson Welles, Luis Bunuel, Jud Apatow, John Ford, Frank Capra, Sajiit Ray, Woody Allen, Jean Luc Godard, Francois Truffaut, David Lynch, Fritz Lang, and George Romero are clearly "author of the movie" directors.

At the other extreme, many TV directors are essential or minimal directors. They shoot scripts exactly as written or almost exactly as written by the show's writers, and as approved by the show's executive producers, who are usually screenwriters, former story editors, etc. These TV directors are surrounded by staff, crews, producers, and production departments that make very many of the decisions that movie directors commonly make while shooting movies. The real job of most TV directors is to "set the shot" and tell the actors where to stand whether to move or not. They tell the cinematographer roughly what the shot is, rehearse the actors, and say "Action" and "Cut" and "Print" and move on to the next shot to "get his (or her) day." The TV director makes sure that all the pages in the script scheduled to be shot that day get shot.

There are other examples of what I call minimal or essential directors. One is the very famous director Elia Kazan, who began his career as an actor and stage director, Kazan was one of the most successful and acclaimed stage directors working on Broadway in the 1940s when he was brought to Hollywood by the movie studios mostly to direct movies made from famous plays. Of course, those plays and screenplays were written by great writers like Tennessee Williams and Bud Schulberg. Kazan worked with some of the greatest actors – Marlon Brando, James Dean, Anthony Quinn, and Warren Beatty. Beatty said that Kazan taught him virtually everything that Beatty knows. Kazan is considered to be one of the very best "actors' directors" or perhaps the very best actor's director ever. He was also a great acting teacher and coach.

Please note that the term "minimal director" that I use is *not* intended as a putdown or a judgment of a director's skill or worth. It is a term I use to describe the width or expanse of the job they are doing or not doing, and how much of the total job of making a movie that they are taking on or sharing or leaving to others such as the screenwriter or cinematographer or producer. As described with Kubrick, all directors are not always a minimal director or "author of the movie" director. The job that they do can change from movie to movie, depending on the given circumstances of particular films.

In 1963, Elia Kazan wrote, directed, and produced *America, America*, a multi-Oscar nominated movie based on his father's experiences immigrating to America. He is clearly the author of that movie. His script and the movie both received Oscar nominations. I've heard from other directors who were in a position to know that when Kazan first came to Hollywood, movie studios' best cinematographer, editors, art directors, and assistant directors set and approved the shots that "covered" the scenes Kazan directed on the set. Kazan was hired to get great performances from great actors and bring out the great drama of great scripts. He operated as the excellent stage director he was.

The distinction between directors who shoot scripts exactly as written by others and directors that create scripts and movies that are expressions of their own point of view toward life, love, money, good and evil, and everything else in the movie has been commented on with much zest and passion by no less of an authority that the great filmmaker Francois Truffaut, whose early observations and analysis on movies formed the basis for the controversial "auteur theory." Truffaut observed in the Introduction of his book Truffaut/Hitchcock that directors like Kazan, who he called "Oscar collectors" were much like stage directors. Truffaut said, "Why establish any distinction between these motion picture directors and their counterparts in theater… They set up a scene, place the actors within the setting and then proceed to film the whole of that scene, which is substantially dialogue…" I'll have more to say in another book about Truffaut's observation and correct distinction between the very few directors that are really "author directors" and the many other directors who are not authors. This distinction between types of directors and directing circumstances is not just an esoteric or theoretical subject. *It has very practical consequences*!

Understanding or misunderstanding what a director's job really is or is not in a real situation can contribute greatly to success or failure. Let's look at some concrete examples. This time we'll look at examples with which I have a sad personal experience.

One gentleman that I knew and tried to help was making a $36,000 micro-budget movie from his own script and his own money. He was also producing and trying to direct that movie. I was giving him free advice and free screenwriting help. I have since realized that there are a lot of people who value everything by money. If you give them free advice, no matter how potentially valuable that advice is, not matter how correct it is, and no matter how much they will eventually agree with your advice, after they have (metaphorically speaking) "put their finger in the electrical socket" that you warned them about, *they will only value advice according to how much it costs them*. Some times they will ignore the advice and only learn the hard way. So the gentleman in question who tried to direct two movies had read a book either by or about Elia Kazan and had heard someone express ideas about Kazan, a director that he idolized. This neophyte director had the idea in his mind that Kazan had said, "All the director has to do is to get great performances from the actors." This would-be director of the $36,000 micro-budget "epic" did not notice that Kazan's circumstances were very, very different (in fact, exactly opposite) from his own. Unlike Kazan, he had no art director, and no art department. The man he'd chosen to be his cinematographer on his second movie was actually not a cinematographer and not even a competent camera operator. Whether this gentleman would-be director knew it or not, whether he liked it or not, whether he wanted it or not, and no matter how much he tried to avoid or deny he was inescapably in an "author of the movie" type directing situation. He was not in a minimal director situation! He did not have the support team or backup to be simply a minimal or essential director, and only focus on actors' performances and leave the other aspects of the director's job to others as Kazan did. He did not have the option or choice to be a minimal director.

Here are some of the very real consequences that resulted from the gentleman's gross misunderstanding of the real definition of the director's job that actually applied to his real situation. He let his non-cinematographer and camera operator set the shots in his movie. This resulted in more garbage and ultra-garbage shots per minute of screen time than in any movie I can ever remember seeing. A "garbage shot" is a shot that does not show the audience or viewer what they need to see when they need to see it in order for them to be drawn into the world of the movie, and for the audience to care about what happens in that world. An "ultra garbage" shot is one that does not show the audience what they need to see but does show them things that they do not need to see, which detract from or destroy the appeal or value of the movie's "world." They look ugly and unprofessional. This type of shot is almost always aesthetically ugly and quickly destroys a movie's production value. They almost always ruin or undermine a movie's "look" and its chances of receiving any real commercial distribution. Placement of the camera and setting a shot is the director's responsibility. Some directors at times "out source" this job to their cinematographer or camera operator, and often that works. Many directors share that responsibility with their cinematographers, but the director is ultimately responsible for any shot, including camera placement and framing on which the director calls "Action" and "Cut" and "Print."

Later, I will have more to say about who really sets the shots on a movie, whether it is the director or cinematographer. Meanwhile, back to the gentleman neophyte director. He tried to direct his $36,000 "epic" and recognized how many garbage shots his movie contained, once it was edited. I commented on the enormous number of garbage shots when viewing his movie, and he blamed the cinematographer and acted like it had nothing to do with him or the director's job. His misunderstanding of the real director's job on his movie (particularly in his circumstances) did not include the director's responsibility for placement of the camera and framing shots. He mistakenly thought that all he had to do was "get good performances" from the actors. That may have been true for Elia Kazan when he was working with a real cinematographer who'd shot many movies and had an Oscar nomination, but it was not true in this gentleman's micro-budget situation.

I remember an actor, Marsha Mason, who said of a Neil Simon play in which she starred on Broadway, that at a specific point in that play there was always a strong and effective reaction from the audience, but in the movie version, this reaction was lost. She said, "Maybe it had to do with where the camera was." Yes, indeed! It has a *lot* to do with where the camera is placed. If the audience cannot see the actor's performance or can only barely see that performance, the effect of even a good performance can be lost to the audience. There is a big difference in the kind of effect that a good performance can have on a movie audience when the camera is properly placed in front of that actor, whether in close-up, medium close-up, or two-shot. Usually, when the actor's face dominates the shot the audience "catches" the full force of the actor's performance, in contrast to a performance that is "almost" captured by a garbage shot or missed by an ultra-garbage shot where the camera is too far away in a wide medium shot and/or at a three-quarter, badly composed angle where you can barely see only one of the actors eyes, and where the set dominates the shot, not the actor's face. In the micro-budget movie in question, the neophyte director gentleman had some fairly good performances (for a low budget movie) in several scenes of his second movie, but I had to watch these scenes a couple of times on an editing machine to focus on the performances, because the camera did not really capture the performances and deliver them strongly to the screen. That was because the camera was set up awkwardly and some times the scene and actors' faces were poorly lit. I had to *work* to study and evaluate these actors' performances because of poor camera presentation of them. The audience or potential distributors won't do that kind of work.

Even the good things this guy had created were ruined and did not reach the viewer because of the important parts of the director's job that he mistakenly ignored, like making sure that the camera and viewer could see the actor's face, eyes, and performance! Under the effect of the incompetence and obstacles, even a very good performance would only have a very weak effect on viewers. The movie was not distributed, and undistributable for many reasons. Rotten camera placement was one of the reasons. The gentleman neophyte director had no art director, or production designer, or art department on his movie. One key location in his movie was supposed to be a stock brokerage. The location was basic to the movie's story. He shot the stock brokerage scenes in a large vacant, severely ugly, office space that had lots of desks and office equipment, and really ugly green bare walls. He did not do anything to dress this location and make it look like a stock brokerage. He mistakenly thought that a few lines of dialogue about the location being a stock brokerage were a substitute for some simply minimal set dressing and of course his non-cinematographer showed as much of this ugly wrong-looking location as he could.

When a director is in an "author of the movie" situation whether he or she wants to be or not, and he or she has no production designer or art director, or even set dresser or real art department, then in reality the director inherits those jobs and any other jobs that are not being filled by others. Because the job description of a director in an "author of the movie" situation or something close is to create a world on the screen that is so real and so interesting that the audience or viewer is drawn into it and cares about what goes on in that world and thus becomes mentally involved with that world.

The physical look of a movie's world is normally the responsibility of the movie's art director or production designer or set dresser who usually has a lot to do with whether the world of the movie *feels real*. The kind of "willing suspension of disbelief" that exists in movies is very different than the tacit mental license an audience grants a stage production in a stage play. If there's a painting of a mountain behind the actors in a stage play and the actors say a couple of lines of dialogue about the mountain, that is usually enough for the audience to accept that in the world of this play the mountain is there. In movies it's very different. It has to actually look like the mountain is really there if that's what the location is supposed to be. In another book I even argue that there is no such thing as the "willing suspension of disbelief" in movies. There is instead and "unwilling acceptance of whatever is believably shown." It is usually the job of the director or art director or production designer or set dresser to make things look like what they are supposed to be in the movie's world.

Well, if you are the director, and you have no production designer, or art director, or set dresser, or functioning art department, who in the hell do you think has the job of making things look like what they are supposed to be? *It's the director!*

Who else is going to do it? If you're an "author of the movie" director movie situation, whether or not you want to be, if something needs to be done to make a good movie, and there is nobody else to do it, it is automatically part of your job description to do it or to get someone to do it!

A director with a great crew can get a lot of help (superb help in some cases). In micro and low budget productions, however, a director does not often have full crew help but still has the full responsibility of creating the movie's world and making it real and interesting to the audience. In his commentary on *Once Upon A Time In Mexico*, Robert Rodriguez talked in a very enlightening way about how he did the production design and art direction on that movie as well as directing it. Because of unusual time pressure, Rodriguez felt he did not have time to explain things to an art director or production designer and also supervise what they did. He instead just did those jobs himself, in a very simple, direct, and uncomplicated way. His commentary on this subject is must viewing for beginning indie directors.

Our $36,000 indie movie did not even have posters or artwork on the ugly green walls of the vacant office "stock brokerage" location. He had no dressing that visually showed it to be a stock brokerage, but his so-called cinematographer "made sure" to show as much of the tacky location as possibly so he could rack up the highest possible count of ultra-garbage shots. What should the director have done? Here are a couple of examples from my own personal experience. One low budget movie that I directed had scenes that were set in a hospital room and the hall of a hospital. When I arrived on location at an abandoned hospital about an hour and a half before crew and cast call time I found a deserted undressed former hospital. Its rooms did not look like hospital rooms. Its main hall did not look like the main hall of a hospital. My art department, set dresser, art director and other crew were missing in action. (Actually, they were burned out, toasted, and fried to a crisp by brutal around the clock production demands of earlier scenes.) I surveyed the location. With me were a production assistant (P.A.), an intern, and a non-hands-on assistant director (A.D.). I went through the hospital, found a bed, and rolled it into a room. I found some medical equipment and sent the P.A. and intern out to find any potential dressings. In about an hour my two helpers and I had dressed the room and hall so that they looked like a functioning hospital. I shot the scenes on these two very realistic looking sets without the help of an art department (that day).

Another incident on this same film also illustrates my point. This movie's opening was on the surface of an alien planet. We built a large model of the surface of the alien planet, complete with a lake of boiling molten metal. This model of the planet's surface was huge. It covered about half of a large warehouse studio's floor. About 40 hours before a very expensive camera crane was due to arrive to shoot the movie's opening shot of the camera swooping across the model of this alien planet's surface, it became painfully obvious to me that the model maker was incapable of finishing off the model with the kind of built-in perspective and detail that would make the model photograph effectively and really look like the surface of an alien planet. The model maker basically admitted that he was in over his head and didn't know how to effectively finish the model and build perspective into it. I took over the finishing of the model and basically worked 40 hours straight through, while putting myself through a trial and error crash course in large model making, using what I already knew of sculpture and model making. I completed the model just before the crane and special camera arrived to shoot the shot.

I encountered another somewhat similar situation on a different sci-fi movie that starred Christopher Lee and Robert Vaughn. It had a series of complex special effects shots that involve suspending a model of a UFO hangar about 40 feet in the air and raising the camera above the model UFO hangar and shooting through the model while Christopher Lee and others walked around in an parking lot that had been dressed to look like a part of the UFO hangar. They were about 50 to 100 yards away from the model and camera. If the camera was placed and aimed just right, the model UFOs that were actually about one foot in diameter would appear to be 40 feet in diameter and Christopher Lee would look like he was walking inside a huge UFO hangar, next to the UFOs. The exact placement and angle of the camera was hypercritical to make this special effect shot work. If the camera was even one-quarter of an inch or less "off" in its positioning the model UFOs would look 20 feet in diameter, not 40 feet in diameter as the should, or if the mistake was made in the opposite direction the UFOs would look like they were 60 to 80 feet in diameter. Christopher Lee would then look ultra-small.

The cinematographer had shot some footage earlier with this special effects setup. He had the camera in the wrong relationship to the model and the model UFOs only looked to be about 12 feet in diameter. So, as Christopher Lee arrived on the set the cinematographer told me that he didn't want to take responsibility for shooting the FX shots with Christopher Lee. Since the last time he tried it, the UFOs came out looking the wrong size. He pointed out to me that it was me and the special effects guy that "cooked this up in camera way" of doing the shot, and that I had more experience in shooting tests of this type of special FX shot than he did so he said that I should climb up the 40 foot scaffold and shoot the special FX shots myself if I wanted to be sure that the UFOs would appear to be 40 feet in diameter. Christopher Lee was standing in the icy wind a few hundred yards from Lake Ontario, shivering and freezing in a flimsy costume. The air was about five degrees. There was a 30-mile an hour wind rolling in off Lake Ontario. The wind chill factor was probably well below zero and the camera operator cinematographer was not going to go up the scaffold. So I did. I climbed up the scaffold in the freezing cold wind and hooked my arms around the bars of the scaffold while setting the camera for the various special effects shots, most of which involved Mr. Lee, and the UFOs did look 40 feet in diameter in the rushes.

Here's another incident that also illustrates my point. On another movie, we were filming inside a flying small airplane. When you are looking through a camera's viewfinder on an airplane or a boat and particularly if you are not pointing forward it greatly increases your chances of getting airsick or seasick, and barfing your guts out. We filmed inside the plane for about an hour and the cinematographer/camera operator started looking sicker and sicker. We landed to reload the camera and prepare to shoot another group of scenes. The cinematographer came up to me and said, "I don't want this to become a habit, but boss, you get to operate the camera on the rest of these flying scenes." He and I had argued about who would operate the camera earlier on this movie. (I would operate on some shots; this was early in my career.) He finally won that argument because he was an excellent camera operator, much better than myself, and he made his point by saying, "You may be a cameraman but you're not *the* cameraman on this movie!" I got his point. After handing me the camera, he went on to tell me that if he went up in the plane again he'd barf all over the inside of the plane. That would probably end our welcome to film inside the plane. I took the camera and shot all day, pointing forward and backward. It took about 20 minutes to start feeling airsick, and after about half an hour I felt like I was about a quarter of an inch from puking violently, but I managed not to. I shot hour after hour, directed the actors, set focus, framed shots, etc. All the time, I felt sick as a dog. I "got the day" (shot everything that was scheduled), and didn't puke. It was all part of the "glitz and glamour" of showbiz and being a pampered, over-credited movie director!

Many people envy movie directors for their supposedly undeserved power or credit or glamour that supposedly just naturally flows with the profession. Well, while climbing up that scaffold and hanging on for dear life in freezing temperatures or building a model on no sleep or keeping from puking in an airplane, I never felt all those supposed undeserved glamour and credit. The moral to these stories is that if you are a director in an "author of the movie" situation, whether you want to be in the situation or not, and something needs to be done for a scene to be shot, or for it to look good, and you are the only one who can do the thing that needs to be done or you are the one who can *best* do the thing that needs to be done, then you need not ask for whom the bell tolls, because that bell is ringing *only* for you!

A movie is not just its script. It also has its graphic aspects, which often are affected heavily by things like camera placement, art direction, and set dressing. The commentary on the DVD for the movie *Juno*, which featured the movie's director Jason Reitman and screenwriter Diablo Cody, has some very interesting sections where they discuss the set dressings in *Juno*'s room and other locations. *Juno* has a strong art director, art department, and set dresser, but it's very interesting to hear Reitman and Cody talk in great detail about the most detailed and minute elements of the set dressing for various sets and how these dressings contributed to the creation of the world of the movie *Juno*.

The graphic aspects of the movie were not the only qualities of Mr. Neophyte Director's $36,000 movie that suffered because of his *basic misunderstanding* of his role as a de facto "author of the movie" director. If a director has a perfect or excellent script, then very often the best thing that a director in that situation can do is to shoot that script exactly as written or almost exactly as written. Scripts that are perfect, however, or truly excellent are very rare, and they are even more rare in low budget or micro budget situations. Mr. Neophyte Director was also the screenwriter of the $36,000 movie, and he had some writing talent. Unfortunately, he also had a lot of very harmful false basic assumptions about screenwriting and movies as well as about directing. His talent as a writer was visible in some scenes, but it was undermined by some weaknesses in his script and ignorance of movie audiences' desires and wants. His attitude verged on contempt for the audience.

When he prepared to direct he did not recognize that he had a very imperfect script, and that as a director in an "author of the movie" situation it was part of his job as a director in that situation to perfect his script and make a movie that could attract interest and satisfy a movie audience, not just shoot every word in his precious script, as if it had been written on stone by God. I would maintain that any director who is in an "author of the movie" situation and is expected to make a good movie and not just shoot the script as written, has as part of his or her job description *the*

11

perfection of the script. That would also mean vouching that the script is as good as it can be made, even in situations where the director receives no screenwriting credit, and is not formally considered to have been one of the movie's screenwriters.

The director may, and often does in reality write the last four real drafts of the movie. Here's what I mean. The director writes the movie's shooting script, detailing shots and scenes. One obvious and extreme, but not at all unique example of this transition to a shooting script involving a major "writing" contribution by the director is the spectacular chase sequence in the movie *The French Connection.* In the script, that major chase sequence was written as "an exciting chase ensues." I've written that exact phrase a few times myself, as have many other screenwriters. The Oscar-winning director of *The French Connection*, William Friedkin, "wrote" that chase sequence during the shooting script phase of pre-production, mostly in the form of storyboards, not words.

In many cases, the writing of the shooting script is an important draft in the progression of the movie's real script, and it's usually written or co-written by the director especially in the case of a director in an "author of the movie" situation. The next real draft of the movie that's typically "written" by the director is in rehearsals. Some times, not a word of the script is changed during rehearsals, and the director's only function is to help the actors develop and perfect their performances. In low budget movies, scenes and dialogue are often perfected, condensed, combined, and embellished, often with actors' improvisations during rehearsals. In some cases, these changes during rehearsals are substantial enough to really constitute the second draft that directors and actors usually "write" via this process.

The third draft that a director commonly develops is during the actual shooting of a movie. Very rarely, but some times, a movie is shot absolutely and exactly as written, but in some cases the actors improvised on takes. Ideas for shots or scenes that are not in the script become apparent during shooting and the director acts upon these ideas and shoots shots, action sequences, scenes, and dialogue that are not in the script, but actually do constitute another real draft of the script in its progression. I enormously recommend John Milius' commentary on the DVD of the Clint Eastwood "Dirty Harry" sequel, *Magnum Force.* Milius is honest and realistic about what actually really happens to a script when it gets made into a movie, even a script from an excellent star screenwriter like Milius. At one point in the commentary during an action sequence, Milius says that you try to write all the details of what happens in these kinds of scenes, but he very realistically and truthfully says when talking about the action on the screen, "You try and write exactly what's gonna go on, but in fact the director, and even if you're gonna direct it, you end up directing, you know what's there." Milius goes on to point out some good things on the screen, like Dirty Harry on the hood of a violently moving car and a villain being killed by driving a car into a crane. He realistically acknowledges that stunt people and others come up with ideas during filming and if the director shoots them they are "written" on film and are part of the movie, not necessarily what's written on the paper of script pages. Milius also admits that the movie's ending scene on an aircraft carrier was *not* in his script. His ending took place in a building. This is why I say that what goes on during shooting actually sometimes constitutes another draft of the script.

I would still say that Milius was the author of Dirty Harry. Some of his script was changed during shooting, but the most important things in the movie were in his script, and most of the important things in the movie were also in his script.

I would say that Ted Post, the movie's director, did an excellent job, and in my opinion he did not operate in a pure "author of the movie" situation on *Magnum Force*, and certainly not as a minimal director. He operated in-between these two extremes as do a very large portion of movie directors.

The fourth and final draft of the movie that the director "writes" is during editing and post-production. Some times, a movie is shot exactly as written, and edited exactly as written, but far more often a movie is enhanced, condensed, perfected, and its story is built and clarified during editing and post-production. Even a writer/director as excellent as Quentin Tarantino made editing changes from the script in his excellent movie *Jackie Brown*. It was his own script and he made changes in it in editing. The published script does not match exactly the movie. The editing of a movie is a final draft of the movie script.

A script is like a drawing of an airplane. It can look beautiful. It can look like it will really fly. A movie is like an actual airplane. It has to contend with reality. It either flies or does not fly. It either works for the audience or it does not. If it does not fly, it will likely crash, no matter how beautiful the drawing (script) on which it was based may have been.

Screenwriters can become "wordified" – meaning hypnotized by the wonderfulness and precious nature of their wonderful words in a script. They can becomes obsessed or enslaved by things in their script that have tremendous significance to them, but mean nothing at all to anyone else in the entire universe, particularly a paying audience. If a screenwriter is to direct his or her own script (and I recommend that they do), I strongly suggest that in most instances the writer/director should adopt a new point of view (POV) and look at their own script critically, and from a mental vantage point separate from the one they held when writing the script. They should take an honest critical look at their script, from an audience POV. If the script is perfect or near perfect like *Clerks* or *She's Gotta Have It*, then the script should be shot as-is, but if the script has weaknesses, or things that are not as fully realized as they should be, the writer/director should not behave like a minimal director enslaved by a weak or flawed script. Before directing their own script, the writer/director needs to abandon the POV of writer and adopt the POV of a moviemaker and/or director.

The multi-Oscar-winning screenwriter and director Paul Haggis, who gave us *Million Dollar Baby*, *Crash*, and *Letters from Iwo Jima*, said that Clint Eastwood did not make changes in his script for *Million Dollar Baby*, but Haggis made changes in his own script when he directed *Crash*.

When Frank Pierson (who wrote *Cool Hand Luke* and has two Oscar nominations for screenwriting) was the President of the Writers Guild of America, west, he gave a lecture in front of a large crowd of Guild screenwriters and talked about his experiences writing and directing for TV. He detailed one revealing incident where he was directing a TV script that he'd written. He wanted to make some changes to the script during production or pre-production and the TV executive would not allow him to make changes in his own script. Pierson thought that this was crazy. He said, "I wrote it, I can rewrite and change it when I'm directing!" The executive continued telling him no because TV executives want to retain "remote control" on every word that has been approved for shooting and make sure that the TV directors never rise above the stature of puppets to the writers who the executive could supervise and control.

Mr. Neophyte director of the $36,000 movie was afflicted with this kind of thinking. He subjugated himself and his role as a director to what he had written as a screenwriter. He did not really take on the role of director that was appropriate to the circumstances under which his movie was being made, and take responsibility for the flaws and imperfections of his script. He acted as a combination "acting coach" and "writer on the set," not as a director perfecting the script during the making of the movie. He made himself a meat puppet to himself as a screenwriter. Some of the very best playwrights, in the history of dramatic writing would typically open their plays "out of town" (not New York); far from famous critics, and often after seeing how an audience reacted to a play they would rewrite it before it opened on Broadway. The playwright often changes some lines of dialogue and edits some scenes after they see actual actors say their written words. Typically in movies, it is the director that presides over rehearsals, and often makes decisions about changes in dialogue or editing or condensing scenes. Some times screenwriters are at rehearsal or on set, and in rare cases they control any script changes but usually the movie's director and the actors take over the late stage of rehearsals or rewriting and often on low budget movies with weak scripts become the de factor screenwriters of last resort.

I used the example of Elia Kazan, a great director but usually a minimal director because he usually shot a very accomplished writer's scripts exactly as written and very able cinematographers, editors, and crew supported him. Simply because a director is supported by very able technicians and artists does not mean that the director is not operating as an "author of the movie." When Orson Welles directed *Citizen Kane*, he was supported by as many fellow geniuses as any director in the history of the movies. Welles is very clearly the author of that movie. His cinematographer was Greg Toland, who at the time was one of the top cinematographers in Hollywood. Toland was a favorite of the best director of the era, John Ford. He is also one of the very best black and white cinematographers of all time. He put all his talents and experience at Welles command, and even expanded the capabilities of the movie camera and lighting and cinematography to accommodate Welles' theater-orientated method of staging scenes. He was enormously "director friendly." He never told Welles he couldn't do something a certain way; he pushed the limits of the movie camera and cinematography to give Welles what he wanted and needed to fully utilize his talents and skills. Toland did not try to curb or confine Welles to conventional cinematography, or to push Welles to stage his scenes in a more ordinary or conventional camera-friendly way. He worked to put Welles' vision on the screen.

Welles co-screenwriter on *Citizen Kane*, Herman J. Mankiewicz, was a veteran writer whose credits dated back to silent movies and early talkies. For about 25 years, Mankiewicz had been, on and off, trying to write a screenplay or a novel about William Randolph Hearst, the person on whom *Citizen Kane* was loosely based. Mankiewicz brought a lot of research and screenwriting experience to his writing partnership with Welles, and contributed a great balance to Welles' youthful enthusiasm and bold, brash, dramatic genius. Welles' vision was embodied in their script.

Welles' musical composer on *Citizen Kane*, Bernard Herman, is one of the greatest and most admired composers in movie history. He also composed the music for *Vertigo* and *Psycho* and many other memorable films. Robert Wise was Welles' editor on *Citizen Kane*, and later became a top director.

Never again would *Welles* be so superbly supported by geniuses and masters and have such absolute carte blanche of resources from a major movie studio. Orson Welles in making *Citizen Kane* is a quintessential example of an "author of the movie" director in action. I'll have a lot more to say about this movie and Welles' method of directing later in this book. For now, I'll just say that Welles is the author of *Citizen Kane*. The common belief is that because Welles directed the movie when he was so young (25), after only recently having arrived on a studio lot, and made a genius movie with "beginner's luck" without any extensive "proper preparation." This couldn't be further from the truth. Welles was actually one of the most thoroughly prepared first-time directors in the history of Hollywood. He supplemented his preparedness with an intense, self-disciplined course of very serious study to fully prepare himself before directing *Citizen Kane*. I will have more to say about this later.

The most minimal case of minimal directing that I have ever heard about was told to me by an assistant director when I was directing *Starship Invasions* in Toronto, Canada. On a hill overlooking the city there is an actual Scottish castle called the Casa Loma. A Scotsman came to Canada, got rich, got homesick, and brought an actual castle over from Scotland that was reassembled brick by brick on that Toronto hill. The assistant director told me about one particular day of filming on a TV movie that happened exterior to the Casa Loma using its exterior as a set. This TV movie was directed by one of Canada's top directors who had directed the biggest beer commercials shot in Canada and also commercials in the USA. And of course, he would be important in Canada, where the only thing more important than beer is hockey. This top director had also directed many TV shows for Canada's privately owned TV network, and he was a highly paid and respected pro. On the day they were shooting those exterior scenes, the air temperature was about 10 degrees. The wind was about 20 miles per hour. The humidity was high, causing a wind chill factor far below zero. It was the kind of day where Canadians come up to you and say "Cold enough for ya, eh?" The director arrived on the set in his heated limo and never left it all day. He called the first assistant director, the cinematographer, and the actors in the first shot into his warm limo and went over the script with them. He told the A.D. and cinematographer and the actors what he wanted. The A.D. and cinematographer and actors left the warm limo and the A.D. set up the shot while communicating with the director via walkie-talkie. When the shot was set, the director had the limo driver drive the limo onto the set and park so that the director's window was near to the camera. The director would then roll his window down about four inches and the A.D. would roll the camera and sound and the director would shout "Action!" The scene would play out and the director would shout "Cut" and "Print." He'd roll the window up. The A.D., the D.P., and the actors for the next scene would again join the director in the warm limo and the whole process would repeat. The director never set foot on the set all that day. This director shot this TV movie exactly from the script. Every word in the script was put on the screen exactly as written. There was a good reason for this exact fidelity to the script. This TV movie was financed partly by Canada's privately owned TV network, and party by a letter of credit form a USA TV syndication distributor by a letter of credit from a foreign sales worldwide TV distributor. These two letters of credit and the distribution agreement that accompanied them all had the TV movie's script attached to them as initialed addendums and I believe that the director's contract also had the script attached as an initialized addendum, and a clause in the contract compelled the director to shoot the script exactly as written.

The reason for all this contractually obligated exact fidelity to the script was that if the TV movie deviated from the script the two distributors could theoretically bail out on their letter of credit, and then the banks would *not* loan money against them. Thus, no money to make the TV movie unless it matched the script exactly.

This top director was not hired to make a good TV movie. He was not hired to make *his* movie. He was hired to put onscreen exactly what was in the script and to make a TV movie that met professional standards and quality. This director was not the author of this TV movie. The TV executives who approved the writing and approved its concept and the screenwriters who wrote it were the authors of the movie, not its "minimal director."

This top director was very well paid, very well treated, and very respected, but on this TV movie he basically worked for the TV executives, and worked to put the screenwriter's vision on the screen exactly as written.

Again, in contrast, on *Citizen Kane*, everyone who worked on the movie including Welles' co-screenwriter really worked for Welles to put Welles' vision on the screen. That's why Welles was clearly the "author of the movie."

I want to reemphasize the word "minimal" is not intended as a putdown and the words essential or necessary can be substituted for the word minimal. Earlier I called Eliz Kazan, on *Streetcar Named Desire*, a non-author of the movie minimal or essential director. Again, Kazan was a very great director who directed some great movies like *On The Waterfront*, *Splendor In The Grass*, *East Of Eden*, and wrote *America, America*. He mostly worked with great writers and put their visions on the movie screen. The top Canadian director, in contrast, routinely directed TV commercials whose budgets were larger than some indie low budget movies.

Here is a story that may illustrate what minimal directors are hired to do and not to do. In Germany, there was a brewery whose beer had begun to taste very sour. The owner of the brewery sent for a brew master to fix the problem. The brew master tasted the sour beer, and then went through the brewery tapping on various pipes. Then he drew a circle on one pipe and his assistant hit the pipe very hard on that circle. A block of yeast came out of the pipe that delivered the finished beer. After that, the beer tasted exactly as it should. When the brew master presented the brewery owner with a bill for $10,010 the brewery owner said "$10,010 for tapping on a pipe?" The brew master replied, "No, $10 for tapping on the pipe and $10,000 for knowing where and how hard to tap, and also for knowing not to do a lot of other things like take your brewery apart pipe by pipe and shut it down for a month!"

Some times minimal or essential directors are hired and very well paid not just because of what they can do, or will do. Sometimes they are partly hired and well paid because it's clearly known what they will *not* do. They will not try to rewrite the script. They will not shoot a movie or TV show that diverges from the script. They will not go off-schedule and over-budget.

Early in my career I was hired to direct some TV shows. My only prior directing experience was on several independent movies, one of which was distributed by Warner Bros. I was eventually fired from that TV director job, partly because all of my previous directing experience on these independent movies that I also wrote or co-wrote, edited and on which I often also operated the camera, was very much as an "author of the movie" director. In directing an episode of a TV show a director is usually expected to be a "minimal" director. On most TV series the crew and staff works on episode after episode and they are there before a director who is directing an episode shoots his or her first shot and they'll be there after he or she shoots the episode's last shot. A TV director usually has to interface with this crew and staff and function smoothly with them and respect their individual territories and egos. This is not always that true for a movie director in an "author of the movie" situation. The crew and staff on a TV show are often used to working in a very specific routine and method and if a director violates that routine and method (which usually involves the director being a minimal director), then the crewmembers or staff members can "cut the director's throat" very easily.

The best-selling writer Robert J. Ringer wrote in on of his most popular books "If you acknowledge reality it automatically works for you and if you fail to acknowledge reality it automatically works against you."

I've detailed how the gentleman who I referred to as the Neophyte director of the $36,000 movie denied reality and tried to avoid the reality that he was in an "author of the movie" directing situation, not a minimal director situation. He did not acknowledge reality and it worked very strongly against him, and did his movie in.

When I was directing TV I did not acknowledge the reality that the TV series director job required a minimal director who could "fit in" with TV production apparatus, and its routines and methods, and that reality worked against me and eventually did me in, on that job.

There are many realities that directors need to acknowledge but among the most important realities directors need to acknowledge are the exact mandate under which they are working and the exact reality of the exact situation in which they are directing. One of the worst barriers to acknowledging reality is *ideology* or an ideological POV about a director's theoretical job can blind a director to a reality that's right in front of his or her face. There are thousands of directors around the worlds directing movies, TV shows, commercials, music videos, educational films, industrial, corporate, or promotional films, and videos. Those who acknowledge the reality of their mandate, and their directing situation, usually have a much better chance of success than those who fail to acknowledge these important realities. All of these thousands of directors (whether they know it or not, or want it to be true or not) are somewhere on this scale that has pure minimal director at one end, and the author of the movie at the other end, and an infinite number of situations and mandates in between these two extremes. A number of situations are alloys of various degrees of these two very clearly defined and different clear-cut directing extreme situations and mandates.

In the earliest days of moviemaking just before and after 1900, some silent movie companies believed that they had a monopoly on the patents of the motion picture camera. They believed or said that they believed those independent moviemakers who were using any camera that was not theirs was violating their patent. So they hired actual gunslingers that would search out independent moviemakers and literally shoot their camera! Pioneering film director Allan Dwan (mentioned in Peter Bogdanovich's must-read book *About Directors: Who The Hell Made It*) tells how when he started directing he wore a holster with a pistol so that he could protect his camera from the "patent gunslingers." One day, a gunslinger showed up near Dwan's set. Dwan and the gunslinger decided to duel to determine his camera's fate. They would not shoot at each other in the duel, but each shoot at a can in the distance. The gunslinger shot at the can and missed. Dwan shot at the can and hit it. The gunslinger honored the rules of the duel and left without trying to destroy Dwan's camera. Dwan went on to make over five hundred movies, most of which were one-reel, ten-minute films, but many of which were very famous popular full-length features. Some were silent and many were sound. Some received Oscar nominations and some were shot as late as 1960.

Any director who carried a gun and chased gunslingers away from the movie camera, may or may not have been an "author of the movie" director but they certainly were not a pure minimal director.

CHAPTER TWO:
SET THE SHOT – GET THE DAY

When a movie's shooting schedule is put together and locked down, a certain number of specific pages of the script are scheduled to be shot each day. If the director shoots all the pages, and shots that are scheduled to be shot on a particularly day, it is said that the director "got the day." Whether a director is an absolute "author of the movie" or a minimal director or something in–between, an intense reality of that director's life, while shooting a movie, is the constant and recurring need to "set the shot and get the day."

Francis Ford Coppola said that directing a movie is like running in front of a train. If you trip and fall it will run over you. When a movie completes shooting, a crew picture is usually taken, including the director. Upon completion of shooting one movie that I truly enjoyed making, which finishing shooting a day ahead of schedule, an assistant corralled me and put me in the center of the assembled crew. I stood there waiting for the still photographer to snap this crew picture. Finally, I looked at my watch, and then realized why the crew were all looking at me. "Snap!" They were waiting for me to do what I'd done so much during the making of the movie, look at my watch. That whole movie was a joy, and it went on to become financially successful and win two major awards.

Satchel Paige, perhaps the greatest baseball pitcher of all-time, once said, "Don't look back, somebody might be gaining on you." Well, if you're a movie director, particularly one on a low budget, you don't have to look back to know that *time* is constantly gaining on you, and if you trip and fall it can roll over you and crush your movie.

Every director needs to know how to set a shot. Directors are usually judged by the crew, and some times by the actors as well, on how expertly or ineptly they set shots or fail to set them. A director has to be able to translate the words on the pages of a script into *specific* shots that tell a movie's story and can be executed by the crew with the equipment at hand within the schedule in alignment with the movie's budget and resources. I am an advocate of a director arriving on set with a "shot list" that the director intends to shoot that day. Some directors do not operate with a shot list. They just block out the scene and decide on "coverage." Blocking refers to positioning the actors and the camera and staging any movements that they may make during the shot. Blocking is like a physical non-dress rehearsal without concentrating on performances, but with great attention to where actors stand and/or move and where the camera is and if it moves, where it moves, and how a particular camera lens frames the shot. Coverage refers to the number and types of shots that are shot to "cover" a scene. As I said earlier, some directors do not operate with a shot list. They just block out a scene, or shot. Virtually always, the "master" (a wide shot that covers all actors and all of the scene) is shot first, then the director and A.D. determine coverage as the master is being lit and the actors are getting into makeup and wardrobe. Typically this process goes something like this:

DIRECTOR

We'll shoot the master from here. Then starting with the second page of the scene, we'll get a two-shot on Bill and Jane from right there, and close-ups on everyone from this line of dialogue to the end of the scene.

The assistant director makes notes on all this.

A.D.

Are you sure you don't want a close-up on Bill for the whole scene?

DIRECTOR

No.

CINEMATOGRAPHER

Are you sure you don't want a tracking shot?

DIRECTOR

I'm sure.

A.D.

How about a zoom in on Bill on this line?

DIRECTOR

Yeah, that's good. Write it down.

A.D.

How about a zoom in on Sally for her reaction?

DIRECTOR

No, it's too much.

A.D.

Okay, I got it.

And the A.D. reads back his notes for the director to be sure that they are on the same page, plan-wise.

Some very successful directors work this way and do not come to the set with a shot list. They and their A.D. make up a shot list on the fly after the blocking of each master scene. However, any director that comes onto the set without a shot list and has trouble deciding on shots, however, or changes his or her mind about shots, or shoots useless or unnecessary shots, should not expect any favors or mercy from the crew, if he or she falls behind schedule and gets himself or herself into desperate or tragic situations. Crew members (and this includes the Director of Photography) will often not read a shot list even if they are given a copy. One really excellent cinematographer interrupted me when I was going through the shot list and said, "Do me a favor, boss. Let's just talk about one scene and one shot at a time." Nevertheless, I still gave a copy of my shot list to all relevant staff, including department heads, first and second assistant directors, the production manager, cinematographer, gaffer, key grip, makeup, wardrobe, stylist, and producer.

At one point I thought about not giving out shot lists because I knew a lot of people who got them did not pay much attention to them. I told the producer that I was going to stop handing out shot lists because I doubted that they got read or used. He said, "No, they read and use them. I heard the AD's on the walkie-talkies talking to makeup, wardrobe, and hair and say 'Ed's combining shots 20 and 21, so get the actors in scene 43 ready for shot 22.'"

The producer went on to tell me how some of the crew was actually following the shots of the day as they were completed, and watched how many remained to "get the day." He felt that following this progress helped some of the crew to know how things were going and helped morale. Even if crew members did not read or follow my progression through my shot list, the fact that I had a shot list, and that I copied it and handed it out made a lot of them feel (correctly) that I'd done my homework and was not wasting or disrespecting their time and efforts. At one point, when I had a nasty dispute with an A.D., a key grip sided with me and cited the fact that I came on the set every day with a shot list and methodically went through it shot by shot as a reason that I was right and the A.D. was wrong.

There is a great scene in the movie *All That Jazz*, a film by Bob Fosse (also a highly successful theater director and choreographer). In the story, the choreographer is trying to work out a dance number with his dancers and he tells them to take a break. He goes into the washroom, locks himself in a stall, and says, "How can I face those dancers? I have no ideas!" His mind is dry. Well, take that horrible feeling and you put a movie director on the set with twenty to forty crew members and actors standing around, knowing that if the director is super-prepared they'll work a 12 to 13-hour day, but if the director is not prepared they can expect to work a 15 to 16-hour day, and they may not even complete the day's scheduled scenes or pages. In a situation like that, see how much sympathy the crew and actors have with an unprepared director. A director who hopes for inspiration on the set and fails to get it is likely to feel an intensely unpleasant, even horrific emotion that is at least a dozen times stronger that what the choreographer in *All That Jazz* is shown to be feeling.

Being a director of a movie that has a limited budget, limited shooting schedule and limited resources, and being on the set surrounded by crew and actors who are there to work and go home, they are looking for you for "What do we do next?" Having your mind draw a blank and being unprepared is a horrific experience. I experienced it a few times early in my directing career and I promised myself that I would never ever be on the set unprepared. I worked out, refined and embellished a method, a step-by-step system for preparing to shoot a movie that would virtually guarantee, if followed, that the director would *not* be on the set unprepared with a blank mind. The system I use is presented in later sections of this book.

A common studio shooting schedule is 16 five-day weeks, or 80 days. A common length of a studio movie is about two hours, 120 minutes. That rate of shooting averages about one minute and a half per day of movie story. Normally, about one page of script equals about one minute of movie screen time. Dialogue usually runs a bit less than a minute per page, and action usually runs a bit more than a minute per page, and some times much more than a minute a page. A studio director who shoots a movie in 11 or 12 weeks, 55 or 60 days, is considered to shoot very fast for a studio director. He or she would be shooting about two pages, or two minutes of story per day at that rate. Low budget indie movies typically have much shorter shooting schedules than studio movies because they have much smaller budgets. They normally do four five-day weeks (20 shooting days), or three six-day weeks (18 days). I shot some of the movies on my resume in 12 or 13 days and one award-winning movie in 17 days. It finished a day ahead of schedule. I shot some movies that are not on my resume on a much shorter schedule. I shot an "art movie" intended for distribution on college campuses called *The Living Target* in four days. It was about 50 minutes long. It didn't get much distribution, but it did get enough distribution to get me another pro directing job. I have even shot movies of a very specific genre over a weekend, and even shot one professionally distributed feature length movie in one shooting day.

The shortest schedule that I ever heard about for any really successful movie is Roger Corman's and Charles B. Griffith's *Little Shop of Horrors*. Its DVD box claims that the movie was shot in two days. Maybe it was, but I suspect it was shot over a weekend, including Friday evening and night and early Monday morning before 8:00 a.m. I'll have more to say about shooting "drive-in movies" over weekends later.

A director who shoots a low budget or micro budget 90-minute movie on an 18 or 20-day schedule has to shoot about four and one-half pages (4.5 minutes screen time) or more per day. That is shooting about three times as fast as a studio director typically shoots. Reportedly, Steven Spielberg shot *Duel*, a 77-minute movie, in 11 or 12 days. I consider *Duel* to be a virtually perfect movie, written by the great screenwriter Richard Mathieson. Shooting a movie of such stellar quality with that much action on that short a shooting schedule is a truly amazing accomplishment. John Carpenter's *Halloween* was, I believe, shot in about 20 days, as was *Monster's Ball*. Supposedly, *Reservoir Dogs* was shot on an even shorter schedule.

A low budget director working on a short or very short shooting schedule is like a tightrope walker working without a safety net below. If a studio director falls a bit behind schedule, they have a much greater chance of making up what they failed to shoot and getting back on schedule than a low budget director has. When a director does not shoot everything that they are scheduled to shoot on a given day, the director is said to be "dragging" whatever they did not shoot. Dragging a shot, or three shots, a page, a scene, or part of a scene, isn't good. Studio movies often shoot in the same location for more than one day, or several days. This gives the studio director multiple chances on subsequent days to shoot whatever they are dragging from earlier days. Low budget movies, because of their much shorter schedules, often only shoot one day in a given location. If a director on a low budget movie fails to get his or her day in one day in a location that is scheduled to shoot only for one day, that shortfall can play grotesque havoc with the production schedule and the movie's resources and staff, particularly if the failure is repeated a few times in a week. It is very difficult to do thorough and complete pre-production on a low budget movie. Even when real and adequate pre-production has been done, all that preparation and planning can be shredded into confetti and blown across the landscape if the director fails to get his or her day repeatedly.

Here's how it can all go to hell without a hand basket.

One: The director fails to get the day on Wednesday, so the staff cancels shooting at Thursday's location, which is owned by Charles. Charles then say, "I told you guys you can only shoot here on Thursday and next Thursday I got something special, but two weeks from now is OK. So the location manager calls the location owner for the location scheduled two weeks from Thursday and moves that day of shooting to the end of the shooting schedule. The location manager feels like a big hero until the second A.D. says that an actor has been told it will be OK to fly to Spain four days before that rescheduled day, because they were scheduled to finish shooting three days before. The location manager has the production manager or producer start investigating recasting the part, and totally offends the actor, who the director happens to think is perfect. Then the producer starts trying to investigate other rescheduling options and right when the production manager thinks that a brilliant solution to the scheduling problem has been devised, the director again fails to get the day, and what was a difficult puzzle now becomes a Rubik's Cube situation. The art department finds out that the location on which they have busted their buns for two days, will not shoot for a week, because of the scheduling change. All because the director has missed the day twice, a scene that they thought would shoot in a week actually shoots the next day, so they have to bust their buns all night to get that ready.

And then the director fails to get another day, and the art department goes from being burned-out to being toast, or "art history." One morning, the director walks onto a set that the art department was only alerted to dress the night before, and the set is undressed. The art department has succumbed to the human need for sleep. The director throws a tantrum and blames everyone but himself or herself for ruining his or her precious movie, despite the fact that the disaster has been caused by the director's inability to get the days and stay on schedule.

On some movies that I directed, a shooting schedule was attached to my directing contract and I had to initial each page of that schedule. On other movies, there was a paragraph where I, the director, promised to shoot the movie on schedule and on budget. Some times, I also have to initial every page of the budget, and in at least one case part of my pay was withheld, pending my finishing the movie on budget and on schedule.

For a director on a low budget movie to fail to stay on schedule is a serious matter that can have dire consequences. It is also no small matter for a director to resort to 16 or 18-hour days to stay on schedule. This burns out the crew and staff and usually leads to a collapse of the production. Don't worry, though. In a latter part of this book I offer a simple action that, if taken, and rigidly enforced by the A.D., director, and D.P. can save almost all low budget production around two hours of shooting time a day.

In order for a director to properly and smoothly set shots, the director must be able and willing to make decisions promptly and must be able to make decisions that they only very rarely rescind. The director must *know what he or she wants* and how to get it with the camera. Once, I asked a special effect (SFX) man whom I was working with, who had worked on a lot of big movies, who was the best director he'd ever worked with. His instant answer, without blinking, was George Miller, the director of *Mad Max, Road Warrior, Babe, The Witches of Eastwick*, and an episode of the ill-fated *Twilight Zone* movie. I asked why Miller was the best, and the SFX man said, "Because he has such a clear and precise idea of exactly what he wants to see, and he tells you so clearly and exactly what he wants to see in each shot. The SFX man then volunteered the name of a very well known TV director/producer as the worst director he'd ever worked with because, "He had no idea what he wanted."

Sometimes a director has to make a decision when he or she really lacks enough information to know what the right decision is or even is likely to be. Some beginning directors can become so afraid of making a mistake or the wrong decision they become mentally paralyzed, and unable to make decisions. I remember once consulting with a struggling director who was deathly afraid to make a mistake. I told him that his indecisiveness was far more destructive to the production that being decisive and accepting the fact that occasionally he would be wrong. I suggested he face the fact that all mistakes cannot be avoided, particularly on low budget movies. A director being indecisive can destroy a movie, or at least quickly put it off schedule.

A director knowing what he or she wants has a lot to do with proper preparation. Just the way that a script can go through a number of drafts or a movie can go from rough cut through a number of stages to fine cut, and "lock" during editing, a director's thoughts about how to shoot a scene can go through a number of "drafts" before the director arrives at the final number and type of shots that the director wants to use to "cover the scene." It's my personal opinion that as much as possible (usually completely), the director should go through these "drafts" of thinking about how to shoot a scene in pre-production, not on the movie set with crew, cast, and staff standing around watching. Time flies by on a set, and suffering a director who did not do his or her homework can turn a crew ugly.

Everything about making a movie takes time. It eats time like a monster with a thousand big sharp teeth. Almost everything takes longer than you at first think it will. There is never enough time on the set of a low budget movie. Time on a set is too precious to waste. Proper preparation is essential to avoid wasting time on the set. I have a specific method of achieving the proper preparation laid out step-by-step later in this book.

Field Marshal Zukov, the Russian army commander in World War II whose armies slaughtered the Nazis and drove them out of Russian and went on to capture Berlin had his own take on this subject. He said, "Train hard, fight easy." Or, to paraphrase

Confucius, "The wise man (or woman), the superior one, believes that all things will be difficult, and prepares for all things as though they will be difficult, and for him (or her) all things are easy. The inferior man (or woman), the foolish one, believes that all things will be easy, and he (or she) prepares for them as though they will be easy or fails to prepare at all," and for him (or her) all things are difficult or impossible.

The director needs to have the movie in his or her mind when filming. There is a trick I have found very useful as the foundation of turning a script into a shot list, and words into images that tell a story. Normally, a movie script has three holes punched on the left-hand side of the page, when the script is open and being read. The pages have backsides, so an open script has blank pages on the left. I have found it very useful to make a director's master shooting script that has three holes punched on the right side of the page, not the left, so that when that script is open, it has the page with the writing on the left side of the open script. On top of the blank pages on the right of that director's master shooting script I insert one or more pages of "storyboard forms." These are a series of rectangular frame shapes running down the page like blank frames of a strip of film. Then, as I read the written words on the script page on the left side of the open notebook containing the director's master shooting script, I draw stick figure images or other drawings of what the images will be on the screen that will cover what the words in the script describe, on the storyboard frames just to the right of the written script. I also have several blank pages on the right side of the notebook, along with the storyboard forms. I write notes and may also make sketches of shots on these pages. I refine this process in and after rehearsals that are videotaped, and after location reconnaissance. Eventually, a final draft of the shots that will cover the scene is on top of the material on the right-hand side next to the page. These pictures and notes can go through drafts just like a script. Thus, when a scene is to be shot, these storyboards can easily be transferred to the shot list, if appropriate, or can form part of the foundation of the shot list. This is a process that helps the director (mostly in private on his or her own time) find out and decide what he or she wants. So then on the set the director will already know what to shoot, and will "know what they want."

Here is a story that dramatically illustrates the difference of situation between an established director making a movie for a major studio, and a beginning director making a low budget or micro budget "indie" movie. When Roman Polanski was directing *Rosemary's Baby* he was walking across the studio lot, and he passed Otto Preminger (a famous director).

Preminger asked him, "Why the long face? You look unhappy. I hear your movie is very good."

Polanski replied that he was "behind."

"Behind what?" Preminger asked.

"Behind schedule," was Polanski's answer.

Preminger then asked, "Are your rushes good?

"Yes."

"Do the studio executives like the rushes?"

"Oh yes, they are very excited about the rushes."

Preminger then told Polanski, "Don't worry. You won't get fired if they like the rushes."

What Preminger told Polanski was true *for Polanski* in his situation. At that point in his career, Polanski was an acknowledged cinematic genius who's already made three movies that I and most critics of that era consider masterpieces – *Knife in the Water*, *Repulsion*, and *Cul de Sac*. Robert Evans, the head of Paramount Pictures, saw *Cul de Sac* and talked Polanski into coming to Hollywood to write and direct *Rosemary's Baby*. (Actually, he tricked him by promising to do a film about skiing.) So Polanski was on safe ground if he fell a bit behind schedule.

That was not so with a low budget indie director whom I tried to help. He thought one day's strong rushes would bring in more investment, which it did not. He cavalierly and arrogantly fell farther and farther behind schedule, and the production collapsed right out from under him and he went deep into filmmaker hell!

There is little margin for error or arrogance on low budget indie movies. There, punishment for failure to "set the shot and get the day" can be swift and merciless.

As I said in the Introduction, many "first time" directors are also "last time" directors. Any director who has directed several movies has the "first time director's curse" removed because it's known that he or she is not a "first time/last time director." Many first time/last time directors fail because they do not prepare and learn how to set up a shot and get the day. They learn the hard way that it takes more than just putting one's name on a camera slate or crew list next to the word director and having a lot of ideas, and "talking a good fight" to actually function as a real movie director. A real director can set shots and usually they can get the day.

CHAPTER THREE:
DIRECTOR ON SET –
BLOCK IT, LIGHT IT, REHEARSE IT, SHOOT IT, AND PRINT IT

Again, blocking refers to where the actors stand or move during a scene and their physical positions and movements in relation to each other and to the audience (or camera). Blocking is a term from the theater. The staging of plays has been going on for well over 2500 years. The first plays that we know of in the West were written and performed by the ancient Greeks in Athens. The playwrights of these plays (known as poets) staged and directed them. They were writer/directors in filmic terms. Aeschylus, probably the very first Western playwright and director, used such shocking visual effects that his plays caused pregnant women to have miscarriages, and after that pregnant women were prohibited from seeing his plays. Even from the very beginning, plays were not just words recited. They had their visual and staging aspects. Thus blocking and picturization are part of the art of drama.

On the DVD of *Who's Afraid of Virginia Woolf*, the movie's multi-Oscar-winning cinematographer Haskell Wexler lays out the professional, standard way that a scene should be shot. First, he says comes a rehearsal not for performance, and not a dress rehearsal. The actors need not be in costume or made up for this rehearsal. He calls it a physical rehearsal to determine the actors' physical positions and movements. This is also called blocking. The camera crew "marks" – puts pieces of tape on the floor to mark – the actors' various positions at various points in the scene. Again, what Wexler calls this physical rehearsal is what I'm calling *blocking*. Blocking is a physical rehearsal. Then Wexler says the actors and director leave the set, and the lighting crew and cinematographer light the scene using stand-ins in place of the actors. They work under the "observance" of the first A.D. During this time, the actors get into full makeup and wardrobe. Wexler says that when lighting is complete the actors and director return and begin rehearsing. When the rehearsals are good enough in terms of camera crew actions and actors' performances the director will begin shooting on film or video and when the director is satisfied with a take he or she will say "Print it" and move on to the next shot and the whole process begins again with a physical rehearsal, blocking the actors and setting the camera in a position for the next shot.

On the DVD, Wexler bemoans how on many movies there has become a common deviation form this clear process. I was surprised to hear that this messing up of this process also occurs on large budget movies and TV of the kind on which Wexler worked at the time he made the commentary for the DVD. Until I heard his commentary I thought that the deviation from the steps of how a scene is shot was pretty much limited to low budget movies, but apparently not.

One of the worst cases of messing up and mixing up the standard process of how to shoot a scene – block it, light it, rehearse it, shoot it, print it – is the sad case of a struggling, suffering "would be" director who would not block out a scene. He would not accomplish a physical rehearsal. Instead, he would describe and discuss the scene. He'd call the actors and cinematographer to the place where the scene was to be shot, and he'd describe the scene with *words only*. He'd say this actor goes over there and says XYZ and that actor stands there and does this or that and then they say or do this or that. Then he'd discuss the scene with the actors about their motivations, and performances philosophically and psychologically and muse about his vision. In short, he'd do anything except work on their physical actions and movements. This discussion was all a major waste of time and could have and should have been done *off set*. Usually, after this time wasting had gone on for a while, the D.P. would say, "I've seen enough. I can light it." And the director and actors would get out of the way and the cinematographer and the lighting crew would throw up a general lighting setup for a "general" camera position. No exact camera position was chosen or marked and no actors' positions in the scenes were marked. Then, when the actors and director came back on set after it was lit, all manner of bad things befell this ill-fated would-be director because he failed to properly physically block out the scene and show everyone a full physical rehearsal.

Instead of discussing what happens when things are done wrongly, let me lay out in detail the how and why of the *block it* (physical rehearsal), *light it, rehearse it, shoot it*, and *print it* method, and why this is the correct way to set up a scene or a shot and to properly and efficiently shoot it. I don't want anyone to accept this method simply because I say it is correct, or because Haskell Wexler says it's the correct way to shoot a scene. I don't believe that just accepting things on the basis of authority is the real road to becoming a successful movie director.

Robert Rodriguez, in the commentary on a DVD of one of his movies, said that before he'd cook a ham he'd cut each end off the ham. His wife asked him why he did that, and he said it was because his mother always did that. He asked his mother why she always cut both ends off a ham before cooking it and she said that, at that time, she only had a pot that was too small to accommodate the entire ham. Rodriguez's point in telling that story was that there are probably a lot of things in the process of how movies get made that were once appropriate to the way those movies were being made, but they continue even though the circumstances of how movies are made have changed and they are no longer appropriate. The golden era of Hollywood, the 1930s, 1940s, and 1950s, was a time that was ruled by the extreme feudalism of movie studios, and there certainly are practices, traditions, and ideas from that period that persist that are not as appropriate as they once were. There is, however, also a different class of methods of doing things that persist because after much trial and error, because these methods have proven workable, useful, and often are the optimum way of doing things.

Here's an example of this from another field. During World War I from 1914 to 1918 the airplane was first used as a weapon of war. When pilots and commanders first experimented with different flying formations, some flew in huge V formations while others flew in a long straight line, or pairs, etc. After 30 or 40 years of war and preparing for war, though, many air forces adopted what is called the "finger four" formation (or some variation of that formation) that approximates the positions of the fingers on the human hand. These air forces, through trial and error and dealing with reality on a life and death basis, had come up with the same solution that "evolution" or "intelligent design" or "God or the "life force" had also arrived at with the human hand. Why? They were both dealing with reality and they came up with a similar solution to the process of dealing with a similar reality. There are certain patterns of action and sequence that grow out of the trial and error process of dealing with reality. These workable patterns of actions often become the "professional" method or pattern of action of accomplishing various tasks.

People who build houses have learned over thousands of years dealing with reality that the first step in building a workable valuable house is virtually always laying down a foundation of some sort. Farmers know from many thousands of years practice that breaking ground and planting seeds is the first step in growing a crop. Similarly, blocking a scene or shot and setting a shot, in the process of shooting a scene corresponds to the laying of a foundation or breaking ground and planting seeds. In making movies and in many other fields difficult tasks that can be overwhelming if faced in total are dealt with successfully by breaking their actions down into sections or steps and assigning a certain pattern of actions and a sequence to each of the steps. You can see this in education, medicine, law, construction, and many other careers.

Blocking in movies is the first step in the very difficult task of shooting a properly composed, framed, lit, acted, and photographed shot or scene. During the first step of blocking the focus of attention is on physical position and movement of the actors and camera, not on performance or lighting or other aspects of the shot or scene. They will be dealt with in later steps of this overall process. The lighting step focuses on lighting only, to the exclusion of all else, and gets everyone not involved in lighting out of the way. The rehearsal step perfects the actors acting and the camera crew's actions to the point approaching perfection. It brings together all that has been done before it is time to shoot the shot. Shooting puts it all together with polish and is for real, and captures the images and sounds of the shot or scene.

In my opinion and experience, I've found that the two times a movie director works hardest and is under the most pressure is (a) during blocking and setting a shot, and (b) at the point of deciding whether to say "Print" and move on to the next shot or to decide to continue to shoot more takes. Directors with long or adequate shooting schedules and large budgets, and large quantities of film or video available are under a lot less pressure at these points of maximum pressure and concentration than directors working on low budgets, or on short or very short shooting schedules. Once a director delivers a blocking, sets the framing of the shot, and puts the actors through a full physical rehearsal and shows that full physical rehearsal to the cinematographer, camera crew, and the A.D., it becomes primarily the first A.D.'s job to push the process forward through lighting, rehearsing, and shooting until the director says "Print!"

This process is specifically designed this way so that during lighting, rehearsals, and shooting the director can be free to concentrate on perfecting the actor's performances and the shot, while the A.D. shoulders the burden of keeping things moving forward. A long time ago, when I was a student at UCLA, a heavily decorated veteran Army sergeant who was definitely a "leader of men" and knew a lot about leadership was teaching an ROTC class. He said that every infantry platoon in the U.S. Army runs a mile before breakfast and if a lieutenant is to lead that platoon and have the respect of the men in that platoon he had to be able to run that mile in front of that platoon. He went on to talk about how running that mile was something *physical* that could be easily seen and easily judged. He acknowledged that what a lieutenant had going on in his mind and brain might be a lot more important in determining how good or bad a custodian of the lives and safety of the men in his platoon that the lieutenant actually was. He was, however, absolute on the subject of the necessity for a lieutenant being able to run a mile leading his platoon to retain or acquire the respect on that platoon. There are about 30 to 40 men in an infantry platoon. It is about the same size as a movie crew, actors and staff. There is something similar to this lieutenant example regarding a movie director, on the set with a crew, cast, and staff. If a director can walk onto the set, and get right down to business and block the first shot in a direct businesslike manner, then block shot after shot and get them in a time frame that is appropriate for the movie's shooting schedule, the crew will tend to believe that the director knows what he or she is doing. Sometimes this demonstration of competence might include humor and joking around, but regardless, a director who operates like this will show he or she has done his or her homework and is professional. That director is *running ahead* of that crew and they will tend to respect and follow that director.

On the other hand, if the director cannot or does not block out a scene or shot and show the D.P. and camera crew and actors and A.D. a physical rehearsal and set, frame the shot and take the lead and *stay ahead* of the crew, the actors will doubt that the director knows what he or she wants and doubt that director has done the necessary homework. Since the time cavemen joined together in small groups to hunt large animals, and cave women formed into groups to gather fruits, berries, and nuts and to better supervise and care for children, people have tended to want to follow competent leaders, and usually after a while they tend to become critical of and would mutiny from and rebel against and cut off the heads of incompetent would-be leaders.

Leading a crew and cast and staff or a motion picture company is part of the director's job. In using the word "company" here, I mean this in the sense of a theatrical company. I've seen a movie crew that was not being paid a cent work very, very hard in pouring rain because they believed that the director who was directing them knew what he was doing, and was leading them properly and was using best efforts to the best advantage to create something good. This company's morale was high. Their pay was zero but they moved forward following the director because of a long time well-developed human instinct to follow competent leadership. I have also seen very well-paid crews that were not being asked to do work that was extraordinarily difficult, become quickly critical, rebellious, and balky because the director was incompetent, unsure of what he wanted, and blatantly wasted the crew's energies and efforts.

It's not true that any director who faces crew or cast criticism, or rebellious attitudes is necessarily incompetent or doing a job badly. There's a certain type of personality that I call the *professional leader of the revolution.* Some crews and movie companies are fortunate to have none of these types of people or to get rid of them early, but many crew, staffs, and cast unfortunately have one or more of these virulent, dangerous pests. I will talk more about these *professional leaders of the revolution* in a later section of this book.

Don't be too sure that because a director is the target of crew or cast criticism that it is the director that is in the wrong. It may be those who are criticizing loudest who are really in the wrong. Almost always, if the director is doing his or her job well and "running ahead" the best people in the crew or cast will follow and respect that director despite what ambient criticism or rebellion may be rattling around. About 20 years ago, a presidential campaign said, "A fish rots from the head down." Almost always, when you see a movie set that has degenerated into a mess, the source of the mess can be traced back to a director that has not properly blocked out the scene or shot and has not shown a full physical rehearsal with the actors' exact positions to the cinematographer, camera crew, and first A.D. The other common cause of a set being a mess is that the first A.D. is grossly incompetent. It is the job of the director to block out the scene or shot and to set and frame the shot, and the job of the first A.D. to push forward the process of block it, light it, rehearse it, shoot in, print it.

When the Director's Guild hands out its awards, they go to both the directors and their assistant directors. Commonly, when a production falls behind schedule, the first A.D. is first to catch the wrath of the producer, or completion bond representative. It is also common practice that the first A.D. directs extras and background action. The director and the first A.D. should work as a team. The director is responsible for what the first A.D. does or does not do. If the first A.D. is not doing his or her job effectively it's the director's job to correct or replace the first A.D. The first A.D. and second A.D.'s should also work as a team transferring the actors and talent onto and off of the set as is appropriate to the block it, light it, rehearse it, shoot it, print it pattern of action. If a director and first A.D. can move through that process productively and deliberately and precisely *once*, then they should be able to repeat that productive pattern of action again and again until the director has shot enough shots to get his or her day. That's how a director can shoot a movie basically on schedule. If a director can not block a scene in a reasonable period of time in relation to the movie's schedule, and the A.D. cannot push the crew and cast through the process in a direct, orderly pattern even once, then the set is likely to degenerate into a mess, and can begin to resemble a fish pulled out of the water, flopping around on dry land. When a set degenerates into a mess, if the movie is being shot on a short shooting schedule and a low budget, the movie's fate quickly comes into question. Whether the movie can or will be completed will quickly come under doubt and the morale of the people working on the movie is likely to plunge as they begin to doubt whether their work will ever yield anything positive or valuable. This is an ugly process. It is a trap no one wants to fall into. When you see a director behind schedule on a set that's become a mess, you will often see a furious, screaming director. The type of director who then blames everything (for which his non-blocking is responsible) on others is the captain of a ship that will soon sink.

The cause of this kind of tragic situation is usually quite simple. The director did not block out and show full physical rehearsals to the D.P., the A.D., and the camera crew, and did not fully and properly set shots in a deliberate manner.

Very many *vital* things in life are based on a very simple pattern of actions repeated many times over and over in virtually the same pattern. The human heart beats millions of times during a person's life, but it does not beat a million different ways. It beats virtually the same way many millions of times. If a human heart deviates even slightly or temporarily from its normal optimum pattern, it can easily threaten the life of the body to which it belongs. The same kind of thing is true of human lungs. It is also true of the internal combustion engine, which repeats a simple pattern of action the same way billions of times as does the flush toilet, and a well-designed wheel.

Our planet Earth has revolved around the sun billions of times pretty much the same way, in pretty much the same pattern of action, and the moon has revolved around the Earth billions of times pretty much in the same pattern of action. This phenomenon of a simple action composed of a simple uncomplicated pattern or smaller actions being repeated a huge number of times is clearly observable in the physical world from things as small as the atom to things as larger as a solar system or galaxy, and this same phenomenon is also clearly observable in many aspects of life and the world of living things and social organizations and many fields of activity.

The legendary German philosopher Fredrich Nietzsche gave this phenomenon a name. He called it the *eternal recurrence* and attached a mystical quality to it, identifying it as one of the codes of how the real world works.

These repetitive patterns of productive action are *not* determined by someone's opinion. They exist because they *work*. They deal with real things in the real world. This is true whether you are talking about the human heart, or lungs, or the internal combustion engine or wheel.

I would say that someone who avoids or tries to circumvent this process of block it, light it, rehearse it, shoot it, print it, is not just in disagreement with me, my experience, my ideas or what Haskell Wexler said on the DVD of *Who's Afraid of Virginia Woolf* or what has been common professional practice in the movie business and has been for a long time. They are probably in a serious disagreement with how the real world works and the method that has been found to deal with the real problems in the real world that relate to setting up and shooting a shot. *Movies are composed of shots!*

When someone tries to ignore or contradict how the real world works, the very real world usually steps on him or her, often very hard. Again, the great writer Robert J. Ringer said, "If you acknowledge reality, it automatically works for you. If you fail to acknowledge reality, it automatically works against you." Many failed and incomplete movies, and many trips to the bottom of "filmmaker hell" are the results of failure to acknowledge the reality of the method outlined in this chapter.

The word *simple* has two very different meanings. This has lead some people to seriously painful and destructive misunderstandings. One meaning of simple is "easy" or "easy to do." Another meaning is "uncomplicated." Some times, what is uncomplicated is very difficult to do. Some times what it uncomplicated is *not* easy to do. When a director first arrives on the set in the morning or when key cast and crew arrive, what is *extremely uncomplicated* is for the director to call for the actors in the first shot, and the A.D. and the D.P. to the location of the first shot and directly, deliberately and full block out and set the first shot of the day. This is also not easy. It's often very difficult, but it also is very productive, and simple in the sense that is not complicated.

How soon the director gets the first shot of the day often has a lot to do with how productive that day will be. When a director finishes shooting a shot and says "Print" it is quite uncomplicated for the director to immediately call for and get the actors for the next shot and without delay deliberately and precisely and fully block out and set the next shot and turn the set over to the A.D. and the lighting crew.

The hardest task that a director faces is to fully block out a scene or shot, and to set a shot but it is also an uncomplicated *simple* task if it is faced directly and dealt with "head on" in a businesslike manner. It's simple, uncomplicated, but not easy. If the director avoids or does not do this vital part of the director's job things will quickly become very complicated. I have seen directors take refuge in complicated crap because they could not face what was uncomplicated and difficult. The way that movies are made is that some people work very hard while others wait for their turn to work. Then, those who worked hard wait for their chance to work again, while those who were waiting work hard. While the actors and director are off the set waiting while the lighting crew is working hard lighting the set, and the lighting crew is off the set or watching, when the director and actors and camera crew are blocking the scene or shot and setting the shot, and the director is working very hard, there are many other alternations of hard work, and waiting that involve just about everyone who works on movies. To some extent, these alternations of hard work and waiting are unavoidable. The great movie actor Jack Lemmon said that if he knew how much time he'd spend waiting while acting in movie, he would have found a way to study various subjects while waiting. He estimated that if he'd done that he would have had at least two or three Ph.D.'s by the later part of his career.

If you can squarely face up to something as simple and as difficult as block it, light it, rehearse it, shoot it, print it, you can probably make a movie. If you can't, then you probably can't make a movie! It's usually that simple.

CHAPTER FOUR:
HOW SUCCESSFUL DIRECTORS PREPARE TO SHOOT MOVIES
AND HOW UNSUCCESSFUL WOULD-BE DIRECTORS
FAIL TO PREPARE

The most thorough and complete process of preparation to direct a movie that I ever heard of a director using is the method of preparation used by legendary filmmaker Luis Bunuel, who was born in 1900. When he was 30, Bunuel made a landmark silent surrealist art movie with the noted surrealist painter Salvador Dali. The movie was *Chien Andalou* (The Andalusian Dog), and it was 18 minutes long. It caused quite a stir and is still virtually mandatory viewing for film students and students of movie history. Bunuel followed this film with *Age De Ore*, 90 minutes long and another surrealist "free form" film that is either a masterpiece or a mess, depending upon your reaction to it. Following that Bunuel, in his native Spain, served as executive producer on mainstream commercial movies. When fascism came to Spain in the 1930s, Bunuel left because he was politically on the far left. He migrated to the USA and worked in the dubbing department of Warner Bros. until he was about 50 and was pretty much forgotten as a tiny oddity footnote in most histories of movies. Then he got a chance to resume his directing career in Mexico. He directed a small Mexican movie *Grand Casino*. The producer was very disappointed with the product of his directing. The cost of film stock and lab processing was a major part of the budget of low budget Mexican movies at that time, and Bunuel shot *only* master shots on *Grand Casino*; there was no coverage.

The film did not work, and Bunuel knew it. He did not get another directing job for two years. When he was allowed to direct another movie, he was determined to succeed. His budget would not allow him to shoot a lot of film, however. He could not shoot a master, some close-ups, two shots, three shots, and reverses on whole scenes, or large parts of scenes. Bunuel knew shooting only masters would not work, so what to do?

His solution to this problem is the most thorough and complete directional preparation I have ever discovered. *Bunuel's method was to memorize the movie's script, every word.* Then he would sit alone in a room, shut his eyes, and say the entire script over and over until he could visualize exactly the entire movie, *shot by shot.* Yes, shot by shot – camera angle to camera angle, cut to cut. When Bunuel had the entire movie in his mind, he felt he was ready to shoot it. This very intense method of preparation served Bunuel very well, and lead to a very prolific, economical, and artistically free, acclaimed and honored career. All starting at age when most men would consider their chances finished. Over the next 25 years, he directed approximately 27 movies, many of which won major awards, including an Oscar in 1973 for Best Foreign Language Movie, for *The Discreet Charm of the Bourgeoisie.* Some of his most honored and acclaimed movies are *Tristana, Belle de Jour* (his most financially successful and widely seen film), *Simon in the Desert, Diary of a Chambermaid, The Exterminating Angle, Viridiana, Nazarin, The Criminal life of Archibaldo de al Cruz, El, Robinson Crusoe, El Bruto,* and *Los Olvidados.* David Chase, the executive producer and creator of *The Sopranos* and director of the pilot episode, and Wes Craven, the "Master of Horror," both name Bunuel as their favorite director. If someone took a poll of very successful directors I'm sure Bunuel would rank very highly, particularly among those who are interested in dreams, and value surrealism.

Daniel Pilon, an actor, was in two of my movies and also had a major role in Luis Bunuel's *The Milky Way*. Daniel told me that Bunuel was very calm on set, almost bored some times. Why not, he'd already seen the movie in his mind! Bunuel's reputation was that he never raised his voice or lost his temper on the set. Daniel Pilon told me that Bunuel would rehearse a lot but only shoot one or two takes and move on very deliberately.

Many of Bunuel's movies had short, or very short shooting schedules. His way of preparing to shoot is the ultimate in pre-production preparation. It is the ultimate of the director having the movie contained in his or her mind. Similarly, Alfred Hitchcock was famous for his use of storyboards, and detailed pre-production preparation and his calmness on the set, often getting a haircut while a shot was being lit.

At the other end of this pre-production preparation is Roman Polanski's way of preparing to shoot a movie. Contrary to the way Bunuel and Hitchcock worked, Polanski said that he tries to arrive on the set *without preconceived ideas* about how he will shoot a scene or what shots he will shoot. I believe Polanski did a lot of study of the script (as a work of dramatic literature) before shooting scenes, but he did not want to deal with shots, camera angles, a shot list, etc. until he had blocked out and rehearsed a scene. Then on the set, after he'd seen the scenes rehearsed, he'd decide how to cover that scene. You can't argue with Polanski's results. In my opinion, six of his films are masterpieces. I don't believe, however, he is noted for short shooting schedules, and anyone who wants to try his way of preparing would do well to be sure that their shooting schedule is long enough to accommodate the "working things out on set" that this method entails. They also might do well to be sure that their level of cinematic genius is equal to Polanski, so that some of the lack of economy inherent in this way of working will be tolerated by the people who are supporting them.

Directors have various ways of preparing or not preparing to shoot movies. Most of these processes of preparation fall somewhere between Bunuel's ultra-preparation and Polanski's desire to avoid preconceived ideas. I'm going to detail the process of preparing to shoot a movie that I use, one I've developed by trial and error over a large number of movies. Different directors may or may not do some of the things I'll list, but usually they will have similar or other methods for dealing with the common problems and tasks directors face in shooting movies. I'm not saying that this method of preparing is the best way, or the only way, but it is a method of preparation that does work. I am a big believer in the importance of *location* and the importance of a director mentality "owning" and "using" the location to advantage. Here is my view on the proper steps for the director to take regarding a location. This view is greatly influenced by low budget movie making.

1. Before a director accepts a location he or she should go to the location and read the actual scenes to be shot in the location and be sure that the scene(s) can be shot as written. He or she also needs to determine whether or not to change the scene(s) to accommodate the location.

That may sound simple, but it's not always as simple as it seems. A location can look good and also be a place where it's impossible to shoot scenes as written. On a movie that an associate of mine was trying to direct, I was functioning as a consultant and trying to dig him out of a huge amount of trouble that he had tripped and fallen into. I started trying to help him on a Sunday after his first week of shooting. He was going to resume shooting the next day. The first thing I did was to ask him to show me the location of the first scene he planned to shoot on Monday. We went to the location with a script and once there I read the first party of the scene to him and asked, "Where's that going to happen?" He explained. I read more of the scene and asked the same question repeatedly, moving forward in the script each time until we came to a part of the scene that could *not* be executed in that room as written. I told him, "You either need to change the scene to fit the location or change the location to fit the script as written." I pointed out that he'd accepted this location and paid a lot of money to rent it and had established it by shooting other scenes in the locations connected to it, without doing what I consider to be Step #1 in a director's job in dealing with locations – *reading the scenes in the location and being sure that the scenes can be shot as written in that location, or changing the scene so that it can be shot in the location as it exists.*

I also pointed out to my associate who was trying with much difficulty to be a director that it was a lot better to discover on the Sunday before the scene was scheduled to shoot that it could not be shot as written in that location, than to discover this difficult problem in the middle of shooting the scene on Monday, with an entire crew watching you.

Locations can look nice or be visually seductive, but the director needs to know whether or not scenes can be shot in them or whether the locations are so good that scenes should be changed to accommodate them. The best way to deal with this reality is for the director to *read the scene at the location* and answer the question, "Where will this be shot?"

2. The next step in the process of the director dealing with locations and the progression of preparing to turn a script into a movie is for the director to be alone in the actual location (or with a low rent assistant who will not cause any time pressure on the director) with the script, and for the director to read the scenes that are to be shot in that location and plan out how to shoot the scenes, and at least to begin to decide on the types of shots that will compose the scenes "coverage" and where and how the various parts of the scene will be staged. It is important for the director to do this process *without time pressure.* The process of a director deciding how to shoot a scene, what types of shots to shoot, what angles to use, what parts of the location to show, where to shoot which parts of the scene, where the actors will stand or move, often goes through "drafts" the way a script starts with a story outline and then a treatment, then a rough draft, to a first draft, to other drafts. Some editors work this way as well. First, they assemble the shots into a rough assembly then a rough cut, and then a fine cut and eventually a final cut and "lock."

Some directors go onto a movie set and set up a shot in one direction, with a particular lens and the actors are standing at certain specific positions and the cinematographer and lighting crew light that shot, and before shooting the shot the director changes his or her mind and changes the camera position and the shot. The cinematographer and lighting crew are very likely to become quite unhappy, and specifically very unhappy with and critical of the director if they have to relight. They are often very vocal about their unhappiness.

That is why I feel that it's very important for the director to spend time at the actual location of a scene with a script and *no time pressure.* If the director is alone on the set with the script, the director is free to go through a number of "drafts" of how to stage, block, and shoot the scene without wasting time, money, energy, goodwill, infuriating the crew, cinematographer, and producer. A director alone on the location or set with the script is free to consider a lot of options, to think freely, and to entertain and reject various approaches to setting the shots that will "cover" the scene.

A director who does not have time alone on the set in pre-production with the script with no time pressure runs the risk of doing some of this creative process, of going through drafts of shots in front of a very unsympathetic crew and a very budget-conscious producer, and possibly some confused and disillusioned actors.

3. The third step which I use in a director's process of preparation to shoot in a location is for the first assistant director and the director to briefly visit the location, and for the director to tell the A.D. roughly how he or she plans to shoot the scene. This step has some benefits for the director, and some for the A.D.

Some of the benefits to the director visiting the major locations with the first A.D. are that it gives the director a chance to bounce his or her ideas off a receptive and hopefully "helpful" associate or comrade. It is one thing to develop ideas in one's mind, but once a person starts to transmit those ideas to even one other person it forces the person transmitting those idea to focus and clarify those ideas. Hopefully, that is a benefit that flows to the director when visiting locations with the A.D. It also provides an opportunity to weed out bad ideas and to accept or reject ideas that the A.D. may present.

Visiting locations with the director gives the A.D. an early chance to start thinking about and dealing with practical matters that will become of great importance on the day of the shoot, things like:

- Where can the vehicles park?
- Are there restrooms?
- Is there electricity or do we need a generator?
- Where can I put makeup and hair, and dressing rooms and wardrobe?
- Where can craft services (food and coffee) go?
- Where can the actors wait?

These practical considerations are front and center in the A.D.'s mind, and the earlier the A.D. thinks about them and knows what the director is planning to do, the better prepared the A.D. can become.

4. The fourth step and last before actual shooting is for the director to visit every major location on a "recon" with the first A.D., the location manager, and maybe the second A.D. Also, with the cinematographer, the gaffer, the sound recordist, the art director, production designer, and set dresser. This recon of all locations is typically done around the last week of pre-production, and usually takes one day, or a bit more. *This is vital!* It is indispensable, and must be done. Any director who does *not* visit every important location on a proper recon with all the proper departments represented is just asking for very, very unpleasant costly time-consuming surprises

and delays on the day of shooting. This recon allows camera, lighting, sound, and art departments to know what kind of additional equipment may be needed for particular scenes. It gives a chance to scrub (cancel) a location because useable sound cannot be recorded there, or other unforeseen problems that could arise. Proper preparation with locations prevents piss-poor performance. The outcome of all contests is determined by previous preparation. Without such preparation failure is assured.

In my opinion, rehearsals during pre-production are a vital part of directorial preparation for shooting a movie, particularly a low budget movie. I am a very big believer in the importance of pre-production rehearsals, particularly for low budget movies. I've learned by much first-hand experience wearing many different "hats" on movie sets that the number of scripts that should be and can be successful shot *exactly as written* is very small in relation to the number of scripts that are written and made into movies. There are few scripts that really should be shot exactly as written into low budget movies. *Reservoir Dogs, Clerks, Coffee and Cigarettes* are some exceptions. Some of the first jobs that I had in the business were editing low budget movies. I soon found that a big part of that job was figuring out ways to cut out *over-written, badly delivered dialogue*. I learned to dump excess, wooden, overly wordy speeches from the screen.

When I started directing movies from my own scripts that were "dialogue rich" I quickly saw in rehearsals that some of the dialogue was too long and over-written. Lines of dialogue that seem indispensable and perfectly perfect, oh so precious to me, the writer, when I was alone in a room writing, reading, and rewriting them, seemed often to be clunky, particularly when I heard these overly long speeches coming out of the mouths of low budget actors. When I was a film student at UCLA, I took a course in screenwriting from the much-admired professor Marvin Borowsky. He addressed the subject of overly written dialogue about as well as anyone I've ever heard. Professor Borowsky was a veteran screenwriter before becoming a teacher of screenwriting. He admitted that he personally had been in screenings of movies he'd written and had the very unpleasant experience of watching a "too long" speech that he'd written play out on the screen in front of an audience. He admitted thinking to himself, "How could I have written something so wordy and over-written?" or "How could I have burdened that poor actor with so many extra words?" and "How could a speech that I thought I'd pruned and polished and cut to the bone and they trimmed in editing seem so much more long and clumsy and unnecessarily wordy when said by an actor and shown on a movie screen?" Professor Borowsky said that on such occasions he'd hoped that nobody at the screening or in the theater knew he was the writer of the overly long speech, and he felt like hiding under his chair and quickly crawling out of the theater, hoping that nobody would see him.

When I was a novice movie editor trying to figure out ways to dump pages of script and minutes of film without losing vital information, all because of long, bad, and badly-delivered dialogue, I definitely remembered Professor Borowsky's very sharp warning to film students and student screenwriters about how easy it is and how embarrassing it is to over-write dialogue. When I began rehearsing actors with scripts that others or I had written, the warnings came back to me again, and were supported by my own memories in the editing room trying to invisibly get rid of dialogue that should have been eliminated *during script rewrites* or *during rehearsals!*

I have observed that this process of dumping, shortening, condensing, and focusing dialogue is a process that usually proceeds through the writing and *rewriting* of the shooting script, through rehearsals, through filming or videotaping, and through editing and re-editing.

I've observed that a script is like a drawing or painting of an airplane and a movie is like an actual plane that either flies or crashes. It's a common practice for airplane pilots to rev their engines up to high power during pre-flight checking to be sure that these engines are not likely to fail on takeoff and cause the plan to crash. I regard one of the major purposes of rehearsals (particularly on low budget movies) is to test out each line of dialogue and see it if flies or if it doesn't fly, then fix it or get rid of it. It's much easier to get rid of dialogue that's not working in rehearsals than on the set or in editing. As I said earlier, there are a few scripts that deserve to be shot exactly as written and can be successfully shot as written, but *almost none of them are available to be shot on low budgets*. Writers who write perfect scripts usually get paid more for a script than a low budget movie's entire budget. In another book about screenwriting, I observed and commented at length that in successful movies a very high percentage of an actor's speeches are one line long. Anyone who has read a lot of scripts (whether filmed or not) will probably notice that the overall body of scripts that are out there bouncing around Hollywood and keeping copy shops prosperous do not have a high percentage of speeches by actors that are one line long. Most of them usually have some dialogue that the writer dearly loves, but will not fly when spoken by actors in front of a movie camera. Shortening, perfecting and testing dialogue in scripts is as important a part of rehearsals as the more obviously important perfection of the performances of actors that includes pushing them to learn and become familiar with their lines.

Dialogue can be of enormous value, and have a unique power to activate emotion in the audience or viewer and portray, reveal and illustrate character, and to go inside character's minds. Screenwriters who resort first to dialogue to tell their story, however, and do not search hard and inventively for visual ways to accomplish that task need to be reminded that movies began and existed (in the nickelodeon phase) for a significant period of time and drew viewers without *any* participation of writers, but simply as a visual medium. That is the genesis and still a basic part of the appeal of *motion pictures*! This is not true of television. In pre-production, the director may have to deal with a script that has been written by a *worrified* writer, whose first instinct is to reach for wooden, wordy dialogue, often over-written, to tell the story. The director may even *be* that worrified writer. Part of the director's job in rehearsals and pre-production is to *think visually* and look for ways that the story can be told *visually*, not just with spoken words. The director needs to bring a fresh visually-oriented, dialogue skeptical POV to the script in pre-production and rehearsals and preparation particularly if he or she were also the movie's writer or co-writer. Often, the director needs to seriously rewrite the script when making the shooting script.

Here are some more true facts about dialogue that are guaranteed to infuriate some screenwriters. There's a British director named Mike Leigh. He makes his movies from treatments and develops his movie's dialogue from actors' improvisations. One of his movies, *Secrets and Lies* (1996) was nominated for Best Picture and Best Writing, Screenplay Written Directly for the Screen despite its tiny budget and non-star actors. He was nominated for Best Writing, Screenplay Written Directly for the Screen for *Topsy Turvey* (1999), and for Best Achievement in Directing, and Best Writing, Original Screenplay for *Vera Drake* (2004), then again for Best

Writing, Screenplay Written Directly for the Screen for *Happy-Go-Lucky* (2008). A screenwriter did *not* write the dialogue for those movies; it grew out of actors' improvisations in rehearsals that were directed by Mike Leigh.

I've used that technique myself in some scenes, never in an entire movie, but brother would I love to try it. John Cassavetes used the technique on a few movies. One of them, *Faces* (1968), was nominated for Best Writing, Story and Screenplay - Written Directly for the Screen. Many movie DVDs show a movie's outtakes (scenes not used in a movie). Many modern directors shoot what's written in the script and also let the actors improvise in other takes and pick and choose what they think is best. Unless a director is girdled into being in a "minimal director" situation where they are obligated or forced to shoot the script as written, the director should recognize that often actors *can* be a resource, and a good line is a good line. Whether it was written alone in a room by a writer or an actor improvises it during rehearsal.

A line that is written on a piece of paper called a page of a script by a writer is not automatically holy or sacred or untouchable just because a writer wrote it. It is as good as it is good or as bad as it is bad. Often in rehearsals actors can improve or fix dialogue. Sometimes actors are more in touch with their own character than the writer was, because the writer had many characters, a plot, and themes to worry about, not just one character like the actor. *By whatever means necessary*, a director needs to put something good on the screen and make a good movie. Rehearsals are potentially a wide-open, multi-faceted *tool* to do this!

Writing really good dialogue is very difficult, and that's why writers who can do it get paid a lot of money and they work for TV or movie studios, and only very rarely is one of their scripts available to be shot on a low budget, but that does not relieve a low budget director of the need for and responsibility for workable, effective, even excellent dialogue. Clunky, overly long, often clumsily delivered dialogue is a jinx or curse of very many low budget movies. *Don't let it happen to you!*

In addition to the obvious uses of rehearsals, directors on low budget movies (or any movie) can also use rehearsals very profitably for other functions to properly and thoroughly prepare to shoot their movie. Directors can use pre-production rehearsals to develop and refine and test and adopt or reject blockings. The director can use a small video camera to virtually rehearse the shooting of the entire movie and to test out various types of coverage of a scene. It is possible for the director in pre-production rehearsals to make a virtual videotape storyboard of at least the movie's dialogue scenes. The director can discuss this video storyboard with the D.P. and others. I know of one case where a struggling director was offered the chance to make a video storyboard and he turned it down, and when making the movie he went down the drain very ingloriously. He should have taken advantage of the opportunity to make a video storyboard. It might have saved him from a quick trip to filmmaker hell.

The way I approach pre-production rehearsals is first I work on the dialogue in the dialogue scenes with the actors. I make sure that the actors are comfortable with the dialogue as the screenwriter wrote it, or if not, I usually ask the same question that John Ford often asked his actors, "How would you say it in your own words?" I change the dialogue to make it work. Some times in rehearsals it's obvious that some lines can be dropped or consolidated, and I do that and have the script supervisor make a record of all dialogue changes. I also videotape all these dialogue changes so that there's a permanent objective record of them. I never ever want to be trapped on a set with an actor struggling with unworkable, uncomfortable, unreal dialogue while a whole crew stands around wondering why this wasn't handled at the writing or rehearsal stage.

The second order of business in pre-production rehearsals is the actor's performance. You don't want to burn actors out in rehearsals. You don't want actors to leave their best performance in rehearsal, but you do want to be sure that the scene works and any potential problems in the scene or the actors' performance have been worked out in rehearsals so it will not unnecessarily delay progress on the set during shooting.

Then I work on blocking. The actors are available to the director during pre-production rehearsals if the director follows anything close to the method of dealing with locations that I outlined the director should have some ideas about how they intend to use the location and how they intend to stage the scene or shot, and rehearsals are the perfect place to test out some of these blocking ideas, and develop and perfect blocking. Hours can be spent in rehearsals developing blockings with little or not real cost to the production and comparatively little time pressure on the director. Rehearsals can be and should be a very creative and productive time! I love rehearsals! Again, a small, hand-held video camera can be used during rehearsals by the director to test and adopt or reject various methods of covering a scene. The director can easily, during rehearsals, see how a scene would look if it were all shot in close-ups or if it was covered only in a master or if the camera moved in various ways or observed the scene from various types of camera positions: high angle, low angle, camera moving toward or away form actors, etc., or if it was all captured in one shot or in many shots.

Pre-production rehearsals when used properly and to full advantage can be a tremendous aid to directors in preparing themselves for the difficult and ultra-important parts of their job that include blocking out a scene and staging it in front of the camera on location and deciding how to cover the scene and how to shoot the shots that are the movie. Low budget movie directors have little time to do these important tasks on the set.

Directors on large budget movies with long shooting schedules have the option to defer a large part of rehearsals to "the day" of actually filming or videotaping. Personally, I don't think that this is a good idea, but it is the way that some directors that are far more successful than I do work. As I mentioned earlier, a common length of shooting schedule of a studio movie is around 16 weeks or approximately 80 shooting days, requiring the director to shoot about one and a half minutes of screen time of story, or pages of script, per shooting day. The highly-regarded director Ivan Pasner, who was of East European origin and a contemporary of directors Roman Polanski and Milos Forman, shot movies in Hollywood by the method of rehearsing in the morning before lunch and then shooting the scene or scenes he'd rehearsed after lunch. He did not care how much or how many people urged him to get his first shot early in the morning. You can shoot a movie that way if you have a studio movie sized shooting schedule, and only have to shoot a minute and a half a day. Pasner is one of the very few directors that I know of who actually threw away a script and improvised a good movie totally from scratch. It was called *Crime and Passion* and starred Omar Sharif and Karen Black, and was one of the most outrageously funny, surreal, absurd, bizarre, and smartly entertaining, unpredictable movies I've ever seen. There are advantages to extensive pre-production rehearsals even for movies with long studio movie size shooting schedules. Jim Cameron, the writer/director/producer of *Titanic*, said that after rehearsals with Kate Winslet and Leonardo Dicaprio, he rewrote his script incorporating what the actors had added that worked, and perfecting what was weak. He took advantage of these pre-production rehearsals to perfect and test his final shooting script. I personally think that is very wise, whatever the size of a movie's budget, or the length of it shooting schedule. On low budget movies with short or very short shooting schedules, it is not just wise to test and perfect the final shooting script in pre-production rehearsals, it is necessary or absolutely necessary. When I was a member of the Writers Guild of America, west I heard Waldo Salt, one of the Oscar-winning screenwriters of *Coming Home*, and the Oscar-winning writer of *Midnight Cowboy*. At one point in his talk, Salt spoke about how during pre-production on *Midnight Cowboy*, Jon Voight and Dustin Hoffman had audio taped their improvisations and how he'd made use of these taped improvisations in the final rewrite of the final shooting script. Salt said that Hoffman and Voight were very great artists and they contributed much to the movie, but he had no doubt that *he* (Salt) was the author of the movie. *Midnight Cowboy* is moviemaking at the very highest level and it profited much from pre-production rehearsals. It had great actors, a great writer, and a great director who all contributed to a great movie.

What director Fritz Lang quoted screenwriter Dudley Nichols as saying is basically *usually* true: "The script is only a blueprint. The director is the one who makes the movie." Some screenwriters feel that it is their job to sit alone in a room, or with another writer, to imagine the movie exactly in detail and write it, and it is other people's jobs to put on the screen exactly what they imagined and wrote. Very few screenwriters are good enough that the above is actually their real job description. Most of the time in movies, and particularly in low budget movies, the script gets changed, refined, perfected, made to work during pre-production while making of the movie. A lot of this process occurs during the writing of the shooting script, which often happens after many major locations have been found.

Let's take an honest look at facts about dramatic writing. Many of the very best dramatic writers of the 20th century wrote plays fro the Broadway stage. Many of these great playwrights changed their dialogue during or after rehearsals, after they saw their words spoken by actors. They changed what they'd written when alone in a room, during the initial writing of the play. It was common practice for these great playwrights to open their plays "out of town" (not in New York), away from the Broadway critics, so they could see how what they had written worked when performed in front of an audience. Often, they would rewrite scenes or sometimes an entire act after these "out of town" tests. Screenwriters who expect every word that they write to go to the screen exactly as they wrote it are claiming an ability of perfection and a privilege that many of the greatest dramatic writers of the 20th century did not possess or claim. TV writers, specifically head writers who are normally writer/producers known as "showrunners", are the only ones who can claim such a privilege, and even they have to deal with network executives and censors. Some screenwriters deserve such privileges due to their brilliance, but they are few. That's why some television is great and a lot of it is "crap".

Many people wonder why there are different versions of William Shakespeare's plays. Nobody knows for sure why this is the case. I have a guess. Shakespeare wrote his plays alone in a room; that was one version. Then, after watching the words performed, seeing actors say his words and watching scenes play out, he perfected the writing, sometimes more than once. I will, however, acknowledge that what I'm saying about pre-production rehearsals is not always true. I heard Robert Vaughn say that on the set of *The Magnificent Seven*, a classic movie derived from Akira Kurosawa's *Seven Samurai*, the pages of the script arrived every night before shooting the next day, and there were no pre-production rehearsals. Some times, that can work, but it's a big gamble, and not at all a good one for low budget filmmaking.

The most extreme (and extremely successful) effective example of the use of pre-production rehearsals I know of is Roger Corman's shooting of *Little Shop of Horrors*. The movie was made in 1960. On the DVD box it says it was shot in two days. I talked with someone who knew Corman from that time period, and he told me that the movie was shot over a weekend, mostly in a studio with two Mitchell cameras on dollies. According to my source, Roger Corman not only rehearsed his actors "to the max" he rehearsed the camera moves and coverage with viewfinder. When he started shooting he just shot and shot and repeated the moves rehearsed. Some of the movie was shot exterior with more mobile cameras (probably second unit). *Little Shop of Horrors* had a talented and ultra-prepared director who used detailed rehearsals and preparation to maximum effect. It also had a very great script, and a very original and outrageous concept! The movie is a "cult classic" and a masterpiece shot in two days. Its budget was microscopic by today's standards. Its shooting schedule was tiny, but the movie that resulted is a product of very talented people, a comic masterpiece in fact. It is a must view for any low budget director. 50 years after it was made, it's still selling briskly in DVD, and may earn more money each year in DVD sales than its original production cost. It will probably be earning money and entertaining viewers 50 years from now. Some times the quality of a movie's concept, its story, its script, and the level of talent and preparedness of its director are more important than the length of a movie's shooting schedule, its budget size, or its resources or lack of resources. The cult classic film noir masterpiece *Detour* was shot in six days by the ultra-prepared director Edgar Ulmer. Early in his career, before becoming a director, Ulmer worked on both *The Cabinet of Dr. Caligari* and *Metropolis* as set dresser and art director. The classic 1956 *Invasion of the Body Snatchers*, directed by the ultra-prepared Don Siegel, was reportedly shot in 14 days, at and around the old Monogram Studios. Many consider this film to be one of the best sci-fi movies ever made. *Reservoir Dogs* was also shot on a short schedule by a very prepared Quentin Tarantino, who reportedly knew exactly what he wanted. *A very prepared Robert Rodriguez shot El Mariachi for a mere $8,000.*

Visiting locations, conducting rehearsals, perfecting a shooting script, making storyboards and notes on how scenes and shots are to be shot, are all ways of getting the movie into the director's mind and getting what is in the director's mind known and understood by the relevant people who are working on the movie. Even making a video storyboard can be part of proper pre-production for a low budget director. From the very beginning of pre-production and as it progresses toward production, the director will be called upon to make decisions that relate to the movie. Some people have great difficulty making decisions, often from fear of making a wrong decision. Such folks can become so indecisive that their inability to make decisions is much more harmful than occasionally making a wrong or non-optimum decision. These kinds of people usually have a very difficult time functioning as movie directors. They typically blame others for their own shortcomings or mistakes. They typically never admit a mistake. In their own minds, for them every mistake is someone else's fault. Since they make no mistakes (in their mind) they can't learn form their shortcomings. For them, all mistakes are someone else's fault because they are "perfect." A director does not have to decide everything when everyone else wants them to decide it, but a director cannot postpone all decisions indefinitely without very bad consequences.

It may be very legitimate to postpone difficult decisions until they can no longer be postponed without serious damage and then make those difficult decisions when the most information is available. One difficulty directors face is that the choices that they come up against are very often not between a good choice and a bad choice. Those decisions are usually easy. It is the decisions that are between a bad choice and a worse one, or between a good choice and a better choice that are more difficult. Also, directors are sometimes forced by necessity to make decisions when not enough information is available to really know what will turn out to be the correct decision. They sometimes just have time to take a best guess or evaluation or analysis and make or act on a hunch and hope for the best. Some times that works, some times it does not, and some times, that's all you can do.

Part of my advice on the subject of directors making decisions is to take a page from Sun Tzu and "Fight the fights you can win" first. If you are sure about a decision early in pre-production, *make that decision* and get out of the way. Turn the decision into an ally and conquered territory when you can. No matter how small it may be, it is now behind you. Make the decisions that can be made with a high degree of confidence. There is a symbiotic interrelationship between the process of making decisions and the process of the director getting the movie in his or her mind. The more clearly and the more focused the director has the movie in his or her mind, the easier that it will be for them to make decisions about that movie. Conversely, the more decisions that have been correctly made, the easier it is for the director to bring into clear and sharp focus the movie in his or her mind. These two activities support each other when they are properly done, and inhibit each other when they are *not* done or avoided.

I have seen indecisive "would be" directors who put off decisions that should have been made in pre-production until the very day of filming, with very bad results. I've seen them try to put off decisions that should have been made during pre-production or during filming until post-production. This also had very bad results. In one case, when I was trying to help a struggling director and I told him flat out, "You are so afraid of making a wrong decision that you are making no decision and that's a lot worse than making decisions and occasionally making a wrong decision or a mistake." For a while, my advice worked. The A.D. commented to me how improved this struggling director was for a while – he acted decisively.

A key point of decision-making or coming face to face with decisions for directors is the first production meeting. I will discuss this first production meeting in more detail in a later section, but now I'll cover some aspects of that very important ritual event that relates most sharply to the director. During the first production meeting, the entire script is read or covered. In this first production meeting, the director is likely to be asked a lot of very pointed questions by the staff key crew and department heads as they proceed through the script. In that first production meeting, the director is likely to be asked how he or she sees this or that, if he or she wants this or that, or if he or she wants "X" done this way or that way. It's not uncommon for a director to have twenty or more key decisions pushed into his or her face in that meeting. The director does

44

not have to make all these decisions on the spot instantly, but they can't be postponed or avoided forever. Excessively avoiding decisions not only robs the staff and crew of information they need to properly complete pre-production, it produces a director who has not been forced during pre-production to clarify and create the movie in his or her mind.

After the first bit of filming on *The French Connection*, the movie's director, William Friedkin, realized that what was on the screen in rushes did not match the movie in his mind. After a bit of thought he identified the cause of the problem. The heavy and immobile Mitchell cameras that he was shooting with were causing what he felt was a phony studio look and feel and the cameras were "cramping" the actors. He called the A.D. and ordered lighter, more mobile cameras, and did some reshooting and got what he wanted – the scenes on the screen matched those in his mind. It is important for the director to have the movie in her or his mind as much as possible before shooting begins.

So far in this chapter, the directorial preparation that I've talked about is preparation to shoot a specific movie. It is important but there is a much broader kind of preparation that a director needs to accomplish to be ready to direct a movie. In the Introduction of this book I outlined five levels of directorial preparation. There is also what I would call "life" or "professional" preparation. Some would-be directors I've talked to have mistakenly used Orson Welles' huge success with *Citizen Kane* at the age of 25 as evidence that diligent preparation is not necessary to be a director. As I said earlier, they mistakenly believed that Welles just walked onto the set and because he was a genius, he made a genius movie without much if any preparation to be a movie director.

The opposite is actually true. Orson Welles was probably one of the most prepared "first time" directors in the history of movies. When Welles was a young teenager he began acting in the theater. While still a teenager, he directed many plays, including classic plays. By the time Welles was 20 he was the highest paid actor in radio. At that time, in the 1930s, radio dramas were very big. Welles would travel in an ambulance from one radio studio to another all day long in New York City to do all his jobs. There was no law that you had to be sick or injured to be in an ambulance, so Welles used the ambulance to maximize the number of jobs he could do. Lots of people know of the radio drama *War of the Worlds* that Welles directed with his Mercury Theater, that caused a huge panic and brought him fame (or infamy, depending on your point of view). Fewer realize that this show brought him to Hollywood to make movies. What far fewer people know is that prior to his radio spectacular, Welles directed one of the most acclaimed and hugely original, unique productions of William Shakespeare's *Macbeth* ever staged. In the 1930s and the 1940s there was something called the Works Progress Administration (WPA). Mostly it is remembered for providing work to people during the Great Depression building parks, roads, and bridges, but it had an arts branch that paid artists to create paintings and murals for public buildings, and it also supported theatrical productions. Young Orson went to the WPA and said, "You want to employ people? I'll show you how to employ people." He staged an all black production of *Macbeth* at the 1,223 set Lafayette Theatre in Harlem. He changed the location of Shakespeare's play from Scotland to Haiti, and used a huge number of amateur actors, probably more than any other production of the play ever. Welles was not yet 21 when this production of the Federal Theater Project's Negro Unit opened on April 14, 1936. It was the beginning of a fantastic New York theater career for the eventual director of *Citizen Kane*. The play was such a must-see attraction, 40¢ tickets were scalped on the street for $3. One reviewer commented that Welles' production reached deeper into the themes of Shakespeare than any other production he'd seen.

When Welles arrived in Hollywood to direct his first movie, he was a very experienced and accomplished stage and radio director, and actor. He acknowledged that up to and through *Citizen Kane* everything that he had done in drama, acting or directing theater, radio, and movies, had been an enormous success. He was clearly a genius, and everyone knew it. Aside from that, Welles had a huge advantage over many other struggling first time directors. Despite all the acclaim, when Welles arrived in Hollywood, *he knew that he did not yet know how to make a movie*, and he knew that if he were to know how to make a movie he would have to study movies and learn. Welles' favorite director was John Ford. He watched one of John Ford's movies over 40 times. He watched many of Ford's movies many times. He studied them completely. He did not simply watch them for enjoyment, but to understand Ford's techniques. He was a student learning from a master. Welles also studied the films of the great silent movie genius, director D.W. Griffith. Many years later, Francois Truffaut said Griffith was the father of the "art form" of movies. Welles admired Griffith enormously as a great artist and studied his movies with serious artistic reverence. In another book I said, "Great writers learn from great writers who went before them, and good writers learn from the great and good writers who went before them." Welles was a very great director who learned by studying two very great directors who went before, D.W. Griffith and John Ford.

Greg Toland, the masterful cinematographer on *Citizen Kane*, during pre-production of the film taught Welles everything a movie director needs to know about the movie camera and photographing a movie in one day. That is a tribute to Toland's ability to teach, and willingness to teach, and willingness and desire to work with a director who was knowledgeable about the camera and cinematography, and it is also a tribute to Welles' ability as a student, and Welles' desire to learn and know the things that a movie director needs to know. Despite his previous accomplishments, Welles realized that he did not innately know everything a movie director needs to know.

Since some of my earliest jobs in the movie business I have encountered and sometimes worked for, or with, people who managed to talk or hustle their way into the job of movie director without having studied or learned how to actually do that job. These people had their names on the crew sheet next to the word director, and on the camera slate next to the word director, but since they did not know how to *do* the director's job. I *do not* consider them directors! Some of them were "first time/last time directors." Some of them, however, managed to stumble through more than one movie while diligently failing to study and learn how to actually do the director's job before crashing and burning, and falling into filmmaker hell in one way or another. Not a single one of these failed directors ever studied a movie they admired by watching it over 40 times. Not a single one of them ever sat down with a cinematographer, or took a course or read a book or shot a bunch of short movies on film or video to learn the things that a director needs to know about a movie camera or movie cinematography. Not one of these people ever read a book or in any other way tried to understand how actors work, or the art of blocking, or picturization or composition.

One of these people who thought that they were a director but never really studied or tried to learn the director's job. One "suffering director" asked me, "What does blocking mean?" That is like someone who thinks he or she is an accountant or wants to be an accountant asking, "What does addition and subtraction mean?" They were would-be directors who think they can make a movie because they could criticize and find fault with movies made by professional, competent directors, movies that have been distributed worldwide. They felt they were automatically better directors than those "mere" professional directors they could find fault with. Virtually everyone of these people were like backseat drivers who have never driven a motor vehicle, and find when they actually get behind the wheel that driving a vehicle is much different an activity than just criticizing another's driving. These ill fated want-to-be's found out that simply being a viewer is very different than *actually directing a film*.

One of the central methods of operations and key themes of this book is to compare and contrast that which has been very successful with that which has been very unsuccessful! Much of this book is organized around looking at and comparing the common denominators of what has been successful with the very different common denominators of what has been very unsuccessful.

Many of these failed directors did not lack intelligence. Some did not lack talent. Many had achieved considerable success in other fields, but all of them had serious *false basic assumptions* of one kind or another. When I say *false basic assumptions* I do *not* only mean a basic assumption that runs counter to what I personally believe. When I say *false basis assumption*, I'm talking about a basic assumption that demonstrably, observably, measurably run against, contrary to, and are the opposite of what is actually observably *fact*, not opinion, over the long history of movies and moviemaking.

One false basic assumption that virtually all failed directors shared was the belief that they did not need to study and learn, and to practice competency at the basic mechanism and important aspects of the director's job in order to be movie professionals. They virtually all also were very big on blaming others. They never admitted a mistake without blaming someone else for the mistake. They either did not learn from mistakes or only learned very slowly. They never seemed to recognize their own lack of knowledge about the director's job or their massive lack of preparation for that job as the real source of all their troubles. Instead, they often blamed those around them who were trying to help get a professional movie made.

Some unprepared directors suffer from what I call "kindergarten finger-painting" with regard to their viewpoint on art and being an artist. As far as I'm concerned, they're still operating under the teacher directive of "Express yourself, children." They usually view the movie they are making as all about them, their tastes, prejudices, ambitions, ego, and not all about the *paying audience*. If you look at very successful directors they usually have a strong connection with and understanding of the paying audience. Hitchcock is the leader of the pack in this arena. When I was a film student, the legendary Oscar-winning director and cinematographer Haskell Wexler spoke to some students including myself about being a dockworker before becoming a cinematographer. He said that as a young longshoreman he was full of political opinions and shared them liberally with fellow workers. Finally, one old salty longshoreman said to the young Wexler, "Kid, before you change the world too much, learn how to tie a bowline knot!" Wexler did well in transmitting that bit of wisdom to young, eager, ideologically oriented full of ourselves film students. It is still great advice.

Many of the failed, suffering, neophyte directors I've seen crash and burn in filmmaker's hell would have been much better off it they had *not* been so hypnotized by their own opinions. Their intense creative impulses made them feel oh so right, as though they knew more than those who had focused on becoming competent and proficient at various vital and important detailed aspects of the movie director's job.

Virtually all of these failed directors seemed to believe that "artists" (read: movie directors) were born, not made. They seemed to be unaware of the many great artists and artisans, famous painters, architects, and others who began their careers as apprentices to masters of various arts who became professionals and learned their art and professionalism from the masters to whom they were apprenticed. Many others including Picasso attending leading art schools. A movie director is a profession that requires talent and intelligence but it also requires study and practice in one form or another as well. I've observed that many failed directors seemed to think that if they admitted they didn't know something about the director's job or moviemaking, they would be admitting there were not a "born artist."

Oddly enough, most of these failed directors were not generally afraid of hard work. Many of them had worked very hard and achieved considerable success in other fields, in some cases in jobs in the movie business. Many of them worked very hard trying to direct movies, but none of them were willing to or did work hard to *learn how to direct a movie*. None of them would study and learn how to do the director's job or even learn the mechanics of it. None of them would properly or thoroughly prepare to direct. All of them seemed to believe, until they smashed into reality with a distinct thud, that inspiration would strike them on the set and as a result they would put something brilliant on the screen.

I never saw that happen once.

In contrast, Orson Welles, who had a lot of directing experience on radio and the stage before coming to Hollywood to make a movie, studied great movies made by great directors until his eyeballs were red. He knew he had a lot to learn and that he was up against a great challenge, and that he was not born knowing what a movie director needs to know. Then Greg Toland taught him about the movie camera, and Welles absorbed it like a smart sponge. The choice of Toland was, in fact, a brilliant piece of pre-production, not just because of his experience. Toland was an extraordinarily friendly cinematographer, and that helped greatly on the set.

One of Welles' major talents was his virtuoso skill and command of the arts of blocking and picturization; he had learned these arts well in the theater. The art of picturization is the placement of actors to create a picture on stage. Welles' placement of actors in *Citizen Kane* and their movement in relation to the viewer to support and reinforce the meaning of scenes was superb. With Greg Toland behind the camera, everything that happened in front of the lens made Welles' production like a great stage play. Much has been said and written about the extraordinary depth of field in *Citizen Kane*, but I've never seen anyone comment on *why* this extraordinary effect was so important to the movie. Since Toland could deliver it, however, it allowed Welles to stage shots with actors in the deep background, the background, the mid-foreground, and the foreground, *all in focus at the same time*. This occurs in very key scenes in the movie, as well as in other scenes. Toland was willing to come up with genius photographic innovations and inventions to push the limits of the movie camera, movie lighting, and cinematography so that Welles talents and storytelling strengths would not be cramped by technical photographic limits. He allowed all of Welles' ideas from the theater to flow out onto the movie screen, unhindered by the commonly accepted technical limitations of movie photography and accepted filmmaking conventions of the day. Toland *never* said to Welles anything like, "That may be how you did it on stage, but here's how we do it in the movies." He instead bent the way the movies did things to accommodate the full scope of Welles' genius, talent, and experience. This kind of director-friendly attitude is not always present, even in excellent cinematographers.

Not coincidentally, Toland was one of John Ford's favorite Directors of Photography. I believe Welles chose him after seeing his work in one or more of Ford's films when Welles was studying them. Toland's attitude made him the perfect choice for D.P. for the "Boy Wonder of Broadway" on stage and radio. Toland saw his job as something not to simply do with virtuoso excellence, but to support and free Orson Welles' genius. It is very important when preparing to make a movie to choose the *right* key people. Toland's lack of ego, probably spawned by security in his ability, is rare among D.P.'s.

Part of proper preparation to shoot a movie is to choose to work with people, particularly in key positions, who will work well as team members and will not unnecessarily sap the director's energies. Choosing Greg Toland was part of great preparation to make *Citizen Kane*. It is as important as the movie's detailed storyboards. During the first few days of the shoot, Welles would shout out directions to the lighting crew about where and how to place the lights. Welles was unaware that, in movies, unlike in the theater, the director does *not* control the placement of lights. That is done by the cinematographer. Toland just nodded to the crew and they followed Welles' instructions with only surreptitious adjustments by Toland behind the scenes, until one day a member of the lighting crew broke the news to Welles about the cinematographer controlling the lights in moviemaking. Welles was severely embarrassed and apologized profusely to Toland, who just chuckled a bit. Then Welles asked, "Why didn't you stop me?"

Toland answered, "I just wanted to see what you'd do, if you'd do anything I hadn't seen before or thought of." Toland was arguably the greatest cinematographer in the world at that time, and he was still eager to learn and see something new!

Orson Welles also learned from his veteran screenwriting partner, Herman Manckiewicz, his editor, Robert Wise, and his composer Bernard Hermann. He knew how to take and use good advice from the best people. In contrast, virtually every failed director that I've seen had a kind of reverse mental compass. They would reject good and sound advice from people with substantial experience and track records, while quickly accepting bad advice from questionable sources! They would often incorporate highly destructive advice (that I call "false wisdom") into their own highly destructive *false basic assumptions*. They often received what they wanted to hear, not what they needed to hear.

"The outcome of all contests is determined by previous preparation. Without such preparation, failure is assured."

"Proper preparation prevents piss-poor performance!"

Remember all that was said earlier about superior people and what they do. That is not only in the movies, but also in vastly different professional fields. General Colin Powell's in-depth preparation for the liberation of Kuwait in the first Gulf war, compared to Donald Rumsfeld's over-confident lack of preparation for the invasion and occupation of Iraq is a study in contrast of advanced preparation. It's one thing to start an activity, yet another to continue it once begun, and to properly complete it.

Orson Welles' storyboards and pre-production notes are included with the latest DVD edition of *Citizen Kane*. The DVD presents the movie's black and white cinematography with incredible beauty and detail. It's a great illustration of how some directors properly prepare and have amazing success.

I'll leave you in this chapter with a quote from a famous poet, Emily Dickinson:

"Luck is not chance, it's toil. Fortune's expensive smile is earned."

CHAPTER FIVE:
PICTURIZATION, COMPOSITION, BLOCKING, SETTING SHOTS, CREATING IMAGES, TELLING AND ENHANCING A STORY WITH IMAGES

When I was in pre-production for *Starship Invasions*, the movie's producers (money men) arranged for a very experienced Hollywood director, Ted Post, to consult with me. I'm very grateful to them for the time I spent learning from Ted. It was some of the most intensely valuable educational minutes and hours of my moviemaking experience. The first subject that I asked Ted about was, "Who sets the shots on your movies and TV shows, you or the D.P.?"

His answer was that he, the director, was the only one that set the shots on his movies and TV shows. When he said that, I looked over at my partner who was one of the producers as if to say, "See, I told you so."

My partner knew about and watched me have disputes with some D.P.'s over setting shots, and saw D.P.'s believe that it is the D.P.'s job to set shots. So when someone with the stature of Ted Post said exactly what I'd repeatedly said in arguments about the role of the director and the D.P., it settled the issues for me and finally for my partner as well. I hoped that this was one argument I would not have again.

Ted Post directed *Hang 'Em High* and *Magnum Force*, two of Clint Eastwood's best movies in the middle of Eastwood's career. He also directed *Go Tell The Spartans*, a Vietnam war movie that was ahead of its time that acquired a cult of admirers. He also directed other movies and TV movies, but a large part of his well-deserved stature was that he was a premiere TV director in the 1950s and 1960s, starting with the series *Danger* in 1950. He began his career in the theater directing plays, I believe, and then directed live television including a large number of episodes of *Armstrong Circle Theatre, Schlitz Playhouse,* and many other shows including *Gunsmoke, Rawhide* (featuring Clint Eastwood as "Rowdy Yates"), *The Rifleman, Peyton Place, Combat,* often alternating directing with Robert Altman. He knew a lot about blocking. He's spent a good deal of time on set blocking out scenes and shots, and setting shots.

A movie director is usually lucky to make one movie a year and usually spends less than one-third of that time on set, often a lot less than one-third of a year. In contrast, a TV director who worked almost constantly the way Ted did would spend a lot of time on set blocking and setting shots. Ted was not a writer-director, or a writer. He was a director. He got the script and shot it. He was very experienced and knowledgeable about blocking, working with actors, and setting shots. William Friedkin, whose *The Exorcist* also came out in 1973, admired *Magnum Force* so much he offered Eastwood the lead in his next movie, *Sorcerer* (which Eastwood turned down, not wanting to travel that year). Ted told me he bumped into Steven Spielberg on the studio lot and Spielberg told him that the scene in *Jaws* in front of the "vandalized" billboard that features Richard Dreyfuss and Roy Scheider and some elegant blocking was homage to Ted's blocking in *Peyton Place*. If you study this superbly blocked scene in *Jaws* and are familiar with the camera work and blocking Spielberg was referring to, it's easy to see their similarity and virtuosity.

The first thing that Ted taught me and wanted to show me related to blocking. He looked at me and said, "Imagine you are the camera, and I'm an actor." He looked straight at me and added, "When my face and body are facing you, that's the full frontal body position." Then he turned his head a bit sideways and said, "This is three-quarters frontal position." Then he pointed his head to the side. "This is the complete profile position." Then he pointed his head partly away from me and said, "This is three-quarters back position." He looked back directly away from me. "This is full back position." Then he slumped over so I could barely see his head. "This is extreme back." Then he said, *"Each of these body positions has a different meaning."*

This made a huge impression on my partner and me. I knew instantly this was important and that I was listening to someone who had very *superior knowledge* compared to what I knew about a subject that was vital to the director's job. Even while I was a student at UCLA making student films, I began to "collect" blockings, picturizations, and camera movement positions from movies I admired. I made stick figured storyboards and diagrams of shots, blockings, picturizations, compositions, camera positions, and movements from movies that I admired. When I first began directing student films, I was hit with the "big questions":

- Where does the camera go?
- Where does it point?
- Does it move?
- Where do the actors stand?
- Do they move?
- If so, where do they move?
- What's the framing?
-

Instinctively, I began studying and "collecting shots" that I admired in movies made by directors I admired. I analyzed and studied how these shots were made, put together, blockings, camera angles, and movie composition, picturization, collecting them in my director's notebook. I was like someone trying to learn a new language by listening to and writing down conversation in that language.

What Ted did when he showed me those body positions and named them was like someone saying, "Here's the alphabet and rules of grammar, and here's how to approach this language in a much more basic, fundamental way."

Years later, when I was advising a young beginning director (who not only became good but also a very successful screenwriter), I told him word for word what Ted told me about actor/camera body positions and when I said, "Each of these body positions has a different meaning" he said "Whoooaaah!" That is just what I thought when Ted presented the alphabet of body positions to me.

Suppose you were going to give a 90 to 120-minute speech to a huge audience in a language that was new to you. Do you think it would be a good idea to study that language and become conversant with its basics and how to use it? Would-be directors that I've watched perish did not study the language of blocking and picturization. Successful directors do study and become expert in those things; in fact, they become fluent in that language.

The next thing that Ted told me was that I must get a copy of a book called *The Five Fundamentals of Play Directing*. He said everything a director needed to know about blocking, picturization, and composition was laid out in detail in that book. He was right; they are! I suggest that anyone reading this book who wants to direct movies get a copy of that book and study the sections on picturization, blocking, composition, actors, and other parts of the book that are relevant to the work of a movie director. It very much is the intention of this chapter, this book, and the course in the back of the book to make the reader indelibly aware that these vital subjects exist, and they are a vital part of a director's job. Codified, very useful knowledge about these subjects is in the book Ted recommended.

If you want to be a successful movie director, a big part of the way to get there is to learn by studying the movies, scenes, and shots made by successful directors who have gone before you. Learn how to be successful from their art. If you at least recognize that blocking, picturization, composition, and setting shots are subjects that a director needs to study and know and you commit to studying and learning these subjects you will be light years ahead of many of the would-be directors that I've seen perish who did not even seem to know that these subjects existed, let alone where codified and written about validly, and were part of a movie director's job and were something that they needed to study and learn if they wanted to be real movie directors and survive, not dive into filmmaker hell.

Movies are still a relatively young art form. They are only a little over 110 years old. TV is just a bit over 60 years old. The theater, painting, sculpture, architecture, and dance are much older art forms. They are thousands of years old.

The subject of picturization and aesthetics of the art and form is thousands of years old and was very well developed in the theater, in painting, in sculpture, in architecture, and in dance long before the first movie was made. Movie directors can learn much that is relevant from a study of these arts.

Here are some quotes from the chapter on picturization in *The Five Fundamentals of Play Directing*. I'm not presenting these quotations as a substitute for reading the book, but hopefully as a stimulant to encourage my readers to study it for themselves.

EFFECT OF COMPOSITION ON AUDIENCE EMOTION

It is a well-known fact that the human being is moved emotionally by shapes. In nature we experience emotion when looking intently at a mountain or when looking at a broad, flat plain.

***

So strong is this effect on the human being that, whether he is conscious or unconscious of it, when viewing a piece of art he feels a kindred association with what he feels when watching excessive shapes in nature. The great perpendicular slabs that form the skyscrapers of New York City, the single shaft of the

Washington monument or the sweeping curve of the great arch in St. Louis all around is man an emotional reaction. Huge masses like the pyramids in Egypt or the Coliseum in Rome affect us differently from the lofty tree or the inspiring tower. The perpendicular line sends us heavenward; the horizontal makes us want to relax. The weight of a large mass may impress us even to terror. The large open courts of the colleges at Oxford affect us very differently from the cramped catacombs in Sicily.

Shapes, then, are made up of line, mass, and forms. The emotional feeling aroused in the spectator from the arrangement of line, mass, and form is known as *mood*. We are not considering, at this time, all the aspects of mood in a dramatic production but merely mood resulting from composition.

***

The factors of line, mass, and form and from them feel an emotional quality that immediately creates a flow of imagery in the spectator's mind an imagery that rises out of or is qualified by the emotional quality. The emotional quality may be one of joy, of pity, of great terrorizing impressiveness, of sorrow and oppression, of loneliness, of peace or turmoil, and the imagery expressed will be in terms of such qualities or mood. This process of stimulus, mood, and imagery is a sudden one; the spectator gets it immediately, or not at all. Almost all physical places and scenes in life, and even the qualities of writing, have a dominant feeling; this mood may be expressed to the spectator by the abstract shapes arrived at from the amount, kind, and dominance of line, mass, and forms.

***

Dominant lines in a stage composition are arrived at from the position of the bodies of the figures.

A dominance of *horizontal lines* creates a restful, an oppressive, a calm, a distant, a languid, or a reposeful feeling in the spectator. Horizontal lines express stability, heaviness, monotony, restfulness, and other similar qualities.

Perpendicular lines express height, grandeur, dignity, regal or forceful impressiveness, frigidity, spiritual or ethereal qualities, or soaring aspirations.

Diagonal lines are seldom used, but on the rare occasions when they are they express a sense of movement or an unreal, an artificial, a vital, an arresting, a bizarre quality, or quaintness.

Straight lines express strength, sternness, formality, severity, simplicity, and regularity.

Curved lines express naturalness, intimacy, quiescence, freedom, gracefulness, and independence.

Obviously, these types are not all distinct and separate. Perpendicular lines may be straight or curved; horizontal lines may be straight or broken; but when the director achieves these combinations, he obtains different and mixed values. Broken perpendicular lines give a feeling of violence; broken horizontal lines, a casual feeling.

***

Form is significant in expressing the mood effect of the subject through compositional arrangement…. Form may be symmetrical or irregular, shallow or deep, compact or diffused.

Each one of these arrangements of form creates a totally different mood effect: the director should give special attention to the expression of a scene in terms of form.

***

As with line, let us analyze the mood effects of the different arrangements of form:

a. *Symmetrical*, regular, or repeated form expresses formality, artificiality, coldness, hardness, and quaintness.

b. *Irregular* form expresses a casual, impersonal, realistic, informal, or free quality.

c. *Shallow* (single-plane) form expresses quaintness, artificiality, shallowness, excitement, and effectual and alert quality.

d. *Deep* (multiplane) form expresses warmth, richness, mellowness, sincerity, and realism.

e. *Compact* form expresses warmth, force, horror, and power.

f. *Diffused* form expresses indifference, coldness, turmoil, defiance, and individualism.

The possible combinations of film, as well as the combinations of line with form, give mixed emotional effects.

***

Composition is the rational arrangement of people in a stage group through the use of emphasis, stability, sequence, and balance, to achieve an instinctively satisfying clarity and beauty.

EMPHASIS

The first factor of composition for us to take up is emphasis. As every art product must have its emphatic element, so every stage group must have its emphasis figure or figures. The director's first problem resolves itself into that of selecting the figure upon whom the eyes of the audience should rest immediately. This is determined by the importance of the character in the scene being played and by the importance and length of the lines being spoken. Naturally, in any written scene, the important speakers should readily be seen as well as heard. The composition should emphasize this figure so that audibility of voice is reinforced by visibility.

THE BODY IN RELATION TO THE AUDIENCE

1. A *full-front* position is one in which the body and head directly face the audience.

2. A *quarter* position is approximately forty-five degrees away from the audience, or the turn from full front toward the audience halfway to profile.

3. A *profile* position is a ninety-degree turn so that the side of the body is toward the audience.

4. A *three-quarter* position is at a point halfway from profile to full back.

5. A *full-back* position is with the back directly to the audience.

***

METHODS OF OBTAINING EMPHASIS

The simplest methods are the uses of the strong body positions.

***

THROUGH BODY POSITION

The strong body position is one of the simplest methods of obtaining emphasis.

***

Full front body position will receive emphasis.

***

TITLE OF THE SCENE (CONCEPT)

We spoke of picturization as embodying the author's concept at each moment of the play. In order to express the concept we should understand what each moment of the play has to say. Analyze the basic purpose, objectives, and attitudes underlying each scene in a play because now, under picturization, he must express graphically the dramatized situation by placing his characters on the stage in storytelling positions and emotional relationships.

***

Now let us work out together the steps in this thought process from title to complete visualization, using a definite situation.

Example: two women before Solomon, each claiming to be the mother of the child.

1. The title of the situation is two people seeking justice of a third. Solomon is justice; the two women are the seekers of justice; the child is the claim.

2. The mood values inherent in the title are impartiality, firmness, appeal, anger, and hatred.

3. The mood values of composition are those of strength, stability, balance, and loftiness of justice, as well as those of vigor and intensity of excitement. One feels a seemingly conflicting note from a diagonal line crossing a broad and strong perpendicular line.

4. The background of the situation is a mother's struggle for the possession of her child whom another woman has claimed as her own. The two women are of law birth, and the scene takes place in Solomon's court.

5. The placement of the figures in the proper parts of the stage and the expression of their emotional relationships are as follows:

Solomon should be placed dead center, high on a level (throne), and should be strongly emphasized by repetition of line coming from guards standing behind him. The mothers should stand before Solomon as far as possible from each other, with their body positions in antagonistic attitudes to each other yet leaning forward toward Solomon (their appeal). One of the women should have an arm raised to give the prolonged diagonal line. The women should be equidistant from Solomon to bring out his impartiality toward them and his inability to decide which is the mother. The child should lie horizontal to Solomon on the floor of his throne; in this position the child is equidistant from the two women and in possession of Solomon; since the child is the motivation of the scene, it should receive secondary emphasis.

**

LENGTH OF MOVEMENT

Walking long distance ordinarily weakens a movement.

**

MOTIVATION OF MOVEMENT

Movement used to express story, background, or character may be motivated out of either inner or arbitrary considerations, depending upon the script that is to be directed. What is motivated out of arbitrary consideration is of a technical and intellectual nature whereas movement motivated from inner considerations has a more emotional basis. For this reason we say that, as a general rule, the movement of comedy is more arbitrary that that of tragedy.

**

TERMINOLOGY OF BODY POSITION

In order to obtain the blended, or pictorial, effect he desires, a director often wishes a change in the body position of his actor. The following terminology wishes a change in the body position of his actor. The following terminology will be used by him to relate an actor's position to other actors and to the picture, or composition.

1. To *open up* is to turn more of the body around toward the audience or, for example, to change from a profile to a quarter of full-front position.

2. To *turn in*, or *close in*, is to turn away from the audience and toward the center of the stage, resulting in giving more profile or back to the audience.

3. To *turn out* is to turn more of the body to the audience.

**

DIAGONAL MOVEMENT

Diagonal movements from down right to up left or from up left to down right or from down left to up right or from up right to down left have four different values and implications.

***

SEVEN STEPS IN CREATING PICTURIZATION

1. *Analyze the scene for purpose, character objectives*, and *attitudes* so that it may be definitely titled, a scene of struggle, of love, of forgiveness, of oppression, of suspicion, and so on.

2. *Determine the mood qualities* that are inherent in the title; if it is a title of suspicion for a situation in which six people are each suspecting the others, we should have awareness, unrest, nervousness.

3. *Express the nature of the mood in terms of mood value of composition such as line, mass, and form*: whether the composition is compact or diffused, large or small, regular or irregular, flat or deep, and so forth, with all the different combinations of these. In the situation of six people suspecting each other, we have isolation in space, diffused mass, and irregular line and form. Now express these in the technical terms of composition, which in the situation under analysis means: diversified emphasis, uneven sequence, and a great deal of counter-focus together with irregular body positions.

4. *Visualize the background of the situation, characters, and setting*: the forces and circumstances about the situation, the social standing of the characters, the environment where the situation takes place, and frequently the time of day and season. The situation of the six people who suspect each other has been brought about by a robbery. The characters might be people of high social standing, and the environment might be the drawing room in the home of one of these people; or the characters might be gangsters, and the environment a hideout, murky and hot. In this second instance the picturization would assume totally different qualities from those in the first.

With a clear knowledge of what the situation is, of the mood qualities inherent in this situation, or the mood values of composition that will express the nature of the mood; and with a clear conception of the entire background (situation, circumstances, characters, and setting), we may now transfer our mental picturization to the actual stage.

5. *Place your characters of composition* that will, in particular, stress the emphatic characters or objects.

Having approximately related our characters, we now work for an articulate and clear-cut quality. We make definite use of our technical knowledge of composition, applying the proper emphasis.

***

7. *The last step is the attitude of the individual actor.*

Have your actors give their emotion body expression and reaction. Individual picturization is more or less instinctive with the actor, as a result of the emotion that he is striving to portray, or it may often be the result of technical skill resulting from his observation. According to normal expectations, if he is defiant, he will express this physically with feet firmly planted and the body erect and forward; if frightened, he will cringe; if humble, he will relax with head bowed. This physical accompaniment of emotion in man is a universal language that he speaks and, as with the picturizing arrangement of the group, arouses in the audience an immediate conception of the emotions and emotional relationships that are in action onstage.

In arriving at our final picturization we have worked from the general to the specific.

***

The excerpts included above are a tiny slice of the useful wisdom available to movie directors, would-be directors, student directors, and those who want to be better directors or are working to become directors. Again, I consider *The Five Fundamentals of Play Directing* to be an absolute must read for movie directors, and those who aspire to the profession. I have not included the quotes as a substituted for reading and studying the book, but hopefully as an encouragement of advertisement for reading and studying the book. It's not the purpose of this chapter to teach all that a director needs to know about picturization, composition, blocking, setting shots, etc. It is the intention of this chapter to burn into the mind of the reader in an indelible fashion these things that are a key, unavoidable part of the movie director's job.

The would-be directors that I have seen perish in the most ugly, inept, awful ways did not seem to know that these things were the core and heart of the director's job. They certainly did not study these things or prepare to do them!

The making of images and the making and positioning of images and sounds to tell a story is the heart and core of the director's job. These images are made by picturization, composition, blocking, and setting shots. Understanding the knowledge of picturization that has evolved from 2,500 years of theater and drama can be very useful to a student director, and so can a study of paintings by great artists, and sculpture, architecture, and dance also be useful. Comic books are a very rich art form in terms of picturization. A lot can be learned from studying the picturization and composition in comic books.

To "block it, light it, rehearse it, shoot it, and print it" the director first needs to be able to know why he or she is trying to block and be able to block it with effective picturization, composition, and to set shots that result in effective storytelling images. Movies are made of images that result from picturization. Thus, picturization and composition are the most basic fundamentals of setting and shooting shots. Proper picturization creates images that tell a movie's story that is right at the center of the heart of a movie director's job, and is at the core of setting shots.

A director who can set effective shots that are images that can engage an audience and tell a story, at least has a chance to make a movie that's worth watching. Those directors who can't do that usually don't have much of a chance.

CHAPTER SIX:
A SUMMARY AND OVERVIEW OF THE VARIOUS ASPECTS OF THE PEOPLE, JOBS, AND ISSUES RELATED TO THE MOVIE DIRECTOR'S JOB

The purpose of this chapter is to take a brief, broad overview of most of the important people, jobs, areas, and subjects that connect with a movie director's job. The very great pioneer movie director Allan Dwan said that a movie is really made by a team (actors, crew, cinematographer, editor, screenwriter, producer etc.) and the director is like the quarterback of that team. Almost always, there is some truth in Dwan's statement about movies being made by a team, and often (depending on the production) there is a lot of truth in it. As with all things in the arts, however, occasionally there are exceptions. Some of the things dealt with briefly in this chapter will be the subject of another chapter later in this book where they will be dealt with in more detail.

Here is a list of people, jobs, and subjects that connect to a movie director's job that will be briefly examined in this chapter; actors and casting, art direction and the production designer or art director, camera, lighting, producer, production manager and office staff, line producer, first assistant and second assistant director, crew, especially key grip and gaffer, screenwriter and script, makeup, wardrobe and hair, location scouts and location manager, special effects, on set mechanical prosthetics, pyrotechnics, and post-production optical and computer-generated effects, script supervisor, music composer, the movie's commercial content, sound recordist, sound effects (SFS), SFX maker and editor, sound mixer, stunt coordinator, second unit director.

You can give the same script to two different directors, and one will make a good movie from that script and the other will make a bad movie from that same script. Part of that difference is a director's style ability to tell a story with a camera and soundtrack, or skill or lack of skill with actors, but part of the difference in directors is how they deal with or fail to deal with, or how *well* they deal with, all the people, jobs, subjects that connect to the director's job. Some directors are tremendously well-supported by huge numbers of very competent, highly skilled and often very talented people in the jobs and areas that connect to the director's job, and some directors are not well-supported or not supported at all. There is a massive difference in the support and the importance of that support between directors who make movies for major studios with budgets in the tens of millions of dollars or now often over one hundred million dollars or more, and directors making low budget or micro-budget or no budget independent movies. How much high quality work a director can get from those whose jobs and workers connect with his or her role as director almost always greatly effects what ends up on the movie or TV screen.

John Schlesinger, the much-acclaimed and honored director of *Midnight Cowboy, Marathon Man*, and many other movies, said, "The main difficulty of any filmmaker is to learn to retain the original intention of his (or her) idea, and manage to put it on film through the necessity of a collaboration with a group of people. That group will include front office, people responsible for overseeing the production, the actor, and technicians. They all form different categories and need different handling. It's easier of course with a small unit, perhaps documentary, which is the way I started off, a four-man crew is easier to communicate with than a thirty-man crew. The problem I had always found is to avoid letting the problems of the people around you influence you too greatly so as to alter what you intend to do. It is so important to resist those pressures."

Another English director said, "Other directors will advise you to involve everyone in the art of creation, so that your vision is fully communicated to everyone, cast and crew, so that they have the opportunity to cooperate in bringing it to life. That does not mean being a dictator on the set. I've never been that because I've always felt the spirit of collaboration was the healthiest atmosphere to engender. Cinema is essentially a collaborative medium but that doesn't mean giving others the chance to do a part of your job. For example, don't ask the cinematographer about specifics like whether an actor should deliver a line standing or laying down. *There is only one director*. The more you are seen to be someone who knows what you want, the more you will be able to involve others in the act of creation, because they get paid for helping you get what you want."

During the course of making a movie, a director is very likely to get innumerable "suggestions" about making the movie, some of which if acted on would ruin the movie. Some times, a suggestion can be a gift, or even a gem, though. John Ford said, "The best things in pictures happen by accident." I think the statement "The harder I work the luckier I get" applies to Ford's statement. The only accidents I've seen unprepared directors get are more like traffic accidents than "the best things in movies." I'm more disposed to the Emily Dickinson quote that "Luck is not good chance; it's toil."

The director's job is to direct, not to dictate (unless necessary) but under optimum conditions to direct. Here are some dictionary definitions and words associated with the verb "to direct" and director: guide, lead, designate motion, regulate, govern, command, control, and aim. A director often has to walk a very fine line in dealing with very many people, on one side of that line is falling into people's bad suggestions or bad ideas and losing control of the movie, and on the other side of the line is shutting one's self off from the possible positive creative contributions of others in order to retain control. The more clearly the director has the movie in his or her mind, the more easily and certainly a director can know which suggestions or input aligns with and strengthens the director's vision and which would harm, ruin, or destroy it.

A big part of a director's job, besides what they themselves bring to a movie, is to be very open to things that are good for the movie (whoever many originate them) and absolutely closed to things that are bad for the movie (whoever may originate them). The director needs to have a clear enough vision for the movie that is being made so that he or she can lead people and guide them toward that vision, and accept and use and build with contributions and "suggestions" that forward, bring into reality, or enhance and develop that vision. They also need a clear vision for the movie that they are making so that they can reject what would weaken, dilute, harm, or ruin that vision.

Part of that has to do with actors and casting. Just choosing the right actor in the right role can be more than half of the battle in getting an excellent performance that enriches or makes the movie. Some times it is much more than half the battle. Casting the wrong actor in a key role can doom a performance or even a movie. The great John Ford said, "The main thing about directing is: photograph people's eyes." The movie critic Kenneth Turnan wrote a book about John Ford called *The Man Who Shot Great Movies*. In an *L.A. Times* article about Ford and Turnan's book, a writer said of Ford's movies, "We always see people's eyes. We see through these windows of their humanity. We see ourselves." The reason that showing actors' eyes can be so powerful is that when a movie or TV camera looks into people's eyes it almost always reveals what is or is not going on behind those eyes. Before I directed *Starship Invasions*, Ken Gord (my partner and co-producer) and I went from Toronto to Los Angeles to take care of final pre-production business, and to meet with Christopher Lee and Robert Vaughn. We met with Lee in his Westwood high-rise apartment, and talked with him about his character, how he'd portray an alien, and about the movie in general, which at that time was titled *Legion of the Winged Serpent*. Lee's character was the leader of that alien legion. At the time, Mr. Lee was best known for his portrayal of Dracula in English and European horror movies and for playing a villain in a James Bond movie. From the first moment that he began to talk about how he wanted to portray his character and from the questions he asked me and the opinions he stated, I realized that there was something extra, something very smart and special about him and his approach to his character and the movie audience, something that gave him star power and the ability to "carry a movie," even though most of the movies he'd carried at that point had been B horror movies. He had a very clear and cutting intelligence, keen knowledge and instincts for drama.

There are very few actors who can "carry a movie" and who really connect with the audience on an emotional level strongly enough to achieve that effect. That emotional connection can be to scare the audience the way Bela Lugosi or Christopher Lee or Robert Englund ("Freddy Krueger") could do, or to impress the audience with physical and/or moral heroism the way Jason Stratham, Bruce Willis, Clint Eastwood, John Wayne, Bruce Lee could do, or to make them laugh like others can, from Laurel and Hardy all the way up to Jim Carrey and Ben Stiller in modern times. Other actors can carry a movie with physical beauty and sexuality, like Marilyn Monroe, Elvis Presley, Sophia Loren, Sharon Stone, or Angelina Jolie. Another method of engaging the audience in such a powerful way is to use introspective intensity, like James Dean, Marlon Brando, Robert DeNiro, Harvey Keitel, or Jim Caveziel ("The Passion of the Christ"). And then, some people are simply interesting to watch, like Mel Gibson, or Brad Pitt, or even the actors in *Clerks*, Brian Ohaliran and Jason Mewes.

In making low budget movies, you will find out how rare it is to find a "star quality" actor who can "carry" your movie, that you can afford on your budget, who may not yet be in the Screen Actors Guild (SAG) or who'll work outside SAG if your production is non-union. On one non-union movie I directed, we auditioned over 1,000 actresses (this included a huge open audition cattle call) and only found our lead when the producer went to New York. It's not hard to find actors that have talent and physical beauty. It is very hard to find actors that can carry a movie who have not yet been noticed or discovered to some degree. While I was trying to package and finance a different movie I saw a very young Nicholas Cage in his first leading role, in *Valley Girl*, the Friday night it was released. I instantly recognized his star quality and that he would be perfect for the lead in the movie I was trying to package. I called his agent the next Monday morning and found Cage was already under contract to a powerful producer. He'd had other small roles in movies before *Valley Girl* and someone much more powerful and "inside Hollywood" than me saw what I saw on the screen.

Some times, real acting talent takes time to blossom, and to be fully recognized. It is, however, usually recognized on some basic level very quickly. Again, it is very difficult to find actors outside SAG who can carry a movie.

Quentin Tarantino said that there are three areas of the world that have healthy movie industries: Hong Kong, India, and the USA. All three of these movie industries have "star systems" that cater to *people who want to see movie stars*. Many people go to the movies or rent them based on stars they want to see. This translates down to the grass roots level.

Some people rail against how much money movie stars are paid, up to $20,000,000 per movie and more when profit participation is factored in. In contrast, I believe that in many cases major stars are often underpaid in regard to their actual financial worth to a movie. While no movie star's name alone can guarantee a hit movie, John Wayne was reported to have never made movie that lost money. He's not making movies any more, and even the biggest stars today have made "disappointing" films, but star names nevertheless can get a movie into theaters, giving those films a chance to step up to the plate and be given a chance to attract a large audience. Usually, it takes a star to give a movie a chance to become a mega-hit. Big star names provide a certain amount of "insurance" for movies. Here's a blunt dollars and cents example. A political movie failed at the box office and was massacred with extreme relish by critics. Some of the reviews were reminiscent of Woody Allen's claim that a movie critic sought to "reconvene the Nuremberg tribunal and charge those who made it with war crimes against humanity." The movie in question reportedly cost $35,000,000 to make but failed miserably at the box office. Allow me to speculate about its income in various markets.

Number One: In U.S. and foreign movie theaters it probably did not recoup its advertising costs. Many people mistakenly judge a movie's financial success by its U.S. theatrical success or failure. U.S. theatrical, in fact, used to be the major "make or break" market for a movie. Now it is just one of several markets. The failed movie in question, with three huge movie stars and an Oscar-winning director/actor, had several large patches of dialogue that were below the quality level of professional screenwriting. Much of this dialogue should have been transcribed and made into a political Weblog, *not* put on a movie screen. Nevertheless, perhaps because of the star power of the movie, I found twelve DVD copies of the movie in my local video store, compared to only fourteen copies of the multi-Oscar-winning *No Country For Old Men*, sixteen copies of *Indiana Jones and the Crystal Skull*, and fifteen copies of *Rambo*. This failed movie sold some DVDs around the world only because it had three major movie stars in the cast. It is only an educated guess on my part, but I would estimate that this theatrical failure, very flawed movie probably would, over time, make back most of its cost in the worldwide DVD and domestic and foreign TV markets, but only because of star power. If the movie had been made without these actors, the money invested would have been much more at risk, because it would not have gotten into theaters in the USA or in foreign markets *at all*. It is likely that it would have been very lucky to get even one DVD into most video stores. Its TV prospects would have been limited to the outer fringes of "TV Siberia."

In case you're wondering, the movie in question was *Lions for Lambs* with Tom Cruise, Meryl Streep, and Robert Redford (who also directed). Do you see the major reasons that I think major movie stars are often actually underpaid in relation to their real financial value? Stars are almost always worth every penny that they are paid. Some of the very best money spent making my movie *Starship Invasions* went to Christopher Lee and Robert Vaughn. This kind of importance of cast and actors' "name value" also exists at a slightly lower level, even a much lower level.

When I have made distribution deals on several of my movies, the first question a distributor always asked was, "Who's in it?" When I was shooting *Starship Invasions*, David Cronenberg was shooting a movie called *Rabid* starring Marilyn Chambers (the late porn star). She was a perfect casting choice, both commercially and aesthetically, for that movie. One of the hallmarks of Cronenberg's prolific and interesting career is wise, original, and very effective casting. He cast actors perfect for roles that often elevate the material from a horror "B" genre to something else entirely. That includes actors like Oliver Reed and Samantha Eggar in *The Brood*, Jennifer O'Neill in *Scanners*, Debbie Harry and James Woods in *Videodrome*, Christopher Walken in *Dead Zone*, Jeremy Irons in *Dead Ringers*, and Jeff Goldblum and Geena Davis in *The Fly*, who are all excellent and represent highly effective casting.

Actors with name value in certain genres or markets can at times be cast in a low budget movie for an affordable price if the actor likes the script or is simply eager to work. This is particularly true if the amount of shooting time for the actor is limited. For example, Robert Rodriguez shot Johnny Depp's part in *Once Upon A Time In Mexico* in eight days. Here's a cruder example. In my local video store I found a copy of the colorfully titled *Zombie Strippers*. It starred porn star Jenna Jameson and Robert "Freddy Krueger" Englund. Without those two names, it is almost certain the DVD would not have been in that store. A name actor has value in certain genres and markets when their name can be put on the packaging and used to advertise the product. Such names can often make the difference in whether a low budget or even micro budget movie gets distributed or not.

The great screenwriter and director Billy Wilder was asked why he put up with Marilyn Monroe's antics, showing up hours late many times, not knowing her lines other times, etc. Wilder's response was that his mother would show up on time, all the time, and even know her lines, but nobody would pay to see his mother in a movie. Nevertheless, in low budget movies like *Clerks*, unknown actors can be more effective than name actors. Perhaps the most important group of people with whom the movie's director connects is the actors, and sometimes those actors can be prime sources of creation in improving the script. While the actor creates and embodies the physical reality of the movie, the movie director operates between the *idea* of the movie on the page and the physical reality created with actors. What they create together is why people watch movies. Screenwriting and acting are two of the most important subjects that connect to the director's job, but in almost all cases, the single most important determining factors in whether a movie has a chance at success is the movie's script, which includes its story and concept. In a TV interview, Steven Spielberg said that after viewing his TV movie *Duel* (which I consider a masterpiece) he realized that he was a good director, and if he got a good script he could make a good movie. Directors with successful careers write, co-write, or get their hands on good scripts and shoot them. Directors who shoot bad scripts don't have good careers, if any kind of a career at all. There is no denying that screenwriters are very important and usually are the authors of movies where the director is not also a co-writer, but some times writers can be very out of touch with reality.

One of the writers was on the set of one movie I was directing. That writer had a minor producing function. He was so very unaware of how movies are actually made that he did not understand "the magic of movies" where a director can use screen direction to shoot two actors against two different walls and make it look like they are looking at each other (if the screen direction is right), or a director (me) could shoot one scene in five different buildings and make it look like it was all one building. This writer, who was a very good dialogue writer and contributed some very good dialogue to the movie but he "knew" that what I was shooting "wouldn't cut." I'd edited most of my own movies, six or seven that are on my resume, and about a dozen that had been distributed and shown at that point. I'd edited about half that many movies that I didn't direct. I had easily made around five thousand working (and often excellent) edits! I'd edited tens of miles of movie film, usually with a splice every six inches or foot. This word-obsessed, word-hypnotized writer, who didn't write the movie I was directing but rewrote and improved the script a lot, severely failed to understand how movies are made or misunderstood how movies are actually made so catastrophically that he literally "freaked out" on set and on the production, and tried to get me fired in the middle of filming! He went to one of the movie's major financiers and told him that what I was shooting would not cut. He'd never spliced two pieces of film together in his life! He didn't know the difference between a socket hole and an asshole, yet he was telling people that what I was shooting would not cut!

There is little you can say about a director that is more insulting and damaging and slanderous than that. He also told the financier I was crazy. I knew how to make a movie and he didn't. Much worse, he didn't know that he didn't know! I have been accused of many things and fortunately, I've actually done some of them, but even going back to my student films at UCLA *I've never shot something that did not cut or could not be cut, or that I could not cut.* When I found out what this writer had done behind my back, I was close to "going medieval" on him. Up to that point, I'd considered him a friendly associate, a comrade working to make a good movie, which he hoped would catapult him into an opportunity to director. I'd been in his home. I'd helped him get paid when a company was going to screw him. I'd met his wife and kid. He'd helped the movie a lot. I was prepared to help him become a director, which could have happened if he hadn't gone nuts.

I would have even been willing to act as his A.D. and help him make his first movie. I'd done it for others. But when someone tries to stick a knife in my back, when I'd worked for over a year (mostly without pay) to get a movie into production. I take it personally and seriously, and it's monumentally insulting to say that a director is shooting something that won't cut, when that's not true. I told the A.D. to get this nutcase word jockey off the set instantly. "Have a P.A. drive him to the nearest bus stop, not back to the production office," I said. "And dump him there."

We were about twenty miles outside downtown Toronto. The good old wind chill factor was well below zero. Then I called the Canadian producer and told him to put this nutcase on the next jet to Hollywood, and not to talk to me about it at all if he wanted the movie done on schedule. "Just do it!" I exclaimed, and he did.

This highly paid development deal writers jackass was gone! Then I called his friends in Hollywood and told them their frozen turkey was coming home to roost, and hung up on them before they could say a word.

After that, everything in the movie "cut" very well. I knew it would! It is a very smoothly edited movie. I edited it. Everything "Mr. Dialogue" freaked out about worked just as I'd planned it, very smoothly, and impressively, just as I'd planned. The Hollywood-based company was a very happy with the movie and made a lot of money, selling it all over the world. The screenwriter blew his change to become a director.

Why do *some* directors not want writers on the set? Why should *some* writers not be on set? Why are *some* writers not qualified to be a director, but just to write development deals that never get made into movies? This guy was a creature of the world of the development deal.

How the movie camera, the cinematographer, director of photography, or camera operator relate to and connect with the director's job will also be covered in depth later. For now, I'll simply say that shooting a movie is "where the rubber meets the road" and it is only partially the job of the cinematographer. The director has a huge responsibility relating to how a movie is photographed. Some directors "out source" a large part of that responsibility but whether that happens or not, a director cannot escape virtually total responsibility for the images that appear on the screen. A movie camera is a basic tool that is key to a director's job, so any director better know certain basic things about it. These basics are not difficult to learn. Typically, the production designer or art director work closely with the director to create and put into physical reality a movie's look, while the director of photography and/or cinematographer work with the director to capture that look, but ultimately it is all the director's responsibility.

On some big studio movies, directors are often very ably and superbly supported by very talented and experienced production designers and art directors and extremely able crew in the art department. With large budget movies the production designer may oversee (usually in consultation with the director) the finding of and choosing locations, designing and building sets, dressing sets, costumes, wardrobe, even makeup, and occasionally special effects. The set dresser is the production designer, or art director's, or art department's representative on set and is present during filming. There may be no people filling some art department positions. Once, I was first assistant director on a film and took the additional job of set dresser because no one else was doing it. On a lower budget movie, if there is no one for certain jobs, *the need to have these jobs filled does not go away.* They become *the director's responsibility.* If you are a movie's director and your movie does not have one of these positions filled, then you inherit it. Some low budget directors on very successful movies have to a greater or lesser degree done jobs like that while directing. Examples are *Once Upon A Time In Mexico, Night of the Living Dead, Clerks, A Polish Vampire in Burbank, The Texas Chainsaw Massacre*, and *Paranormal Activity*.

Producers, production managers, and line producers are people who usually play a major role in the life of a movie director when they are making a movie. The legendary director of *Metropolis*, Fritz Lang, played himself in Jean Luc Godard's masterpiece *Contempt*, which starred Bridget Bardot and is one of the best movies about making a movie ever made. In that movie, Lang said, "Producers are something I can very easily do without." Often, I would agree with him, but not always. George Lucas said that his job as producer on *Indiana Jones and the Crystal Skull* was to get everything for Steven Spielberg that he needed to make *his* movie and make sure that it was on set for him when he needed it. That's a very director-friendly view, and defines the producer's job. Star directors like Spielberg will often only work with producers, line producers, and production managers that share Lucas's definition of their jobs.

Directors that do not share Spielberg's stellar star status and power may deal with producers that have a very different director-*unfriendly* and sometimes very negative and *destructive* concept of their jobs as producers, and their relationship to directors. Many directors do not realize or even suspect the degree to which they are at times targets of camouflaged and sometimes not so well camouflaged hatred and envy, just because they are doing the best job on the movie. Many people who would like to be directors lack the guts, discipline, talent, knowledge, or willingness to be responsible that it takes to be a movie director, so they get a job that is *close* to being a movie director but doesn't have as much potential for *blame* as the director. Some producers for whom I've worked saw the definition of their job as producers as a job that was in *opposition* to the director, not in support of him or her. They sought to undercut the director's authority and power, and felt their role was to "police" the movie, meaning to interfere with, thwart, and even imprison the "evil director." Some producers I worked for actually hated directors and begrudgingly saw them as a necessary evil. This is not a good or positive, effective or cost-effective way to make a movie!

In contrast, the very best producer with whom I worked was Barry Pearson. At the time we produced *Plague*, an award-winning financial success (later titled *M-3: The Gemini Strain*) that I co-wrote and directed, Barry was working full-time as a writer for the Canadian Broadcasting Company (CBC). He was rewriting a script under a tight deadline, and often meeting with CBC executives, all day or for at least several hours. He had limitations on how much time he could spend producing *Plague*. What made Barry the best producer I worked with was that *he never contributed any negative energy at all to the production*. That made him very unique as a producer, putting him far ahead of others with whom I've worked. Barry never did a single thing to make my life as a director harder or worse. He did very many things that helped, and always backed me up. Long after I worked with Barry, I saw Jerry Bruckheimer being interviewed on TV. Bruckheimer may be the most successful producer of all time. He was explaining the producer's job as he saw it, and talked about the importance of backing up and supporting the director. I thought that indeed, I had rarely experienced that, but I knew what he was talking about because of working with Barry Pearson.

Although someone watching what Barry did on *Plague* in his producing role might say he didn't do that much, what with having another full-time job, but the kind of things Barry did were very valuable. He brought world-class editor Ron Wisman to our $200,000 production, and a great line producer Gwen Iveson as well. Barry focused like a laser on things that were important, that a director might not have time to emphasize, or that staff might forget. Some times when I'd be ready to shoot something or get it set to shoot that day, I'd worry over not having what I'd need to shoot the scene. In every case, Barry had backed me up and foreseen the possibilities and made sure the appropriate person had the situation covered. I always had what I needed. What is often important on a movie is what might not be accomplished if things are not made ready in advance. Barry covered any potentially disastrous holes in the production. It was his backup and support that allowed me to shoot every strip off the production board in exact scheduling order. That was no small thing because we were shooting in Toronto, where you didn't get enough light to shoot until 10:00 a.m. and lost it by 4:00 p.m. I finished one day ahead of the movie's 18-day schedule. *Plague* had been written in only six days, so this was an accelerated production all-around. Nevertheless, it won the Grand Prize and Best Screenplay awards at the second most prestigious film festival for sci-fi, horror, and fantasy movies in the world. Another kudo for me came when the CEO of Film House, Toronto's major movie lab, told me that every year, "the guys in the lab" screened all the movies made in Canada that went through their lab, and voted on which movie was the best to go through their lab. *Plague* was up against some big American productions that year, directed by famous directors, but the guys in the lab voted my movie the best.

It is rare for a producer to contribute *only* positive energy to a production and see their job as backup and support of the director. When I look back on various movies I directed, one thing that stands out about *Plague* that makes it unusual is nobody was trying to constantly stick a knife in my back because of envy or some other negative feeling. The money man (executive producer) did his job and raised the financing and didn't mess with the production. Barry did his job superbly, and Gwen Iveson was the very best and most supportive line producer I've ever worked with (she was also production manager).

The worst production manager I ever worked with is a person I'll call "Mr. Take It Apart." He had the biggest reputation of any P.M. I'd ever been around, but was the worst at his job. I'd put things together and he'd take them apart! He was worse than useless, a negative detriment to the entire production. Here are a couple of examples, though I could give many more. One scene in the movie was the aftermath of a UFO crash. I wanted the crash scene to have smoke and fire as the military arrived and began to seal off the area and collect the metal wreckage, while a high-ranking military officer arrived and surveyed the scene. In the pre-production meeting and in a special prep meeting with the SFX and art department, I said that I wanted lots and lots of old tires that I could burn to send black smoke across the field where the crash was supposed to have happened. I said 50 tires was not too many because I was not sure how many takes and how many shots would be used to cover the whole scene. I also asked for lots of motor oil to burn and gasoline to burn the tires.

Well, I arrived on the location early in the morning and began setting up the first shot. The amount of wreckage was less than what I asked for and the knuckleheads in the SFX department had only six to eight old tires. I was furious. I had specified how many tires and they did something else. I asked why. Their answer was that Mr. Take It Apart thought that six to eight tires would be sufficient. This jerk had not even seen the location! It was hundreds of yards of open field in several directions. Lots of tires needed to be burned to *make the scene look good*, not "El Cheapo". I told my business partner, who was also one of the movie's producers, to send productions assistants out to buy tires, good new expensive tires that I knew they could find, and motor oil and gasoline from local service stations, to get what I needed to shoot the scene and make it look good. An editor out of my control later cut the scene much shorter than I had in mind, but it still looked good. The cost of the tires, oil, and gasoline ended up being five times what it should have been if my original instructions had been followed. Certain penny-pinching fools, two of the movie's producers (money men) and Mr. Take It Apart the production manager were so busy squeezing pennies that the dollars jumped down a sewer. The art department and SFX folks had played what I call the "Shopping For Less Difficult Instructions" gambit. They got an instruction from the director that would require them to do their jobs, but that entailed doing more work than they wanted to do. So they simply went shopping for different instructions that were more to their liking, and found someone in the chain of command that gladly countermanded my instructions.

Guess who became the "go to" guy for anyone who wanted to avoid or alter the director's instructions? Mr. Take It Apart was always there willing and eager to undercut anything I put together. Here's another example of the trouble caused by this humanoid-looking, walking, talking piece of dinosaur crap. On another scene I arrived on set after lunch. There was a change in the schedule and right after lunch we were shooting a scene originally scheduled for the end of the day. My business partner and producer told me, "We can't shoot it." I asked why. He explained that Mr. Take It Apart had struck again, and we had no sound person. Without consulting the first assistant director or director, the jerk had told the sound person he could take a couple of hours off after lunch for personal errands because the scenes to be shot right after lunch was MOS ("mit out sound" – a play on a German-accented pronunciation of English "without sound" from the early days of sound movies). In short, the scenes would not require sync sound, according the resident idiot, who was totally wrong. Again, I was furious. First, the sound person should not have asked that of the P.M. but he should have asked the A.D. or myself, the director. I *never* would have cut him loose. So the entire crew got to sit around in the wind and snow for an hour (this was before cell phones) waiting. When you are making a movie, things happen, and the anticipated order of shooting can be changed on short notice, but I never would have agreed to leave the crew without a sound person!

These two examples are not isolated incidents. They are consistent with the standard operating procedure of Mr. Take It Apart. His entire vibe was to countermand, undermine, and generally infuriate the director, all the time with a phony smile pasted on his duplicitous face. I believe he was following the money men's instructions to frustrate or annoy the "evil director." When this flaming turkey wasn't taking things apart he was constantly turning out "projections" for the moneymen of how much over-budget I was going to be. In actuality, I finished this very complex and difficult movie slightly under budget. Mr. Take It Apart's projections were based on faulty, stupid assumptions, such as the idea I would shoot the same shooting ratio on every scene or type of scene. He reported that I would likely print the same number of takes on dialogue scenes as on action scenes. While I don't have specific evidence that the money men specifically instructed the jerk to undermine me, I'm pretty sure they did, and I'm positive they did not instruct him to get me the things I needed to shoot the movie, which is the real job of a production manager.

To a degree, I am certain the moneymen viewed me as their enemy, and Mr. Take It Apart knew he was working for them, not me. His primary concern should have been to make the movie as good as it could be, as efficiently as it could be made, as cheaply as possible with due consideration to budget and quality, but he didn't do that. And the producers had long-term grievances in their minds against directors with whom they had clashed. To an extent, they were still fighting old battles with directors no longer around. It is common for the director and lead actors of a movie to be insured for the cost of the movie. If they are killed or severely injured, or become severely ill during the making of the movie and are unable to complete their job, the production can collect the insurance. As soon as I was insured, one of the producers came to me and said gleefully to me, "Now that you're insured, if we don't like the rushes we can just kill you and get our money back, ha ha ha." I wasn't amused. I'm sure that if they no longer felt they needed me to finish the movie, nothing could have made them happier. There was a clause in my directing contract that said any dispute between the moneymen producers and the director would automatically always be resolved in their favor. Even though I should have been grateful to them for financing my movie, after I signed that contract. It was, unfortunately, very hard to feel positively toward them.

There's a sentence in a police interrogation manual that I read a long time ago that I copied in my director's notebook. It says: "If you conduct yourself in a way that is above reproach you will not have to spend time defending yourself." When directing *Starship Invasions*, I did *not* conduct myself in a way that was beyond reproach and I paid the consequences. I would embellish the statement in the police interrogation manual to say that, when directing a movie, if you do not conduct yourself in a way that is above reproach, you will leave yourself open to extra attacks and may provoke extra attacks, and constantly you are likely to have various sleazy sharks trying to bite you in the back. As I've said, many people would like to be director, but they are afraid or know that they lack what it takes, so deep down they hate directors and wish them ill, and often actively and covertly oppose the director.

Directors are human. They have faults, varying degrees of competence, incompetence, and a limited amount of physical, mental, and emotional energy and preparation or lack of same. Nevertheless, they are all making movies or TV shows or trying to make them. In the real world, there are people who do things, and people who criticize people who do things. There are people who help people do things, and there are people who get in the way of people who do things. A movie director needs to be able to tell which of these four categories the people in their cast and crew belong. Some producers are very helpful and do a lot, and that's very valuable. They see their role just as George Lucas described his role as a producer: to get the director everything the director needs to make the director's movie.

I've made enough movies to know that some people act like they would like to see the director (the person making the movie they're being paid to help) dead. This dichotomy is also true of line producers and production managers. The line producer typically supervises or handles the logistics of the movie; getting people and things and moving people and things onto the set. People may tell you that "you don't want to direct *and* produce" at the same time. That's total bunk. It's often easier to direct and produce than simply direct. Directing and doing the line producer's job is hell! I did it on several movies, including two on my resume. Directing and line producing at the same time is something that I strongly recommend avoiding it if at all possible. Directing and being one of the movie's producers, however, can make directing a lot easier. On *Plague* I signed everyone's check. People are a lot more likely to make sure that the director has what the director needs if the director's name is on their check! Here is a quote from film critic Pauline Kael about how much power a director should have and another reason that it is important for a director to have much power.

> "The Director should be in control not because he is the sole creative intelligence but because only if he is in control can he liberate and utilize the talents of his co-workers, who languish (as directors do) in studio-factory productions. The best interpretation to put on it when a director says that a movie is totally his is not that he did it all himself but that he wasn't interfered with, that he made the choices and the ultimate decisions, that the whole thing isn't an unhappy compromise for which no one is responsible; not that he was the sole creator but almost the reverse-

that he was free to use all the best ideas offered him." – Pauline Kael from "Raising Kane" in *The Citizen Kane Book*)

Ms. Kael was writing about something very real, when a director has power, and some security he or she is much more free to entertain and to either use or reject the ideas of others if he or she thinks that they will improve the movie, but a director who is under constant attack, or fending off covert attempts to knife him or her in the back cannot accept valid criticism or suggestions because to do so can weaken him or her and cause openings to further attacks or back-stabbings.

"The director is the one who makes the movie," and often directors make their movies despite a lot of director hatred and envy.

Ted Turner had a saying on a plaque on his desk: "Led, follow, or get out of the way." I'll adapt that. If you hate or envy directors, either become a director yourself or learn to follow and help the director, or get the hell out of the way! Director who strike back ruthlessly and definitely against this kind of director envy have my admiration. The director's job is hard enough without tolerating those who make that job harder by undercutting the director and are not bold enough to be a director.

Here's a story about John Ford that is relevant. Ford and his movie company were on location. In the evening in a large tent, people would do skits to entertain the group. This was before television. One guy did a skit imitating John Ford, making fun of him, wearing a hat like he wore, barking orders, shouting loudly, etc. A lot of people laughed. Telling people what to do and getting them to do it can build a lot of resentment over a period of time. Ford happened to look in on the skits and he was not amused. Basically, all the people in that tent had jobs because of him and men like him. The next day, the Ford imitator was on a train back to Los Angeles without a job. That's where he belonged.

On a movie, Henry Fonda tried to show Ford how to direct actors and said, "This is how we did this scene in the play."

"Oh," Ford replied. "That's how you did it in the play." Ford then punched Fond in the chin and knocked him out. That is a little different method of directing actors than Stanislavski used.

Hitchcock may have said that actors were "cattle" but at least he didn't confuse them with punching bags. If you think you're better than the director, walk the walk, don't just talk the talk. *Direct yourself*, but then follow and help the director or get out of the way. Snide, constant criticism or undercutting the director is not harmless. It is really also aimed at the movie. Damaging the director damages the movie. There is a lot of director hatred and envy out there. It's bullshit! Don't be part of it. Lead, follow, or get out of the way.

The writers at the Writers Guild are leaders of the pack when it comes to director hatred and envy. Some of these writers write good, very good, and excellent dialogue. When it's in my movies I'm grateful, but boy do these folks ever create their own hell. Most are afraid to direct. Even the worst director at least had the guts to try to do the job.

Hollywood legend David O. Selznick, when producing *Rebecca*, made Alfred Hitchcock "show" him each scene on the movie before it was filmed. Hitchcock would rehearse the actors and the shot until he was ready to film, then someone would go get Selznick and the director and actors and crew would do one last rehearsal. If Selznick approved, Hitchcock would then film the scene. So, sometimes the director works *for* the producer, and sometimes the producer works for the director (as in the Lucas/Spielberg example). I will have more to say about that later. Hitchcock so strongly resented what he considered to be Selznick's disrespect that he tried to get even with Selznick when he made *Rear Window*. He cast Raymond burr as the movie's villain, a wife murderer. Burr had a resemblance to Selznick. Hitchcock had Burr dye his hair white like Selznick's and wear glasses like Selznick, to make the resemblance very striking. Hitchcock felt that Selznick's compulsive gambling and womanizing had driven the producer's wife to commit suicide; therefore, he considered Selznick something of a "wife murderer" which to Hitchcock was almost as bad as a meddling producer. It didn't matter that Selznick had brought Hitchcock from England to Hollywood, given him the Oscar-winning *Rebecca* to direct, and integrated the director into the Hollywood community; Hitchcock deeply resented the way Selznick treated him and regarded his years under contract to Selznick as a form of artistic slavery. Hitchcock vowed to become a producer, so that a producer could never mistreat him again. Selznick paid Hitchcock $800,000 to direct four movies, a huge amount to pay a director at that time, but money alone is not why or how people make movies.

If you are a director it is not always easy to feel good about or get along with people who give you money or opportunities to make movies, but it's very important to also look at things from their point of view, try to get along as best you can, and not unnecessarily antagonize them.

Now let's take a look at some who are even closer to the director's back and even more able to protect and cover or stick a knife in it, depending on their choice. That would be the first assistant director (A.D. or "first"), and second assistant director ("second"). The main body of the first assistant director's job is to control the set and deal directly with the crew and keep things productively flowing on the set *and* help the director get his or her shots, and get the day. Typically, the A.D. is on set most of the time, during blocking, lighting, rehearsals, and shooting.

The second is typically off set near makeup, wardrobe, the actors' dressing rooms, or the area where actors are waiting for their turn to shoot their scenes. The second makes up the next day's "call sheet" so people know when to arrive. (I'll discuss call sheets thoroughly later in the book.) The second usually makes the call sheet in the morning, in pencil or on a computer, and then locks it in after the director approves it. I personally recommend that the director sign off on the call sheet at lunch.

I've only worked with one first that I considered really good, and some who were adequate. A lot were pretty useless and some were bad to the point of being a detriment or obstacle, or seriously potential lethally dangerous. The really good first A.D.'s are in the Directors Guild of America (DGA) and are very able and helpful to directors. They work mostly on studio movies and television, not very much on independent films. I've done the first A.D. job myself a few times to help out associates that ventured into directing. I've seen the first A.D.'s job from both sides, just as I've seen the director's job from both sides.

The second A.D. deals with "talent" actors. This means he or she deal with SAG paperwork and the Guild itself on union shoots. The second's job includes verifying actor's time worked, and during filming is to keep a "handle" on the actors and always deliver the actors to the set just before they are needed. The correct way for a set to run is block it, light it, rehearse it, shoot it, print it, then block again! A typical number of setups (shots) in a day on a low budget movie are around 25 to 30. A setup is a change of camera position to shoot a new shot. If just five minutes on average is wasted between the time the director says "cut" and "print" and the beginning of blocking the next shot for the next setup, that adds up to over 120 minutes a day, over two hours. That means the difference between a ten to twelve hour day or a twelve to fourteen or even fifteen-hour day.

In baseball there is something called a double play. When there is a runner on first base, the third baseman, shortstop, or second baseman grabs a ground ball and throws it to a teammate at second base before the runner gets there. When the ball is caught, the fielder tags the base and throws to the base to his left to get another runner out. Ideally, this is the kind of teamwork a director, a first, and a second should have as they repeatedly pass through this process of block it, light it, rehearse it, shoot it, print it, then the same sequence again. A good first can help a director a lot in various ways and even save a director's backside and be his or her BFF (best friend forever). Or that first can be a giant thorn in the director's posterior. When the aforementioned proper setups are done, the first is usually someone doing his job like a member of a great double play combo.

Directors have a relationship to the crews with whom they work. That relationship usually flows through the D.P. and the camera operator and the key grip, and gaffer. Grips physically move things that need to get moved, like the lights and cable, etc. The key grip directs the other grips and moves the camera. The gaffer handles lighting and electric and theoretically and usually works for the D.P. The A.D. is usually a buffer between the crew and the director. A good relationship with a crew can make things flow more smoothly but a good or bad judgment by the crew about a director is not always a good indicator of how good or bad the movie will be in the end. On *The Godfather* the crew, particularly the D.P., Gordon Willis, had a very critical opinion of the director, Francis Ford Coppola. At one point on set, in front of the crew and actors, Wills reportedly shouted at Coppola, "Can't you ever do anything right, even once?!" Coppola had his own logic about this. He admitted that he purposely got the production into a big mess every Friday so the producers would be afraid to fire him and bring in a new director. It is almost impossible to believe when you look at the spectacular excellence on many levels of the finished movie, but Coppola was apparently on the verge of being fired for much of the filming of *The Godfather*. He was held in very low esteem by many of the crew, who had no idea that they were working for a great director on a great movie, probably the best movie they would ever work on. Coppola had a great movie *in his mind* that he successfully put on the screen. In the end, that's what mattered, not the crewmembers' or D.P.'s opinion of him.

Other times, everyone knows when they're working on a hit. One editor who recut my movie *Starship Invasions* went on to edit *Saturday Night Fever*, John Travolta's breakthrough feature film. An editing assistant visited this editor in the cutting room of the Travolta movie while the production was still filming. He told me that everyone from the Teamster drivers to the interns in the editing room to the extras and actors and A.D.'s, to the hard crew and producers, were sure the movie would be a big hit and a great movie. The assistant said he'd never seen that kind of morale on any other movie set. They were right what they felt was very real.

One very important group of people for a director to be connected with (who are some times forgotten when making a movie) is the movie's audience. An associate of mine who was an A.D. for me later became a very successful screenwriter. He told me, "There's only two types of people who need to have a good time on a movie, *the audience and the investors!*" And he was right. Something that relates sharply to the director's real job and to whether the audience and investors will or will not have a good time is *commercial content*. This varies from genre to genre. The simplest definition of commercial content is *anything that an audience will pay to see on the screen or hear on the soundtrack.* I write further about this idea from the writer's point of view in another book, and later in this one. For now, I'll just say that it is often the major responsibility of the director to know what is and is not commercial content in the genre of the movie that is being made. It is the director's responsibility to deliver in abundance to the audience, high quality commercial content, whatever the genre. Directors that have successful careers virtually always deliver lots of excellent audience-pleasing genre-appropriate commercial content to the audience. It helps when that content is explicitly present in great detail in the script but some times it is simply created while filming. As mentioned previously, the long chase sequence in *The French Connection*, which is a major part of that movie's commercial content, was written in the script only as "An exciting chase ensues." This classic sequence that set the standard for other movie chases that followed, *was the director's creation.*

In the other direction, although Steven Spielberg has received and deserves enormous credit for the chase sequences in his TV movie *Duel*, I've been told that very much of the action in the script was written out in serious detail. Commercial content is what the audience and many viewers watch movies to see. It is at the root of the director's relationship to the audience and usually also at the heart of a director's relationship to the movie's investors, distributor, or studio.

In some genres, the stunt coordinator, second unit director, and stunt people are a serious part of a director's life during filming, and contribute much to a movie's commercial content. Many deaths, accidents and serious injuries that occur when making movies are unnecessary. Since potential accidents are simply part of filming, the director needs to understand them, because not properly knowing about them is a dereliction of duty.

In the director's world, the most important person on the office staff is virtually always the production secretary. I've had the good fortune to work with some excellent production secretaries, the people who organize and control the P.A.'s, particularly during pre-production. A production secretary has certain key specific tasks that are part of the job, and when done well, can catalyze the production office into an efficient production machine, and that is particularly important in pre-production. One producer with whom I worked very much fit Fritz Lang's description of producers – "Something that I can very easily do without." He decided to save money by tasking my movie's production secretary with also keeping the books of his production company and the financial activity of his other movie. He had his name as producer, co-producer, executive producer, on 50 to 100 movies, but by tasking the production secretary with bookkeeping on his production company he made sure my movie was de facto without a production secretary. Anything I wanted done that related to *making a movie* was put on the back burner and *did not* get done. Anything useful was second to numbers, and the money game of his company and other movies. He basically decapitated the production office and the movie's staff. It is this experience that led me to recommend that *no person who is expected to do anything that causes the movie to get made should be given a detailed accounting or primary "keeping track of money" responsibility job on a movie, or they will sink into a black hole of money and numbers and become totally useless to the production and not do their primary job related to making the movie.*

If you run into a situation anything like the above, *get an accountant*. Give him or her an associate producer's credit and let him or her sink into the black hole of numbers and money and periodically emerge to let the producer, production manager, or director know what's going on in detail with the movie's finances. This admonishment about *not* letting staff get too deeply involved in accounting, while simultaneously expecting them to do work that relates to production also applies deeply and thoroughly to production managers, line producers, etc. Money and numbers are a full-time job for someone. If you give that to someone who is needed to make the movie, they are gone from the world of people who are useful to the director in the task of making the movie.

Makeup, wardrobe, and hair often play a role in a director's life during production and even the production. On one movie I directed an actress came to the cutting room to look at some of her scenes on the editing machine. When she left to get ready to re-record some of her dialogue, the assistant editor turned to me and said, "Wow, why doesn't she look like that in our movie?"

I asked what he meant and he pointed out that her hair was normally fluffy and curly. I had her straighten it and comb it to a particular style for the movie, which was evidently opposite to the taste of this assistant editor. I don't know who was right and who was wrong, but I do know that if he'd directed the movie instead of me, that actress (the movie's female lead) would have had a very different look. In a commentary about *Chinatown*, Roman Polanski talked in detail about how he modeled Faye Dunaway's makeup in the movie on the exact style of makeup that his mother wore in the 1930s, the time frame in which *Chinatown* is set. Typically, the director approves every piece of each cast member's wardrobe and assigns the scenes where each piece of wardrobe will be worn. This same kind of thing usually happens with makeup and hairstyle changes if they are serious. A movie's wardrobe is seriously valuable, particularly if it is gathered from thrift shops or other not easily replaceable sources. On one production, the wardrobe lady drove the wardrobe van to a party. That's a no-no. The wardrobe van needs to be in a safe and protected place. This party was in a very bad section of downtown L.A. She partied it up and by dawn's early light when she staggered out onto the street she found that the van had been broken into and vandalized.

Big surprise! In that area of the city, she was lucky they didn't also take the tires, or the whole van. The vandals took some of the wardrobe, and cut up or spray-painted some of the wardrobe before leaving. Many of the pieces of wardrobe were from thrift shops, or clothes borrowed from the actors. We could not simply go to a store and replace them. Most of the missing or destroyed wardrobe had already been "established" in the movie. They had been worn in one or more scenes that had already been filmed. In movies, scenes that are next to each other in the script can be filmed at very different times in the shooting schedule. Let's say an actor is in a number of scenes inside a house, and they wear a certain costume or wardrobe in those scenes, then in the movie, they walk outside the house and scenes follow outside. Those outside scenes may be filmed days or weeks after those inside the house were shot. Still, the audience expects to see the actor wearing the same clothes they wore in the interior scene. If that piece of wardrobe is missing when you try to shoot the outside scene, you have major sorrows. When I arrived on set after this wardrobe fiasco, I found the line producer working with wardrobe people, interns, and P.A.'s, as well as the script supervisor, to identify which pieces of wardrobe were gone or ruined, and which could be replaced, depending on if those pieces of clothing had been "established" in prior shooting. If wardrobe could not be replaced, we would have to reshoot those scenes. It was a total nightmare, and all because of a thoughtless night out.

Locations are often key to a movie's look and value. Location scouts and location managers play a big role in director's lives during the pre-production, when the director selects locations. A bad choice of a location can ruin a scene, and also a bad location can stress out a director or an entire crew. One very important thing about a location is that during filming and if necessary during pre-filming dressing the production must "own" the location. *Beware of locations that have too many restrictive conditions on them.* A second very important thing about a location is that, if at all possible, a location needs to have a "time cushion." If you are supposed to shoot in a location from 9:00 a.m. to 12:00 p.m. and the shoot runs over and you need two more hours to finish shooting the scene, make sure that the world does not end at 12:00 p.m. or the whole movie does not turn into a rotten pumpkin if you shoot over the timeline. Location scouts and location managers should *not* lowball time estimates of shooting when talking to the location owners. Don't say, "It'll only take two hours, tops." Say, "We think it will take two hours, but it might run over a bit." Do not make ironclad promises. Beware of locations where you are "just barely there" before you have to leave. One of the major disasters that can happen with low budget moviemaking is the "unsecured location" or being thrown out of a location with only half a scene shot.

There are several types of special effects in movies: pyrotechnics, prosthetics, on set mechanical, post-production optical, and post-production computer-generated images (CGI). Pyrotechnics includes anything that involves fire or explosions, setting stunt people on fire, blowing up cars or buildings, bullet hits and squibs. One pyro guy I worked with thought nothing of showering me, and the camera crew with small bits of sharp metal. It was small but it drew blood and could have taken out someone's eye. He'd been in a war, and his attitude was "What's a little sharp metal." When the gaffer complained that he was unsafe, and she threatened to walk with the whole electrical crew, he threatened to sodomize her with extreme brutality in front of the whole crew. I graduated from UCLA's film school, but I missed the class where they teach you what to do when the pyro effects guy at three in the morning threatens someone like this. Perhaps not uncoincidentally, this pyro guy worked on the commercial where Michael Jackson's hair caught on fire. The stunt coordinator and I managed to calm the pyro guy down and I convinced the gaffer and her electrical crew to stay and finish the all-night shoot.

On another shoot with a different pyro guy, I was the first A.D. and second unit director. I was shooting a multi-camera setup where a large part of a set was blown up along with a non-working life-sized model of a helicopter. I asked the pyro guys where it was safe to put cameras and camera operators. This pyro guy told me what was supposed to be a safe distance. I set the camera positions, chose the lenses, framed the shots, started rolling, and on my command he set off a huge explosion. The fireball from the explosion probably went 150 feet in the air. For a few seconds the heat that hit the camera crew and me was intense, like a short-lived instant sunburn. Then, after the explosion faded, I heard a thud behind me. After I called "Cut" I looked to see what had caused the sound. It was a large piece of metal that was still smoking, sticking up in the dirt nearby. I picked it up and the camera operator saw it and said, "Holy shit!" It had landed about twenty yards behind us and could have landed right on top of us. It weighed at least 40 pounds. I walked over to the pyro guy holding the chunk of metal and told him where it landed. "This could have killed someone," I said. "You said the camera positions were safe." He looked at me like I was too dumb to talk to, which did not make me happy. I grew even unhappier when I visualized what would have happened if the chunk of metal had come down on my head, or on the head of one of the camera crew. But this pyro guy was annoyed with me. He and his assistants were in euphoric celebration with a few others about how beautiful and wonderful the fireball and explosion looked. On their scale of importance the beauty of the fireball and the explosion were all-important and the fact that their irresponsibility could have easily killed someone mattered not at all to them. They even appeared pissed off that I was spoiling their celebration.

Some times when you are making a movie, you are confronted by something that is so ridiculous, so much in absolute defiance of common sense, and so obviously *wrong*, but it just seems A–OK to someone else that you ask yourself "Is this a joke?" The pyrotechnics gentleman and I exchanged a few unkind words then he shouted at me that the movie's producer/director had told him that he "wanted to see lots of wreckage fly." The producer/director's request to see lots of wreckage fly was legitimate, but it could have been accomplished more visually effectively and infinitely more safely with cardboard and balsa wood, even rolled up newspapers. That would have read much better on film than the potentially deadly piece of metal that landed behind the camera crew and did not add to the shot at all. That piece of metal went through frame so quickly I'm sure nobody saw it. So the pyro guy added extra danger for no reason. Such explosions only last a few seconds, and they are virtually always shot in serious slow motion or extreme "slo mo." Even in slow motion, no one saw that metal fly.

The pyro guy complained to the director/producer about me, saying, "For what you're payin' me you oughta kiss my ass at Hollywood and Vine, not let that stupid f'in' A.D. give me shit!

Later, a crewmember told me about some of the close calls he'd had with this guy and others. One incident that stood out was on a movie where they blew up an actual house. A real porcelain toilet landed right behind the camera crew, only missing them by a few feet. Some pyro "genius" had apparently put a charge directly under the toilet. The crewmember remarked to me that pyro guys are usually nuts. "They just don't care," he said.

Any producer, director, assistant director, second unit director, actor (except for stars), or crew member that thinks that their safety or the safety of others figures high on the agenda of pyrotechnics people may be seriously mistaken, and such an assumption can have serious or even fatal consequences. When the pyro people are "doing their thing" you are responsible for the safety of those in your charge, and if you're the director you're responsible for everyone. The pyro people have "more important" things to be concerned about, like how good the fireball will look. Most pyro people will tell you about other pyro people who they knew well (in many cases, those who were their mentors) who have been killed or seriously injured doing their job. So watch out.

Prosthetic effects are things that actors wear to make them look like aliens or monsters, or even like someone else. Mechanical effects are something that will perform on set in front of the camera, like a motorized remote controlled monster or model, or flying an actor through the air on a cable. Special FX people who do some types of on set work often feel that if an effect works *once* in their workshop, it works but for a special effect to really work it has to work reliably every time or most of the time on command, and be available for a second, third, fourth, or fifth take if needed. This is often outside their frame of reference of FX people. Any director who sees a mechanical effect tested for the first time on set with crew and actors standing around is running a huge risk of being very disappointed. The SFX person's definition of "It works" may be much different that what the director envisions. My advice: *See it in the SFSX workshop. Don't be unpleasantly surprised on set when it's too late to do anything about it.* If you see it for the first time on the set, you may have to "eat it." So make sure it's thoroughly demonstrated in the workshop and be sure.

Nowadays, computer-generated effects can accomplish very amazing things. In Robert Rodriguez's commentary on *Once Upon A Time In Mexico*, he revealed that the motorcycle riders in one very effective exciting chase sequence were put in digitally. They were computer-generated. I'd watched the movie several times and it never occurred to me at all they were not real. When I rewatched the movie again, I still could not find fault at all with how these computer-generated motorcycle riders looked. Rodriguez said that he used digital images because he knew that if he shot it with real stunt people, some of his guys would get hurt.

On one movie we were set to shoot a special FX shot of a UFO flying out of control, into a model of a famous high rise building in downtown Toronto. Our call time was 10:00 in the morning. The entire camera crew, lighting crew, and special FX crew were there on time. The special effects person decided that he wanted to break the model apart and glue it back together in key places so it would disintegrate and break apart just right when the model UFO hit. Well, everyone sat around and watched for hours while he did that. Then he wanted to strain the magnesium powder into an even finer dust so that the flash of light when the explosion ignited would be just perfect. We watched him strain the magnesium dust and some other chemicals into piles on the warehouse (studio) floor and repeat this process for hours. Then he practiced with the slingshot and wire device that would throw the model UFO across frame and into the model building just before it would explode. He futzed around with one thing and another hour after hour until it was about 3:00 or 4:00 *the next morning*. That's right, about 17 hours after our call time from the previous day!

The D.P. on this shoot was a very fast-moving "cut to the chase" type guy. At this point, he was not just ready to leave the set. He was ready to leave the planet without the assistance of a rocket! He told me to get a new D.P. for the rest of the shoot. He'd shot principal photography and some of the model shots but now was at "no more." Some of the SFX man's eccentricities were too much for him. He went on to bigger and better things while I slogged out the model shots on my own.

We would shoot this special effects shot with a special *very* high-speed camera. It would run at over 280 frames per second, over ten times the speed of a normal 35mm camera. Everyone was finally set to "do" the shot. We rolled the camera and the camera assistant tried to gradually bring it up to full speed. It sounded like a propeller airplane engine revving up to full power. Then just as the camera assistant called "speed," just as I was about to call "Action!" and send the UFO model flying into the model building, the camera jammed and the camera assistant yelled, "Jam! Cut!" By the time this high-speed camera stopped, film was so tightly packed inside the camera's main body that it was as thick as a piece of wood. I told him, "Clean it out. We are going to shoot this shot before we go home. The camera assistant took a tool that was like an ice pick and began chipping the pieces of film out of the camera, once he got the ruined film out of the camera (almost an entire roll). He cleaned out the entire camera so it was perfectly polished clean and reloaded. We tried the shot again around 6:00 in the morning, now twenty hours after our call time. This time everything went perfectly, the camera hit "speed" and held it without jamming. I called "Action!" and the model UFO flew across frame, hit the model building perfectly, and the explosion was perfect. We did not know how it looked in ultra "slo mo" until we saw it the next day projected in the lab's screening room. *It looked great!* I suspect this shot contributed to Warner Bros. acquiring the movie for North American theatrical and TV distribution. They used the shot in the movie's trailer and in its TV commercials.

Some times special effects shots cause a lot of hell and are hell to get but sometimes they're worth it because they are what will draw an audience to see the movie, and what will please and satisfy the audience. They are exactly what the audience pays to see.

A movie's editor is one of the very most important people with whom a director works. I have edited many of the movies that I've directed and I've at least co-edited most of the movies I've directed. I've also edited many movies that were shot by other directors, and I've had other editors cut movies that I've directed. I've seen and participated in the director/editor relationship from both sides. The great playwright and writer-director David Mamet said that everyone except the editor is doing their job and trying to tell a story, but the editor *is just trying to tell a story*. That is the editor's job. The European credit for editor usually reads *montage* or some variation of that word, depending on the language. The word edit or editor has a connotation of cutting things out, trimming things down. It's true that's often part of editing, but the more basic substance of the editing process is usually about putting images and sounds together to create meaning, to make a montage or sequence and to tell a story, to create interest in an audience, or to cause emotion in a viewer and pull him or her into a movie's story and cause them to care about its outcome. When I was a film student at UCLA, a film professor talked about how the process that a director goes through in turning a script into a series of shots and visualizing how those shots can or will go together is very similar (in a reverse way) to the process that an editor goes through in putting various shots together to tell a story.

He was right. Many directors have a strong background in editing, from editing their own early movies or working as an editor. Robert Wise was a great editor (he edited *Citizen Kane*) who went on to become a great director. There are others. Another film professor at UCLA when I was a student was a union editor. He'd cut a lot of TV shows. He said "If you're an editor and you really can't cut a scene call the director and tell him his or her scene won't cut. The director will usually come in and cut the scene for you and tell you that you're a "lousy editor." Most directors, but not all, do have some (and often, very good) idea of what they are doing in relation to editing or they often won't last long as directors. Many beginning directors are, however, very deficient in knowledge and experience at editing.

At times, I've had very good experience with editors, particularly with world-class editors like Ron Wisman on *Plague*. Often enough, I've had to take over editing myself. Two times on two different movies the process of editing and finishing a movie was taken away from me. Once on a horror movie, the producer recut the movie, moved scenes around in it, and generally had an editor of questionable ability hack away at it. Still, it was profitably distributed in theaters and video and in foreign territories, but it's by far my least favorite movie that I directed. The other case where a movie was taken away from me in post-production was on *Starship Invasion*. Earlier in this book I quoted Confucius saying "The outcome of all contests is determined by previous preparation; without such preparation failure is assured." When I began writing the script for that movie, which was originally called *Legion of the Winged Serpent*, I was not prepared to write a script for a world class major league movie, and the script I went into production with was a script that was weak, unfocused, and not full developed. It was not well unified or rooted in a thorough fully thought-out conceptualization. My partial unpreparation as a screenwriter left me in a bad position in post-production. After the first rough cut screening, the reaction was pretty positive, because there were some good scenes and good production value in the movie, and everyone could see that there was a possibility for a movie, but the reaction in subsequent screenings grew more and more negative. The Canadian editor on that movie could not cut a dramatic scene. Most of the real editing was being done by me, while I was still shooting second unit models and UFO FX footage. I was working around the clock, and it was killing me.

Much to the money men's credit, they always saw the movie as world class. My original conceptualization was as a low budget exploitation film. The budget grew a bit, the ambitions for the movie grew a lot, but its concept and script did not grow that much. In the editing room, you often face what you didn't solve or create when writing the script so again, much to the producer's credit (which I did not appreciate at the time), they brought in some pros from Hollywood to finish the movie's editing, and let me devote my time to shooting the remaining model shots, special FX shots, and UFO effects shots. They had a writer rewrite one group of alien's dialogue. These aliens spoke telepathically and did not move their lips, so the new writers were free to introduce far more information and story through these alien's dialogue than I had in the original story. Also, much to the moneymen producers' credit, they brought in a top Hollywood editor to recut the movie. He hated being in Toronto in frigid winter. He hated the movie. He hated that I'd directed the movie, but he was a very good, very talented, extremely knowledgeable experienced editor who knew a lot about movie storytelling. He was also (at least in my dealings with him) the most sarcastic human being I've ever met. Watching what he did with the movie and answering his questions and listening to his comments was not pleasant, but it was a crash course and learning experience. At one point on the editing machine, he was playing a shot of a female alien with a ray gun. Visually it was a very nice shot, and I was proud of it. He asked "Where's she going?" I told him, and also explained in great detail the importance to the story of what her character was going to do. With tremendous sarcasm, he responded, "Well, you are going to have to go to all theaters where the movie is shown, every screening, and tell the audience exactly what you told me, or they're not going to know what you just told me, and they're not going to know what's going on in the damn movie, because it's not in the movie, and if the audience doesn't know that, they aren't going to care if that character gets where she's going or what happens in that scene. They will wonder why they're being show this shot."

I had fallen deep into one of the worst traps that is always a danger for screenwriters and movie directors. I was so close to the story and script that I'd been dealing with for so long and that was so familiar to me that I tacitly assumed the audience knew things because I knew them, even though these things had not been *shown* to the audience earlier in the movie. I've watched other screenwriters and directors fall into this same trap, mostly beginners and on low budget, often resulting in undistributable movies. This trap is not just a danger to beginners and people making movies on low budgets. Ridley Scott on *Blade Runner*, and Francis ford Coppola on *Apocalypse Now* both fell into this same trap. In the pre-release screenings, the audiences could not understand or follow either of these movies and voiceover narration had to be added to give the audience more information to make the movies both work for the audience and cause them to understand what was going on in the story, and care about what would or would not happen in the movie.

James Cameron avoided this trap on *The Terminator* with the movie's opening crawl, and prologue sequence that was *not* in an early draft of the script that I read. Cameron avoided the trap but I don't know whether it was during the writing, filming, or editing phase of the moviemaking process.

One thing that the top Hollywood editor on *Starship Invasion* shouted at me that I still remember to this day is his description of the editor's job. He said that for him as an editor shots were "just strips of film and these strips of films were just pieces of information." He said it was his job to put these pieces of information in line in a way that would tell a story and pull the audience into that story. After a while, he left for New York to work on *Saturday Night Fever*, and another top Hollywood editor took over the re-editing. The first editor had been working in editing rooms since he was a teenager. His father had been an editor and had taught him the trade. He was a repository of Hollywood editing storytelling know-how that started with silent movies, ran through the Golden Era of studio films, and led to the time of my movie.

Once that I'd shot the last of the model and UFO shots and the money men producers no longer needed me, and they fired me and told me that I was not allowed in the editing room and would have no say or participation at all in how the movie was finished, and added how really awful I was on several levels. The next thing I heard about *Starship Invasion* was many months later. My business partner, Ken Gord, one of the movie's producers, called me and told me that the movie was picked up for distribution by Warner Bros. in Hollywood! I was stunned. He told me that there was a screening of the movie the next morning for cast and crew at one of Toronto's finest theaters, and I was invited. When I saw the finished movie screened, it "played." I would have cut some things differently in some places and I really hated some of the music. To me, a lot of it sounded like cheap elevator music. My thought while watching the movie was that after all the work, after all the hell of filming it, and the models and UFO effects, the editing frustration, what really came through and made the movie play was the original story and its commercial aspects that I had written years before with a Bic pen on a stack of the absolutely cheapest yellow paper. What was good in the script was good in the movie. After all the sound and fury had died out, what was missing or not perfected or developed that made the movie not as good as it could have been was because the script limited the movie. *Starship Invasion* changed my awareness on the importance and value of scripts. Up until that time I thought of scripts as just something you had to have to get the money to make the movie. When making the movie, was when things got worked out. Now I agree with Sam Goldwyn, who said, "If it's on paper you got a prayer, if not, you got nothing but air."

Recording sync sound to go with image greatly increased and changed the dramatic and comic power of movies, and altered their direction and destiny as an art form. The recording of sync sound (basically, dialogue) is an important part of a director's life while filming a movie. My attitude about recording dialogue is pretty much "old school." I think that unless it's absolutely impossible because of location noise the director and sound person should get usable sound recording of a dialogue when filming, or videotaping a picture, if at all possible. There is a process called ADR, Automatic Dialogue Replacement. Studio movies use it a lot. In this post-production process the actor sees the picture of him or herself on a screen and while wearing headphones they can hear exactly what they said on set as they repeat the replacement dialogue in a sound-controlled environment. Some actors are very skilled and experienced with ADR, and can replicate virtually exactly or even improve on the performance that they gave in front of the camera. Some studio movies (many, in fact) are 100% ADR. On some studio movies that often makes sense. They just record a "guide track" of dialogue (a recording that's not useable in the final movie). The guide track is an accurate recording of what's said. They often figure that it's better to plan to, and budget for ADR from the start, than to burden the director with trying to get usable recordings of dialogue while filming in environments where that will slow filming and may even be impossible. Low budget movies often don't have that option, though. They may not have the budget for ADR or the experienced post-production personnel who know how to prepare and set up the materials required to do proper ADR. Also, actors in low budget movies are likely not to be as experienced or not experienced at all in doing ADR.

Something a director needs to know about sound is that our environment has a lot more ambient noise than anyone not familiar with the profession of sound recording and a tape recorder, and recording professional quality sound would usually expect. The human ear, and the human brain tend to filter out what they don't want to hear and they tend to focus in on what they want to hear or are trying to hear. In most urban areas, you could be inside a house and think it's pretty quiet, but if you record the actual ambient sound with a tape recorder you may find out that the freeway half a mile away sounds like a waterfall just outside the house or the refrigerator sounds like a sewing machine and the camera itself can sound like a car engine. Recording clean sound, clear usable dialogue, often requires sound blankets, other equipment and materials, and a skilled good sound person and assistant (boom person).

Usually, but not always, the sound effects – footsteps, cars, punches, explosions, falls, etc. – recorded during production almost always need to be replaced in post-production. Why? Because they are "off mic" and usually have to be "off mic" if you are going to get the shot, get the picture, get the image, without a mic in the middle of the shot. I usually tell the sound person that I want him or her to get all the usable dialogue possible during production. I don't want to deal with ADR unless it's absolutely necessary. I also stipulate that any sound effects that we get are "gravy" and I don't spoil a shot to get them.

As previously discussed, the term MOS means the shot was taken without sync sound recorded. Some editors and directors wasn't sound recorded on every shot, no matter if that sound has a snowball in hell's chance of being in the final movie. I'm not talking about dialogue. All dialogue, every time an actor opens his or her mouth, what they say must be recorded if only to make a record of what the actual line spoken is and how it was said, so that it can be replaced if necessary. Other directors and editors (myself included) feel that if the shot is not going to have any usable production sounds and it has no dialogue why waste the time and money dealing with sound that will all be replaced in post-production. Why worry about the boom person being in the shot? Why transfer it? Why sync it up? Why deal with that in editing when only the picture of the shot will be used in the end? Some directors shoot a lot of MOS and some shoot only sync.

A lot of people who have spent a lot of time working on movie sets and no time working in the cutting room make really absurd statements about when sound needs to roll, because they don't understand post-production and how movies actually get completed. Roman Polanski's use of sound effects to create mood and for artistic effect is about the best that I've studied. Luis Bunuel's use of sound effects usually instead of a music track is also great.

Sound effects either come from the original production soundtrack, or a sound FX library or are recorded specifically in post-production custom made for the movie, or are done to picture in a process known as "foley." I have recorded a lot of sound effects and cut them and mixed them usually for the movies I've directed or edited. "Foley" is a process where scenes in a movie are projected and a sound person in a sound studio usually equipped with all kinds of things to make the appropriate noises makes those noises in sync with what's going on on the screen. Footsteps are often done this way as are fights, sword fights, etc. When the movie's dialogue track is completely cut and "cleaned" (all inappropriate sounds removed), sound effects tracks are completely cut into sync with the picture and the music track is also put into proper relationship to the picture. All these tracks are then mixed together at proper levels in relationship to each other and to the movie's picture. The director usually presides over "the mix" which results in the movie's final soundtrack.

A script supervisor's job includes keeping continuity. Some times their job is called continuity. A good "script sup" can be a tremendous help to a director, and to the editor. Copies of the script sup's notes go to the editing room with the rushes. Here is an example of continuity. An actor is wearing a red sweater in a scene inside a house. The scene ends with the actor walking out the door. In the next scene in the movie, the actor walks out the door and into the backyard. That exterior scene in the backyard is shot two weeks after the one inside the house. In the finished movie, the two scenes will be right next to each other. If the actor walks out of the house wearing a red sweater, the audience expects the actor to walk into the backyard wearing that same red sweater. If the actor does, you have continuity. If the actor is wearing something other than the same red sweater, you have a major continuity error, and major continuity errors are not acceptable even in low budget movies. So if you have a major continuity error you probably have unusable footage, which means wasted money, wasted time, wasted effort, and probably bad morale and frustration. Continuity can extend down to minor details. If one camera angle of a scene is shot with an actor repeatedly scratching his head, and then when the same scene is shot from a different angle the same actor has his hands in his pockets at the points in the scene where he previously had his hands on his head these are continuity errors and can make it difficult or impossible for the editor to cut the scene. If objects on a table are in a shot or objects are behind an actor such as a plant or decorations and then another shot is taken from another angle of this scene and these objects are moved or removed they can seem to appear or disappear or jump around as the editor cuts from angle to angle. This is *bad continuity*.

Continuity is not just the responsibility of the script supervisor. A director can set up and cover a scene in such a way that they are just begging for continuity problems, or a director can set up a scene in such a way that they are to a large degree immune from continuity problems.

I rarely if ever have suffered from continuity problems! I have worked with very experienced, and totally inexperienced script supervisors some times. One key task I assign to script supervisors at the beginning of the last week of filming (production) is to go through the script, the shooting schedule and make note of what has been shot and make sure that when that last week is shot out that what was scheduled for principal photography has indeed been shot. Sometimes this search uncovers little surprises, but its better to get these "surprises" in the last week of production than after one has very embarrassingly wrapped principal photography, without completing it. The music composer is of vital importance to most movies. The movie's music sets a scene's mood and often stirs or enhances emotions in the audience. Getting effective music onto a movie is one of a director's most important tasks, as is choosing an working with the movie's composer.

Lots of money goes into making movies, and lots of hard work from a lot of people also goes into making a movie, and in the end it's usually the movie's *concept, story, script* and the director's work that will determine the movie's quality, value, and fate.

CHAPTER SEVEN:
THE MOVIE CAMERA AND THE DIRECTOR

One of the first things that a movie director encounters when dealing with a movie camera and filming a scene is something called *depth of field*. What that relates to is whether an actor or object in the foreground of a shot (near the camera) and an actor or object in the background (far from the camera) are *in focus at the same time*, or whether one will be out of focus while the other is in focus. When actors who are at different distances from the camera and are both or all *in focus* at the same time, *the camera's depth of field* is said to be a wide depth of field. Depth of field is determined by the size of the lens on the camera and the amount of light shining on the scene and reflected into the camera, and how wide open or partly closed the lens is. It is affected by how much light is being projected onto the film or videotape.

A wide-angle lens tends to have wide depth of field. When using 35mm film a 25mm lens or an 18mm lens are wide-angle lenses. The 16mm lenses are about half the size of the 35mm lens. A 12mm lens is wide angle when shooting 16mm. Any millimeter lower than 18mm when shooting 35mm film is usually an extreme wide angle or "fisheye" lens. I've seen 9.8mm fisheye lenses used and I believe 12mm or 13mm lenses as well. Even lower millimeter lenses are available.

The wide angle, very wide angle, or ultra-wide angle lenses usually provide a wide or very wide depth of field, depending on lighting conditions. *Telephoto lenses typically have the opposite effect*. Telephoto lenses are *long* lenses, typically with 35mm film, 100mm is telephoto. 150mm, 200mm, and 250mm telephoto lenses are common and even longer lenses exist. They typically have shallow or narrow or very shallow depth of fields. For instance, with a telephoto lens, you could have a situation where an actor who was eight feet from the camera would be in focus but another actor that was ten feet from the camera in the same shot would be out of focus, or slightly out of focus, depending on light. If that same scene was shot with a wide angle lens and lots of light, you could have an actor that was in focus five feet from the camera and another actor who was twenty feet from the camera and also in focus at the same time. Generally speaking, the more light that is falling on a scene and being reflected into the camera, the *wider* the depth of field (allowing for the type of lens being used). For example, if you are shooting outside in very bright sunlight with a wide angel lens, you will usually have a *very wide* depth of field. Actors close to the camera and very far from the camera will both be in focus at the same time. In an opposite kind of situation, however, where you are shooting with a telephoto or "long" lens, *not* a wide angle or neutral lens in a *low light situation*, you can have a situation where the depth of field is shallow or very shallow.

One D.P. told me of a situation where he was shooting with a telephoto lens in a low light situation and if he put the tip of the actor's nose in focus the actor's eyes would be out of focus. If he put the actor's eyes in focus his nose tip would be out of focus. That is a *shallow depth of field*.

Filming in 35mm, a 50mm lens is usually considered neutral. Some consider a 35mm or 40mm lens to also be neutral. A 75mm lens is usually considered mild telephoto or just "A-75". Again, when you get into millimeters of 100 or above when shooting 35mm film, you are dealing with a telephoto or extreme telephoto lens. 25mm to 250mm or 25mm to 200mm lenses are common to use in filming in 35mm. Commonly nowadays, these zoom lenses are not used much to actually zoom in or zoom out during a shot. They are often used to provide a large number of lens size choices. Some D.P.'s like to use zoom lenses this way. Others prefer to use fixed lenses (lenses of one and only one specific millimeter length), because fixed lenses often can shoot with much less light than zoom lenses can and fixed lenses are also often sharper than zoom lenses.

The millimeters I've listed for wide angle, neutral, and telephoto lenses are usually about half that amount for 16mm cameras and also are different for various video cameras. I have shot a fair bit of film with a 500mm or longer extreme telephoto lenses outside in bright sunlight where they have a substantial depth of field particularly at a distance. Telephoto and extreme telephoto lenses tend to compress the people and objects that are in an image. Long telephoto lenses can be used to make things look close together that are actually far apart. One common use of these kind of lenses and their compression effect is to have actors run toward the camera and set off a large explosion behind them at a great distance (I should add, *a safe distance*), behind them and it will look like the explosion is right behind them. I shot one scene like that with a very, very long telephoto lens and the explosion looked like it was right behind the actors. Actually, it was over a football field's length away from them. This telephoto compression effect is very observable in major league TV broadcasts of baseball games. One of the angles these games are typically covered from is with a telephoto lens from center field shooting over the pitcher's shoulder at the batter, catcher, and umpire. In these telephoto shots the pitcher and batter do not look 60 feet apart because of *telephoto compression*. They look like they are right on top of each other.

In the movie *Lawrence of Arabia*, there is a shot where Omar Sharif's character first appears in the distance. He's riding a camel toward the camera. He is on a flat desert landscape. Gradually, Sharif comes into focus. The air seems to be bubbling like water, and there seems to be a thin layer of reflective water on the ground in front of him. This is the compression effect of this extreme telephoto lens acting on the air. *Visually*, it is compressing this air into a visual liquid. At the temperature in the desert, the air is *visually a boiling liquid when visually compressed*.

Wide-angle lenses can have the opposite effect. They can make things in the background seem farther away than they are, and they can make things in the foreground look bigger than they are. This effect is often used with a pistol or gun barrel in the foreground. This effect can be used to make rooms or sets or exteriors look bigger or more spacious than they are in reality, or things in the foreground look larger, more imposing or threatening, and when using such a lens, movement toward the camera will look more dynamic. Roger Corman on the DVD commentaries of his Edgar Allan Poe movies is very frank abut how he used wide angle lenses to make sets and rooms look bigger than they were, and how he used a very wide lens to make the pit in *The Pit and the Pendulum* look much deeper than it really was.

The term "F stop" can be intimidating to a non-photographic person. All a director needs to know about this term is that it refers to how wide open or how shut the camera's lens is, meaning how much light is let in or kept out. A high F stop like F22 or F11 or F16 means that the scene is brightly lit, and is reflecting lots of light, so the lens is "shut down" and it limits the amount of light hitting the film. A low F-stop like F1.4 or F2.2 means that the amount of light falling on the scene and reflected at the camera is very slight. So the camera lens needs to be wide open or almost wide open to let in all the light possible. Shooting at a high F-stop widens depth of field, and shooting at a low F-stop decreases depth of field.

Low F stop means you are shooting at a low light level. High F-stop means that you are shooting at a high light level.

Don't make it more complicated than that unless you want to get into the nuts and bolts of photography or cinematography.

"F stop" can also relate to the reading on the light meter that tells how much light is being reflected toward the camera, as well as the setting of the opening of the lens. Again, when shooting at low F-stops, depth of field is typically very shallow because the light level is also low and focus is typically very "critical." The assistant cameraperson, or "focus puller," must have the actors' distance virtually exactly right or the actors will be out of focus. At high F-stops where there's lots of light, the focus puller's job is much easier, as the depth of field is considerably wider.

Allow me to simplify and summarize.

One: When you shoot with lots of light you will tend to have wide depth of field.

Two: When you shoot with little light you will tend to have a shallow or short depth of field.

Three: When you shoot with a wide-angle lens you will tend to have a wide depth of field.

Four: When you shoot with a telephoto lens you will tend to have a shallower, narrow depth of field, unless you are shooting with lots of light.

Five: Telephoto lenses compress things, and make them look close together.

Six: Wide angle lenses tend to make things look farther apart and add space to locations and make things in the foreground look bigger and things in the background look smaller, and also tend to make motions toward and away from the camera look more rapid and extreme.

Seven: The two things that determine depth of field are type of lens (wide angle, neutral, or telephoto) and the amount of light falling on the scene and reflected into the camera.

A few hours or minutes with an actual camera can aid the understanding of depth of field and the aesthetic effect of lenses more than any words on a page can, but I hope I've made a start.

Another aspect of movie camera use that will smack the director right in the face as soon as the director starts trying to capture images with it is *the actual position of the camera in relation to the actors*, or whatever else is being photographed. Should the camera be placed low? Waist high? Knee high? Right on the ground? Shoulder level? Eye level? A high angle, or overhead? All of these different camera positions have different types of aesthetic effects and different "looks," particularly with different types of lenses, because each type of lens tends to create a specific type of aesthetic effect and look. The best way for a beginning director to become familiar with the aesthetic effect of various types of lenses, and various camera positions and combinations of lenses and camera positions is to get a home movie video or film camera and go out and *shoot some film or video of people and objects from various angles and lenses and then watch some very successful movies with an improved awareness and hands-on experience of the look of various lenses and camera positions*. This method can aid an aspiring director in moving from audience member to a student who is eager to learn from professionals who have preceded him or her. This process of shooting film or video from various angles with various lenses and then watching successful movies repeatedly and studying them over and over, *not just watching them to be entertained*, is incorporated in the do-it-yourself course in a latter part of this book.

I'll have a lot more to say about this later. For now, here are some broad generalizations about various types of camera positions and types of lenses. Low angles and extreme low angles make actors and objects look imposing or more menacing or dangerous or important. Such angles can create gravitas. There are a lot of low angle and very low angle shots in *Citizen Kane*. These kind of shots are very, very appropriate to a movie about a very rich and powerful man who metaphorically towers over ordinary people and is "larger than life." The movie is about war, peace, political power, wealth, and power. The ideas in the movie are *big*. Low angle shots with a wide-angle lens makes things look even more imposing. It's used in *Citizen Kane* but it's also used in *Gangs of New York* on Daniel Day-Lewis's character that is a murderous gang leader and criminal. Low angle wide-angle shots of him advancing toward a retreating camera are very effective in making him and his tall top hat look super-menacing and super-imposing.

Normally, most of the good directors I've studied shoot close-ups from chest level of the actor being photographed, *not* from eye level. Close-ups *usually* look better when shot from the actor's chest level or lower. In contrast, in specific shots in *Stagecoach*, John Ford, as did Alfred Hitchcock in *The Birds*, shot a couple of close-ups on characters that are *under pressure* from an angle that is slightly higher than the actors' foreheads. This tends to make the actor look vulnerable, weak, and unimposing. This slight high angle was extremely appropriate and effective, subtly, in the way that these two master directors used it in two classic movies.

Close-ups are sometimes shot with longer lenses, sometimes telephoto lenses, to put the actor's face in sharp focus and cause the background to be partly out of focus ("soft" focus). This draws more attention directly to the actor's face.

Later, I will talk more about the effect of actor's motion in relationship to the camera, and the camera's motion in relationship to actors, and the relationships and effects caused by mutual motion of camera and actors. Whether to move a camera or not is a key director's decision. Will the director move the camera toward the actor, or away from the actor, or along with the actor, or will the director hold the camera stationary and have the actors move within or through the frame? These are very directorial decisions. They all create different aesthetic effects.

All of these types of camera moves cause different effects on the viewer or audience and cause different directorial "comments" with the camera. I will discuss this in more detail later. The camera is a vital tool. No camera = no movies! Its use is an important part of a director's job. A movie director should become as comfortable and familiar with a movie camera as an artist is with a paintbrush and paint, or a writer is comfortable with a pen, or pencil and paper, a typewriter or computer. And the best way that a director or beginning director can learn how to properly use a camera to tell a story is to *use a camera*!

CHAPTER EIGHT:
THE FOUR MAJOR METHODS OF
USING A MOVIE CAMERA TO TELL A STORY

In studying many financially and critically acclaimed movies, I have observed four major methods of telling a story with a movie camera:

One: Observational

Two: Directorial comment with the camera

Three: "Looking good" or visually poetic

Four: Montage

Some very successful movies that use an observational style or method of telling a story with a camera are *Clerks*, *The Pianist*, *Alphaville*, *Chinatown*, *Rosemary's Baby*, *Blue Velvet*, *Little Shop of Horrors*, *Coffee and Cigarettes*, and to a large degree, *Belle de Jour*. The observational styles is based on the camera always or almost always being in the best possible (optimum) place to observe the scene, parts of the scene, or various characters at various points in the scene. In this method, the camera does not move to provide emphasis. It only moves to provide a new, more appropriate vantage point from which to observe. Extreme high angles and low angles are usually not used in this method of telling a story.

The directorial comment method of using a camera to tell a story is a readily present in *Casablanca*, directed by Michael Curtiz, in Orson Welles's *Citizen Kane*, and in many of Steven Spielberg's movies. It can be seen in *Gangs of New York*, *Mulholland Drive*, and many other films. The extreme low angle shots in *Citizen Kane* are "directorial comment" making the characters look more imposing. The same is true of the many low angle wide-angle shots of Daniel Day-Lewis approaching the camera in a menacing manner in *Gangs of New York*. When John Ford moves his camera abruptly toward John Wayne until his face dominates the frame when in introduces Wayne's character in *Stagecoach*, this "track in" shot is directorial comment, basically telling the audience, "This guy is important to this movie."

In *Casablanca*, Michael Curtiz moves the camera in rapidly, closer to the actors more than once, to emphasize dramatic points in the final scene and several other scenes. Spielberg credits Curtiz as one of his major directorial influences. Accordingly, Spielberg in many dramatic points in many of his movies rapidly or slowly moves the camera in closer to the actors just as Curtiz often did for dramatic emphasis. When Hitchcock cuts close and closer three times in *The Birds* to show the dead man who has been horrifically pecked to death by birds, he is commenting and shoving this horror right at the audience. This is a shocking series of shots, and the directorial comment is that this is overwhelmingly horrific. It is a shocking horror slap in the face of the audience. George Romero does virtually the same thing with a decayed partially eaten body, pushing in with a fast zoom lens in *Night of the Living Dead*. The camera tilting in to produce diagonal images and add to a bizarre feeling is also directorial comment. Romero used it very effectively in *Night of the Living Dead* and in *Creepshow*, and Hitchcock used it on *Strangers On A Train*.

The "looking good" or cinematic poetry method has its low end and its high end. The lower end of this looking good method is fully in operation on the TV series *CSI: Miami*. In many shots on the show, the camera moves simply because the shot *looks* better with the camera moving. The camera is not moving for a better place to observe or to cause directional emphasis, or comment. Many of the shots in *CSI: Miami* are framed to show off a great-looking location, or cool clothes that the actors are wearing, or gorgeous bodies, natural beauty, or architecture. The camera angles, movements, lighting, and framing are chosen and executed to look good. The job of TV directors is often to keep the shots visually interesting while dialogue tells the story.

Examples of the high end, cinematic poetry end of this looking good method are many poetically composed outdoor shots in John Ford's Westerns. Most directors who came to their profession during the era of silent movies did not set out to be movie directors. John Ford, when young thought he would either be a painter or a sailor. He became a director with the eye of a painter and the point of view toward life of a sailor. Ridley Scott's movie *Blade Runner* is another example of the cinematic poetry method of telling a story. I would say that the currently premier practitioner of this method of movie storytelling is Robert Rodriguez. His films *Sin City* (co-directed with Frank Miller), *El Mariachi*, *Once Upon a Time in Mexico*, and *Dusk Till Dawn*, are prime examples of this poetic style. John Woo's *The Killer* is an extremely archetypal example of great cinematic poetry. Rodriguez's shots, often evolve within the shot. They start off showing one thing – the action moves. The camera moves and the shot and often ends up showing more than one thing. Some of Rodriguez's shots are mini-masterpieces of poetic cinematic art in themselves. Spielberg also has many sections in his movies that are guided by this method, particularly in *E.T.* It is not surprising to me that Rodriguez also composes music. Some of his shots are like visual music. Rodriguez has a high degree of feel for aesthetic knowingness that means knowing what looks good.

The fourth method of movie storytelling is montage, which is putting one image next to another or one sequence of images next to another in sequence, to create meaning. Alfred Hitchcock said that some people think that cinema is action or movement, and some think it is spectacle, but what the cinema really is more than anything else, is *montage*. Hitchcock uses montage exactly this way in many of his best movies such as *Vertigo*, *Psycho*, and *Rear Window*. The famous Russian director and cinematic theoretician of the silent movie era, Sergei Eisenstein, conducted an experiment around the subject of montage. He took a shot of an actor looking off-camera at something and intercut this same close-up with something sad like a funeral. Then on a different strip of film he had the same close-up of the actor "looking" at something happy like children playing. He also cut this same close-up of the same actor with other shots of things that elicited other emotions. Eisenstein then showed these different montages to separate audiences and questioned them about the actor's performance. The audience that saw the "look" at something sad commented on what a great job the actor had done portraying sadness. The audience seeing the same shot of the actor looking, with the close-up on something joyful, remarked on how the actor had done a great job of portraying joy. The other comparisons elicited the same type of praise from audiences.

The masterpiece cinematic sequences in great movies like the previously mentioned Hitchcock films are constructed on a more complex and sophisticated application of this same basic principle of montage; meaning and storytelling arising from the combining of shots. Robert Rodriguez used this principle to cut Selma Hayek into a "shoot out" scene when she was not actually present when the action of the scene was shot. Montages are often used in battles, fights, and chases. A Native American shooting an arrow with a bow might cut to the arrow impacting a cavalry soldier's chest, when in actuality the soldier shot his portion of the scene shot five days earlier. The audience assumes that the brave shot the soldier because the two shots are spliced together. A soldier fires a rifle through a hole in the wall, a Native American flies off his horse (it could even be stock footage shot years before), someone looks through the hole in the wall, and the audience assumes that what is shown is what the character sees.

In *Chinatown*, Roman Polanski goes beyond the observational method of movie storytelling to what I would call an ultra-observational movie. In *Chinatown*, except for one shot, a P.O.V. shot through binoculars, all or almost all of the shots in *Chinatown* are shot with the same or almost the same millimeter lens. If Polanski wanted a close-up he'd move the camera closer before shooting the shot. If he wanted a wider shot he'd move the camera back before shooting the shot. It is simplicity *uber alles* (over all) but as it continues, it builds a very strong and effective consistency of space. Using this same or almost the same lens all through the movie (which I believe is about a 35mm lens) causes the viewer to feel quite close to the actors, and in some scenes virtually like an on-set observer. I told an associate of screenwriter, a teacher, and mine about what I called this "consistency of space" phenomenon that results in an almost tangible feeling as proximity to the actors. I commented that the use of this one lens over and over made me feel like I was sitting at a table in a restaurant a few feet from Faye Dunaway, and Jack Nicholson, watching them talk back and forth. My associate commented that was how he also felt when he was watching the same scene.

Polanski said, "I never design the movement of the camera first and then try to fit the actors… or the situation into this movement. I do the opposite. I start with the actors, and I let them to go through the scene and then I try to follow what they do with the camera. I think doing the reverse is like having a ready suit and trying to find a man that fit it."

Richard Sylbert, the production designer on *Rosemary's Baby* and *Chinatown*, said of Polanski that "He knows more about lenses than cameramen do." Here's a story told by *Rosemary's Baby* cinematographer William Fraker that illustrates the effect of this "consistency of space" technique on a movie. There's a scene in the movie where John Cassavetes goes into another room to answer a phone and talks on the phone. He goes behind a wall and out of the audience's view while he talks on the phone The cinematographer wanted to move the camera forward to follow Cassavetes into the other room so that the audience could see Cassavetes while he talked on the phone. Polanski said no, and moved the camera to the side. The scene plays better, more mysterious and from the character Rosemary's POV with Cassavetes hidden from view and only his voice being heard (not the other side of the phone call). Fraker did not fully understand what Polanski was up to until he saw the movie projected for a large audience. When Cassavetes disappeared behind the wall and the camera moved to the side (the right of the screen), the entire audience leaned to look around the wall as if it existed in three-dimensional space, not just in two dimensions on a movie screen. That is how effective Polanski's creation of the illusion of the consistency of space had been in that movie.

Polanski uses the camera for directorial comment only once in *Chinatown*. He moves the camera in on Jack Nicholson's face when he realizes that the movie's "showdown" will take place in Chinatown. This camera move foreshadows the movie's outcome, and its meaning.

Another of Polanski's masterpieces, *The Pianist*, is also a very observational movie. Just like in *Chinatown*, there is almost no directorial comment with the camera. In movies like these, Polanski seems to remove the director's "style" or personal comment from being any kind of filter between the viewer and the actors. He puts the viewer and the actors in direct observational connection. The director, and his comments, opinions, and emphasis seem to be absent. Only the actors and the viewer seem to be present. In *The Pianist*, Polanski has a scene where the old man in a wheelchair is pushed off a balcony of a tall building. Men are executed by pistol shot at close range as they lay face down on the ground. Tanks and infantry battles, fiery explosions occur, bombs destroy buildings, yet Polanski never uses the camera to complement or visually enhance each scene. The camera merely observes. He does *not* use camera angles or the camera to comment on this very intense material. He usually observes from a P.O.V. similar to that in *The Pianist*.

David Lynch in *Blue Velvet* shot in an observational style. That movie is about the "good points" of being a Peeping Tom in a criminal environment, much like the scenario in *Rear Window*. This style fits with the subject matter of both movies. On a different Lynch movie, *Mulholland Drive*, the camera method used is far more subjective and there is a good deal of directorial comment as well as poetic imagery. *Blue Velvet* also occasionally used poetic imagery, particularly in the opening sequence. *Mulholland Drive* is basically a "death dream" or two interconnected death dreams. Subjective, poetic imagery and directorial commentary are each appropriate to the movie's subject and both are used very effectively.

Some directors on some movies, or even in a whole series of movies throughout a career, use predominantly or even exclusively one of these methods of using the camera to tell a movie story. Many directors use some of the methods, or all of the methods on different movies, or even within the same scene. My purpose is simply to point out that they exist.

Most directors don't analyze their use of the camera as introspectively and self-consciously as I have in this chapter. They just set a shot a certain way because it feels right and aligns with their own personal tastes and because they feel that it suits the subject of the scene or the movie that they are directing. That's what I did until I spent about 30 years on and off researching another book about screenwriting, during which times I studied movies over and over while at the same time making movies, working on movies, and writing scripts. While studying a huge number of successful and very successful movies doing research to write a book about screenwriting, I noticed the things about directing that I've written about in this chapter, and I hope that presenting these different ways that directors use a movie camera to tell a story is something that you find helpful and useful.

CHAPTER NINE:
THE SIX MOST COMMON METHODS
OF SHOOTING A SCENE

A great many directors use the "master and coverage" method of shooting a scene. The purist definition of a "master shot" is a scene that shows the entire scene, all the actors in it, and everything that happens during the course of the scene. Silent movies were originally filmed completely or almost mostly completely using master shots. The legendary silent movie director D.W. Griffith is said to have invented and perfected the close-up, complete with soft light reflected in the actor's eyes, though some dispute this. Griffith definitely popularized use of the close-up and other "closer than master" shots. By doing so, he established the basic "grammar" of the art form of motion pictures. In very early silent films, directors felt they had to show all actors head to toe or the audience might ask for their money back.

Virtually all studio movies made from the silent era to the advent of sound (1930) and up into the 1960s, used the "master and coverage" method of shooting a scene. This method is still so common that many believe it is the only way to shoot a movie. Well, it is not. It is just the most common way to shoot a scene.

The word "coverage" refers to shots other than the master, close-up, two-shot, medium close-up, three-shot, single shot (showing one actor full or half body). P.O.V. (point of view shots as though seen from a character's eyes), over the shoulder shots, reverse shots (two opposing camera positions, as in shoot-outs) also figure into the coverage of the scene.

Master and coverage filming gave studio executives like Irving Thalberg much opportunity to change or recut scenes. The master shot was always available to cut to, and several other overlapping other types of shots were usually available also, at least for key parts of the scene. The editor could cut away from the master to a close-up or two-shot to a closer two-shot, and if the editor or producer or studio executive wanted to, there was usually a way to cut back and forth and remove a part of an actor's performance, some dialogue, or part of a scene if those exalted feudal toads (executives) that normally interfere with those who make the movies wanted to do so. Coverage, many different shots on the same scene, allows the scene to be edited, shortened, condensed, or for the audience attention to be directed to specific aspects of a scene at a given point. An obvious example of this is playing a certain part of a scene in a close-up on a certain actor, "showcasing" that actor's performance. When a scene is covered with lots of angles, lots of types of shots, many key decisions about how that scene will appear in the final movie can be made with the benefit of hindsight, in the cutting room or screening room, by looking and relooking at the footage that actually exists. Some times, the part of a scene that a director or writer thinks will be good before shooting does not turn out that way during filming, and looks even worse when screened. The same thing often happens with actors or actors' performances. These things can often be fixed with the advantage of hindsight in the cutting room if there is enough coverage. Another advantage of the master and coverage method of shooting a scene is that crews, actors, producers, movie and TV executives, assistant directors, editors, script supervisors, and others are familiar with this system or method of shooting a scene, and *very many of them consider it to be the only professional way to shoot a scene.*

It is not!

I heard a story about what happened when John Carpenter (director of *Halloween*) directed a TV movie about Elvis Presley that starred Kurt Russell. The TV executive overseeing the project totally panicked when he saw the rushes and reportedly called Carpenter in and asked, "Where's the masters in these rushes. How do these shots fit together? Are you sure it will cut?" The story I heard was that Carpenter told the executive that he'd show him how it would cut by going to the editing room, putting the rushes on the editing machine, and cutting a couple of scenes together that looked excellent. After that, the executives left Carpenter alone and he made an excellent movie. At that time, Carpenter's background was in low budget independent movies. He knew that you don't always have to shoot everything by the master and coverage method *as long as you shoot it so that it works, and you can cut it!*

Typically, when a master is shot, all other coverage of the scene is "slaved" to the master. If an actor moved to a certain place on a certain line in the master, he or she must move to that same place on that same line in all other coverage shots. If an actor raises his or her hand on a specific line in the master, then they must do it on all other shots that cover that portion of the scene. Francis Ford Coppola violates this standard Hollywood "professional" rule by "matching up" rather than matching "down." If the actors do something one way in the master but a different better way in a three-shot, Coppola will match subsequent shots to the better three-shot, not to the inferior master. If something even better happens in a close-up or two-shot he will match to what's best and most likely to be in the final movie.

Another major way to shoot a scene that I have seen in some very successful movies is what I call "shooting in sequential units." I'll explain this by example. Suppose there is a scene that is as follow. Joe is sitting alone in his apartment. There is a knocking at the door. He gets up and walks to the door. He opens it. Sally is standing on the other side of the doorway. Joe and Sally talk for half a page of dialogue, about half a minute. Then Joe and Sally walk into the apartment and sit on the couch and talk for a minute then Sally gets up and walks to the window and Joe follows her and they stand by the window and talk.

One way to "cover" this scene with the master and coverage method would be to shoot a master that covers the entire scene, then a two-shot of Joe and Sally at the door, then close-ups of both Joe and Sally when they are sitting down on the couch talking, then close-ups of Joe and Sally when they're talking at the window. That is a total of six shots including the master. That is six "set ups" to cover that scene with the master and coverage method.

Here's how this scene could be covered in the "shooting in sequential units" method:

Shot One – Open on Joe sitting on the couch. There's a knock at the door. When he walks to the door the camera tracks with him and the shot turns into a two-shot of him and Sally at the door. When Joe and Sally walk back to the couch, they walk out of frame.

Shot Two – A medium shot on the couch as Joe and Sally sit on the couch and talk and the camera moves into a tight two-shot and maybe moves in further into close-ups that pan back from Joe to Sally and back featuring each character when their dialogue is most important to the scene. Then Sally gets up and walks out of frame. Joe follows.

Shot Three – Sally walks into frame, Joe follows her, and the camera follows them both to a window and covers their dialogue in a two-shot. This is *one* way to cover this scene with *three* shots. These three shots are probably more difficult and they do not allow for much, if any, editing or recutting or postponing decisions to the cutting room. In the shooting in sequential method, the editor usually simply has to attach the beginning of shot two to the end of shot one, and the end of shot two to the beginning of shot three and the scene is basically cut.

The six shots described in the master and coverage method, however, can be cut together and intercut in various ways that would likely involve a dozen or dozens of edits. The two directors that I've studied that I admire who use the shoot in sequential units method extensively in their movies are Roman Polanski and Luis Bunuel. As I mentioned in another chapter, Polanski has made several movies I consider to be masterpieces, and so did Bunuel. Some of the most elegantly simple and seemingly completely effortless uses of this shooting in sequential unites method that I've seen and studied are in Luis Bunuel's surreal erotic masterpiece *Belle de Jour*.

I first became aware of this method of shooting sequential unites when I was watching a martial arts movie that starred Jet Li. There was a long fight sequence between Jet Li and many opponents. When I watched the fighting several times I realized that (a) there was no overall master shot, and (b) there were a very large number of shots where the camera was in the exactly perfect position to capture some spectacular martial arts move. When I analyzed the scene, I saw how the director shot it. First, he broke the scene into three sections, then he shot the first section with three cameras, each of which was strategically placed to capture at least one great a martial arts move. He repeated this process on the middle and end sections of the scene. This gave him at least nine great camera placements to perfectly capture at least nine great martial arts moves. He just cut from camera angle to camera angle and intercut them, using the angles in preferences that gave best coverage of particular parts of the scene. I realized that he'd shot the scene *in sequential units* and with multiple cameras. I went back and looked at some of Bunuel's and Polanski's films that I'd long admired and realized that to a very large degree they had done the same thing. They had shot these movies that I had admired so much mostly or completely in some cases in sequential units. They shot shots that only overlapped slightly so that they could be connected. These movies had not really been shot in the master and coverage method so common in Hollywood. What is a bit amazing to me is that Bunuel and Polasnki shot so many scenes with such exact precision that they were almost literally cut in the camera at a time when there was no video feed as it now commonly used. They did not see a TV image of the scene on the set. They did not see how these scenes actually looked through the camera lens until they viewed the rushes. To make a movie this way required a lot of confidence, skill, talent, mental directorial preparation, and yes, some experience, judgment, and an appreciation for the value of and limited supply of resources. Knowing exactly what they wanted was obviously present.

The third common method of shooting a scene, the montage method, is most readily evident in Alfred Hitchcock films like his masterpiece, *Vertigo*. In that movie, James Stewart's character follows Kim Novak's character by car and on foot, presenting excellent examples of this way of shooting scenes that creates meaning in the scenes by the method itself. Hitchcock often uses a one, two, three, step montage that works this way:

Shot One – He shows a character looking at something.

Shot Two – He shows what the character is looking at.

Shot Three – He cuts back to the original camera angle in shot one, and lets that shot continue to show the character's reaction to what happened and what he or she has seen in shot two.

Some ill-informed people who have their head parked firmly where the sun don't shine and have not studied enough successful movies believe and will say with very certain and imposing authoritative *ignorance* that you can't cut back to the same shot, or it looks bad, cheap, etc. These people are saying something that is not true, and I'll have more to say about that in a later chapter about false information in filmmaking. In the meantime, I'll simply say that these ill-informed people need to watch *Vertigo* a few hundred times, as well as Hitchcock's *Psycho*. Sam Raimi's horror classic *The Evil Dead* should also be watched many times, as should Lynch's *Mulholland Drive*. You'll find evidence of what I'm saying in them all. Another excellent example of the use of montage to shoot a scene is in *Dusk to Dawn*, the crime/psycho vampire stripper movie made by Robert Rodriguez and Quentin Tarantino. My vote for best scene in any vampire movie is in the "Titty Twister Bar" when Selma Hayek is introduced as Santanico Pandemonium and she appears scantily clad except for a very large python that she is "wearing." She does a very sexy dance, python and all, and pours wine into Tarantino's mouth via her leg and foot. Tarintino and George Clooney are confronted by some thugs whom they kill, but they come back to life – vampires do that. Tarantino is stabbed in the hand and the sight of the blood causes Ms. Hayek's character to morph from sexy babe to a half-snake vampire, and then as written in the script, *all hell breaks loose* and the movie's major characters as well as bar patrons played in cameo by famous horror and action stars from the 1970s engage in an all-out battle against the resident vampires (mostly vampire strippers). This battle has some very original "touches" that align perfectly with vampire lore. The method of shooting this scene from its beginning is montage. The shots of Selma Hayek dancing with the python are intercut with each other and with shots of the bar's patrons, Tarantino, Clooney, and the band. This is all great montage. Then when the battle breaks out, a huge number of exquisitely perfect and very rapidly-paced edits, joining shot to shot to shot to create this non-stop, hellish, life and death battle that is guided by the rules of vampire lore, and still very much shows the audience a lot of things that have never been seen before in a film.

Montage is the method of shooting of most battle scenes and chases and fights. On a movie I was directing, I had a scene where one character picks up a brick and throws it at another character, and the brick hits that second character in the face and kills him. Here's how I shot the scene:

Shot One – First, I show the two actors facing each other in a duel, gunfighter style, in a two–shot.

Shot Two – A character picks up a real brick and throws it. This was a full shot, a single shot of only the first character, shot from the side in profile.

Shot Three – This character held a piece of balsa wood that was painted to look exactly like the brick. He threw the balsa wood "brick" right at the camera, right at the front of the lens. I was holding the camera with my left arm. It was on a tripod, my eye was in the eyepiece, and in my right hand I held a clipboard, just out of frame. As the balsa wood brick came at the camera and me, I brought the clipboard down to protect the lens just before it hit. The balsa wood brick bounced off the clipboard just before it would have hit the camera. I has a great shot. It looked like the actor threw a brick right at the face of the other actor.

Shot Four – I shot the actor who was supposed to be hit by the brick holding the balsa wood brick at his forehead. I had him flip the brick into the air while throwing his head back and then fall out of frame onto a mattress that was out of frame.

Here's how this sequence went when it was cut together. I had a tie-in or sort of master shot or two-shot that showed the two character's physical positions in relationship to each other, and the general geography of the location. Then I cut to the side shot I described where the brick thrower picks up the real brick and throws it out of frame. Then, cut to the brick flying right at the audience (or the second character), and cut to the other actor with the brick bouncing off his head as he falls. I followed this up with a shot of the second character's head falling back into frame with blood on his forehead and fake blood gushing from his head via a hidden tube.

The essence of montage is often to put shots together so that it *looks* like something happened that never actually happened. The brick throwing sequence was in an "art" movie I made with money I saved while driving a cab. It's not on my resume, but this brick-throwing sequence was seen by a theater owner, distributor, producer who bought a script of mine and hired me to director and edit it for his production company. I think a major reason he trusted me to direct a feature movie (the first on my resume) was the extreme effectiveness of this brick-throwing sequence. Most viewers of the film flinched back when they saw the sequence.

Montage is a powerful tool. Some times you don't need a lot of budget to use it. Roger Corman's statement that whether a director is in a studio with a large crew and lots of equipment or in a back alley holding the camera himself or herself, *it all boils down to an actor in front of a lens, a director, and a script and a story.* This rings very true to me because I've shot movies in studios with large crews and lots of equipment, and I've also shot movies in back alleys holding the camera myself, and it does really all boil down to actors in front of a lens and a director, a script and a story.

There are other important uses of montage besides chases, battles, action sequences, and fights. In Hitchcock's *Vertigo*, there are places in the movie where Hitchcock shows Jimmy Stewart's character thinking and the scene shows the memory in his mind, as an image of something the audience has seen earlier in the film. This shows the audience a character's inner life, what Stewart was thinking, by use of montage.

There is a similar use of image in the movie *The Fountainhead* that shows what Patricia Neal is thinking (she's remembering Gary Cooper drilling rock with a drill) after she first meets Gary Cooper's character and is strongly attracted to him and obsessed by him.

In *Psycho*, there is a scene where Janet Leigh's character is driving out of town with $40,000 in cash that she has stolen. She's stopped at a stoplight and her boss walks in front of her car and gives her a puzzled look because she's out driving at that time of day, when she's supposed to be at home resting. His look and the close-ups on Leigh are an exquisite use of montage, as is the shot of the policeman wearing dark sunglasses looking down on her when she wakes up after sleeping in her car. The ultimate in montage as a method of shooting a scene is the murder in the shower scene in *Psycho*, which consists of many images put together to make a scene that intensely impacts the audience. The same is true of the first shootout scene in John Woo's *The Killer*. In *Psycho* there is also a voiceover montage of Janet Leigh's character hearing in her mind what she imagines that her boss is saying about her.

The fifth method of shooting a scene that I've observed being used regularly, is what I'll call *get it all in one shot* or *almost all in one shot*. The opening of *Boogie Nights* is an example of this as is the opening of Brian DePalma's *Femme Fatale* and *Snake Eyes*. Orson Welles got *almost* all of a couple very important scenes in one or two shots in *Citizen Kane* then he cuts to close-ups for emphasis and to punctuate the ending of two important scenes in *Citizen Kane*. He saves the "Cut To" to use it for dramatic emphasis. Welles does the same kind of thing in the opening of his film noir masterpiece *Touch of Evil*.

An interesting and related way of shooting a scene that is similar to *get it all in one shot* is *get it all or almost all of it in one shot with two cameras* running at the same time and with these two cameras positioned at between 45 and 90 degree angles of separation in how they are pointed at the actors. Roger Corman used this method to shoot most of the scenes in *Little Shop of Horrors*. Typically, neither of his two cameras held a complete master by itself, but together what both cameras covered was virtually always a complete master. Since both cameras were running in sync for the whole scene, Corman could cut back and forth at will to whichever angle most favored what he thought most important to show, without worrying about any matching problem.

As far as I'm concerned, the four most meaningless stupid and ridiculous words any screenwriter ever wrote are – CUT TO: ANOTHER ANGLE. Although I do admit that I have seen those words written in scripts by writers who are far more successful and highly paid than I am, I still don't understand how anyone who knows how movies are actually made could write that, except in TV where many episodes are partly directed by "remote control" by the writing staff and the executive producers, who are "overgrown" writers. If you give a scene in a movie to one director, he or she may shoot five, ten, or fifteen angles on that scene. Another director may shoot three angles and yet another director may decide to just move the actors and the camera around rather than cutting to other angles, and shoot it *all in one shot* or almost all in one shot. Alfred Hitchcock tried an experiment when he made a movie called *Rope*. He tried to make a movie without cutting except to put a new ten or twenty minute roll of film into the camera. All his experiment proved was the severe limitation of the *get it all in one shot* method of shooting, and how obnoxiously ineffective it becomes when it's too over-used, and how important cutting, editing, and montage are to building an effective movie in most cases. Some classic scenes, however, have been shot by this method.

The sixth common method of shooting a scene or even an entire movie is what I call "documentary style." The American TV series *Homicide*, created by Barry Levinson, featured relentless handheld documentary-style camera work. This gave the show a kind of "cinema verite" (truth) and an "it's really happening" feel for the viewer. Danish filmmaker Lars von Trier, whose best-known movie is the award-winning *Dancer in the Dark*, developed an entire avant-garde filmmaking theory after seeing Homicide. He and another Danish director, Thomas Vinterberg, called this the "Dogme 95" method of making movies. It became more popularly known as the "Dogma" style.

Almost all movies until recently are primarily *machine movies* because the governing element in making these movies was *the camera*, and the camera's needs ruled. This is true for *Citizen Kane, Casablanca, Vertigo* and many other movies, all the way through the first *Star Wars* movie. The actors in all these great movies and all the way back to silent movies had to think about "hitting their mark" (standing on or moving to a specific marked spot on the floor at a certain point in a scene so that they would be in focus or out of focus, as intended or "in the light" or "partly in the light" or in the dark. Customarily, in a mammoth number of movies including almost all of the greatest movies ever made, the camera, and the camera's needs, were and are of *prime importance* and the actors were "slaved" to the camera. Thus, I call all these movies no matter how great they are and how great the actors' performance in the movies are, films that are all or primarily "machine movies" because the movie camera is a machine. At times, an actor will be called upon to turn his or her head at an exact angle or the light will not properly illuminate the actor's face. Other times, if they turn the face as much as a quarter of an inch the wrong way, it will spoil the shot. Many times, an actor "misses his mark" by even a few inches and it spoils the shot. No matter how "pro" or experienced actors are, shooting movies where the needs of the camera are of prime importance forces actors to put at least some of their attention to *things dictated by the needs of the camera.*

The only exception to this that I know of in any early movie is the films made by Charlie Chaplin, which he also directed. His instructions to his cinematographer, Rolley Totherot, were to keep him in the center of the frame all the time. Chaplin did what he wanted and the camera was his slave, not the reverse. It worked out pretty well; Chaplin is a legend. He would throw out his performance and Mr. Tothenrot had to catch it.

The massive number of machine movies, some of which are very great, are only one way of making a movie and of shooting scenes; putting the camera's needs and capabilities first. This method is so dominant that many people think it's the only way to make movies or the only professional way to make movies.

What Lars von Trier did in his Dogma movies (and he was not the first with this philosophy, take a look at John Cassavetes' *Faces*) was something very different from how machine movies are made. He cut the actors loose from the shackles of the camera's needs. He used a type of lighting and lens that allowed the actor to move very freely and still be in focus and properly lit. The hand-held camera operator could move around during the scene and pan the camera to catch the actors' performance and von Trier just coached the actors to play the scene all out at each other and the camera operator has to "catch the performance." I call this "actor first" or "documentary style" method of shooting a movie or scene. Von Trier shoots the scene several times with this documentary method, covering different parts of the scene in close-ups or two-shots or panning to one character or the other at different parts of the scene, some times back and forth, and then he sorts it all out in the cutting room, and he's not afraid to use jump cuts, which are now in style. Von Trier gets away with this sometimes rough jerky jumpy non-elegant camera work because his movies have some absolutely real and spontaneous, great performances, and the camera catches them. These performances are shot on limited budgets intended for small select audiences, and von Trier is a great dramatic writer in the same league with the famous Scandinavian dramatists Henrik Ibsen and August Strindberg, and he reminds me in some ways of Doestevsky.

Von Trier operated the camera himself on *Dancer in the Dark* and on *Dogsville*. By his own admission, he's not a good camera operator, which is a major understatement. One filmmaker who will remain nameless told me of his repulsion to von Trier's shaky hand-held camera work on *Dancer in the Dark*. He said that the movie "looked like it was shot by someone embarking on an epileptic seizure, during an earthquake, while trying to stand on one leg and jumping a rope." Although von Trier's movies are mostly seen by select art movie audiences, they are seen and admired by a lot of big time mainstream directors. They are very influential. *The Bourne Identity*, *The Bourne Ultimatum*, and *The Bourne Supremacy* were all shot more or less in this documentary ultra-realist style, as was *Traffic*, for which Stephen Soderbergh deservedly won the Oscar for Best Director. Soderbergh also operated the camera himself on *Traffic*. His decision to go with a hand-held documentary style was key to making the movie very effective with the audience and acclaimed by critics.

The Dogma style has become standard on many TV programs and contributes to their feel of realism, and it's also quite popular and growing in popularity in many studio movies, perhaps because it's very liberating in style. A pure Dogme 95 style, however, has certain stipulations like using natural light only.

See http://en.wikipedia.org/wiki/Dogme_95 for a full explanation.

This style may or may not last in TV and movies because styles change, and perhaps too many TV shows these days wallow in this style. A couple of decades ago, when the Steadicam came into use, it was considered necessary for the camera to never shake, only glide smoothly, and it was considered equally important that no edit was ever seen as a jump cut. Now on television, in music videos, in big budget star vehicle studio movies, with hand-held style, jump cuts are okay and hip, and under-lighting is in vogue. As I watched the mega-budget Will Smith vehicle *Hancock*, I thought the cinematographer and director were on top of the studio heap, but the cinematographic effect was not much different than what I used to feel guilty about putting on the screen with a "B movie" I was filming hand-held and with poor lighting in the late 1960s or early 1970s.

So styles change, fads come and go. When Godard used jump cuts in *Breathless* he shocked the movie world. Now they are common and accepted. *Some times, everything old is new again.*

The six methods of shooting scenes and movies and TV shows that I've mentioned in this chapter are commonly used. Some directors hate some of these methods and prefer others. Some directors use only one of these methods on a movie, while others use several within one movie. Some stories, scripts, and movies are very suited to some of these methods and not others. Often, choosing a method to shoot a scene is a mater of personal taste, preference, familiarity and comfort, or suitability to a specific scene. Many different tools and methods are available to directors to shoot scenes and movies. The director has to choose which of these methods to use and how to use them. In the end, philosophical or ideological arguments don't matter much. What does matter is *does it work? Does it attract and please a movie audience in large numbers compared to the movie's cost of production?* These are not real *rules*. They are conventions, which come and go and change a lot. The real rules of storytelling and drama don't really change that much and in truth haven't changed that much from Shakespeare's time or the time of Greek drama, 2,500 years ago. When the rules seem to be broken successfully they are usually actually being transcended by deeper, even more basic rules of entertainment or storytelling, or even human nature or the human mind. The basic rules of storytelling and drama transcend conventions and work through these conventions when they work. The six methods discussed in this chapter of shooting a scene are largely conventions and the rules of drama and storytelling work through them, *when they work!*

CHAPTER TEN:
THE DIRECTOR'S ROLE IN CASTING
AND IN DEALING WITH ACTORS
AND HELPING ACTORS PUT THEIR BEST POSSIBLE
PERFORMANCE ONTO THE SCREEN

"They don't need to act. They need to be."
- F.W. Murnau (from *Shadow of a Vampire*)

One would-be director who I tried to help was terrified that a Method actor would ask him what his or her motivation was for this or that action that the director wanted the actor to do. He felt that these actors' questions were unnecessary and were an annoyance, a hindrance and a threat to him, because he could not answer them. He saw these questions about motivation as "out of line" and just something to make his job harder. Roman Polanski also commented in a documentary about the making of *Rosemary's Baby* that he appreciated that Mia Farrow was not a Method actor, and he disparaged the Method a bit.

Personally, I love it when a Method actor asks what his or her motivation is for this or that action, because I know that if I give them a good, helpful, logical, and useful answer the probabilities are very good that this will help them put a good performance on the screen. It almost always works that way. Helping the actors put a good performance on the screen is a big part of the director's job. I told this struggling director who was besieged by and felt hectored by actors' requests for their *motivations* about an incident that happened when I was in Arizona and Utah directing a TV episode of a Biblical saga. The late actor Vic Morrow (best known for his starring role in the TV series *Combat*) was playing a Roman centurion in my show. I wanted Vic to look off to the left toward the ending of a shot and then continue looking left as one of two cameras slowly zoomed in on him. This was the last shot of the day. He was a bit stiff and uncharacteristically unnatural when he made that move in rehearsal. Before I could shoot the shot he said to me, "I'm having trouble with this. It doesn't feel right. What's my motivation for turning and looking left?" I could have been unhelpful and not done the director's job and said something destructive like "Your motivation is your paycheck" or "Your motivation is so the camera can see your face" or "Your motivation is so we can shoot this shot and go home." I didn't say any of those things, however. I did the director's job and helped the actor do his job. I tried to give Vic something to work with.

"You are looking left because that's where Rome is," I said. "Rome is where your wife and children are. That's where your ancestors lived, where the emperor who is a god is located. That's the heart of all the power and glory and splendor of the Roman empire, which you serve as a soldier. You are part of that empire."

"Okay, give me a minute," he replied. He took about 20 seconds to think about it and said, "I'm ready."

We shot the shot, and his turn was perfect. The look on his face was great and very natural. I said "Cut" and "Print" and "That's a wrap" and we all went home early.

Any director who has written a script, co-written a script, or even read the script that they are directing should be able to see a motivation in the script that aligns with any action or performance aspect that they are asking an actor to do. Any director should be able to find a motivation or they should be able to manufacture one that aligns with the script. If he or she cannot, there's a need to ask why they are asking the actor to do what they are asking them to do. Even more basically, why are they directing? Why do they think they're qualified or suited to be a director?

What I had told Vic Morrow was made up on the spot, but *it helped him do his job, and what I told him aligned with the script*. The script was a piece of TV garbage that I did not write, but I read it, and its dramatic flow and intentions were obvious. One of its writers was an Oscar-nominated screenwriter that was a major writer of film noir movies.

An actor I knew in Toronto who became a producer and produced movies, was an admirer of some of my movies and he talked with me about a PBS behind the scenes show that showed Arthur Penn (director of *Bonnie and Clyde*) directing Dustin Hoffman in the movie *Little Big Man*. In that movie, Hoffman played a white man who was with the Indians and was dressed like and looked like a member of a tribe. The section of the behind the scenes documentary that captured the attention of myself and my actor friend was Penn giving Hoffman something to use when he was pleading with an actor playing Lt. Col. George Armstrong Custer for the life of Hoffman's character. The scene took place before the disaster at Little Big Horn and Custer was joyously massacring Native Americans. Penn told Hoffman, "He's Hitler. Custer is Hitler and you're a Jew pleading for your life trying to convince him that you're not a Jew." The actor/producer was very impressed. He said, "Talk about something an actor can *use*, something that would help an actor, something he could hang onto." He really admired Penn's advice.

I'll discuss more on Method acting and the Stanislavski Method later. For now, let's look at the very beginning of a director's contact with actors – casting. I firmly believe that if a production can actually afford it, a movie should have a casting director. There are lots of assistant casting directors who want to get a casting credit on a feature movie. Some will work for just the credit, while many of them are talented and quite knowledgeable. I think it is a highly destructive mistake for the director to be deeply involved in the nuts and bolts beginning of the broad casting process. Casting typically begins by placing notices in the proper trade papers and Internet sights. What follows from this is an avalanche of pictures and resumes and a relentless march of actors and would-be actors, and calls from agents and managers. There are hordes of people out there that want to be movie stars, or at least professional actors. The overwhelming majority of them are and will be disappointed and frustrated in this quest. Casting an independent low budget movie is usually a process that's like a prospector who digs through a lot of dirt and rock to hopefully find a nugget or a few nuggets of gold. I believe that even the lowest budget independent production should make every effort to have a casting person do the movie's first auditions, the preliminary first step in casting.

Personally, I do not think that the director should be present at these preliminary first auditions. The casting person should audition these actors and have an assistant that reads with these actors. The casting person should keep an accurate log of each actor's name and contact phone number, agent's phone number if they have an agent, and the casting person's brief notes about their opinion of the audition. The actor should be videotaped and when they are taped they should say their name and their contact phone number, and agent's name and phone number. They should also state which role or roles they are reading for, and the video should including a full body shot of the actor, and the dialogue scene or scenes that they read in the audition should be shot in at least medium close-up or close-up, *not* wide shot. The video camera should be in front of the actor, *not to the side*. The person reading with the actor should stand near the camera or behind the camera, so that the actor being auditioned will tend to look in the general direction of the camera. The actor auditioning should not be shot in extreme profile. The actor's face should be properly lit, particularly so that their eyes can be seen. The purpose of the casting person videotaping these auditioning actors is to present these videotape auditions to the director along with the casting person's recommendations about which actors should be called back to read for the director. If the casting director makes good notes in the log, the director and casting director can review a whole day of preliminary auditions (eight or ten hours) in half an hour or an hour or less, and the director can make an educated decision about which actors that they personally want to see, and which ones they don't want to see, or which ones they want the casting person to work with and videotape again.

Directors are human beings. They have *a limited amount of physical, emotional, mental, analytic, and creative energy*. To my way of thinking, and from my experience, it is a major destructive squandering of the director's vital energies for the director to be present during the avalanche of preliminary auditions. I also do not feel that it is good for a director who will eventually have to direct these scenes, *with the actors who are eventually cast*, to see a scene or scenes poorly acted, or overacted or even slaughtered and murdered by dozens or hundreds of some of the most amateur actors in the city, perhaps hundreds of times. Ideally, the casting director or casting person does the "prospecting" so hopefully the director can view and polish the nuggets that are found. If the director gets pulled too deeply into the more laborious and energy-draining effects of preliminary casting, this can easily burn up vital energies that the director will need when they are actually shooting the movie, or completing other aspects of the production. After all, most directors don't sleep much during a production and get a chance to recharge their "batteries."

Now let's take a look at some of the most basic fundamentals that underlie the process of casting. There are certain ideas in this book that recur, because I consider them to be of prime importance in the making of movies. One of these is obviously the important of *proper preparation*. Here is another such idea that I consider to be of primary importance. The legendary playwright and screenwriter George S. Kaufman reportedly told a young playwright whose play he'd read, "The trouble with the end of your play is your play's beginning." This valuable concept, that the final result of something is usually determined by or greatly affected by its beginning, often its very beginning, is an idea that has a tremendous amount of validity in many aspects of moviemaking and in the making of many movies. In another book I emphasize how important a movie's basic concept is to the prospects for success or failure of a movie. Casting has the same type of emphasis.

The first thing every distributor asks when you approach them to view your newly completed indie movie is "Who is in it?" Distributors tend to want movies with name actors and tend to *not* want movies with no-names. When your movie has no name actors, it usually has two strikes against it when it auditions for a distributor. Some movies are actually aesthetically stronger with unknown actors, however. The basic premise of *Clerks* is that the audience is observing the ordinary life of two weird guys and the people they deal with daily, and that is greatly enhanced by very good and believable performances by unknown actors. The same kind of thing, in a horrific direction, works in *The Texas Chainsaw Massacre*, *The Evil Dead*, *Night of the Living Dead* and the original *Dawn of t he Dead*, as well as *The Blair Witch Project*. I saw a movie critic on TV talking about *The Texas Chainsaw Massacre*. He said, "You can't tell, are these just strange people who are not actors, just put in front of the camera, or are they actors who are just acting very realistically and strangely?" The use of unknown, or little known actors in *The Passion of the Christ* is also very effective. It makes it more real if the actors are not familiar. The same is true with the actors in *Slumdog Millionaire*. The basic choice of whether to use name actors or unknown actors is one of the most important of all casting decisions. Often on micro budget or no budget or low budget movies, this decision is made by financial realities, not be choice!

Another very basic casting decision with far-reading consequences is will the production be SAG, meaning you sign a contract with the Screen Actors Guild and use union actors and abide by the union's rules and pay scale, or not. Despite the fact that SAG repeatedly touts their new rules for low budget movies and rolls out one "low budget" program after another, going SAG can in some cases can cripple, crush, or destroy micro budget or low budget movie's productions. There are many very tangible and very valuable advantages to working with SAG and union actors. When I was in pre-production on the third movie on my resume, I was meeting with the head of the Canadian actors union. The first two movies on my resume used non-union actors. I was bemoaning to the union head some of the union's very unfriendly rules and he said, "Yes, but if you go union you can hire any actor in the world who wants to be in your movie and who you can pay and that can add tremendous value and quality to your movie." *He was right!* I still agree with his point, which is something very important to consider when deciding to go SAG or not.

There are also important things that run in the opposite direction for a low budget or micro budget movie that need to be considered. Before you can begin production with union actors, you need to "post a bond" with SAG (or whatever union you're working with) to cover part or all of what *they* estimate the total amount of money that will be owed by the production company to actors will be at the end of production. You may calculate that amount to be $20,000 but they might estimate it to be as much as $100,000 and demand a bond of a size they feel is appropriate. The stated purpose of causing the production company to post a bond before they can use union actors is to ensure that the actors will be paid promptly for their work. That is one purpose of the bond, because the bond is held until all actors are paid *to SAG's satisfaction!* Actors are *not* paid out of the bond except as a last resort.

The production company is expected to pay the actors out of its production funds and then when all actors are paid *to SAG's satisfaction* the bond is refunded, and *not* always that promptly. What this bond system actually ensures is that in virtually every case on low budget productions where there is any dispute with any actor about hours and days worked and money owed that the dispute will be settled in the actor's favor, because *production companies making low budget movies need their bond back to pay for post-production and finish the movie.* I know of *no case* where a production company making a low budget movie ever held out and fought long drawn-out arbitration with an actor and finished the movie without getting their SAG bond back. They will settle the dispute in the actor's favor to get the bond money back. SAG has control of something very valuable - virtually all of the very best and most valuable actors in the world, or at least in the United States. If you have a really good script with a good or great role, some of these great or very valuable actors may be within your reach, even if your budget is minor league. With most actors who are excellent, the absolute highest currency of the realm *is a great script with an imaginative director*. If you go SAG with a great script all those great actors are very open to your approach. That is the major plus side of going SAG. Your movie can be a "sleeper" and hit a home run.

There are other downsides to SAG and other actor unions that the low budget producer and director need to be aware of. Some of these downsides are specific and tangible and others are more general. Many of SAG's rules and regulations and attitudes make a great deal of sense if you are talking about a TV series that is being shot by a major studio or a TV network. That type of production entity has budgets of tens of millions of dollars but some of these rules and regulations and attitudes are real "bone crushers" when they are dumped onto the backs of low budget or micro budget movies during their production. SAG officials are often struggling or failed actors. Many of them resent or hate or want to punish producers, directors, and production companies. Nothing is simple when dealing with SAG. They never miss an opportunity to hurt or punish you for making a movie. They turn the simplest things into a hassle.

One of the first things that should be done when almost any production decides that they will go SAG is to look through the production directory books and find name actors who may fit various roles. There are actors out there whose quality work is on display in past movies and TV shows and whose career may be in a "valley" and they would be open to acting in a low budget or not so low budget movie if the role that they are offered is attractive. The producer and director need to carefully weigh how important a name and quality actor is to that particular production when they decide to go union or non-union. On one movie that I made, a monster was the real star. I decided to spend a large amount of money to go union to get better actors. The producer's instinct was the opposite. He wanted to use non-union actors, and spend the money that would be saved on a more spectacular monster and special effects. If I had it to do again in the exact same situation I would go in the direction that the producer originally wanted to take, if I was sure that I could used the money saved by going non-union to make a more spectacular impressive monster. I have since learned that people who go to see or rent monster movies in DVD are usually far more concerned about and impressed by the quality of the movie's monster than they are by the quality of the movie actor's performances.

Now let's look at the actual process of the director working with actors once they are cast, and during the making of the movie. I think that at a minimum, a director should know what the Stanislavsky method of acting is and should have read Stanislavsky's major books, and should also be aware that the Stanislavski method is *not* the *only* acting discipline or way for an actor to approach their craft. Method actors refer to their body as their instrument. I'm not going to present myself as any kind of expert on Stanislavski or the Method, but I have read his major books, and I have studied them and cut out what I consider to be the most useful and important parts of these books and put them in my director's notebook. I often refer to them when dealing with actors, and even when writing scripts. I have found Stanislavski's ideas very helpful in screenwriting. For example, as a writer or director you should know that a Method actor does *not* play an emotion. They play an *action*. They do *not* try to conjure up of force an emotion like anger by saying internally, "I'm angry, so angry, got to get real angry." The Method actor plays an action and what they encounter in playing that action hopefully causes a valid emotion to develop in them, not artificial emotion to rise up inside. Here's an example. An actor is playing a scene where someone is trying to throw her "movie daughter" off a cliff. The movie mother's action is to stop her movie daughter from being thrown off the cliff. Someone is restraining her and preventing her from saving her daughter. The emotion that the actor displays and feels is supposed to come spontaneously and genuinely from inside the actor as she tries to play her action only to have it blocked. Again, Stanislavski-trained actors do *not* play the emotion. They play the *action* and if the other major aspects of the Stanislavski method are working for them, then they are likely to be "in the moment" and the emotion they portray will be genuine however it is expressed. In the above example, the actor who was trying to save her daughter and being prevented from doing so could respond with violent *anger*, or *panic* with crippling grief. These are the actor's choices. Many directors including myself are far more concerned that the actor's emotions and performance appear genuine and real than if they take a specific direction.

One very useful piece of advice that I received from Ted Post (who was a great director of actors), was to *not* give an actor any specific detailed directions until after you first see the actor's own interpretation of the character and scene. Often when auditioning actors or rehearsing actors, they will ask questions like, "How do you want me to play it, angry, sad, ironic, crazy, subdued, over the top?" Ted Post's excellent and very useful advice was to say to the actor, "Show me *your* interpretation. Let me see how *you* see it first, before I start giving specific directions." The reason Ted advised me to work that way was that he quite correctly said that sometimes the actor will come up with something that is just great and totally different that how you (the director) would have originally directed them. He said that if you give actors a lot of specific directions before you see *their interpretation* of the scene, you risk robbing yourself of a great "gift" from the actor and you cramp or stifle the actor from doing that initial part of building their performance. Ted pointed out that if you don't like the choices the actor is making and their interpretation you can always *direct* them in a direction that you like.

Don't rob yourself of the actor's original interpretation was Ted's advice. You can build on that original interpretation or discard it.

Roman Polanski said something similar to what Ted told me: "I direct this way. I let actors rehearse. I never tell them where should they go, or what should they do in the scene. I let them do it first, and usually what they do instinctively is the right thing." Actress Mia Farrow said something that is complimentary to this and is an enlightening view from the other side of this issue. She said: "I do my homework. I think about it."

I saw John Travolta being interviewed on the Actors Studio cable TV show. He said that when he asked Brian DePalma how he wanted him to play a scene, and which direction he should take, DePalma said, "You're the actor. I'm paying you a lot of money to make those decisions." That's similar to the approach suggested by Ted Post. When Hitchcock was directing *Vertigo*, Kim Novak asked him detailed questions about acting decisions. Hitchcock told her that he trusted her to make those decisions or he would not have hired her. The key point is, don't hire actors that you don't trust to make acting decisions. Hitchcock also told Barbara Bel Geddes to remember *not* to act. He wanted her to *be* natural, not stagy. Movie "acting" requires a high degree of naturalness.

The fact that this book mentions or summarizes some aspects of the Stanislavski method is not in any way intended to be a substitute for reading Stanislavski's books. Exactly the opposite is true! These references and quotes are intended to point and push the reader toward reading them. Two Stanislavski terms - "given circumstances" and "the magic if" - need a slight bit of definition for the purposes of this book but the slight definitions here are *not* a substitute for reading what Stanislavski says about his own concepts. The "given circumstances" are the actual situation in detail that surrounds the actor's character. These "given circumstances" could be that the actor's character is about to be cruelly executed and tortured to death, or that the actor's character is deciding whether to take advantage of an opportunity to kill the king and become king himself, or the character is a graduating high school senior who is spending the night trying to find the beautiful woman who waved and smiled at him, or that he's a policeman on an island and a shark is killing people and destroying the economy of that island, and if he doesn't destroy the shark the shark will continue. These are all "given circumstances" of various characters in well-known dramas and movies. The "magic if" is another of Stanislavski's concepts. Basically, it asks the actor how would he or she *really* act and feel *if* actually in the situation, the "given circumstances" of the character in the script.

Not all actors work internally using the Stanislavski method or similar internal methods. Robert Blake, who played "Baretta" on TV, was a child actor and had a role in the classic movie *The Treasure of the Sierra Madre*, starring Humphrey Bogart. On TV, Blake told of spying on Bogart as "Bogie" prepared for each day's work. Bogart worked *completely externally*. Early each morning, he would stand in front of a mirror and say each of his character's lines in the scenes that would be shot that day. He'd say these lines over and over until he could *at will* deliver the exactly line delivery and facial expression that he wanted, then he'd move on to the next series of lines or the next scene until he had his performance for the day's scenes rehearsed, perfected and previewed by himself. There is a great consistency in Bogart's performance, probably because of the way he prepared.

Different actors may work in different ways and use different methods, techniques, processes, or disciplines to create their performances. Directors need to be aware of this and sensitive to it, and understand that they and the actors are "on the same side," on the same team, with the same goals, that being the best possible performances.

Some of the worst examples of *bad* directing of actors that I've seen occurred when I saw a director who had no awareness or understanding of *any method* or process that actors use and he'd try to direct them, targeting and calling for emotions. All that he succeeded in causing was a lot of phony over-acting, a lot of which ended up on the cutting room floor. Unfortunately, it was not possible for *all* of it to end up there. Painfully for the audience, too much of it made it to the screen. Two movies where I witnessed this kind of bad directing got no distribution. The other wasn't really released – it just escaped to a few video stores.

Here are some quotes from Stanislavski's books:

There are no accidents in art – only the fruits of long labor.

The most important thing is to build the life of the human spirit.

Art establishes the basic human truths that must serve as the touchstones of our judgment.

Do nothing in general.

Stanislavski felt that generality was the enemy of art. One very practical aspect of this statement is to give an actor something specific to look at when he or she is supposed to be looking at something in the movie.

Stanislavski was quick to praise, and praise is important. He found the conscious means to the subconscious. He said, "I consider good manners as an actor's creativity." Stanislavski warns the actor not to try to "squeeze emotions which he has no personal reason to experience, but to act logically and truthfully. The more an actor forces an emotion, the less he [or she] is likely to stir it. He realized that an actor has to learn anew to see and not just *pretend to see*, to hear and not just *pretend to hear*, etc. In short, the actor needs to *think* and *feel*.

"There is uninteresting truth as well as interesting and unusual truth," he said. "In executing his [or her] actions, inner and physical, an actor must always look for the unexpected and the true at the same time. His [her] actions must be free from unattractive details. They must be real…. Actions will be impressive if they are unusual, different. To find such unusual forms of truth, an actor must see and watch, absorbing all possible impressions around him [or her]."

Here are some more relevant Stanislavski quotes:

"An actor should not practice dialogue without another person; otherwise he can become accustomed to receiving no reaction and might have difficulty in communication… with a person (actor) who does react."

"An actor must learn to respond to his fellow actor, for it is what happens between characters that is important and interesting to the audience."

Of course, if we believe Robert Blake, that didn't seem to be a problem with Humphrey Bogart. But back to Stanislavski.

"There is no inner experience without external physical expression; it is with our bodies that we transmit to our inner experiences."

Sometimes complete external immobility may be an expression of inner activity; upon hearing tragic news a person may remain physically still." (There is a great example of this in Jill Clayburgh's performance in *An Unmarried Woman*.)

"Given circumstances include the plot of the play, the epoch, the time and place of the action, the conditions of life, the director's and the actor's interpretation, the setting, the properties, lighting, sound effects – all that an actor encounters while he creates a role. A person's psychological and physical behavior is subject to the external influence of his environment, and an action makes clear what a certain character does in given circumstances of the play and why he does it."

"All attention must be directed to the execution of physical actions, to their logical consecutiveness. Only truthful, concretely executed physical actions involve true emotions."

"The 'small truth' of physical actions stirs the 'great truth' of thoughts, emotions, experiences, and a 'small untruth' of physical actions gives birth to a 'great untruth' in the region of emotions, thoughts, and imagination."

With regard to "the magic if," Stanislavski did not think that an actor could honestly believe in the truth and reality of events on stage (or in front of a camera) but he said that an actor can believe in the *possibility of events*. An actor must only try to answer the question, "What would I do *if* I were in King Lear's position?" With this "magic if" as Stanislavski called it, all the actions must lead to the fulfillment of the main idea of the play and the role.

I presented these quotes from Stanislavski's works to give the reader a taste of the useful wisdom available, and to encourage the reader to read and study these original sources fully and completely. Much of what Stanislavski writes about goes right to the core of what is valuable in art and what creates valid dramatic art. Stanislavski's ideas and observations cut very deeply. Serious actors deserve respect. They are doing something that is very difficult, and very vital to making good and successful movies. Stanislavski respected and helped them, and good directors do the same. In one of his movies Ingmar Bergman, the great screenwriter and stage and movie director, has a circus and a stage company of actors. One of his characters says that actors are much braver than circus performers, because the circus performers only risk death, while the actor risk humiliation. Without actors, there is no theater, and there are no movies.

Now a few words about actors and dialogue and improvisation. Many superstars have very quick inventive minds and love to improvise. On *Ocean's Eleven* in the movie's ending scene where George Clooney emerges from prison wearing a tuxedo (which he was wearing when he was arrested), Brad Pitt improvises and says, "I hope you were the groom." Clooney responds with his own improvised line referring to Pitt's gaudy shirt and responds, "Ted Nugent called. He wants his shirt back." These lines are very good but they are also very authentic and the actors' own. In movies, that kind of ability counts a lot.

The requirements for dialogue in movies are actually more stringent than in plays or novels. Movie dialogue has to work. It needs to seem natural and real when it comes out of actors' mouths in front of the camera. Ted Griffin, the screenwriter for *Ocean's Eleven*, is an excellent writer. The script is great. The fact that two very sharp, quick, in character, in the moment actors put a "little icing on the cake" and improvised a few lines does not mean the writer was defective or wronged. It's not the cause for hari kari or a samurai banzai charge that some members of the Writers Guild of America would urge. Just before the writers' strike in which I participated in Los Angeles, there was one particular prolific mediocre TV writer that was a real leader in urging the strike. Well after the strike, this motor-mouth had a new cause celebre. He and others were riding a fantasy to stop any director, actor, or other writer, or editor from ever changing anything a writer wrote, without that writer's permission. I think he'd vacationed a bit too long in *Alice in Wonderland* or his computer fell on his head when he tried to plug it in. He loved to launch out on his impassioned self-righteous oratory like he was Patrick Henry or Thomas Paine in the Revolutionary War. He'd say, "What right does a director or actor or other writer have to change a word of *my script*!" I felt like shouting at him, "Then direct it yourself!" But I didn't.

What happened to Mr. motor-mouth TV writer? I can only guess, but I have a good idea. What has happened to a lot of "written TV" – particularly mediocre TV – is that reality shows have massacred them and washed them and their writers away. Doug McIntyre, an L.A. radio talk show host and former sitcom staff writer lamented on his radio program that all his TV writer friends were losing everything, their houses, their cars, their wives, because the reality TV shows he'd hated so much had more than decimated over half of written TV and most sitcoms. What is reality TV? It is the improvisations of amateur actors. About half of written TV, the most mediocre half was less able to attract and entertain an audience than shows that rely on the improvisations of amateur actors.

Sir Motormouth declared that actors are not writers. In retrospect, his oratory looks like Colonel Custer declaring "Those Indians can't fight; they have no uniforms!" Then he gets an arrow in his ass and he and his men are wiped out at the Battle of Little Bighorn!

Artificial power cannot be sustained for long and is very vulnerable to anything that is more in touch with reality and the audience "desires to see." TV is controlled by writers. When you have a great writer with dictatorial control, you get great TV like *The Sopranos*, *West Wing*, *Twilight Zone*, *Lost*, *Desperate Housewives*, and *Sex in the City*. When you have mediocre writers in dictatorial control, who have turned directors into little more than traffic directors, and actors into little more than ventriloquists' dummies, you have artificial, unearned power in the hands of those mediocre writers. In that case you don't get great TV; you get *TV crap* that is very vulnerable to reality TV.

If you want to know what movies would look like if the writers got their way, look at television. TV is a very writer-friendly medium, unlike movies. Mario Puzo, the acclaimed novelist that wrote *The Godfather* and co-wrote the screenplay for the movie with Francis Ford Coppola, had a piece of dialogue about how a lawyer with a pen and paper could steal more than all the thieves. He put it in the script. Marlon Brando, playing the godfather, did not want to say the line. Coppola, who was also the movie's director, backed Brando up and skipped the line. Puzo went nuts. He threw a tantrum vocally and in writing. He went on about how people all over the world had written him to tell him what a great line he'd written. Novelist Puzo did not understand that motion pictures are a different art form than novels. With his tantrum, he was broadcasting his lack of understanding about movies. A line that can be great in a novel (and Puzo was a very accomplished novelist), can be wrong for movies, or wrong for a specific actor, or wrong for a special scene in a movie.

I think Brando's instinct was right. That line was too "on point" preachy for movies, and I'm sure Coppola was right not to force an "iffy" line on an actor that felt bad about that line.

Sometimes, whether an actor can or cannot make a line his or her "own" is far more important than all but the most important story information carrying indispensable lines. Puzo went on and on about how Hollywood disrespects writers and mistreats them because the director had allowed a *mere actor* (who was light years ahead of Puzo in artistic accomplishment in movies) not to say a writer's pet line of wonderful words.

Many times, dialogue has to be changed not because there is anything wrong with it, but so that it will fit the actual normal speech pattern of the actor that will say it, so the actor can say it comfortably and easily. *Chinatown* is an exception to this and actually runs in the opposite direction on this point. Robert Towne and Jack Nicholson were friends for a long time before the movie, I believe going back to their days working for Roger Corman. Towne wrote the script for *The Last Detail*, a very good movie in which Nicholson starred. Towne was nominated for a Best Screenplay Oscar for that script, a year before *Chinatown*. He knew Nicholson's personality, his character, his persona, his speech patterns, his sense of humor, and his charm. Towne wrote the script exactly for Nicholson; it fits him like a glove. Towne would not write the ending for the movie that Polanski demanded though, so Polanski had to write it himself. The first thing Polanski did when he finished that ending was to take it to Nicholson and have him rewrite, change dialogue, and cross out dialogue until it was all in Nicholson's own way of talking. Do not under-estimate the power of actors to improve or fix dialogue.

CHAPTER ELEVEN:
HOW TO SHOOT STUNTS AND ACTION TO LOOK DANGEROUS
WITH A LOW PROBABILITY OF DEATH
OR SERIOUS INJURY

There are two very different points of view about the director's role in shooting stunts and action scenes or sequences. One philosophy sees the director or second unit director or stunt coordinator's role regarding action and stunts to simply create something that *actually is very dangerous*, and have it play out safely and capture it with (usually) several cameras. The other point of view sees the director's role regarding stunts and action as akin to the job description of an illusionist or magician. The aim is to make the audience think that they saw something that was very dangerous when actually what really happened was relatively safe. That job description can be summarized as to make the audience believe that they saw something very dangerous that did not actually happen in reality. Earlier, when I was discussing montage I told of how I shot a scene in an alley were an actor threw a balsa wood brick right at the camera, and I edited together a series of shots that make it look like one actor had thrown a brick into another actor's head and killed him in bloody fashion. What actually went on during the filming of that scene was extremely non-dangerous. One actor threw a real brick out of frame, an actor held a balsa wood brick next to his head and flipped it into the air and fell out of frame onto two mattresses. An actor threw a balsa wood brick right at the camera and I blocked it from hitting the camera with a clipboard, an actor lay back on the ground with bloody makeup on his head. When I edited these shots together with precision, the scene was very effective. I showed this scene to several people, one at a time, on an editing machine that had a large screen right in front of the viewer's face. Every person who watched that scene flinched or reacted or fell back at the impact point in the scene. Almost all of these people were sophisticated movie viewers. This scene is a small example of director's job in action or stunt scenes as illusionist, using moviemaking tools like montage, camera angles, P.O.V., motion, composition, framing, etc. to make an effective visual illusion. Here is an equally stark albeit smaller example of the opposite P.O.V. or philosophy of the director's role in shooting action. I was A.D. on a micro budget movie. There was a scene where a female actor was fighting with another actor and the other actor was to grab a rake and swing it at the female actor. First off, a real rake was being used which was *unsafe*. There should have been a "double" rake with rubber claws, but that would have required *proper preparation*, and this micro budget movie's neophyte director had no concept of *proper preparation*. In the middle of the shot the neophyte director shouted for the actor to swing the rake *closer* to the female actor's beautiful and soft and vulnerable face. The camera operator and I both yelled "Cut!" at the same time. I reflexively reached into frame and grabbed the rake handle blocking its progression toward the female actor.

The camera operator stopped shooting and held the camera with only his right hand and put his left hand in front of the female actor's face. Then the camera operator and I spontaneously proceeded to give this neophyte director a lecture on how "out of line" and *unsafe* he was trying to shoot this scene this way and shouting such a direction like that mid-scene. He responded immediately with a raw blunt skeletal statement of what I call the "macho phallic you're a pussy" argument. He said that in order to get good footage that would look good onscreen you had to subject actors to danger and hardship, "make 'em suffer," and that's what made great scenes. "That's how it's always done in great movies." This argument holds that *you have to do dangerous things* and hope they turn out safely, and if you try to avoid doing dangerous things or putting actors at serious risk, you're not "a real man director" but a pussy.

This neophyte director had many false basic assumptions, and his numerous false basic assumptions about moviemaking and screenwriting destroyed the value of his movies and his chances of ever becoming a real movie director or screenwriter despite whatever talent he may have had. It is a paradox – something contrary to natural belief but actually true – that very often the best way to make something look really dangerous is to use to the fullest extent possible the tools needed to make the action in reality relatively safe, so that the actors or stunt people are free to "play up" what looks dangerous. This method of making things look dangerous by actually making them safe requires *work* on the director's part, specifically mental work and proper preparation and imagination. It requires no mental work or imagination or preparation for a director to simply stage something very dangerous in a very dangerous way in front of a camera.

For a director to make things *look* dangerous when they are actually shot in a very safe way requires a director who can visualize shots and edit them in his or her mind and create a montage in the director's mind and figure things out. Safety often requires a director that can figure out how shots will look when cut together and how they will affect an audience or viewer as a montage. This method requires a director with imagination who is not afraid of the very difficult mental work of proper preparation, and detailed visualization and montage planning.

There is a sharp actual contrast between how I shot the scene in the alley and how the neophyte director thought that it was necessary to shoot the scene with the rake. At the heart of this contrast and conflict between these two opposite philosophies, or methods of shooting action or stunts was the neophyte director's *very false* belief that simply doing something dangerous would cause that thing to look dangerous on the screen.

This neophyte director paid no attention to the camera's position. He could have had the rake miss the actor's face by an 1/8 of an inch and the camera would not have shown in as that dangerous because of his lack of attention to camera position. He felt it was his job as a "macho phallicer" to have the guts to do it dangerously and to have the luck to get out of it safely, and he falsely assumed that if it was dangerous it would look dangerous on the screen. He had a totally different view of the director's job than mine. I didn't realize it until I began to outline this chapter, but the reason why I repeatedly clashed when directing, being an A.D., or second unit director with such persons who insinuated I was a coward was because of my reluctance to take risks with actors was because *our most basic assumptions were opposite.* They wanted to place the main burden of danger directly on the actors in real life situations during filming at the expense of the actors or stunt people's safety. My assumption is the opposite. I place the actors' safety in the first position whenever possible, and put the burden on the director to use filmmaking tools. The director has to prepare to create the look of danger, as safely as possible.

Our basic assumptions and points of view and assignment of importance were opposite; that's why we conflicted. They didn't understand me, and I didn't understand them until I though the whole thing through while writing this book.

The scene with the rake could have been shot very effectively and safely with the same philosophy and method as the scene I shot in the alley, but that would have required a director who could really do the director's job – visualize, plan, and prepare, and use montage effectively. The paying audience does not know or see whether things are done all in one shot or with a series of cuts, if they are done well.

At one point I wrote a script for a *Road Warrior* style hyper-action type movie. I tried for years to get it financed, and eventually lost interest in directing it. I sold it to a producer who wanted to be a director. Part of the deal of the sale of the script (and I was "mucho" happy to get the money from selling it) was for me to be the movie's A.D. and second unit director and to help with the shooting of the movie's numerous action sequences. I had storyboarded some action sequences, sometimes in great detail, during previous attempts to finance the movie. Other scenes and sequences only had sketchy descriptions in the script, such as "A long exciting chase ensures" or "The fight turns into a battle and all hell breaks loose."

We shot the first part of the movie inside a building in the city and then moved to motels in the desert where some of the movie's major action sequences would be shot. I found myself face to face with the problem of *how* to shoot all the ultra-violent fast-paced spectacle a go-go action scenes on a low budget and short shooting schedule. The director's views on actor safety were the opposite of mine. I had to figure out how to shoot those scenes and not get anyone killed. It was easy to write some of these things, but putting them on film so that they would *look good*, and doing that with a low budget and some inexperienced people got more and more scary as the time to shoot them approached. I decided to do what I've recommended here already – *learn from what has gone before you and been successful*. I rented a video copy of *Road Warrior* and spent all night studying that classic action movie in great detail. I learned a great deal about shooting action from doing that, and I also learned why a special FX man who told me that George Miller, the director of *Road Warrior* and *Mad Max* was the best director with whom he'd ever worked, because he had such a clear specific idea of exactly what he wanted to see in each shot. At the time that I studied *Road Warrior*, I'd directed more than fifteen movies and I'd edited more than twenty. I'd also worked quite a bit as a camera operator. I was not a stranger to shooting or editing action sequences, but during my first couple of viewings of *Road Warrior* I was very much watching from an audience member's P.O.V. What I saw was totally dominated by George Miller's *illusions*. Repeatedly, my reaction was, "Shit, how'd he shoot that?! Someone could have gotten killed doing that!" It was only when I began to rerun these action scenes in slow motion and stop and start them before and after key edits and watch these edits in slow motion that I began to form opinions as to how Miller shot these scenes and created these illusions. It was through repeated viewings of key sections of the movie, often a frame at a time, my own version of slow motion that I moved from being an audience member under the spell of a master illusionist to the very different P.O.V. of a student studying *how* a master created these illusions.

Here are some things I observed. As I watched the close shots of star actors supposedly on top of vehicles traveling around 100 miles an hour, I began to notice that the position of the clouds in the background did not move as you'd expect with a vehicle traveling at high speed over a period of time. I cannot say for sure, as I never talked to anyone with the production, but I strongly suspect that the closer shots with the star actors supposedly standing on fast moving vehicles were actually shot with these vehicles stationary, being shaken slightly by off-camera grips, and with a wind machine blowing on the actors, with sky as the background. I believe that these shots were intercut with wider shots of stunt doubles or photo-doubles of the star actors actually on top of the vehicles traveling at high speeds. These shots were wide enough to allow for safety lines to come out of the bottom of these double actors' pants leg and secure them to the vehicle, so that if they fell during the fight sequences they would not fall off the vehicle and hit the pavement at 100 miles per hour. There's one sequence in the movie where two actors are fighting on top of a vehicle traveling at a very high speed, and one actor appears to grab the other and throw the other actor head first onto the pavement below the high speeding vehicle. The first couple of times I watched this sequence I was completely enveloped by its illusion, but when I took it a part watching it in slow motion several times stopping before and after each cut I saw clearly that it was a long way from being one shot that captured something that actually happened. It was a series of shots that were expertly edited together in a seamless flow and the last shot in that sequence was an over the shoulder shot (designated as "OTS") that showed an actor throwing a dummy headfirst into the road. The "matches" of action and choice of angles and edit points was so flawless that on first viewing, even to an experienced eye, it really looked like one actor had thrown the other off a speeding vehicle face first into the road.

There was another sequences involving a motorcycle where it looked like a stunt man rode the cycle through a major spectacular wipeout. Upon closer examination, I determined the sequence was composed of shots skillfully edited and one key shot appeared to be a dummy strapped to the cycle, launched up a ramp and flying through the air with zero risk to human life, but a good deal of spectacle on the screen and apparent danger. I don't want to ignore or deny the level of unavoidable ambient danger in shooting a movie like *Road Warrior*. Having vehicles race along the highway at 100 miles per hour and having camera crews or camera truck race with them is never very safe. Things can go wrong and when they go wrong at high speeds they can be lethal.

What I did see when I studied *Road Warrior* was a great deal of proper preparation and exquisite use of the tools of filmmaking to maximize the spectacular, spectacle of stunts and action and where possible to minimize the real danger to actors and stunt people. After I watched the movie over and over and studied it in great detail, I could say that I did not believe that there was any apparent *unnecessary* danger in the way things were filmed, only absolutely necessary danger. My definition of necessary danger in filming a movie is *that which you have to do to give the paying customer his or her money's worth."* It is that which you have to do to give the paying customers what they came to see.

Some times this level of necessary danger can be very low because of the director's imagination and creative use of filmmaking tools to create an illusion of danger, and sometimes the level of necessary danger can be unavoidably high, because sometimes in some situations the only way to get something that looks appropriately dangerous on the screen is to do something that's actually dangerous in front of the camera. *Sometimes, not always!*

In Alfred Hitchcock's movie *The Birds* there is a sequence where Tippi Hedren, the movie's lead actor, is trapped in a room and repeatedly attacked by a relentless, never-ending swarm of birds. The way the scene was shot was for the effects people and bird wranglers to throw live birds by the dozens right at Tippi Hedren in front of a camera over and over for a long time until she became hysterical. Reportedly, she had a nervous breakdown after filming the scene this way. It posed a lot of danger and hardship, even cruelty. Ms. Hedren could have easily lost an eye or had her incredibly perfect beautiful face permanently scarred. A strong case can be made, however, that this danger was necessary because there was no other way to get the strong audience horrific effect that was achieved on the screen in this classic scene.

Every day we accept a certain amount of necessary danger in things like driving to work, even though we know with certainty that every day and probably every hour or minute, someone somewhere in the world is killed or seriously injured in a traffic accident. We know that periodically airplanes will crash and kill a lot of people, yet we accept that as a necessary unavoidable danger that is part of traveling long distances in short periods of time. For over a hundred years people have been doing dangerous things in front of movie cameras to entertain people, and to make money. Some of these people have been horribly injured and killed. Some of these injuries and deaths are part of making movies just like airplane crashes are part of air travel and traffic accidents are part of people driving to work, but some of these deaths and injuries are the result of unnecessary danger, unnecessary risks, often taken because directors did not fully do their job "to the max" and were not using their imagination, tools, and homework to achieve audience satisfying screen images while putting actor's safety first wherever possible.

It's one thing for someone to be killed or injured when a driver is driving safely, carefully obeying the rules of the road, and is properly trained to drive a vehicle. It is quite something else if someone is killed or injured because a driver has not properly learned to drive a car or is violating the "rules of the road" or driving recklessly.

The same kind of thing is true of people who are killed or injured during the making of movies. It is one thing for someone to be killed or injured because of the unavoidable, necessary risk and danger that is part of making some movies. It is quite another thing, though, for people to be killed or injured because a director was not properly trained or prepared or did not do his or her homework to come up with a safe way of shooting an action scene or stunt sequence that only *looks* dangerous on the screen when properly edited, if that possibility was actually available to the director.

Right now, in my own mind I can hear some readers (the irresponsible ones) who seek to avoid responsibility and reality objecting and thinking it's all luck, or accidents can happen. Nobody wants accidents to happen, and you can plan and prepare as much as you want and things can still go wrong, but if you are unprepared and sloppy the odds are that sooner or later someone will get killed or injured. In fact, the odds are pretty high that will happen.

How do you think those odds would be if you properly learn the director's job, master the filmmaking tools available to the director, put the actors and stunt people's safety first and put the burden of making things *look* dangerous on the director, and wherever possible by the full use of filmmaking tools and do not shoot things is really dangerous or risky ways and do not dump danger on the actors and stunt people. What are the odds of death or serious injury if the director properly prepares and carefully deals with and respects danger and potential danger? The odds are manageable, and tolerable, even over a long period of time and the shooting of lots of stunts and action. Probabilities are real! Probabilities matter!

Recently, I heard a scientist talking about string theory, the most advanced cutting edge theory in physics. He said that the theory would not predict the position of an electron in an atom; it would only predict the *probable* position of an electron. It could only predict a *probability*. It seems very likely to me that the physical world and the rules and laws that run it may very well be simply be the result of the interaction of probabilities. Reality consists of probabilities.

The only certainties and absolutes that I've found in the arts and humanities are in people's minds. Usually, the more absolutes and certainties someone has in their mind the more psycho they are likely to be and the less useful they are likely to be. Gamblers rely on luck and chance, and in the end, gamblers usually lose. Professionals are aware of probability and they use that awareness and take advantage and usually win over a period of time. Gamblers and amateurs are usually punished, often severely, for ignoring or trying to negate or cross and collide with the reality of probabilities, while just hoping things will turn out positively. When shooting stunts and action, an accurate judgment of probabilities is vital.

There is no area of moviemaking where Confucius' axioms about the outcome of contests and that the wise men believe all things will be difficult apply more intensely that in shooting action and stunts. The outcome of all contests is determined by previous preparation. Without such preparation failure is assured. Now let's go back to that motel room in the desert with the VCR and the video of *Road Warrior* and my script with all those stunts and action that needed to be filmed. After studying *Road Warrior* action and stunt sequences in great detail repeatedly, I storyboarded (with stick figures) the sequences in my script and then made shot lists based on these storyboards and broke the shot lists down into separate days of shooting. I went over all this with the director. At that point we were a bit behind schedule, and the completion bonder's representative was repeatedly harassing the director, and hoping we'd stumble and he'd get to take over and finish the movie. The director and I broke the company into two units, one for him, one for me, and we shot stunts from sunrise to sunset and finished pretty much back on schedule, and nobody got hurt or killed, and the action on the screen was "OK" for a low budget movie, and was a major factor in securing distribution for the movie.

Here is a kind of reverse illustration of the paradox that some times the way to make stunts and action look dangerous is to actually make them safe. A director bragged to me that in the swordfight scenes in his movie he was going to have the actors fight with real swords. That sounded weird to me. He had a look of relish on his face when he said it. Now I understand why. He mistakenly believed (probably subconsciously) that the more dangerous, the more risky something was when it was shot, the better and more dangerous it would appear on the screen. I watched the rehearsals of these poor actors "fighting" with real swords, and I watched the scenes being shot, and then saw them in the final movie.

They were awful!

The visibly scared and clumsy actors were pussyfooting around, trying not to hurt each other or get hurt. Their attention was as much on the actual danger in filming with real swords as it was on the action, so they didn't "play up" the scene. The director shot mostly in masters with no use of safe, exciting, fast close-ups to "zip the scene up." The result of this really dangerous way of shooting the scenes ended up looking about as dangerous as a bunch of sorority girls in pajamas engaging in a pillow fight.

How should it have been shot? First, you need safe doubles for the swords. Establish the real swords, but in the "fighting" do it with safe doubles made of plastic or a light and safe metal. Second, stunt doubles in wide shots help, and well-planned, well shot, well edited, very safe close-ups where the actors can act and play up the scene are vital to inject life and the feel of reality and excitement into the scene. If properly planned for and shot, these vital close-ups would have been the safest of shots and perhaps the most visually valuable. Most likely, this director did not shoot them that way because he *mistakenly* thought that only shots that were dangerous that would look dangerous.

I heard of an incident where simply because of sloppiness and lack of preparation, a very famous martial arts star was doing a fight scene with a part-time actor with real knives because the prop person did not provide doubles. The part-time actor lost an eye because of this unprofessional use of real knives. He was a soldier in the U.S. Army and the loss of his eye ended his career. On another movie I watched a director trying to stage a fistfight and make it look more and more violent. He kept berating the actors and the stunt coordinator to be more violent and go "all out." He wanted the fight in his movie to be as violent as his memory of a violent fight in the movie *Scream*. He kept shouting for the actor to go all out, slamming into the wall. He never got a scene that was as violent as he wanted. Why? The scene needed an *actual director*. The fight scene in *Scream* that he remembered was not just a master. It had a violent master but what really juiced up the fight scene was closer shots that were cut into the master and intercut with each other. If this director wanted a fight scene that was as violent as the one in that movie, he needed to be a *real director* who knew how to use the tools of filmmaking as well as the director of *Scream*, Wes Craven. Instead, this neophyte director just kept shouting at the actors and stunt coordinator and it was impossible to create a master shot that was as violent as the scene in *Scream* whose look was the results not only of the level of violence in its master shot but the very real result of the synergy of the master and closer shots. One shot I remember from that movie is of a character flying through frame and falling out of frame (I presume onto a mattress). One thing that makes scenes like that look so violent is that the director imagined and executed shots that looked ultra-violent when they were cut into the masters, and when they were cut together, the director didn't try to do it all in a master and put an unrealistic burden on the actors. The amateur I began discussing did it in just the opposite way.

Low budget movies can easily be disproportionately *dangerous*. One of the greatest stunt men who ever appeared in movies died in an accident on a low budget movie in which he was acting. He was not doing a stunt; he was only doing precision motorcycle riding when an accident happened, and he basically bled to death before the company got him to the hospital. Ironically, this stunt man had done some incredible stunts in large budget movies and survived them all. Some times it's necessary for directors to be protective of stunt people, and in my opinion it is not always okay to let stunt people be exclusively responsible for their own safety, and let them do anything and everything that they feel is safe. The director and A.D. have a certain amount of inescapable responsibility for everything that happens or doesn't happen on their set. I would never push a stunt person to do more than they felt was safe.

Here's an incident that illustrates my point. On a horror movie that I was directing there was a scene where a character drives a car off a small ledge and it falls about ten to fifteen feet. A stunt man wanted to drive the car off the ledge and "ride" it down. I wanted to use a dummy in the car and wire the gas pedal down. There was an argument and a lot of discussion of the pros and cons of each way of doing the scene. One guy said, "What if the car hits and keeps rolling, then you got a runaway car with no driver." On and on and back and forth the argument and discussion went until I realized what my personal bottom line was. I did not feel comfortable about having a human being with a human body in that car when it fell about fifteen feet, and it didn't matter what anyone said, even the human being who wanted to be in the car. So I just said, "We are going to use the dummy in the car, and we'll lock off the camera, no operator, no crew in front of the car. We shot the shot, the car went over the ledge, wedged nose first into the ground, and a grip came in from the side and pulled the keys out of the ignition, and everyone let out a cheer. One of the grips looked over the car, and came and got me.

"I want to show you something," he said. He opened the car door and I saw the steering column in the car. It had snapped like a twig. "You were right. That coulda been the stunt driver's back," he said.

Some times, you have to take an overview and not always go along with stunt people's desire to solve every problem with a stunt. Sometimes there are safer, better ways to do things. As I pointed out earlier, in the commentary on *Once Upon A Time In Mexico*, Robert Rodriguez reveals that the motorcycle riders in a major chase sequence are computer-generated images (CGI) that he used because if he shot the scenes in reality, people probably would have gotten hurt. I watched the movie a couple of times before listening to the commentary, never suspecting the CGI. I rewatched the scenes after viewing the commentary and I still could not fault the look of the riders – it looked real. Rodriguez's decision illustrates that it's important for a director to care about the safety of the people who work for him or her.

Here's a story about John Ford and how he felt about the safety of his actors. Ford was shooting a Western and some actors were eating lunch in a covered wagon when something spooked the team of horses attached to the covered wagon and the horses ran toward a cliff, pulling the covered wagon with actors in it toward the cliff. Ford saw this and yelled in horror. The whole crew watched in horror, then a young wrangler saw what was happening and jumped on a horse and (just like in the movies) caught up to the covered wagon and stopped the runaway horse team just before they ran off the cliff. The wrangler was Ben Johnson. Ford ran up to Johnson and with tears in his eyes said, "Son, as long as I make movies, you'll have a job." Ford felt so indebted to Johnson, he not only employed him, and he cast him in small parts and mentored him into an acting career. I saw Johnson in an interview say that when he was starting out as an actor in Ford's movies, Ford would shoot two pages of dialogue with John Wayne, the movie's star, in half an hour, and spend two hours with Johnson working to get him to say a line or two of dialogue at a professional level of acting. Ben Johnson's supporting performance in the classic Western *Shane* is superb. He eventually won an Oscar for Best Supporting Actor in Peter Bogdonavitch's *The Last Picture Show*.

Other "old Hollywood" stories didn't turn out so well, because some directors did not care as much about people. I read and "oral history" of an old-time cinematographer who said he once refused to shoot a scene because it was too dangerous for those in front of the camera. He told of a scene that was being directed by Michael Curtiz (the director of *Casablanca*), in a movie being produced by the legendary Daryl Zanuck. This was in the 1930s during the Great Depression when it was easy to get extras to do just about anything for a few dollars. The scene that the cinematographer refused to shoot involved a dam breaking and a huge quantity of water and debris smashing into a crowd of people. Curtiz and Zanuck set the scene up in front of a huge water tank that had debris positioned in front of it, then let the cameras roll as the floodgates opened on those extras, who were *not* stunt people. A torrent of water and debris smashed into them and the cinematographer, who refused to shoot the scene, said many people's arms and legs were broken. People lost limbs and some were crippled and maimed. Many were seriously injured in other ways. According to this cinematographer, Curtiz took a sadistic relish in the spectacularly gruesome images that the cameras captured at the expense of the suffering and tragedy of these extras.

After I read the cinematographer's account of Curtiz's reactions I could no longer look at any of Curtiz's excellent movies, including *Casablanca*, with the same frame of mind I had before reading that interview. Many people now justifiably rail against the omnipresence of lawsuits, but the current litigious environment we live in is a pendulum swing outgrowth of decades of abuse by those in power. The Curtiz incident is not the only case I know of where a cinematographer refused to shoot a scene that he felt was too dangerous. Jock Brandis, a gaffer and technician on many of my movies, was also a cinematographer. He told me of a case where a director of an ultra low budget movie had a young man who was an "eager beaver" aspiring stunt man who was all set to run off a 20-foot cliff and the director admonished this brave and foolish daredevil to "keep running" when he hit the ground. Jock not only refused to shoot the scene, he threatened to return the camera to the equipment house to make sure nobody else shot the scene. In the field of stunts and action being out of touch with reality can have tragic results unless someone protects the deluded from himself or herself. Just because movies are not real does not mean that danger is not real, just because what is really dangerous is being done in front of a movie camera for a movie does not make it not really dangerous.

The director Fritz Lang had a reputation for "Prussian sadism" and taking delight in images of pain and suffering he created by causing real pain and suffering to actors and others in front of the camera. In one of his Westerns, he caused the death of many horses and at least one stunt man. In one of his movies there was a scene where the great Western movie star, Randolph Scott, had his hands tied behind his back and he put the cord tying his hands together into a campfire to burn the cord and break free. Lang shot this scene for real and reportedly took delight in the real looks of pain on Scott's face that the camera captured when his hands were actually being burned. The micro budget director with the scene with the rake with whom the camera operator and I clashed is not unique or one of a kind in the movie business. That micro director had soul brother predecessors like Lang and Curtiz, who made famous movies.

There is a saying that "The sure way to tell if a stunt man is lying about the stunts on his resume or his sexual adventures is to check really close and see if his lips are moving." I don't know if this also applies to stunt women. I was working on a movie and the stunt coordinator invited me to sit in on a callback interview of a stunt man who wanted to be hired as a stunt driver on the movie. The stunt coordinator said, "We're gonna have some fun. This is gonna be fun." About half a dozen of the stunt coordinator's men and women buddies showed up with big smiles on their faces to also sit in on the callback interview. The stunt driver showed up and the stunt coordinator asked the driver to tell him again about the car jump that he did in the ultra stunt-laden, action spectacular Burt Reynolds movie *Hooper*. The driver proceeded to tell us in graphic detail about this harrowing and famous stunt that he'd supposedly performed, which involved a car flying a huge distance in the air. He said he injured his back and had to have a chiropractor fix it and he was on pain pills for a while. He had all sorts of authentic-sounding detail.

Well, some of the stunt people were unable to restrain themselves from chuckling. The stunt coordinator then dropped a bomb when he said, "That's all a bit strange. You see, the stunt coordinator on *Hooper* is a friend of mine and I asked him about that car jump and he said they *put it in optically and there was no stunt*." An optical effect is where images are combined in an optical printer. This was common prior to CGI.

Talk about your embarrassing moments, but the stunt people surely enjoyed it. Everyone enjoyed getting that guy, not for lying, but telling such an inept, easy to check out lie. They were offended by the guy's lack of class. Stunt people have a particular point of view and way of relating to things that grows out of the realities (good and bad) that go with their job. During pre-production, my A.D. and I were sitting on the ground in the corner of a parking lot near the street and a stunt driver/stunt coordinator was moving old tennis shoes around on the ground, showing us how he planned to move cars during some car stunts we would soon be shooting. We were planning camera positions, disguising what types of cameras and lenses to use, and how to shoot these stunts, with how many cameras, when a real "yahoo" went ripping past us on the city street in a car at an excessive speed and just missed hitting the curb by inches.

The stunt coordinator was instantly angry. "That asshole is really irresponsible and that was really dangerous," he said.

My A.D. chuckled and I looked at him as if to say, 'What's so funny?" The stunt coordinator went on moving around the shoes that represented cars and the A.D. and I finalized our notes on camera positions, lenses and cameras and equipment. After this meeting ended, I asked the A.D. what he was chuckling about during the meeting.

He responded, "I just thought it was funny that here's this stunt coordinator/stunt driver talking about flipping this car at high speed with him inside it, and the car sliding along the street, for fifty yards, and where's the best position to film the sparks that will be shooting off the car as it slides along the street upside down, and also about blowing up a car and these other stunts, and a car drives by a bit too fast and too close to the curb and he says, "That's dangerous. It just seemed funny."

I thought about what the A.D. said and after awhile I realized something about the stunt coordinator's way of looking at things. He was very willing even eager to do things that were potentially very dangerous, or even *potentially lethal*, but he was only willing to do these potentially dangerous or lethal things very carefully, very well-planned out and in a very controlled way. The "yahoo" driving past us too fast and to close to the curb was doing something that should have been safe (driving on a city street) but he was doing it carelessly and recklessly, the opposite of the stunt coordinator's method. That's why the yahoo's action grossed him out as dangerous and irresponsible. Good stunt people will do things that are potentially lethal and potentially very dangerous, but they do them as carefully and safely as possible or they will get hurt and killed. It is important when shooting stunts and action not to allow or engage in unnecessary rehearsals or to shoot extra takes after one "has the shot" (a good take).

Stunt people should only be allowed to do the rehearsals that they actually need to do, in order to do the stunt properly and safely, but they should *not* be allowed to do unnecessary rehearsals simply to show off or to pass the boring time while waiting to do their stunt. On PBS, I saw a documentary of the making of *Raiders of the Lost Ark*. It showed the behind the scenes activities during the shooting of the famous shot where a moving truck blows up behind Harrison Ford and he believes that his love interest has been killed in the explosion. Spielberg loved the first take. He loved the look on Ford's face and the way the truck "realistically" almost flipped completely over. The stunt coordinator wanted to do another take to have the truck flip completely and he lobbied Spielberg hard to do another take for a more extreme truck flip, but Spielberg refused. He "had" the shot. He knew he had it and just because the stunt coordinator wanted another take was not a good reason for extra risk.

For me, it's an axiom for shooting action or stunts to not take extra risks and not to tempt fate. Luck grows thin when you take extra unnecessary risks. Here is a true story that tragically goes in the opposite direction. First, let me emphasize that I had nothing to do with this movie. I never even met the director of this movie. I was not even in the same county where this movie was being shot when a tragedy happened. A producer with whom I worked on two movies and three scripts told me this story. Two stunt men on the movie had met a young twenty-one year-old man who wanted to become a stunt man and they arranged for him to do a stunt where he jumped from a bridge and landed in the back of the truck. They had cardboard boxes to break his fall. They rehearsed the fall a few times while the director shot other scenes. They were ready. The director kept shooting other scenes and planned to shoot the stunt later that night. The stunt people and the young men rehearsed stunts *unnecessarily* to break the boredom of waiting. A couple hours passed and the producer said he heard a horrible crash. He went to see what happened. The young man had "rehearsed" the fall again, only someone had removed the boxes from the back of the truck. The young man had landed flat on his back on the metal bed of the truck. He broke his neck.

The stunt man lived, but he would be paralyzed from the neck down for the rest of his life! The producer and director and movie company were sued for $10,000,000. The suit was settled for a mere $100,000. Apparently, the paralyzed young man, who'd dreamed of a career as a Hollywood stunt man, had a bad lawyer or desperately needed the money, probably for his medical bills and care.

When the producer told me this sickening and tragic story, I responded in a pretty accusatory fashion, blaming him and the director for allowing this kind of unprofessional *crap* to go on. He got very upset and defensive of himself and the director. "Accidents happen," he said. "The director didn't want this kid paralyzed. It wasn't his fault."

I didn't press it. He was very livid in his defense of the director, who was a well-known, very prolific low budget director, producer, and actor. About three days later, the producer came up to me and said, "You were right. That accident happened because that director doesn't give a shit about anything. He doesn't give a shit." Then the producer told me of another scary incident. This same director was shooting a scene where stunt men would jump from a high-rise apartment building into a swimming pool. This director didn't stop these stunt me from "rehearsing" (showing off) this jump many unnecessary times before the actual filming of the stunt. The producer said their heads just barely missed the concrete edge of the pool by less than a foot. "If they'd slipped, the results would have been another 'accidental' tragedy," he said.

Some times when you tempt fate and take unnecessary risks, you get away with it and *sometimes you don't!*

I've watched stunt people, men and women, on my movies and other movies on which I've worked. I've observed them flip cars, do high falls, light themselves on fire, do fights, and I've seen how their temperament and mindset changes as the time to do the stunt approaches. I've talked about how professional stunt people are careful and precise about planning and doing dangerous, even potentially lethal things. This method reminds me of a quote from the legendary investment banker, Nathan Rothschild, who said, "To amass a great fortune, it was necessary to act with incredible boldness, take great risks, and act with extreme caution at the same time."

Many people have written and talked about bravery and courage that feel that does not mean a person lacks fear, or is not afraid, it means that they overcame their fear and did their job, *despite fear*. I trust stunt people's evaluations of what's safe and what's not safe a lot more when you're a week or two away from shooting the stunt than their judgment in the heat of the moment right before shooting the stunt, because at that point, their mindset is to "steam roll" their fear, rather than to carefully evaluate.

Again, I would never pressure a stunt person to do anything more dangerous than what is comfortable for him or her. When close to doing a stunt, I do not regard a stunt person's willingness to do a stunt, or do a stunt in a certain way as conclusive evidence that it's necessarily okay or safe to do that. They may simply be in a steamroll their fear mode, and might accept risks that in a calmer time they would consider unsafe. One stunt man told me that on the day that he'd done a legitimately death-defying stunt, he would not drive. He'd be too hyper.

I said, "Okay, I'll send a P.A. to bring you to the set, and take you home after the stunt."

He agreed the P.A. could bring him to the set, but after the stunt, he'd either leave in an ambulance, a hearse, or with at least two of the best-looking women on the set. He was not wrong, and he did not leave in an ambulance or hearse. He also had a serious collection of detailed graphic stories about his sexual adventures with some fairly famous female actors after previous death-defying stunts. Maybe they were true, or just very well crafted.

There are a lot of emotion and pressure on stunt people to do the stunt, even if everything is not exactly right. It's very hard for them to back out. The director has to be aware of this, and ultimately responsible for safety. It's okay for a director to look like a "pussy" and pull the plug on an unsatisfactory stunt when a stunt person's mindset won't let them back out. I have been extremely lucky and blessed that nobody has been killed or seriously injured on any movie that I've directed on worked on. I do not want to falsely present myself as someone totally clean hands that's never put people at risk, however. Here are some close calls that could have resulted in death and possible manslaughter charges, very easily.

One: From the earliest phase of the first incarnations or the *Road Warrior* style movies I wrote, assistant directed, and second unit directed, I had storyboarded a sequence during a vehicle battle sequence. This storyboard detailed shot by shot the climax of a vehicle battle sequence. These shots depicted the movie's final showdown where the movie villain "gets what's coming to him." Good guy vehicles approach bad guy vehicles and as the vehicles cross, the good guy throws a three-pronged grappling hook on a chain that goes into the villain's chest. As the vehicles pass each other, the chain is pulled taut and yanks the villain out of his vehicle and he flies about twenty feet in the air and is dragged behind the good guy's vehicle.

We were shooting this vehicle battle on a dry lakebed in the desert north of Los Angeles. The last shot in the scene that we were trying to get was the shot where the villain is yanked by the grappling hook out of his vehicle. The villain was being played in this shot by a cloth dummy, not a human-looking dummy. The first two times we tried to get the shot, the rope doubling for the chain attached to the dummy and the good guy's vehicle broke when the dummy caught on the car door and did not fly out of the villain's car. A grip brought over a long one-inch thick metal cable to use instead of the rope. I said, "Okay, use it, it won't break." I was directing the shot as a second unit shot. We tried again with this metal cable. When the vehicles crossed and the cable was pulled taut, one of the vehicles bucked as the cloth dummy had again caught and the metal cable snapped loose as the vehicle completed its buck and that long metal cable whistled across the desert like a metal bullwhip. It was probably traveling hundreds of miles per hour and it barely missed me and about ten other people standing near the cameras. It missed us by less than fifteen feet. Thinking about it still makes me shiver. If it had hit anyone it certainly would have seriously injured or killed them and it might have cut them in half. I felt very lucky, protected, and blessed that nobody was hurt, and very scared when I visualized what could have happened. We went back to using ropes. They might break but they weren't going to kill anyone. Finally, we got the shot. The dummy flew beautifully out of the vehicle and arched twenty-five feet into the air. When the scene was cut together, it pretty much matched my storyboard and when the movie was shown to an audience, they broke into a spontaneous cheer as the villain flew out of the vehicle through the air and was dragged.

Two: At the end of a monumentally hectic day of filming which I'll describe in detail in an upcoming chapter called *Momentum, Inertia, and Win or Lose*, we were racing to beat the setting sun and to get a shot of a car going off a 150 foot cliff so it would smash into the floor of the canyon below. This was in Hamilton, Ontario. I was on one side of the canyon with the cameras, and the key grip and some other grips were on the other side of the canyon, preparing to launch the car forward and over the cliff while hiding themselves from view of the camera. I got the camera set, the key grip was ready to send the car off the cliff, and the sun was about to set, but we beat it. I looked down into the canyon floor and I saw just about the worst thing that I could see – people! Hikers, nature lovers, were in the bottom of the canyon walking directly toward where the car would impact if it went off the cliff. The camera was running, the car was moving toward the edge of the cliff. I began yelling across the canyon that was about as big as a football field, yelling "No! No! Back it up, there's people down there!"

The key grip got the message barely in the nick of time, and looked down into the canyon and joined me in yelling at the hikers to leave the canyon, which they promptly did and we safely shot the car going off the cliff and crashing. That was really close. Theoretically it was the A.D.'s responsibility to secure the area, but I could not blame him. He was running like a mad man the last hour to help me "get the day." I also still get a major shiver when I think about that incident.

Three: I was shooting a car chase in rural Ontario. Part of the chase involved two cars whipping through a small tunnel. I was all set to launch the two cars toward the tunnel and I did a final check on the walkie-talkie. I asked the A.D. who was on the other side of the tunnel down the road a bit, "Is it all clear? Are the intersections on the other side locked off? Is the road totally clear?" With every question, the A.D. said yes, and I was about to call "Action!" and launch the stunt cars with the two eager beaver hellion stunt drivers when the camera operator began yelling "Cut! Cut! Damn it, cut, and don't send the cars! Cut forever, man, cut!"

The camera operator was looking through a slightly telephoto lens and he had a better view into the tunnel than we did, but it wasn't long until we saw what he was yelling about. Out of the tunnel driving slowly toward us came a little put-put car driven by a sweet-looking little white-haired old lady, and next to her in the passenger seat was a sweet little of white-haired man, probably her husband. They smiled at us as they drove past. I was extremely unhappy. I just about fell down. I had a stunt driver take me to the other side of the tunnel. I found the A.D., took his walkie-talkie, and told him he was no longer A.D. on this car chase sequence. I fired him a couple of days later. I personally placed P.A.s at every intersection, and personally checked to make sure the road was clear. Then I went back and continued shooting the chase again, thinking, "That was close."

There were other close calls like the three discussed above, but not as bad. I'll include one last close call of a different character. We were shooting in a semi rural location. The Scarborough bluff cliffs that border on Lake Ontario. We were on the beach, having been shooting there all day, and we were ahead of schedule. I decided to wait for "magic hour" – the time just before sunset when the light looks really nice – before shooting the last shot. We had about an hour to wait. The female script supervisor asked if she could go into the forest and shoot some stills. I said sure. She went off into the forest with her still camera. The whole cast and crew just relaxed on the beach, enjoying the Canadian summer as the sun slowly moved lower in the sky. Some time passed, and then we heard someone screaming and yelling. It was Liz, the script supervisor. She was screaming and yelling, "They tried to rape me!"

She slid down the side of a dirt slope and when she hit the bottom she started running toward us repeatedly yelling, "They tried to rape me!" A car came around the side of the mountain on a dirt road and began chasing Liz. By the time she got to us, the car was about 100 yards away. It stopped when the driver saw an entire movie crew and all our vehicles. Liz was out of breath, crying and looking panicked. She reached us and gasped, "They tried to rape me!" Several crewmembers picked up rocks and were ready to stone the evildoers if they came closer, but suddenly the car backed up, whipped around and peeled out in the opposite direction. Jock Brandis, the gaffer, and the producer had jumped into the equipment van. Jock was driving right at these would-be rapists like a Japanese officer in World War II leading a banzai charge. The van chased the car up the dirt road and onto the city streets full of rush hour traffic. I'm sure Jock just wanted to make contact with them and "raise their consciousness." Liz said that she hoped Jock and the producer did not catch them because to her they looked like hardcore criminals and she feared that if they had caught her and raped her, she thought they would also have killer her.

About an hour and a half later, Jock and the producer returned. They'd chased the criminals in rush hour traffic, but lost them. The producer told me that at times Jock was going over 100 miles per hour on the wrong side of the road, running red lights. So much for close calls.

I have almost a superstitious reluctance to point the finger of blame at unfortunate or irresponsible directors whose luck has run out and have had the horrific experience of presiding over a tragedy. I'm going to override that superstitious reluctance in the last part of this chapter to make an important point. In the 1980s, one of the most notorious fatal accidents in movie history was in the news and in the minds of many in Hollywood. It was the *Twilight Zone* movie helicopter that killed actor Vic Morrow and some small children. That movie was composed of separate episodes, each based on a famous *Twilight Zone* episode. Each section of the movie was directed by a different director, some of the top names in Hollywood at the time.

The episode that killed Vic Morrow and the kids was set during the Vietnam war. Morrow was playing an American soldier shielding some Vietnamese children in a river, while a helicopter flew above them, and explosions went on around them. The director's way of shooting the scene was to do the action with real danger and capture it with several cameras. It was the exact same method as the micro budget director with the rake had used, based on the same erroneous belief that to make the scene truly look dangerous one would make it look really dangerous. So well after midnight, Vic Morrow and some small children were standing in an artificial river. A real helicopter was hovering above them and real explosions went off around them, while several cameras rolled. One of the explosions destroyed the helicopter's air worthiness and it fell straight down onto Vic Morrow and the children and killed them. The director had chosen an extraordinarily dangerous, unsafe way to shoot the scene.

In the state of California at the time of this filming, there was a law that prohibited the filming of children after midnight. I've shot movies with child actors and have had social workers walk into the middle of a shot two minutes before midnight and pull the child actors off set with the camera still rolling. No grace period, no leeway, no discussion, just "It's 12:00 and tough luck." How they managed to go around this law on the *Twilight Zone* set I don't know; I can't even imagine it. There is also a law in California that a social worker is to be present on the set when child actors are working and the social worker has the power and duty to stop filming if they feel that the child's health or safety is at risk. How a social worker would ever allow a helicopter to hover over those children is a mystery to me.

On one movie, I had a scene where two kids were fighting. They slipped, and one kid got a scratch. The social worker descended on me like I as a combination of Charles Manson and Jack the Ripper. As a result of that incident, I no longer write parts for child actors in my scripts, and I no longer cast actors under eighteen years of age.

In case you're not familiar with the case, the director of the scene in the *Twilight Zone* movie, was charged and tried criminally after the accident, but his lawyer successfully persuaded the jury not to convict him.

Here is an alternate way that the scene could have been shot with the same amount of audience satisfaction or more than the dangerous way in which it was shot. The "tie in" shot showing the helicopter and the actors would have used prosthetic mannequins that would have been exact replicas for the actors. Cables could have been run under the water to these mannequins to run mechanisms inside them to make them move. If you doubt that this could have been done, look at the mechanical prosthetics from John Carpenter's *The Thing*, which was made in the same time period. If the tie-in shot between the helicopter and the actors would be wide enough to show the helicopter and the actors at the same time. It would have been wide enough that nobody could have seen that the mechanical prosthetic mannequin doubles of the actors were not real actors, particularly if for instance Morrow's mannequin moved its head up to look at the helicopter, then cut to Morrow in a close shot looking out of frame in an exact match with the mannequin, and the children's mannequins had moved their arms to hold onto Morrow's mannequin. Cut to the real children in a close shot-matching Morrow reaching to hold onto Morrow. The closer shots of Morrow and the children could have been shot with no helicopter, and no explosions but with a wind machine (utterly safe, off-camera) and arc light flashing and sound effects added later to register as explosions. The actual explosions could begin in the wide tie-in shot. A crane shot almost above the actors could have been a safe helicopter P.O.V. shot of the actors, complete with wind machine and arc light flashes (safe substitutes for explosions), and locked-off cameras with no operator pointing up at the helicopter and at real explosions could have been the actor's P.O.V. of their supposed surroundings could also have been shot very safely. Good footage shot from these various camera positions in the ways described above could have given a skilled editor more than enough footage to make a very exciting scene, probably much more exciting than what resulted from the director's very dangerous choices.

Why did the director choose such a dangerous way to shoot this scene? Nobody knows for sure. This director was certainly smart enough to imagine a safer way to film the scene. He directed one of my all-time favorite movies. The director entered the movie business as a stunt man. It's my guess that he may have still thought like a stunt person or wanted to impress stunt people and action directors and was not simply aiming to do what was necessary go impress moviegoers, who do not know whether what they see is a series of shots cut together or all one shot, or all one real time action caught with a lot of cameras. I doubt that the actors' safety was as important to this director as impressing himself, stunt people, and fellow action directors, with a really dangerous "macho uber alles" stunt.

The next chapter is about importance. Here's a choice that I faced while shooting a stunt in a horror movie. I shot a scene inside a studio where a female actor is attacked in her room by a monster "in her mind" and she backs away from the monster and smashes backward into a window that's supposed to be on the third or fourth story of a building. The shot that comes after this in the movie is the exterior stunt shot of a stuntwoman smashing out of a window and falling three stories out of frame into some out of frame boxes. I shot the studio shot two weeks before shooting the stunt. When preparing to shoot the stunt, the stunt coordinator came up to me and said, "I don't think it's safe for her to go out of the window backwards. She doesn't want to go out of the window backwards." The shot with the female actor in the studio could not be reshot she had gone into the window backwards. If the stuntwoman jumped through the window frontward it would not match. I had two bad choices to choose from, something that is not uncommon for low budget directors. I could choose either a mismatch or extra risk for the stuntwoman. I choose the mismatch and I'm sure 99% of the paying public never sees it. A magazine writer for a horror movie magazine in Toronto told me that this movie has become a cult classic and plays regularly on the local cable horror movie channel. It was also profitable for all involved, and the stuntwoman was *not* hurt.

Sometimes, directors have to choose what's most important to them and what's not!

CHAPTER TWELVE:
IMPORTANCES AND UNIMPORTANCES

Rarely, but sometimes, one sees a movie where absolutely everything in the film is completely perfect. I would say this is true for me of Orson Welles' *Citizen Kane*, Michael Curtiz's *Casablanca*, Billy Wilder's *Sunset Boulevard* and *Double Indemnity*, Stanley Kubrick's *Paths of Glory, Dr. Strangelove, Full Metal Jacket, 2001: A Space Odyssey*, Roman Polanski's *Rosemary's Baby, Chinatown, Repulsion, The Pianist*, Luis Bunuel's *Belle de Jour*, Akira Kurosawa's *Red Beard* and *Seven Samurai*, David Lean's *Lawrence of Arabia*, and Catherine Hardwicke's recent *Twilight*.

These movies are *not* made on low budgets with short shooting schedules. There are very few, if any, low budget movies shot on short shooting schedules that seem over-archingly perfect in every detail. Some you might possibly put in that category, to my mind, would be *Reservoir Dogs, Little Shop of Horrors, Breaking the Waves,* and *Sex, Lies, and Videotape*. There are, however, a number of very successful low budget "breakout" movies that launched major director's careers that contain imperfections that can be criticized but these imperfections do not stop the movies from succeeding enormously. I've studied a lot of low budget breakout movies to find a common denominator and realized that, despite imperfections, they all do the most important things very well, often with more excellence than mediocre studio movies. Examples are *Night of the Living Dead, The Evil Dead, Clerks, El Mariachi, Kentucky Fried Movie, Texas Chainsaw Massacre, Last House on the Left, The Hills Have Eyes, Faces, Breathless, Dancer in the Dark, Targets, Mean Streets*, and *The Blair Witch Project*.

When making low budget movies on short shooting schedules the director usually does not have enough resources and time to make everything "perfect." I watched one poor suffering and struggling would-be director who mistakenly believed that the way to make a good movie was to make everything "perfect" particularly the most *unimportant* details. He squandered his time and budget and crashed and burned horribly and plunged into the lower depths of filmmaker hell by obsessing on unimportant details.

Here's how I look at the continuum of importance and unimportance. There are things that are *vital*, and *very important*, *important*, *less important*, and *unimportant*, as well as things that *do not matter at all*. There are also things I call rotten dinosaur crap. That's my scale of importance of items involved in moviemaking. Allow me to give you some examples.

Things that are *vital* must be done well or very well or they will destroy or severely damage a movie's value. *Concept* is vital. *Audience interest in and identification with lead actors* is vital. Every one of these low budget breakout movies mentioned above had excellent editing and an excellent concept. A movie's *story* and *script* are vital. Its *commercial content* (particularly genre-appropriate content) is vital. Virtually all of the low budget breakout movies mentioned have excellent genre-appropriate commercial content. If they are comedies, they are very funny and have lots of laugh out loud moments. If they are horror movies they are scary and have excellent horror content. If they are "art movies" they deliver that in bucket loads.

It is *very important* to have hot coffee on the set. Some people can't wake up or move quickly or talk civilly without their caffeine fix. It's very important for the crew to be fed good food that they like, and to have drinking water readily available. Accordingly, professional production values are very important.

The general quality of acting in a movie is *important*. Competent art direction is important.

It is *less important* for actors to be scheduled so that they have time off to go to auditions to try and get their next acting job, or to run personal errands than it is to get the movie made in the best, most efficient possible way, with the best possible result.

Some people will tell you that you "can't cut back to the same angle." Or that "It's bad or looks bad to cut back to the same angle." In a later chapter I will fittingly destroy this absolute erroneous claim. For now, I'll simply say that in *Psycho, Vertigo*, and *Rear Window* Hitchcock "cut back to the same angle" a lot, and Sam Raimi did it seven times in more than one instance in *The Evil Dead*. David Lynch also did it many times in *Mulholland Drive*, as have many other great directors in many successful movies. It is purely a matter of personal taste and is *unimportant* whether one "cuts back to the same angle" or not.

Beneath the level of *unimportant* are *things that do not matter at all*. Here are some examples. On the movie *Night of the Living Dead* there is a brief shot of a second story window that is not boarded up. The audience does not know that it is not a first story window, to which the zombies would have access. On the DVD commentary, some actors reveal that this was a hotly debated issue during production as to whether the audience would wonder why the zombies didn't come through that unboarded window that was glimpsed for an instant. George Romero apparently ignored this weighty debate and just made a great movie by concentrating on things that were vital, very important, and important, and ignored things that do not matter at all. In the DVD commentary of *The Evil Dead*, Sam Raimi talks about how the shot of the moon in one sequence bothers him and he still doesn't like it. I can't see what he thinks is wrong with it, and I know a lot of people who have seen the movie, and none of them see anything wrong with the shot. *The Evil Dead* has so many very important and vital things done very well that whatever Raimi sees as wrong with the shot of the moon *does not matter at all*. In the move *The Godfather* there is a scene where Al Pacino's character returns from Sicily and asks Diane Keaton's character to marry him. In that scene, there's a shot where Diane Keaton looks much taller than Al Pacino. This scene was shot early in the shooting schedule and many of the crew took this shot as proof that Francis Ford Coppola was incompetent and would soon be fired. When the movie was finished, that shot was in the middle of the movie, and by that point in the movie the audience was so deeply *emotionally involved* with the story and its characters that Diane Keaton could have looked like the stand-in for the female lead in *Attack of the Fifty-Foot Woman* and the audience would have scarcely noticed. The shot that some on the crew thought proved Coppola was an incompetent goner did not matter at all.

At the very bottom of the scale of unimportance are things that I call *rotten dinosaur crap*. For an example, on a horror movie I directed in Los Angeles the cinematographer wanted to shoot a shot at 10:00 a.m. simply because it happened at that time in the script. He wanted the right "10:00 a.m. light" and oddly enough, the producer granted him this favor despite my protest that it would turn the first day's shooting schedule upside down. And because of this oddity I did not get my day the first day of the shoot. I was dragging a couple shots, because of the goofy idea that it was necessary to shoot in "10:00 a.m. light." Every day of the first week of shooting I'd come up in a couple of shots short and had to drag a couple shots because of this cinematographer's "idea." For a whole week I shot under intense time pressure, all the time hearing from the favor-granting producer that I was behind schedule, needed to make my day that day, and the completion bonder was watching and wanting me to get back on schedule. I was also reminded that if we shot an extra day we'd go over-budget. Constant time pressure and significant harassment resulted from "10:00 a.m. light." It was like being at bat in a baseball game against tough pitching, while someone is throwing tennis balls at you from the side. I'm sure you get the picture, and this is an example of *rotten dinosaur crap* – something that causes an expenditure of significant valuable resources or significant inconvenience or distraction yet doesn't mean anything at all to any significant portion of the paying movie audience. Try to imagine sitting in a theater and saying, "Wow, that looks just like 10:00 a.m. light!"

On another occasion, a writer who was also a neophyte director producer had written something into his script about a special kind of fireplace. He drove the whole crew and actors half a day to a distant location on the other side of the Inland Empire in southern California to shoot a rare location that had this special kind of fireplace that meant so much to him, but nothing at all to anyone else in the entire universe. He made a royal mess of that day's shooting. I worked with him on the script, and I did not understand the significance of this fireplace.

Ultimately, he was making a movie for himself, and the film never got distribution. He was its only paying customer.

To risk actor's lives and safety to impress stunt people and other action directors by shooting scenes in a very unnecessarily dangerous way that will not add to the satisfaction of the paying audience at all is *severely rotten dinosaur crap*. It wastes things that are valuable, people's lives and safety for something that means nothing to the paying audience, but means something to one person or a few people. This perfectly illustrates that *the judgment of and assignment of importance matters*.

Being sloppy, hasty, cavalier, incompetent, or inept, or making bad decisions, or failing to deliver excellence in things that are vital or very important destroy the value of a movie. On the other hand, obsessing about or throwing resources at or taking valuable time to perfect or be terrorized by worries about things that do not matter at all, or are unimportant or even rotten dinosaur crap can also easily destroy a production. Directors need to be able to judge importance and act accordingly, particularly if they want to make low budget movies that are successful and break out and launch careers. Directors that succeed in making low budget breakout movies put their time, energy, and financing into doing things that are vital or very important very well, and do not get suckered into or stumble into obsessively sinking into pouring time, money, energy, and resources into unimportance.

135

CHAPTER THIRTEEN:
IF IT'S NOT IN THE FRAME IT DOESN'T EXIST!

The title of this chapter came from a line of dialogue in the Oscar-nominated movie *Shadow of the Vampire*. The line was spoken by John Malkovich, who was portraying the great silent movie director F.W. Murnau, who directed *Nosferatu* and *Faust*. I was watching a movie on an editing machine that was non-directed by a neophyte director and it had a poorly-framed shot that ran for a very boring twenty seconds or so featuring a car driving out of a parking lot in one screen direction and then cut to the car driving in the opposite direction on a highway. It was an ugly, unaesthetic amateur a-go-go edit. I asked the neophyte director, "Why did you show the car doing all that driving and then a jarring, ugly cut to the car going in the opposite screen direction?"

He said, "That was the only exit out of the parking lot."

He was trapped in reality!

I asked why he didn't just have the car drive out of frame in the correct screen direction. The audience, after all, wouldn't know that there's no exit in that direction in that parking lot. If he'd done what I suggested, the cut to the car on the highway would have worked smoothly. This poor gentleman was captured by the circumstances of his location, a slave to the real world. He was not an effective creator of a movie world of his own that overpowered and superceded reality. Earlier in this book I quoted the great writer Robert J. Ringer saying, "If you acknowledge reality it automatically works for you. If you fail to acknowledge reality it automatically works against you." Acknowledging reality is *not* the same thing as submitting to reality, obeying reality, agreeing with reality, or being its slave or prisoner. The director is "god of the frame" and creator of the image.

Shakespeare said that "All the world's a stage." Similarly, I'd say that all of reality is but potential movie sets upon which a director can stage scenes and create images and show or not show what he or she wants of that reality. The director chooses what part of reality he or she will allow into the precious frame and what he or she will keep out of the frame, and what he or she will allow into the movie's world. A director needs to be a master of reality and have an imagination that supercedes reality and creates the aesthetic reality of his or her movie. First, acknowledge reality, face it head-on, then become its master. On one movie I directed, I was complimented several times on the great building I'd found for the movie's central location. Well, that building *only existed in the movie*. It was composed of parts of *five* different buildings that existed in reality. I shot scenes in five places and wove them together in editing so that it looked like one building. I chose what I wanted from reality and within the rules and conventions of moviemaking and the grammar of film, I had an exterior that looked great, a boiler room that came from a large school, some great large areas from the Ontario Science Center, and some rooms in a studio. An actor would walk out of frame in one location then walk into frame in front of an appropriate background in another building, yet it would look onscreen like the same building. When an actor disappeared around a corner and appeared traveling in the same direction in another building, it was easy to make it all look like the same place.

Doing something like this requires a director to have the movie in his or her mind. My view of screen direction is what some might call "old school." I would say it's actually post-modern. Lars von Trier in a DVD commentary said screen direction does not matter to the modern audience, and he may be right that is does not matter to a *sophisticated audience* as *a rule that must be obeyed.* So let me roughly define screen direction.

If an actor is in a close-up or medium shot looking from right to left and another actor is in a similar shot looking from left to right, they will look like they are looking at each other. Even if these shots are shot miles or weeks apart from each other, that's how it will look onscreen. If you are shooting a chase and the person being chased is moving left to right and the person chasing is also moving left to right, it will look like the chase is in progress. If actors really are looking at each other or really are chasing each other and *you keep the camera on one side of them,* what's going on in reality will appear on the screen. On the other hand, even if they are actually looking at each other or chasing each other and you move the camera to the other side of one actor, the screen direction will look wrong – like they are not looking at each other or chasing and being chased. That is wrong direction. It is often called *crossing the axis.* Lars von Trier is right in that modern director often gets away with crossing the axis. Discussing this is like diving into a pit of quicksand, but what von Trier was mostly talking about was in a dialogue scene shooting on either side of actors and then cutting these shots together without regard to screen direction and letting the audience do the mental work of determining if the actors were still facing each other, or if the audience was seeing things from the other side. Again, von Trier is right in that modern audiences are rarely circumscribed by screen direction as a rule that must be obeyed.

With old school proper screen direction, however, I have a very effective and useful tool that can be used to instinctively and reflexively pull audience members into a scene or movie. My attitude is why not use every tool at your command? Life is rough enough. Moviemaking is hard enough. Why make the paying audience do extra work? Why not make it easier for them to enter and stay in the movie's world?

Sometimes, director purposefully violate screen direction to purposefully disorient the audience. There is a shot in *Night of the Living Dead* during the first zombie attack in the cemetery where the zombie looks at the movie's female lead in the wrong screen direction at a key point in that scene. I had long wondered whether George Romero did that on purpose or if he accidentally crossed the axis. On the DVD commentary Romero, in a rare stroke of complete honesty not rare for him but for directors in general, admitted that at that point in his career, his first movie, he didn't know about proper screen direction. A director can do all kind of things with the movie frame. He or she can pan and reveal and change a shot, and have a shot evolve. He or she can shoot a shot miles away from the rest of a scene and if the background is right, he or she can make that shot look like it was part of the scene. The director can have an actor walk out of a house in L.A. left to right, exit frame right, and walk into frame in front of the Great Wall of China and it can work. When John Malcovich as F.W. Murnau said, "If it's not in the frame it doesn't exist!" he was not just playing a great director, *he was talking like a real director who truly understood the art of movies on a very basic and fundamental level!* A line like that reveals someone who knows that the director is the "god" of a movie's world and the frame is a window into that world.

CHAPTER FOURTEEN:
THINGS THAT ARE NOT TRUE
BUT SOME PEOPLE BELIEVE THAT THEY ARE TRUE

The idea that you can't cut back to the same angle in the continuation of a shot is the most obvious and obnoxious of things that are not true, because it doesn't necessarily look bad to cut back to the same angle. As I mentioned earlier, Alfred Hitchcock repeatedly used that in many of his great films, as did David Lynch, Sam Raimi, and others. There is not a shortage of people out there, however, that will tell you with complete false certainty (though they believe it) that you can't cut back to the same angle, or that doing so looks bad. I would have absolutely no quarrel with these people if they simply said that they did not like the look or style of cutting back to the same shot. They are totally entitled to express their personal opinions or personal tastes, if they will simply label their statements as personal opinion and/or taste, and not try to pass opinions off as absolute aesthetic or metaphysical truisms that apply to all filmmaking.

Here's another example of things that some people dearly believe are true that are not. When I was directing a TV show, the production company making the TV series that included my show had a script supervisor that believed a close-up could only be cut to another close-up, not a medium shot or a wider shot. She also believed that a medium shot could only be intercut with a medium shot. Anyone who has studied movies knows that this script supervisor's pronouncement was totally false, as can be demonstrated to be false by simply studying many successful movies. The "cinematic geniuses" in control of this production company probably had never studied a single movie, and they treated the script sup's absurd ideas like they were God's words written on stone. They "slaved" the director's coverage to this script sup's false commandments. If I shot a close-up on one character in a scene I had to shoot close-ups on all characters in that scene. If I shot a medium shot of one character in a scene I had to shoot medium shots on all those in the scene. If I violated the stupid assumptions and the demands of the script sup, she'd scream to the producer that I was being unprofessional and that what I was shooting would not cut. The producer didn't know the nuts and bolts of how movies are actually made or put together. At that time I'd probably cut a dozen professional movies and the script sup had probably never touched a splicing block or editing machine, or even a piece of film, but she "knew" what would cut and I didn't!

Idiots often get power and idiots often follow other idiots. Telling someone who can't make personal judgments that something won't cut is like telling them that a house has termites or mold. It's scary. When she yelled, "Won't cut!" I was ordered to align my coverage with this script sup's insanity and false ideas. Eventually, I was mercifully fired (probably with a good deal of help from the script sup) and I left that outpost of cinematic Siberia and flew home. The first thing I did at home was watch some movies on TV, starting with *Rocky* and *Gone with the Wind*. Each of these very successful movies had many sequences that blatantly violated the script sup's mighty edicts, yet the cinematic illiterates in Tele-Siberia were so intimidated by the false pronouncements I was overruled. How this script sup got her false ideas, I don't know. She might have gotten them from a book, a professor, an editor, or generated them herself. In any event, she projected them with such certainty and an "everybody who's a pro knows this" attitude that she totally intimidated the producer.

There are many other easily provable falsities that are sincerely believed and passed around with great certainty, usually passed around by people who don't have the level of professionalism and experience to know. So how do you separate what is true from what is false? The only way I've found to separate truth from falsity is in two steps:

One – Study in great depth and quantity movies and drama that have been successful and compare what's asserted to be true to what you see on the screen, or read on the page in the case of plays.

Two – Look at very unsuccessful movies and scripts and compare what's wrong with them and what doesn't work in them with what's right and what works in successful movies.

Do not accept anything as true simply because some authority, book (including this one), teacher, professor, writer, director, producer or other authority say it's true. *Make successful movies the ultimate judge, not some authority.* Many people will ask what comprises a successful movie, and I have a definition for that. It is not a movie that I personally like, but something that I believe has four parts:

One – A successful movie is one that has made a lot of money in relation to its cost. Such a movie is financially successful no matter how much anyone hates or disparages it.

Two – A successful movie can be a movie that receives strong critical acclaim, particularly Oscar nominations or other major acclaim, and propels its director, producer, writer, actors and others' careers forward, making it easier for them to make movies. It doesn't matter who hates the movie if it is critically successful.

Three – A successful movie is one that becomes a classic and continues to draw viewers and make money in significant numbers long after it was made and released, no matter how it was received when originally released.

Four – Low budget movies that breakout financially or critically and launch their maker's careers are successful movies.

Movies that qualify in two or more of these categories are by my criteria very successful movies, whether they are liked or not by you, me, or anyone else. Some examples are *Titanic, Forrest Gump, American Graffiti, Clerks, E.T., Schindler's List*, and many old movies like *Shane*. I'll provide more examples in the directing course later in this book. A serious study of successful and very successful movies is your best protection as an aspiring or actual director or screenwriter against false assumptions. While writing this book and another one, I reflected back on the careers and successes and failures of various associates of mine and others I'd come in contact with who wanted to be directors or screenwriters and those that actually became directors and screenwriters. I came to the conclusion that talent, desire, the ability and willingness to work very hard are not always the only determinative factors in success or failure. I've watched people who have achieved a lot of success in other fields (and even in the movie business) fail utterly when trying to become movie director . These people were not stupid. In some cases, I think they had some talent. They had tremendous desire and worked very hard. In every case, they also had *false basic assumptions* and were to some important degree or in some important way out of touch with reality.

When I look at people who succeeded in directing and in screenwriting, I see people with talent, sharp intelligence, and find they are very willing and able to work hard. In every case, however, I realized that the people who succeeded had an *absence of false basic assumptions and they were also all in effective touch with reality.*

When I used the term "false basic assumption" I do not mean something with which I personally disagree or think is wrong or false personally. I use the term to apply to something very basic, very important, easily observable (with serious study and repeated observation) that is dramatically out of sync with and opposed by a large body of successful and very successful movies, and contrary to how these movies were written and made. Again, when I use the term, I'm not talking about something superficial or trivial, and it is *not* based on my personal opinion, tastes, or my favorite movies.

I believe that people that respect authority or are hypnotized by authority or controlled by it, are more susceptible to inhaling ideas that are false but come from an authority that they respect or that impresses them. They do not test the ideas that contradict the realities contained in successful movies, because the bad ideas came from some "authority." The authority figures that usually propagate such false ideas, like the aforementioned script supervisor, build intellectual insulation around their ideas and the bad information takes root in the core of people's minds, thus becoming false basic assumptions.

There is a great line in the superb Western *Red Sun* – "Men need ideas to live by." Some of the ideas that some people live by and try to use when trying to direct movies or write scripts are quite at odds with what usually causes success and false destructive ideas are usually difficult to dislodge and very destructive. If a person does not know something, and knows that they don't know that thing, then it's pretty straightforward for them to study and learn it. On the other hand, if they *think they know* what needs to be known about something and what they "know" is actually false, then it is usually very hard for them to arrive at a workable truth. Even if people in this situation have enough intelligence to normally learn, they usually cannot learn to do what will cause success over a false basic assumption. These people are virtually impossible to teach to do things correctly as long as they hold on dearly to the false information in their mind.

Often, people with false basic assumptions have a know-it-all attitude and can be very arrogant. To me, it seems that their gullibility and vulnerability and willingness to blindly accept authoritative "data" without checking things against reality has a bad downside in that they have an expectation that anything they think is right is inviolable and that if something fails it is someone else's fault. And thus, with false information in place, they keep marching down the path to failure and blaming others. Something that human beings do not easily want to do and will do almost anything to avoid is to examine where they might be wrong. To that end, I do not want or expect anyone to accept anything in this or any other book, or anything told to them about filmmaking without first checking it against successful movies, and when they start making them, against their own moviemaking experience. Don't be afraid to look; false basic assumptions about making movies is a sure ticket to moviemaker hell.

Let's take another more in-depth look at the idea of cutting back to the same camera angle or the continuation of the same shot. Earlier, when talking about montage, I pointed out how Hitchcock would often cut back to the same angle in a one, two, three sequence by (a) showing a character looking at something, (b) showing what the character is looking at, and (c) showing the character's reaction to what they've seen. Personally, I'm not in favor of cutting back to the same angle or against cutting back to the same angle. For me, it's up to the director's own personally taste or style whether to cut back to the same angle or not. Some successful directors like Kubrick avoid it and only use that technique sparingly. Orson Welles avoid it almost completely. I use it sometimes, but only when I think it works well.

Here I will argue that. Cutting back to the same angle is a good thing, just to kick sand in the faces of the bozos that say it's bad and should not be done. No director in the history of movies can legitimately claim to be more successfully in touch with the mass audience that Hitchcock. He may actually be at the very top of directors most in touch with the mass moviegoing audience. I think Hitchcock's use of the same angle technique is so that the average viewer does not have to refocus. The view is already adjusted to that angle and the size of the image of the actor's face, when the camera comes back to the actor the eyes of the viewer are automatically drawn to the character's reaction and the movie's story is not interrupted. Hitchcock believed in doing the work for the audience so that they could easily and effortlessly be drawn into the movie's world and story and (in Hitchcock's case) emotionally involving game. He worked hard to make things easy for the paying customer. He did not set his coverage to please film students or film professionals who were making notes on camera techniques. Hitchcock wanted his movies to be as effortlessly entertaining as possible for the movie audience, and he succeeded enormously, with many of his movies being on the American Film Institute's list of One Hundred Best Movies.

Successful movies are the ultimate judge and arbiter of what's good and what's not, what works and what doesn't, what you should do and not do, *not what anyone says!* Become an expert on successful movies that you admire, particularly those that are very successful in the genre in which you are working or hope to work, and become a skeptic about all authoritative pronouncements that don't match the reality of successful movies. Probably the most disrespectful action against established authority in the history of the human race, and one of the most successful, was the American Revolution, which defied "the divine right of kings" conventional wisdom at the time, which held that the king was God's representative on Earth and had maximum authority over everyone in the kingdom. Thomas Jefferson and his friends saluted that idea with one raised finger when they signed the Declaration of Independence.

Conventional wisdom and authority of virtually any age has been and will be proven wrong by the advance of time and knowledge. What is proven right over and over is what works and succeeds. Learn from observing what succeeds, and forget what any authority says unless it *proves true, by working!*

CHAPTER FIFTEEN:
AUDIENCE AND VIEWER REALITY AND DESIRES TO SEE
AND THE DIRECTOR'S NEED TO BE AWARE OF SAME
WHILE PULLING THE AUDIENCE
INTO THE WORLD OF THE MOVIE

It is very important for a movie director to be in touch with the reality of the paying audience or a significant segment of same and to be very aware of genre-specific viewing desires of that paying audience or audience segment and to not be stuck in or blinded by the director's own opinions, tastes, and prejudices and make a movie only for the director's desires. This is easier said than done, but it is vital that it be done if a director is to have a successful career.

CHAPTER SIXTEEN:
ALWAYS READ THE SCRIPT BEFORE YOU SHOOT THE SCENE

I emphasize to directors and writers that when they are writing a shooting script that they should put everything, every good idea, into it and they should not assume that they will remember those good ideas on the set in the chaos of the making the movie. Write those ideas! It is hard enough to come up with them, and it's a shame when they don't make it into the movie because they were not written down in the shooting script, or the director did not read the shooting script before shooting the scene.

One director that I constantly advised to read the script constantly told me, "I don't have to read it; I wrote it." Later, he confessed to me that he'd forgotten to put into the movie some things that were in the script that he dearly loved. He said that when he did read the script on the set, it often seemed like a script written by someone else. The motion and commotion and rapid-fire questions and decisions and time pressure and stress of making the movie dimmed his memory of his own script. Instead, he had to focus his attention on the immediate realities of the production. That's why it is vital to always read the script just before you shoot the scene.

There's a funny story about John Ford *not* reading the script before he shot a scene. This was in the 1920s during silent movies. Ford arrived on set in the morning, a bit hung over, and asked the A.D., "What's this scene about?" The A.D. said, "That guy over there kisses this girl over there."

So Ford calls "Action!" and the actor kisses the actress with a little peck on the cheek. Ford says, "Cut! You call that a kiss? Bend her back and really kiss her like you really mean it!" Ford calls for another take and the actor very aggressively followed the director's instruction. Ford calls "Cut" and is pretty proud of his direction until he showed up at the rushes, and much to his intense embarrassment found out that the actor doing the kissing was in the movie's story the father of the girl he was kissing. He was supposed to be consoling her over the death of his wife, the girl's mother. Ford said later that after that regrettable incident he always read the script before shooting a scene!

PART TWO

BACKGROUND AND BRIEF HISTORY
OF INDEPENDENT LOW BUDGET MOVIES

CHAPTER SEVENTEEN:
A BRIEF SUMMARY OF SOME OF THE HIGHLIGHTS OF
THE HISTORY OF INDEPENDENT MOVIES
AND AN ANALYSIS OF THE
CURRENT INDIE MOVIEMAKING SCENE
AND ITS FUTURE

The first movie that I'll single out as a highlight in the history of independent movies is a Spanish art movie written and directed by Luis Bunuel in collaboration with legendary 20th century artist Salvador Dali. It was 18 minutes long, shot in black and white in 1929. This surrealist cinematic masterpiece, *Un chien andalou* (An Andalusian Dog), is required viewing in most film school movie history courses. The movie begins with Bunuel sharpening a straight razor. He moves toward a young woman and brings the razor toward her eye. Cut to the razor blade cutting a grape, but it looks like it is cutting the young woman's eye. As the entire audience flinches, a parade of surrealist images follow. *Un chien andalou* is a very important movie because it is the first one made by Luis Bunuel, one of the most important independent writer-directors of the 20th century. It is also a pure attempt to make a movie that is solely a work of art "for art's sake."

In 1917, D.W. Griffith set out to make a movie that he hoped would end World War I and bring about a raised awareness in the human race of the real brotherhood of all men and women and drive home the futility of war and other forms of inhumanity. The movie's title was *Intolerance: Love's Struggle Through The Ages* and cost an estimated $386,000, which was an astonishing budget for a movie at the time. Griffith spent his considerable personal fortune making the movie, and that is one reason I consider it an independent movie, despite its huge cost and astonishing spectacle. To give you some idea of how enormous the sets were, the Babylon Court, featuring mammoth pillars topped by marble elephants, in the massive courtyard of the "Hollywood Highland Center" adjacent to the Kodak Theater in Hollywood (the place where the Academy Awards take place today), was designed as a homage to the Babylon set in *Intolerance*. Nevertheless, I consider *Intolerance* an independent movie because of the intense spirit of independence in the film. And it is the unique, personal, and independent vision of one man, D.W. Griffith. *Intolerance* is an epic and episodic movie, composed of several stories that include the life and betrayal of Jesus, the betrayal and destruction of ancient Babylon, a religious massacre in France, and a 1917 story of a young woman who is persecuted in the name of righteousness (only it's self-righteousness). These stories are intercut, and each story is tinted with different coloration to make it easy for the audience to follow each story, despite the intercutting. Steven Soderbergh used this same technique of different coloration for different storylines in his film *Traffic*, reminiscent of the idea "Everything old is new again."

The unifying image that binds these various stories of different types of intolerance together is the hand of a woman rocking a cradle and that woman protecting the baby in that cradle, who symbolizes the future. Griffith told his fellow filmmakers, "The people of the world will see the movies that you make here, and they will understand them." He very idealistically saw movies as a new universal language that would cut across cultures, various spoken languages, and bring about wide understanding among peoples and make war obsolete. Accordingly, *Intolerance* ends with a mass "realization" and a rise of human awareness on a battlefield and an end of warfare as well as the end of World War I. Griffith was a great artist in addition to his idealism. Orson Welles said, based largely on his enormous admiration and respect for the film, that Griffith was one of the greatest men who ever lived.

Intolerance is not just one of the greatest movies ever made, it is one of the most intellectually, visually, and physically ambitious independent movies ever, and is acknowledged as the best silent film of all-time. As I mentioned earlier, around 1900 in the very early days of moviemaking some companies held patents on movie cameras and felt that all other moviemakers (all independents at the time) were violating their patents by merely using a movie camera to make movies. Accordingly, these companies sent gunslingers out to literally shoot and destroy the cameras of the independents. In the early days of film most movies were "one-reelers" only ten minutes long. Very many of these movies were made by independents who simply went out with a hand-cranked camera, shot a movie from a scenario (in the beginning of movies, a list of scene ideas) or script they wrote, or even made up on the spot, developed the film in a tub (with no "work print"), and cut the negative with no editing machine, just a splicer (and later a handheld magnifying glass to "cut in hand"). They would then ship the cut negative to the distributor, who would strike prints and ship them to 5¢ movie parlors known as nickelodeons, and to movie theaters. As today, the distributor would send part of any profits to the indie moviemakers, who would make more movies.

The movie business grew rapidly. Filmmakers coalesced into movie studios, which produced an even steadier flow of movies into theaters, set up their own distribution, and began building their own movie theaters. The 1920s to the early 1950s was the golden age of the studios, which owned chains of theaters and produced huge numbers of very popular movies, which were the center of popular culture. Even during these times, however, independent movie production persisted, usually in the form of small independent studios like Monogram, with some independent producers who worked with many studios. There was even a "poverty row" of independent producers in Los Angeles that ran south from Sunset Boulevard near Gower. Many of these indie movies were horror movies, Westerns, or crime dramas.

In the 1950s, "drive-in" movies became very popular. Many movies shown in drive-in theaters were major studio films, in wider release after first opening in more prestigious indoor venues. Many of the drive-in movies, though, were indie low budget movies like the kind very accurately depicted in the film *Ed Wood*, also comically and nostalgically referenced in the ultra-cult classic mini-masterpiece *Hollywood Blvd.* One king of these drive-in movies was Roger Corman. He wrote a book, *I Made A Hundred Movies And Never Lost A Dime*. Corman has at least one thing in common with Jean Luc Godard. They both made some very bad movies, and some very good movies. If you only see one or a few of their very bad movies, you can easily feel the sentiment "Why the hell does anyone think this guy was a good director?" Corman began his career in the 1950s as a producer of "ultra creepo" drive-in indie movies like *Attack of the Crab Monsters*. He became a director of "el cheapo" drive-in indie Westerns, monster, and horror movies. One of them was about Viking women battling a sea serpent, complete with all the Freudian implications. He made them quickly, too. The DVD box on *Little Shop of Horrors* which Corman directed and produced in 1960 says that it was shot in two days, but as I've said before, I think this comic masterpiece cult classic that became a Broadway hit onstage was shot over a full weekend, starting on Friday. It's Corman's best movie and not just because of his inspired and totally appropriate off-the-wall direction. It's a great little movie largely because of Charles B. Griffith's absolutely superb absurdist black comedy screenplay masterpiece.

Some of Corman's best movies, the ones on which his strong reputation largely rests, are his Edgar Allen Poe films made between 1960 and 1964, in widescreen color and on comparatively luxurious shooting schedules of around 15 days. These movies include *Fall of the House of Usher, The Pit and the Pendulum, The Premature Burial, The Tomb of Ligea*, and *The Masque of Red Death*. Stephen King has credited Roger Corman's horror movies as a major early influence on his development as a master of horror. Corman probably had the sharpest eye for young undiscovered talent of anyone in the history of Hollywood. Huge numbers of major movie stars, actors, writers, directors, cinematographers, and others in the movie business got their start or advanced their careers working for or with Roger Corman. Here's a partial list: *Jack Nicholson* was in many Corman movies including an unforgettable "over the top" comic cameo in *Little Shop of Horrors*. *Vincent Price, Peter Lorre*, and *Boris Karloff* all had second careers working for Corman. *Peter Fonda* and *Dennis Hopper* are Corman alumni, as is *Robert DeNiro*. *Jim Cameron, Martin Scorcese, Joe Dante, Monte Hellman, Francis Ford Coppola, Peter Bogdonavitch*, and *Ron Howard* all trace their directing roots to working with Corman. *The Masque of Red Death* was photographed by *Nicholas Roeg*, who went onto become a director. *The Tomb of Ligea* was written by Robert Towne, the Oscar-winning screenwriter of *Chinatown* and many other fine films. *Richard Matheson*, who wrote Steven Spielberg's TV movie *Duel* and the book *I Am Legend* (that has been filmed several times) wrote *The Pit and the Pendulum* for Corman.

In some ways, Roger Corman's inventive, imaginative, audience pleasing and satisfying vibrant, vivid, unashamed "B" movies formed a minor league in Hollywood where major talent got started and developed their craft. The major reason Corman could brag that his movies never lost a dime is not as some would say, that they didn't cost a dime to make, but that Corman had an exact fix on what slots for movies were open distribution-wise and waiting to be filled, starting at first with drive-ins. He also knew exactly what it would take to fill those slots to the waiting audience's satisfaction. His movie often had a monster, or some Wild West shoot 'em up action, a sci-fi or horror theme, or a story about something crazy like buxom Viking women. Corman knew how much each of these open slots would pay at a minimum and he made his movies for less than what he was basically sure they would earn.

There were many independent filmmakers who made these indie drive-in movies in the 1950s and 1960s. Many of these movies were Westerns, sci-fi, or horror (like atomic mutated insects). Corman stands tallest of all these filmmakers, and Ed Wood's *Plan 9 From Outer Space* stands lowest in that fraternity of film. In the 1950s, Stanley Kubrick got a camera and went out and made a movie. That was unusual then, and considered by some to be a revolution. Even more influential was the French "New Wave" movement that gave indie moviemaking more stature, backbone, and audience octane, but before that, other foreign films began showing up in "art house" movie theaters in major cities, usually near college campuses. Ingmar Bergman's masterful Swedish art movies pioneered the audience in America for art movies in the late 1950s and early 1960s, as did movies from Luis Bunuel and Federico Fellini (his *La Dolce Vita* stands out). All these movies were unapologetic about being works of art and making serious statements about life and the human condition, and often about sex and sensuality. Many of them came straight out of a long elite European artistic tradition. They were much more sophisticated and frank and adult and "meaningful" than American movies of that time and set the stage for the French New Wave.

The most intense and important example of an independent moviemaker and successful revolutionary filmmaking from that movement is the making of Jean Luc Godard's first movie, *Breathless*. Godard was a movie critic for a French movie magazine and a college dropout. He and fellow movie critic Francois Truffaut wrote continuously about what was good in movies and what the disliked in film. Both of them also had minor league criminal pasts. Godard stole the petty cash of the magazine where they worked and based on a treatment written by Truffaut they went out and shot part of a movie until they ran out of cash. Godard was the director and Truffaut was his assistant. When they ran out of money, Godard confronted the owners of the magazine and told them that they had two choices: (a) turn him in to the police for theft and lose the money they "invested" in his film, or (b) raise more money to finish the movie, and possibly get their money back and even make a profit. He emphasized that they could just go on endlessly talking about revolutionizing the cinema, or they could take action to back up the words they put in print.

Well, they raised the money to finish *Breathless* and it turned out to be one of the most revolutionary and influential movie ever made. It was a major hit and launched the French New Wave. It's easy to see the influence of that movie in films like *Bonnie and Clyde*, *Traffic*, *Dancer in the Dark*, *Boogie Nights*, *The Wrestler*, and innumerable music videos and TV shows. When *Breathless* first opened in Paris, the lines of people waiting to see it stretched for blocks. The movie had a metaphorical finger on the pulse of an *alienated* movie going public fed up with the French government's two useless colonial wars, one in Indochina (Vietnam), the other in Algeria, involving lots of torture by the French military, and other hypocrisies of the dominant social order.

Truffaut and Godard had written a movie about a very alienated, anti-authority, petty thief, and they had financed the movie with their own chicanery. Their protagonist was obsessed with an American woman played by Jean Seberg, and Godard and Truffaut were obsessed by American movies about American gangsters. Godard dedicated *Breathless* to Monogram Pictures, a "poverty row" type indie studio that shot many of its pictures on tiny budgets in real locations, just like Godard had shot *Breathless*. Godard made several other excellent movies like *Vivir Se Vie (My Life To Live)*, *Alphaville* (one of the most prophetic film ever made, the "godfather" thematically of *Blade Runner*), and one of the most intelligent sci-fi films ever made, *Contempt* starring Brigitte Bardot. Unfortunately, Godard not only made great movies, he also made some conspicuously not so great movies. The huge financial and critical success of *Breathless*, and its blatant and highly successful disrespect for conventional filmmaking grammar caused a cinematic earthquake in the French movie industry, and later in all the movie industries of the world including Hollywood.

Truffaut soon got a chance to direct a film, and his first two were the best he'd ever made. *The Four Hundred Blows* and *Jules and Jim* are masterpieces that helped move the French New Wave into the center of the world of cinema. Other former movie critics like Claude Chabrol, Erk Rohmer, and Louis Malle were soon also making outrageously intelligent and superlatively excellent movies and the French New Wave began repeatedly breaking across the shores of the Atlantic in American art house theaters near colleges and otherwise. These movies had a huge effect on the Baby Boom generation movie directors who later revolutionized Hollywood. In the late 1960s, each new Godard film was a major cultural event for just about everyone at UCLA's film school.

It is almost true to say that virtually all modern independent movies are descended from the French New Wave. Much of what Godard, Truffaut, and others of the French New Wave introduced and put forward was in brash defiance of the stodgy filmmaking and screenwriting and directing conventions of that time (1950s and 1960s). Much of what was so original and so defiant then has been inhaled and digested and has become a part of mainstream modern TV shows and movies. It's now easy not to know and credit these bold cinematic revolutionaries for the huge amount of liberation that they delivered to the art form of cinema or movies, and which modern directors now routinely enjoy. The French New Wave rescued the art form of movies from an ossifying stodgy decline that was the last gasp of the feudal studio system and studio system movies that had a sound-based, word-based vice grip on the neck of an art form that began as an image-based art in the era of silent movies.

If you watch current TV shows or movies you are likely to be seeing a lot of filmic freedom and liberation that is now common but was far outside the mainstream when Godard, Truffaut, and others ignored and defied convention, and instead looked deep into the nature of the actual essence of the art form of movies, delving into their methods of telling stories on a movie screen. There is a very direct connection between silent movies and the French New Wave, especially between *Jules and Jim* and D.W. Griffith.

The French New Wave invigorated the art form of movies and it leapfrogged a lot of very accepted, very professional bullshit. They liberated the process of making a movie from the feudal studio system and they *correctly* put the director, not the studio or producer, right at the core of that process. They moved the screenwriter's function from working for the studio or producer to *correctly* being the director or to working for or with the director. They recognized that the true axis of creativity in moviemaking is between the director and writer, who are sometimes the same person, not between the producer or studio and the writer. Godard's best movies, *Alphaville*, *Contempt*, and *Breathless* are great works of cinematic art, and he is one of the 20th century's most original artists and movie directors.

Studio movies are made by studios. The movies I like best have been made by directors. All modern directors owe the French New Wave a great debt.

In 1968, Pittsburgh-based TV commercial director George Romero formed an alliance with other local filmmakers and recruited some professional actors and local "film people" and friends to make "a horror movie with a bit more" for $114,000 on a 28-day shooting schedule. This black and white 35mm film shot in areas around Pittsburgh, *Night of the Living Dead*, was truly indie. Romero operated the camera himself, and not coincidentally the movie has the best framing and composition of any of his movies. He also lit and edited the movie, and did both beautifully, although he used very primitive editing equipment. I have edited two feature length movies and a short student film on that equipment, a Moviescope, and will say that it is a "caveman" piece of equipment, barely better than "cutting in hand" as the silent movies used. *Night of the Living Dead* has some of the best, most precise and highly skilled editing you can find in any movie. Romero is a great editor as well as a great director and cinematographer. To achieve the superb editing that Romero accomplished with a Moviescope and rewinds is amazing filmmaking. *Night of the Living Dead* is not just a very scary horror movie, it is a major work of art, a masterpiece that captures the "things gone wrong" reality of the 1960s in a metaphorical way better than any other movie of that era, with the possible exception of Godard's *Weekend*. Wes Craven, famous for directing horror classics like *Nightmare on Elm Street* and *Scream*, said *Night of the Living Dead* made "a real political statement" and showed that "a horror movie could go as high as you could take it, and as deep as you can take it." Romero has said that all his zombie movies are "people movies" really about revolution and social conflicts. *Night of the Living Dead* is about old ideas rising up to kill the living. The movie has something that most indie movies lack, and the ones that succeed and breakout have – an excellent script. The film was written by Romero and John Russo, and to this day remains Romero's best movie. The music came from a canned music library, but was so effective because of the way Romero edited it, that it sounds like a completely original score. *Night of the Living Dead* has a continuing ability to attract viewers and still sells well on DVD. It is a landmark indie movie because it was made outside Hollywood completely with local people before and behind the camera. In 1968, that was a very rare occurrence.

The film was originally distributed on the "B" movie circuit as just another horror movie. After its initial release, it began to build an audience by word of mouth an midnight screenings in the major cities of the world. It was an effective balance of French "cinema verite" (movie truth) and classic black and white Universal Studios style horror. When the video store boom hit in the 1980s, virtually every video store that had any kind of horror section had at least one copy of *Night of the Living Dead* and its status as a horror classic was solidified. I first saw the movie at the World Theater on Hollywood Boulevard at 2:00 in the morning on a weekend in 1968. That theater was open almost 24 hours a day and always showed three to four big hits a day, with two or three of them usually being indie movies. I had been editing or cutting sound FX all day and late into the night, and I decided to catch a movie at the World on my way home. When I walked into the packed auditorium, hot dog and popcorn in hand, an ethnic group that commonly shouts instructions and commands to characters in a horror movie was "overly represented" in this audience. People were shouting things at the screen like, "There's a zombie in the closet, man!" They wouldn't stop with the warnings. A guy behind me said to his friend, "Heavy movie!"

Earlier in this book I defined the job description of an "author of the movie" style director as someone who creates a world on the movie screen that makes that world so interesting and compelling that the audience becomes more interested in the world on the screen than the actual circumstances of their own life and their immediate surrounding. George Romero in his first and best movie certainly accomplished that to a very high degree – that audience at the World was scared to death!

Hitchcock said that some directors direct the camera, and some direct the actors, but really good directors direct the audience's attention. Romero's direction was a supreme example of what Hitchcock considered the very best directing. *Night of the Living Dead* is an intense and stellar example of what a talented and prepared director operating with limited resources but with an excellent concept, story, script, and clear vision, along with the knowledge of how to use a camera and montage and a soundtrack can accomplish despite limited resources and actual limitations.

In the mid-1960s, John Cassevetes made a startlingly realistic looking and excellent indie movie, *Faces*. I don't have definite proof but from what I've been told, that was a "no budget" movie. Cassavetes apparently went out with a 16mm camera and some black and white film and began shooting scenes with his very talented friends who were under-employed or unemployed actors, in much the way that Michael Moore began filming *Roger and Me*, his breakthrough documentary. *Faces* features shockingly realistic and powerful improvisational acting. It deals with emotionally powerful things under the surface of people's lives that they usually don't talk about. It was sort of like a European cinema verite movie, only it was also very American. When the film was nominated for a Best Screenplay Oscar, it shook up Hollywood and people's standards as to what they considered to be excellent acting. Judd Apatow commented on a DVD commentary that Cassavetes had heavily influenced his way of making movies.

During this time period, Peter Bogdonavitch directed his first movie. Roger Corman produced it on a $150,000 budget. It starred Boris Karloff in a cameo role, a modern horror movie about a random crazy killer. *Targets* was a mixture of intellect and intelligence and social awareness and exploitation movie basics, and commercial content and suspense. Paramount Studios bought it for much more than it cost.

Another far more influential and successful movie of this time period was a very high octane mixture of an exploitation movie façade with deep social insight and the French New Wave mandate to make movies that addressed the actual human condition of the audience. That movie was *Easy Rider*. It starred Jack Nicholson, Peter Fonda, and Dennis Hopper, who also directed the movie. All three were veterans of Roger Corman's low budget movies, with Nicholson having made many movies with Corman. *Easy Rider* flipped the violent motorcycle genre on its head. Its motorcycle riding protagonists were basically drug transporters who fancied themselves "men of peace" as they crossed America on bikes. It was a very introspective movie filled with the kind of self-criticism common to European art movies, yet it became a very successful mainstream American hit. In the late 1960s the mood of younger Baby Boomers was alienation and disillusionment, mostly due to the war in Vietnam, which was increasingly becoming very unpopular. The 1960s was also the decade of political assassinations, with John and Robert Kennedy, Martin Luther King, and Malcom X murdered within years of each other. For very many young people, this social environment seemed sick and absurd, a screwed-up reality. The idea of "flipping the bird" to authority and riding across the country, using a drug deal to gain freedom and autonomy, seemed thrilling. When the anti-heroes of *Easy Rider* met their end at the hands of intolerant and violent Southern rednecks that was considered a very real metaphor to many young Americans. The film tapped an emotional nerve of a huge segment of young moviegoers. At a cost of $300,000 it didn't matter than its actors had mostly been in indie movies. The movie had the right ethos and was excellently shot by the now legendary Laslo Kovacs and edited by Donn Cambern, who became one of the most successful editors in Hollywood history. The movie's box office was enormous in comparison to its cost. The film played endlessly, and for about a year in one prestigious theater in Toronto. It became *the* movie that many people in Hollywood wished they'd made. Low budget independent movies were no longer stragglers relegated to drive-in Siberia. They had a spine and a brain and a heart. The ending of *Easy Rider* hit me like a ton of emotional lead. I remember watching the last shot and walking out of the theater as the end credits rolled thinking, "That movie said it. It didn't flinch. It said it." Many people saw *Easy Rider* as simply a drug movie and some tried to copy that aspect in other movies, but those failed. They missed the most important core of what the movie was about and what caused its success. Those who made copies failed to see that *Easy Rider* was unlike any movie that had gone before.

Another very interesting indie movie from this time period is Haskell Wexler's *Medium Cool*. Its title is a play on Marshall McLuhan's statement that TV is a "cool" medium. The multi-Oscar winning cinematographer shot the movie himself, in Chicago at the 1968 Democratic party convention, with a focus on the epic clash between the anti-war protestors and police. Robert Forester is the movie's protagonist, playing a TV camera operator. A major movie studio picked up the film because they wanted to distribute a counter-culture movie. At that time, Paramount was owned by Gulf & Western, a huge oil company. The executives wanted counter-culture, but they didn't want their bosses to think that they'd "gone native" in revolutionary fashion, though, and an early cut of the film had some very brutal and bloody shots of police beatings in Chicago, over-reacting to demonstrators who were simply exercising Constitutional rights. Senator Abraham Ribicoff from the speaker's platform at the convention basically called Chicago Mayor Daley's police "Nazis" to which Daley responded in full view of TV cameras broadcasting the convention across the country that Ribicoff was a "f'ing Jew" who should engage himself sexually. Given that atmosphere, you don't need much imagination to figure out what the Chicago police were doing to protestors when they thought no cameras were rolling. Wexler's cameras captured some of the worst actions of the police and he put those in *Medium Cool*. His shots showed what actually happened, documentary style.

Wexler refused to cut the truth out of his movie, so the executives began negotiating with him to put provocative words and taunts from the demonstrators to justify police brutality. Several telegrams went back and forth during this negotiation that said things like, "I'll trade you three mother f'ers on the soundtrack for the shot of the kid with the bloody face being hit in the head with a policeman's nightstick" and "You can keep the shot of the guy on the ground being kicked by the cop if you put in four 'shitheads' on the soundtrack." *Medium Cool* was an American New Wave movie. It had a very fluid use of camera and editing, and its style aligned with optimum film grammar, not studio-based rules. It demonstrated that the New Wave was rising in America with full force.

During the 1960s, there was a film underground in New York that made experimental films. Andy Warhol made some feature-length movies that were mostly improvised by so called superstar actors with interesting and sometimes bizarre personalities. Two relics that survive from Warhol's filmmaking are his indie versions of *Dracula* and *Frankenstein*, but many of his most interesting movies have disappeared. One highly irreverent, very counter-culture and yet successful black comedy was made for just $40,000. It was directed by Brian DePalma, starred Robert DeNiro, and Harvey Keitel. The title was *Greetings*, the first word in a military draft notice. The movie features one of the blackest comedy scenes ever as the protagonist's mark President John Kennedy's wounds on the body of a nude woman and "proves" that he could not have been shot by a "lone gunman." A lot of the movie is shot in a "one angle, one take" style.

One of the most jarring scenes I've ever seen in a movie is when a real Vietnam war vet, who matter of factly describes how one night in 'Nam when everyone had a few beers, two GIs decided to shoot it out Old West quick draw style to decide which one of them would get to sleep with a nurse. They shot it out, a bullet went through one soldier's neck, and he was paralyzed for the rest of his life.

In 1977, another very successful comic movie with a blackly comic scene about the JFK assassination and the cover-up of the "truth" was released. Its budget was about fifteen times that of *Greetings*. Its poster correctly bragged that it was fresh, frantic, funny, refreshingly rebellious, ribald, lavish, rude, hilarious, zany, and brilliant. The movie was *Kentucky Fried Movie* and it launched the careers of the Zucker brothers and Jim Abrams, who went on to make *Airplane*, *The Naked Gun*, and many other funny and successful movies. It also launched John Landis into making *Animal House* and other comedies.

Another phenomenon of independent moviemaking of the 1970s was "black exploitation" movies. A highly acclaimed African-America still photographer, Gordon Parks, went into Harlem with a movie camera and $70,000 and made a movie about people and a way of life that moviegoers had not really previously seen. The movie was *Superfly* and it was a huge hit. That and other blaxploitation movies like *Sweet Sweetback's Baadasssss Song* launched an avalanche of similar films, many of which were made independently, while some like *Shaft* were made by major studios.

In the late 1970s, John Carpenter made *Halloween* for $300,000. It was a huge hit and spawned many sequels as did *Friday the 13th*, which was also independently produced but distributed by a major studio.

The decade of the 1980s was a time when independently made horror movies flourished. George Romero made a blackly comic yet horrific "thinking person's" vampire movie called *Martin* for about $100,000 that caused reviewer from *Newsweek* magazine to say "Romero has become a dazzling stylist…. His balance of wit and horror is the best." Sam Raimi launched his career with the indie cult classic horror masterpiece *The Evil Dead*. He and college friends went south with a camera and some lights and money, found a farm house, and with a little unaccredited help from H.P. Lovecraft, made a movie that many Raimi fans still consider to be his best.

Wes Craven, a veteran of early low budget indie horror movies like *Last House on the Left* and *The Hills Have Eyes*, made a big splash early in the 1980s with *A Nightmare on Elm Street*, which he wrote and directed, for a small movie distribution company for $1.8 million. Now there are ten "Freddy Krueger" movies, and the small indie distributor, New Line Cinema, became a major studio that produced the *Lord of the Rings* trilogy.

Italian horror cinema director Dario Argento financed George Romero's *Dawn of the Dead*, a zombie sequel to *Night of the Living Dead*. Argento's exceptional and bizarre horror movies include *Suspia*, *Creepers*, *Demons*, and others. Romero teamed with Stephen King to make the highly entertaining *Creepshow* and completed his zombie trilogy with the more intelligent and haunting but less successful *Day of the Dead*.

The Re-Animator based on H.P. Lovercraft's story was a low budget indie movie shot mostly in a small studio. It was a huge hit, and one of the many horror movies the dominated most indie movie production in the 1980s.

Toward the end of the decade, an associate of mine who was a screenwriter told me that he'd seen this great movie, and the guy who made it was like a "black Woody Allen." The movie was *She's Gotta Have It*, written and directed by Spike Lee. It was made in 16mm for $100,000 independently. The film was new, different, and original as well as being very funny and insightful. It became a huge hit and launched Lee's career.

Stephen Soderbergh's *Sex, Lies, and Videotape*, also independently made, won a major award at the Cannes Film Festival before becoming a huge hit that launched Soderbergh's career.

During this same time period, Jim Jarmusch emerged as an important moviemaker with movies like *Night on Earth*. In the early 21st century, he made one of my all-time favorite indie movies, which in one 15-minute sequence sums up the entirety of one major aspect of the movie business. That movie is the very original and unique *Coffee and Cigarettes*.

In the early 1990s, with the making of *Reservoir Dogs* on a short shooting schedule and very limited budget in stringent circumstances, Quentin Tarantino emerged as a very important and fiercely independent writer-director, and he embellished and advanced that stature with *Pulp Fiction*, a maxi-successful movie smash.

After film school, Robert Rodriguez correctly calculated that if he'd made a student film that was about ten minutes long for less than $1,000 he could make a feature suitable for the Spanish language video market in the USA and foreign for about $8,000. So Rodriguez checked into a drug company facility where new drugs are tested on paid subjects. While Rodriguez was being paid for allowing the drug company to use his body as a test site, he wrote the script for *El Mariachi*, and with the $8,000 he was paid, he went out with a group of friends and associates and made a feature length movie in 16mm. *El Mariachi* won a major award at the Sundance Film Festival and it became obvious that it deserved and could get wider distribution than just the Spanish language video market. One point, however, needs to be made clear. While Rodriguez made the movie for $8,000 and could have delivered a finished movie to its intended market for that price, there was around $40,000 in extra post-production costs to blow up the film to 35mm and improve the sound for theatrical release in Spanish language theaters. I first saw the movie in Santa Fe Springs, California with a largely Spanish-speaking audience. They really loved it and got it in depth. Later, *El Mariachi* was distributed widely in English in video and DVD and its two sequels, *Desperado* and *Once Upon A Time In Mexico*, propelled Rodriguez's career into indie moviemaking Heaven. He put together his own studio in Texas and began making his movies with full creative control, writing, directing, photographing, and even musically scoring and art directing his films. He began dealing with distributors in the way that moviemakers did in the silent movie era. Rodriguez is so in touch with major segments of the movie audience that all his movies have been profitable. He gained real independent moviemaking power and freedom.

In the published versions of the scripts for his movies *Clerks* and *Chasing Amy*, Kevin Smith thanked Spike lee and Jim Jarmusch for pointing the way. In another book I've referred to *Clerks* as a $35,000 movie made from a million-dollar script. It is one of the very best scripts of the 1990s. It is also a very well-directed and acted indie movie. It is by far Kevin Smith's best movie and the admiration and affection that movie audiences and people in the movie business have for the film propelled Smith's career through seven subsequent movies, none of which are as good as *Clerks*, whose budget was tiny compared to the later films. This proves to me my contention that often the quality of a movie's script is much more important than the size of its budget. Kevin Smith worked at a convenience store depicted in *Clerks* while making the movie and shot the film after hours, until 4:00 a.m. in the morning, after which he would get a couple of hours sleep before reporting for work. He did this for 21 days. He maxed out his credit cards and sold his comic book collection to finance the movie, among other things. After the movie won some important film festival awards, it got excellent and aggressive distribution and enjoyed excellent "word of mouth." Like *El Mariachi*, *Clerks* was a rags to riches story as great as any that exists in indie moviemaking.

During the 1980s and early 1990s there was a video store boom as movie viewers experienced an extraordinary explosion in the level of movie choices and access to huge quantities of movies to view at home any time they wanted to watch them. That boom still exists to some degree with DVDs today and distribution outlets like Netflix. There was a "direct to video movie" boom that paralleled the rise of video stores and many were very profitable. Some were shot in 16mm and transferred directly to video. The video boom cut deeply into the dwindling existence of drive-ins and direct-to-video movies resided in genres that were like the "B" movies popular at drive-ins in days gone by. After the huge success of *Basic Instinct*, for example, there was an avalanche in direct-to-video erotic thrillers.

In 1982, Mark Pirro shot and starred in a satirical horror comedy, *Polish Vampire in Burbank*. He shot it on 8mm film and transferred it to video. The movie cost only $2,500 to make, the lowest budget of any feature I know about that received effective distribution in professional markets. It was also shown on cable TV, and sold a lot of videotapes as well. The movie is reported to have made over $500,000. One very important point worth repeating here is that the major limiting factor on that movie was the quality of its script, which was simply "OK." If it had a better script of the quality of *Clerks*, or even *El Mariachi*, I think it might have been much more of a breakout movie and not just a very successful curiosity.

In the 1990s, the independent divisions of major studios increasingly became major players in the production and distribution of high quality, acclaimed and honored movies. Miramax began as a quality-minded indie distributor and became an indie division of Buena Vista (Disney) while forming its own more obviously commercial and less artistically-oriented division, Dimension. I saw a promo celebrating its 25th anniversary of existence that claimed movies produced and/or distributed by Miramax had received over 200 Academy Award nominations. That's a lot of excellence for an indie producer and distributor. I doubt there is a year in the 1990s or early "aughts" of the 21st century where Miramax did not have some horses running seriously in the Oscar race. Other studio indie divisions like Fox Searchlight, Sony Classics, and Grammery also made and distributed many highly acclaimed movies. Indie in effect became mainstream.

Before his death, the superb actor-director-producer Sydney Pollack said while appearing in a TV forum that the kind of movies that he used to make at major studios were no longer being made at major studios. He claimed that most of the movies up for Oscars that year had at least "one foot in the independent camp." There is a big difference between so-called independent studio movies like *Slumdog Millionaire*, *Juno*, *Sideways*, and *No Country For Old Men* that are made with established movie industry professionals, studio budgets, and truly independent films that are made with the limitations and budgets of films like *Clerks*, *El Mariachi*, *The Blair Witch Project*, and *Paranormal Activities.* Nobody told those filmmakers that they were green lighted by the powers that be. They weren't given a few million to make an "independent" movie in a studio's subdivision, knowing the studio would distribute it. The makers of truly independent movies did not need permission to make their movies. They just found a way to get them made.

Nora Ephron, the screenwriter of *When Harry Met Sally* and writer-director of *Sleepless In Seattle*, said in a TV interview that she had many friends and associates in Hollywood that she talks with regularly, and what the studios are about now is all *money*. That's why fewer studio major movies get nominated for Oscars, and more indies like *Crash* are nominated for and win Oscars.

Large budget movies often are filled with very expensive CGI, with stories that often originated in comic books, old TV series, or even video games. These movies are aimed at the widest possible worldwide market, usually aiming at a youth market. While studios have been cutting back or eliminating their indie divisions, those remaining also have an eye toward the same audiences that the big budget films attract. Usually big studio movies are packaged with stars and a director to go with a script by an A-list screenwriter. Studio movie producers usually have considerable political skills, and the movie has usually wended its way through a considerable "development" process at the studio, some times past executives who are no longer working there by the time the movie is released. Thus major studio films are more product than passionate artistic vision. Still, movies like *Little Miss Sunshine*, *Good Night and Good Luck,* and *Milk* do show the passionate vision of the filmmakers.

This is also true for two of the most dynamic and financially profitable, as well as critically acclaimed and decried indie movies of recent years. Both Mel Gibson's *The Passion of the Christ* and Michael Moore's *Fahrenheit 911*, coming from opposite ends of the political spectrum, appealed to specific movie audiences, and they were both very successful compared to their cost. Both movies were excellently made with a gusto that the success of independent movies usually require. They were films that their viewers *strongly desired to see*, and both delivered content *that was not being delivered by major movie studios*. That is a very strong and common denominator of very many successful indie movies.

When desired content is not being delivered to the movie viewing public by major studios, an indie movie that fills that void can become very successful. When *Crash* won the Oscar for Best Picture, there was a reason. It spoke to things people think but do not talk about until they crash into others and the ideas come spewing out. How many studio movies deal with complex important issues with the kind of insight, intelligence, honesty, and intentionally ambiguous artistic flair like *Crash*? The movie was, no surprise, turned down by everyone as a script, before it was independently financed and made. Some times scripts are turned down by studios because they are not good enough for a studio film, and some times they are turned down because they are too original to be made there. These great original scripts that studios will not touch are what turn into hugely successful breakout indie films. If you set out to make an indie movie with a camera and some friends and not that much more in the way of resources, but you have a truly excellent concept, story, and script, if you have done the proper study and practice how to make a movie and set shots and put them together to make an effective montage and you have a strong and clear *vision* of your movie and know how to put that vision on the screen and soundtrack, then you are not really so alone. You are, among other things, the latest extension of a long tradition of independent filmmakers that extends all the way back to the early silent one-real moviemakers with hand-cranked cameras who had to protect those cameras from real gunslingers. That line of indie filmmakers has current players like the makers of *Once*, a great inide film shot in 17 days in Dublin, Ireland for $100,000, whose theme song won an Academy Award for Best Song in 2007, and the creators of *Paranormal Activity*, a $15,000 indie distributed by Paramount that is still making millions as this book is written.

If you properly prepare and have a good script or story, even a good concept, and you don't let anyone have the power to say "No you can't make a movie" and you go out and make your movie, you are a kindred spirit with film legends like Allen Dwan, D.W. Griffith, Fritz Lang, Orson Welles, Luis Bunuel, Stanley Kubrick, Roger Corman, Jean Luc Godard, John Cassavetes, Francois Truffaut, Roman Polanski, Quentin Tarantino, Spike Lee, Stephen Soderbergh, the Coen brothers, Paul Haggis, and many other very successful indie filmmakers.

On the other hand…

If you don't prepare properly, don't study and practice, don't learn, don't find or create a good story or script, and simply go out and make a movie anyway, unprepared and with no clear vision, without the ability to put a vision onscreen, you are a soul brother to Ed Wood, who is widely considered to be the worst indie moviemaker of all-time.

Everyone with a camera is not always a moviemaker. The current situation facing indie low budget, micro budget and no budget film artists is almost an inversion of the situation that existed in the past. Currently, there are far more people going out with a video camera to make a "movie" than there are people who have taken the time and expended the creative energy necessary to develop a great concept, story, and script that has the potential to appeal to satisfy some significant segment of the movie viewing public. Many of these so-called films that I refer to as "calling card movies" are made by beginners hoping to make a mark at some film festival that matters or get them a job with a production company. I took that route at the beginning of my career, but circumstances are different now.

Filmmaking studies are no longer limited to major film schools on the east and west coasts. Colleges, universities, community colleges, even technical and private schools teach the basics of video and movie production, to anyone who pays the tuition. Legions of corporate and promotional videos are being made, while some areas of the San Fernando Valley in Los Angeles are teeming with people churning out porn movies. Video and lighting equipment is everywhere. It has never been easier to seize the means of production and make a movie. Technically it has gotten much easier, and a lot of people are doing it.

The basic job of the storyteller has *not* gotten any easier than it was during the day of cave paintings, oral storytelling, Greek playwrights, or 19th century novelists. Effective storytellers must still transfix their audience. As such, the greatest challenge facing today's indie moviemaker is to identify some segment of the movie viewing public that he or she can appeal to and to distinguish his or her movie from the sea of so-called movies that may never see any kind of meaningful distribution. While opportunity and potential is exploding for indie moviemakers, imagination still rules the world. If you have it and connect to a sizeable segment of the movie audience with your product, you will rise above the hordes of those who create worthless, non-career advancing so-called movies.

Every time that there has been a major shift in the way that movies are distributed and consumed by the public, that shift widens the choice and ease of the public and the world of opportunities of independent moviemaking expands. Smart indie moviemakers profit from that expansion. The latest "tectonic shift" in how movies are distributed and consumed is the home viewing revolution, which has given viewers incredible choices and control over what movies they see and when they choose to see them. The Internet is verging on being yet another "earthquake" in how movies are distributed and consumed. People post their own short movies on YouTube and have instant worldwide distribution, some times to millions of viewers if that movie "goes viral." People download movies by the hundreds, and not just from YouTube. It's not unusual for a savvy Web user to have dozens of feature-length films (legal or illegal) on their computer, downloaded from all over the world. This situation accelerates the power of "word of mouth" far beyond where any hype generated by studio PR machines can go, and in fact studios now work hard to use this type of marketing for all their movies.

The future is bright and the potential even brighter for indie moviemakers. It all depends on the artist's ability as a storyteller to connect to some significant segment of the movie viewing public. To paraphrase Roger Corman's observation, it all comes down to actors in front of a lens, a director, and a good concept, story, and script. Virtually all the significant breakout indie movies that I've mentioned here that have contributed much to the history of movies, and in many cases to the advancement of movies as an art form, whatever their budget, resources, or lack thereof, have excellent concepts, stories, and scripts. Things haven't changed at their basics. The movie *Paranormal Activity* was reportedly made for $15,000. Picked up and released by Paramount Studios, it grossed $151,000,000 at the box office and a sequel was planned with the director of *Saw VI*. That is a stunning testament to what is possible in the vividly opportunity rich area of micro budget movies, and it is a sharp illustration of the foundational, prime importance of concept, story, and script!

PART THREE

MAKING INDEPENDENT MOVIES
AND
BEING A MOVIE PRODUCER

CHAPTER EIGHTEEN:
THREE COMPETENT AND COMMITTED PEOPLE

It is possible to make an independent movie with only one competent and committed person. I had done it more than once. Unfortunately, it is barely possible, very unpleasant, and on the border of a death-inducing activity to try to make a movie solo, unsupported. I have directed movies where I was also doing the first, or first and second assistant director jobs, and the line producer and production manager jobs as well. That kind of thing is, no joke, *pure hell*. It should be avoided, if at all possible. The quality of the movie definitely suffers when a director is not properly supported by competent, committed people, or at least some people who are competent and committed to some degree.

Sometimes, the only thing worse than making a movie without support is not to make a movie. I've chosen the lesser of two evils, which is to make the movie no matter how much hell I have to go through. If you want to avoid that kind of mental and physical torture, I suggest you get at least two competent, committed people to help, so that you can create a somewhat sane, humane, potentially successful moviemaking environment that is not the cruel and unusual punishment of going alone. These people, as well as the director, should be grounded in the realities of time, and what actually happens on a movie set.

In his great novel *Moby Dick*, Herman Melville has a chapter entitled "Knights and Squires." It is about how those who are on the cutting edge, the point men who are doing the most important task that is the determinative action of the whole enterprise need to spring to that task unhindered by the cares and obstacles of the mundane world. Thus, knights have squires to assist them. Melville establishes that the whaling ship harpooners in *Moby Dick* are similar to knights and are similarly assisted. On a movie set, there are logistics and mundane but important activities, and there is also *artistic creation*. The first assistant director handles the logistics, and the mundane things. *The director handles the artistic creation.* If a director is not properly assisted he or she will be drawn into logistics and the mundane, and this will draw attention and energy away from the artistic creation. Directors, like all humans, have a limited amount of attention and energy. If that creative energy or attention is squandered on logistical or mundane tasks or dispersed by disorganization on set, it often shows negatively on the screen.

Military organizations are the result of thousands of years of trial and error in the crucible of mortal combat. The human body is the result of millions of years of evolution. There is a reason humans have *two* legs to walk and run. One leg supports the body's weight while the other moves forward and then the other leg does the same. A director on a set who is not properly assisted is like a body with only one leg, hopping around exhausted. Typically, people have a dominant hand that takes the lead in doing important tasks, with the other hand offering support. Keep that in mind when trying to make a movie. An infantry squad typically has two fire teams, one that fires in support while the other maneuvers. Similarly, an infantry platoon is commanded by a lieutenant, and is run by a platoon sergeant.

The reason why the human body and military organizations are organized on this bi-operative basis, with one dominant and handling higher functions while the other supports is that they both have spent a lot of time dealing with reality and learning what is effective. This same kind of reality exists on a movie set and in the making of a movie. Thus, you need two competent and committed people to properly run a movie set. What do I mean by "competent"? That is someone who can solve problems that are appropriate for them to solve, who can recognize and pass on and if necessary supervise or assist in the solving of problems that are appropriate for others to solve. My definition of "committed" is someone that sees his or her own personal future well-being or advancement directly connected to the movie's quality and/or success.

The reality of time itself dictates the need for a *third* competent committed person. There is the here and now on the movie set, and there is the future which arrives relentlessly and turns into the here and now every day. A movie production that lacks this third competent committed person usually gets into serious trouble because it lacks someone to "trouble shoot" problems and disasters off the set and to deal with approaching situations that might paralyze the production or disperse the director, crew, and actors. You need this third person to deal with the future and also, off set realities. Typically, this person is the producer, line producer, or production manager.

During the earliest phases of pre-production anyone seeking to make a movie, particularly an independent movie, should do his or her absolute best to pull together a central core of at least three competent committed people. One is the director. The other person can be called producer, co-producer, line producer, associate producer, production manager, or assistant director. Any such person on set doing the job of the A.D. can also be a producer – there's no prescription against wearing more than one "hat" particularly on low budget movies.

With a core of three or more competent committed people involved in making a movie early in pre pre-production, or at least before production begins, you have *proper preparation* that will likely contribute greatly to the ultimate outcome of the process of making a good movie. A production that lacks at least three competent committed people, however, almost always suffers because of the deficiency of personnel. In *Day for Night*, Francois Truffaut's fabulous movie about making movies, he says that first you start out wanting to make a great movie, then you'll be happy if you make a good movie, then you'll just be happy if you get the movie made, then you'll be happy to just live through and survive the making of the movie. If you lack the three people I think you need at the very least, you may arrive at the last position that Truffaut postulates very quickly!

CHAPTER NINETEEN:
THE SIX PHASES OF MOVIE PRODUCTION
AND THE FOUR KINDS OF SEQUENTIAL ACTIVITY
WHEN MAKING A MOVIE

My definition here might not fit with previously described phases of movie production that you've read or been told. The phases of movie production I've lived through repeatedly are:

One – Inspiration

Two – Engagement

Three – Panic

Four – Search for the guilty ones

Five – Punish the innocent ones

Six – Reward the non-participants

On a more serious note, the four sequential activities when making a movie are:

One – Writing, creating, preparing, perfecting or polishing a movie treatment and/or script

Two – Pre-production, preparing to shoot the movie, which can be divided into pre-pre-production and pre-production proper

Three – Production, actually shooting the movie

Four – Post-production, editing, sound editing, music, perhaps special visual FX, sound mix, negative cutting, final coloration, and all the other things it takes to finish the movie.

CHAPTER TWENTY:
TWO PRODUCTION MEETINGS AND THE JOBS OF THE PRODUCTION MANAGER, LINE PRODUCER, AND PRODUCER DURING PRE-PRODUCTION

I have never seen a low budget independent movie run at all smoothly during production if it did *not* follow exactly the system of two production meetings during pre-production. I have seen numerous low budget movie productions turn into total messes, result in undistributable movies, and in some cases founder, break apart, splatter and stop and die because they did not use the exact two production meeting system. Here's how it works, ideally.

Production meeting #1 should occur about ten days to two weeks before the first day of production (and by that I mean, first day of principal photography). The first production meeting is a very "heavy duty" industrial-strength nuts and bolts detailed meeting that lasts an entire day. Some run into the evening. In some of these meetings *every word* of the script is read out loud, usually by the A.D., sometimes by the line producer, but usually *not* by the director. Typically, the A.D. or line producer presides over the meeting and the production secretary takes very detailed notes. Typically, the A.D., line producer, director, producer, production manager, and second A.D. sit at the head of a long table. A representative of each department sits along the sides of the table. The departments represented usually include camera, lighting, grip, props, wardrobe, makeup, special FX, art department, sound, stunts, casting, location manager, script supervisor, transportation. Some times the screenwriter is present, and sometimes others are present as well.

The A.D. or line producer starts at the very beginning of the script and reads it through, often reading every single word, while in some meetings dialogue is not read and in others only parts of the scenes are read, usually in summary or description. Every time something in the script states something that requires production or pre-production, a location, a prop, a special effect, a costume that an actor will wear, extras, sets, special camera or lighting equipment, anything that will be needed during production, the person reading the script stops and inquires of the relevant department as to the status of that piece of production or pre-production. For example, the first scene is exterior at a park (EXT. PARK). The question might be: "Do we have that location?" If so, then it would need to be established when it shoots, if the director has approved it, if the paperwork is signed (to rent the property), etc. If a prop is mentioned, questions would be about whether the prop is in hand and if the director has approved it. Questions might come up about whether a character has been cast, how a special effect will be achieved, or if special equipment is needed for a stunt. That might include the need for a stunt double. Wardrobe needed and location questions like using location or building a set for various scenes might come up. This kind of thing goes on all day as the person reading the script moves word for word through the scenes, detail by detail, assessing what has been accomplished and what is yet to be done. *The production secretary makes notes on all this.*

The most important aspect of this first production meeting is that nothing at all that still needs to be accomplished is left until someone's name is attached to an item, and that assigned person promises to accomplish it. The prime purpose of this meeting is to uncover absolutely everything that remains to be done to complete pre-production, totally and thoroughly, and to assign a person or persons to accomplish each of these remaining tasks and to record the name of the person(s) assigned to each task. There are also secondary purposes for this meeting. One of them is to expose, communicate, clarify, develop, and force the director to think about the director's ideas and vision as to exactly what the director wants specifically for various detailed aspects of the production. At the end of the main production meeting, the director usually has "sidebar" meetings with the various departments about things that have come up in the main meeting, but would be a waste of others' time to discuss in detail at that point. Get ready to order takeout – these sidebar meetings usually go on late into the evening.

These first production meetings are enormously productive in many ways. They are vital and essential, propel pre-production forward, and eliminate lack of focus. They offer a reality check of what has been done and what has not been done. They are also a reality check of what has been decided and what has *not*, offering a wakeup call to the overall production. I remember walking into one production meeting for a movie that I was directing and producing, one I had written. I felt like a lot of pre-production had been accomplished and not that much remained to do. It was two weeks before the movie would begin shooting. All day, thing after thing had not been accomplished or decided came up. The production secretary was a seasoned professional who took detailed notes of everything. I walked out of that meeting shaken. One hundred and fifteen things remained to be accomplished or decided. I personally got a list with my name at the top with 25 to 30 major things that I had to accomplish or decide. *What a wakeup call!* Only two weeks until we started shooting, and I had all this to do, wow! Not just my stuff, mind you, but all that the production company had to accomplish – it looked overwhelming!

A good, well-run, well-recorded first production meeting can wash away a lot of PR and bullshit and complacency. It provides reality. It can let the key people know in an undeniable form what the actual condition and status of the production and pre-production actually is. If the entire pre-production schedule is four to five weeks (a common length of pre-production for many low budget movies), about two weeks to ten days before the first day of shooting is usually a good time to have this first production meeting.

The second production meeting usually occurs three to five days before shooting starts. The second production meeting is usually short and swift. It usually takes a morning at most. They usually start at 8:00 a.m. to 9:00 a.m. and are over well before lunch. The master list of things remaining to be done that comes out of the first production meeting is moved through item by item and the person whose name is attached to each item is asked if something is really, truly done. If it's not completely done, accurate notes are made as to what needs to be done to complete it, and who will take responsibility and/or join the team promising to accomplish it.

Let me point out that for a prop to be moved into the done category that prop needs to be *seen by and approved by the director*, not just gathered by the prop person. For a location to be moved to the done column, it needs not only for the director to have seen it and approved it, the proper paperwork giving the production company the necessary access to that location has to have been signed by the person that owns or legally controls the location. For a costume or piece of wardrobe to be done it not only needs to be in the possession of the wardrobe person, and approved by the actor who will wear it, the director must have seen and approved it for the scene or scenes in question. For the casting of a role to be cast and done, the director has to have definitely chosen the actor for that role and the actor or actor's agent has to have agreed, including the amount of pay, and time frame for rehearsals etc. Done means *really done*, for real, not some problem that can, like Count Dracula, rise from the grave to terrorize the production.

Usually, at the second production meeting there will be some things remaining to be done, usually about 10% to 20% of the things that were uncovered in the first production meeting. These things remaining to be done are double-teamed or triple-teamed or avalanched to get them accomplished. Example: A key location has not been found by the location manager when the second production meeting begins. When it ends, the location manager, the production manager, the line producer, the producer, two production assistants, two interns, and if necessary even an ex–boyfriend of the wardrobe lady who worked on a similar movie are assigned to do what is necessary to secure that needed location and put it in the done column, pronto. If the line producer, producer, and/or production manager are doing their jobs *properly* the production will not arrived at the second production meeting with a lot of outstanding "yet to be done" important items and the production should not arrive at this second production meeting with many (or even, any) outstanding items that shoot on the first day of production, or first week of shooting.

After the first production meeting the production manager should have highlighting markers of three different colors, one for items that shoot the first day of shooting, one for items that shoot the first week of shooting, and one for items that shoot the second week of shooting. The first production meeting is when things that are remaining to be done are written down and made clear. Right after that meeting (usually the next day), the producer, line producer, and the production manager (people individually and collectively responsible for the proper accomplishment of all aspects of pre-production) should have a separate meeting and go through every item on the list of things remaining to be done. Among themselves, they should be brutally honest, and totally without illusion or self-deception or complacency, about what's been done, what remains to be done, and the level of competence or incompetence that they see or feel in each department head. They should pool their collective knowledge, experience, wisdom, and contacts.

Here's the kind of thing that might typically happen in that meeting. The production manager notices a location that remains to be found and suggests someone he knows of that scouted many locations like the one described, for another movie. He offers that person's phone number. Or the line producer sees some wardrobe items that have not been acquired and offers a similar solution that might be had by contacting another wardrobe person she knows who might have those items. The line producer then transmits those phone numbers to the proper personnel within the existing production. It is the responsibility of the production manager, line producer, and producer to follow up what has been written down and made clear in the first production meeting. By follow up I mean help when help is needed or advantageous or appropriate, or supervise when supervision is needed or advantageous. Sometimes, in rare cases, following up includes firing a staff member that is just not doing the job or is unable or unwilling to do the job. In some very rare cases, following up requires that you must do the job or part of the job yourself. The best working definition of following something up is to make sure that something that needs to get done is done, and properly, on schedule, in a realistic and optimum manner.

The staff members or department heads that had their names attached to various things that remain to be done are responsible to accomplish what the committed to accomplish, but they are not the only ones responsible for the accomplishment of these things. The movie's producer, line producer, and production manager are individually and collectively responsible for the complete and thorough and proper and workable accomplishment of all pre-production during the pre-production phase of making a movie. The producer, line producer, and production manager are the mainspring of the production that pushes forward pre-production to proper completion. It should *not* be the job of the director to push forward pre-production and oversee its completion.

The director's job during pre-production is to make decisions and give guidance as to his or her vision of the movie, and to properly prepare to direct the movie as I described in an earlier chapter on that subject. The director needs to visit locations and approve them, rehearse the actors and complete casting, design the storyboard (if the director uses them), plan shots and lay out how to shoot scenes, and clearly convey the director's vision to key people in the production. During pre-production the director has a huge job simply to prepare properly to direct the movie, and to also burden the director with following up, pushing forward, and accomplish the other aspects of pre-production will cause a director to be burned out before shooting starts. His or her's is the vital job of *properly and thoroughly preparing to direct the movie and to form and transmit his or her vision of the movie.*

One thing that the producer, line producer, and production manager have to watch closely and control with finesse is that everything necessary for the first day of shooting and the first week of shooting gets secured as soon and as properly as possible. It is very dangerous if the staff gets the false but seductive idea that during pre-production only the things necessary to shot the first week need to be accomplished before shooting starts. This is a seductive but *very* dangerous idea. Few low budget productions actually accomplish all pre-production during pre-production and they usually pay for it "through the nose." Not completing pre-production necessities during pre-production is like asking the director and others key people to put a foot inside the gates of filmmaker hell. Here's how it works. When pre-production is not completed before shooting starts and the attitude is adopted that a role only has to be cast just before it shoots, or a location only has to be found just before shooting it, you are saying to the director and other key people that working twelve to eighteen hours a day isn't enough. You're giving them a sentence of many extra hours, perhaps including their day off, just because things weren't totally nailed down during pre-production.

To begin shooting without completing pre-production also opens the production to very real danger. What happens if some unforeseen things go wrong during production? If you have properly completed pre-production before starting shooting and something goes wrong during the production, resources and people can easily switch gears to deal with the problem. On the other hand, if resources and personnel are thinned to take care of the results of incomplete pre-production, and when something unexpected goes wrong it can easily develop into a state of overwhelm, one decimated by the "slings and arrows of outrageous fortune." The road to filmmaker hell is often paved with incomplete pre-production before shooting starts.

A movie production, particularly low budget, often is motivated by emotions, either fear of disaster, or hope, or enthusiasm, yet starting out, every production wants to do something excellent, exceptional, or at least successful. If things that must be done for the first day of shooting or first week of shooting remain undone, they become fear-producing invitations to disaster. That is why the producer, line producer, and production manager should make it a major objective to get things necessary for the first day and week of production excellently completed as soon as possible, so that they do not become distracting. As soon after the first production meeting as possible, the production manager should review his or her notes from the meeting, go over the master list of things remaining to be done. Each individual list of things that each department head has agreed to do should be gone over with that person by the production manager in a follow up on the first production meeting. If areas of trouble remain, it's best to catch them immediately, and every person on the staff or crew should be told to *call when in trouble.*

Call when in trouble works several ways. If department heads or staff members are having trouble accomplishing their tasks, they need to call the production manager or line producer for guidance. If the production manager or line producer notices an area of trouble in the production they need to call those in charge of that area and find out what is going on and what needs to be done for a resolution. They may need to call someone with more experience or resources to solve the problem.

The two pre-production meeting system provides a spine and focus for prioritization and accountability, support and structure, to the very difficult and vital action of properly addressing and completing pre-production. *It is an absolute must!*

CHAPTER TWENTY-ONE:
WRITE IT DOWN AND MAKE IT CLEAR,
FOLLOW IT UP, CALL WHEN IN TROUBLE,
AND THE
"MOMMY, DADDY SHOPPING FOR EASIER INSTRUCTIONS" GAME

When I look back on the major disasters that occurred on movies I made and movies on which I worked, its obvious to me that *almost* all of the production disasters and almost all production problems can be traced back to *failure to write it down, make it clear, follow it up, call when in trouble*, and failure to stop the "Mommy, Daddy shopping for easier instructions" game. The other sources of production disasters and problem are very few, and they are usually "one of a kind" things that are not easily susceptible to being handled by policy. Many people will resist being told to write it down. They will say "I can remember." Maybe in ordinary life they can, but working on a movie is a different reality. Here's why.

In ordinary life, a person may have to remember three to five things a day, maybe a dozen or so things to do a week. When making a movie, anyone in a key position, and almost anyone working on the production, can temporarily be in a key position, can be hit with a dozen things to do in an hour or even half an hour. This often happens in the last week of pre-production or during shooting. A person working on a movie can easily be presented with 50 or more important things to be done within a week. If they don't write these things down, using a notebook or paper or an electronic device or small pocket notebook or some other method of recording a reminder, they will forget some of the items. A chain is only as strong as its weakest link. That's where it breaks under pressure. A production will only run as smoothly as the most important disaster producing thing that goes forgotten and remains undone, sometimes by a very junior person on the production. So *write it down and make it clear* so it won't be forgotten and will get done!

Sun Tzu, the author of *The Art of War*, one of the clearest thinkers in human history, said that when orders are not clear and are not carried out it is the general or commander's fault. If the orders are clear and are not carried out, it is the soldier's fault. It is important to try to make instructions so clear that they cannot be misunderstood. Sometimes that level of clarity is necessary, because some people have a tendency to alter or avoid instructions. When you write them down, instructions are hard to argue with.

On a very low budget movie once, I had a scene to shoot that involved an optical effect I had never used before. I knew in theory how this effect worked but I wasn't sure about the exact dos and don'ts of shooting the shots to make it. I was in trouble so I called for help. I told the producer that I needed to talk to someone who had actually done this type of optical effect. He made calls and eventually reached a veteran elderly gentleman who had done just this kind of effect for the original *Star Trek* TV series. He was very generous with his time and knowledge and told me in detail exactly how he'd done the optical effect in question many times. He revealed what to watch for and what I should be careful with. He also told me some very interesting stories about his participation in the original *Star Trek* series. After talking to him, I knew how to do the effect and was no longer guessing.

Call when in trouble works. Often in situations of emergency or unexpected change or challenge, junior staff or crew people find themselves dealing with something important or crucial to the production, and they have to make a decision on something that's normally "above their pay grade" or about which they are unsure. They cannot be faulted for not knowing the correct decision, but they certainly can be faulted for *not calling someone more senior* in the production and turning the task of making that decision over to the appropriate decision-maker. Call when in trouble!

I define "Mommy, Daddy shopping for easier instructions" by presenting an example of it in action. Mommy tells the kids "You can't watch any TV at all until all your homework is done." The kids don't like these instructions so they go "shopping" for easier instructions from Daddy. They tell him they have half their homework done and promise to do the rest right after dinner, and he says okay. Then Mommy catches the kids watching TV and gets all over them, and they reply, "Daddy said we could watch TV if we finished our homework right after dinner." What they don't tell her is that they didn't tell Daddy about Mommy's instructions, because if he'd known about those, he wouldn't have contradicted them.

Here's how that works on a movie set. On my movie *Starship Invasions* I had one week of shooting with Christopher Lee. The first day of shooting on the movie was the first day of the week we shot scenes with Mr. Lee. The day began at Lake Shore Studios in Toronto, a large facility equal in size to many Hollywood studios. The sets in which Lee's scenes would be shot were already built. Other sets were under construction. It was very exciting to shoot in a big studio, with a big star, on a larger budget. The young cinematographer and I were going over my shot list for the first day of shooting and discussing and setting up the first shot, when the wardrobe lady ran out of the dressing room and up to me. She couldn't finish a sentence without laughing.

"You have to come to the dressing room!" she exclaimed.

"Why"?

"Christopher Lee won't come out of the dressing room."

"What?"

"Just come into the dressing room. Talk to him. You'll see."

So I went into the dressing room. The first thing Christopher Lee said was, "My fan, my fans. I can't let them see me like this." He pointed to the ridiculous two-foot long shoulder extensions on his costume that were stuffed with wadded-up newspapers   extensions that had *not* been approved by me. More importantly, I had told the costume department's tailor to go to Christopher Lee's hotel room Sunday afternoon, a day before shooting began, and show him all his costumes and make sure that they fit and that he was happy with them.

I told Mr. Lee that the tailor would alter his costume exactly to his tasted and specifications, and apologized for the costume fiasco. Then I went and confronted the tailor and repeated the instructions I'd told him. Well, naturally, he'd been told to do something else by my enemy, "Mr. Take It Apart." The tailor probably didn't want to "schlep" Mr. Lee's costumes to the hotel room and back on a Sunday afternoon and "Mr. Take It Apart," the worse than useless "production manager" was more than glad to give the tailor new instructions not to go to Mr. Lee's room Sunday and an opening to play the Mommy, Daddy shopping for easier instructions game and ignore my instructions. No one informed me of the change, of course, probably because they knew I would not allow that kind of crappy, creeping insubordination on my production. This is what happens when money men undercut the director and take joy in trying to make the director powerless, then a*holes are able to avoid instructions and cause disasters and fiascos and make it a lot harder to make movies, but the director still has to get the day no matter how much horse crap has been dumped in his or her path.

Sometimes when I tell people about the Mommy, Daddy shopping for easier instructions game, they respond that the solution to this problem is chain of command, or to work through department heads. Neither of these are workable solutions to this highly destructive game in the arena of movie production. The chain of command on movies is not as rigid or sharply-defined as it is in the military, and you can't always work through department heads. The only real solution or inoculation against the b.s. and frustration that this game generates is to viciously enforce the rule that when a person in authority gives a junior person an instruction, that instruction must either be carried out exactly as given or, if it is to be altered or abandoned in favor of contradictory instructions from another person in authority, *the person who gave the original instructions must be informed that their instructions are being altered or countermanded of contradicted*, and the two people giving instructions can work out one set of instructions to be followed. The person in authority who gave the original instructions must be notified when their original instructions are altered or countermanded, contradicted, or negated!

The person in authority that gave the original instruction has to know when those instructions are in jeopardy of not being followed. Some instructions at times should be changed, altered, or cancelled. Every instruction ever given by anyone in authority should *not always* be followed blindly without question. Blind obedience to all instructions from people in authority is *not* a valid solution to the problems caused by this "Mommy, Daddy, shopping for easier instructions" game that some people play. Often, the person who issued the original instructions will *not* disagree with changing them if they are faced with valid reasons to change. When persons who are in authority have actually issued contradictory instructions they need to immediately be put in touch with the person that issued the original instructions and told of these "cross orders." Usually, they can resolve the situation quickly and easily. It is when the contradiction remains unknown to one or both parties that real grade A hell can be quickly generated.

Ignoring my instructions to show Christopher Lee his costumes the day before filming began generated grade A hell. The first day of shooting was heavily scheduled, with a company move in the middle of the day. The entire first week of shooting was very heavily scheduled because I only had Christopher Lee for one week, and I had to shoot all his scenes then. It took over two hours to fix his costume, which caused us to be shooting well after midnight on a day that began before 9:00 in the morning. I was fortunate to have a loyal and director-friendly cinematographer, who supported me through the crushing results of lost time. He simply said, "I'm with ya, boss." The veteran gaffer was equally supportive, and we managed to finish the day with a significant use of overtime, costly but not shredded due to the subversive efforts of "Mr. Take It Apart" production manager and the tailor who ignored my instructions.

Here's another concrete example from a different movie of what can happen when people do not write things down and follow up. During rehearsals, dialogue often changes from what is written in the script. It gets rephrased by the actors to make it more conversational and easier to say. The script supervisor makes note of the changes and the production secretary usually types them up and issues them as "blue pages." (There are various colors issued as pages are changed during production. Usually it would go like this - white, blue, pink, yellow, green, gold, salmon, cherry, white called "double white", and blue called "double blue".) That's what happened on this movie after rehearsing a scene with an actor. I told the first A.D. to deliver the blue pages to the actor so that he could study them and be familiar with his new lines before we would shoot his scene. Time passed and it was the day to shoot that scene, and I found out the actor *never got the blue pages, so he didn't know his lines*. He kept blowing the lines he was learning on the set. I was already put under unnecessary time pressure because of the "rotten dinosaur crap" behavior of the D.P., so rather than fall further behind schedule, I elected to cover the scene with one less shot than I'd planned.

When we edited the scene I found that we really did not that shot, however. We recut and recut the scene many times but it never worked as well as it would have with the needed shot. Finally, the scene was as good as it would get without that shot, but the repercussions of this screw-up did not end in the editing room. Because we had re-edited and recut the scene so many times, the film of the work print was tattered and covered with splicing tape in several places. When you mixed the sound of a movie back then, you ran that work print back and forth in a projector, sometimes at high speed. Now it is common to mix pictures to video, or DVD. Well, because this scene had been re-edited so much, with heavy tape in some places and tattered in others, the work print caught in the projector and the film ripped right down the middle for about ten feet, then jammed in the projector, shattered, and before the projectionist stopped it, the projector "spit" pieces of film out, all over the projection room. I ran from the mixing theater into the projection room and saw small bits of the work print all over the floor. I was stunned. At that time, you needed a perfect work print to mix and complete a movie. The editor, the assistant editor, and I spent about an hour splicing back together and repairing the work print while being charged the full price for the mixing theater and mixers. Finally, we got it to run through the projector, as we held our collective breaths and completed the mix.

If you think this was the end of the repercussions of the "blue page screw-up" think again. While we were waiting for the lab to make a complete composite print (called an "answer print") of the movie, I got a call from the negative cutter, the person that cuts the actual film negative that ran through the camera when the movie was being shot. The negative cutter can not make *any* mistakes cutting the movie's one and only negative, and so negative cutting is a serious business. I've done it. There is no margin for error. So on the phone, the negative cutter says, "You've gotta come down to the negative cutting room. Something's wrong with these edge numbers."

I found out she was right. Edge numbers are on the edge of the work print and the negative, and they are used to conform the cut negative to the work print. It turned out that when the editor and I had put the work print back together, splicing and taping as fast as we could, we got a couple of pieces of the jigsaw puzzle that the jumbled-up work print had become in the wrong order. It didn't show when projected, but some edge numbers were in the wrong position in comparison to the negative. I had to take the work print apart and put it into the exactly correct order. Then I thanked the negative cutter for being so exacting and calling me. Even then, the sad saga of the blue page screw-up does not end, but let's just say this particular horror movie is my *personal* least favorite movie of all the films I've made for a number of reasons. Nevertheless, it received reasonably wide distribution, very wide for a movie of its low budget – theatrical distribution and very wide video distribution. At one point I think most video stores in North America with a significant horror section had a copy of it. I saw it in store in Manhattan, Toronto, Brooklyn, Los Angeles, and in other California cites – Whittier, La Mirada, and La Habra.

I recognize that it is not a tragedy of a magnitude that will alter the destiny of the known universe but it is a pain in the backside that every one of these people who paid to see the movie on video or in theaters saw a scene that was not nearly as good as it would have been *if the damned blue pages had been delivered*. Here's the why and how of the blue pages *not* being delivered. First, I told the first A.D. to deliver the blue pages to the actor. The first A.D. told the second A.D. to deliver the blue pages. So the second A.D. told the head production assistant (P.A.) to deliver them. Down the chain it went; the head P.A., who is kind of a third A.D., told a mid-level P.A. to deliver the blue pages to the actor. And that person told the *lowest level P.A. on the production* to deliver them. Naturally, the lowest level P.A. was already up to his neck in other work because he had nobody to pass work on to. He had to actually *do everything he was told*, that everyone was dumping on him. He had to clean out the Winnebago and empty its septic tank, for example, so maybe his hands were too dirty to write down "Deliver the blue pages." And of course, he forgot to do it, because he was so overworked!

That's why you have to write things down when you're working on movies. The workload and the number of things to be done and remembered can become intense and acute, and normal memory will fail under that pressure. Write it down, or screw-ups will occur!

Who was at fault? Lots of people, and the whole production apparatus deserves a trophy in the "Incompetence Hall of Shame." *Nobody*, including myself, followed-up. When you are responsible for doing something, and you tell someone else to do that thing, your responsibility does *not* end there! You still have a responsibility to follow up and make sure that the thing gets done on time, on budget, and correctly.

I remember an interview with the legendary producer/director Stanley Kubrick in which he related severely endangering his popularity with staff and crew because he repeatedly emphasized to them that it was not just their responsibility to *tell* someone to do something, but to follow up and make sure that thing got done well and correctly and on time and budget. Kubrick himself also repeatedly followed up personally, checking on the progress of various things, much to the annoyance of some of his staff.

Screw-ups that sometimes result from failure to write it down, make it clear, follow it up, call when in trouble, or to end the Mommy, Daddy shopping for better instructions game are not just a one-time fiasco. Like the failure to deliver the blue pages mess, they have repercussions that are like the clearly visible phenomenon that happens when a python eats a small animal that forms a lump in the snake's body that moves through its digestive tract. Bad consequences of these screw-ups are like ghosts haunting a production, or a vampire that you think is dead that rises up to attack you again. Some times these screw-ups reverberate off each other and turn a production into a total mess. Make sure the people working for you follow the steps outlined here, and make sure that you also adhere to them. Write it down, make it clear, call when in trouble, and stop the Mommy, Daddy shopping for easier instructions game dead in its tracks and follow up, and make sure that others also follow up.

CHAPTER TWENTY-TWO:
THE IMPORTANCE OF PROPER SEQUENCE

I've found it difficult on some productions to understand how things go wrong. For example, it seemed that everything that was under the control or direction of one producer with whom I worked usually became a relentless mess. It was not until I wrote this book that I realized it was the producer's *compulsion to violate proper sequence* that made such a large contribution to these messes and caused them to be so dispersing, disorienting, and so hard to bring under control. Proper sequence violated will mess you up as quickly as anything. When cutting the sound effects of a movie, the proper way of doing sound FX is to go through the entire movie and list every sound effect in the movie, and note if that sound effect exists and the production has it, or needs to get it. If the production needs to get the effect, list how it will be acquired; from the production track, or from a SFX library or recording, or it will be recorded in post-production or will be done to picture as "Foley." Then, virtually ever effect should be gathered. Only after all effects are gathered should cutting begin. Once the effects are cut to the picture, it is mixed with dialogue and music. So the proper sequence is *list, gather, cut.*

So let's go back to the go-wrong producer. On this movie, the producer talked me into cutting the sound FX we had before completing listing and gathering. I went along because proper listing and gathering of sound FX are difficult to confront, so I took the easy way and started cutting the sound FX we had. *Big mistake!* The process of doing the SFX on this movie eventually devolved into a dispersing disorienting mess because I'd violated proper sequence. I was only able to complete the SFX on that movie when I went back to proper sequence. I made a complete list, gathered everything that remained to be gathered then cut the effects to completion with the help of other FX cutters.

This producer became a director, and his compulsion to do things out of sequence haunted him intensely in his attempts to direct. It's my opinion that the proper sequence in directing a movie is: (a) learn to direct by study and practice, usually involving making short movies; (b) write or get a good script; (c) get financing; and (d) direct the movie. This poor gentleman took a swan dive to filmmaker hell because he violated this sequence. He got a good script, got some money, then started directing the movie and tried to learn to direct and complete financing of the movie while directing. Some people instinctively do things in proper sequence, but others compulsively do things out of proper sequence, leave steps out, or jump to a later step, thinking that they don't have time to do all the steps, or that they are "getting ahead of the game" by jumping. If things are turning into a mess, and you feel dispersed, disoriented, stuck in quicksand, check and see if you are doing things in proper sequence. Be sure that all the proper sequential steps leading up to what you are doing have been properly and full completed. Very many low budget movies experience a lot of hell during production because pre-production was never fully complete. A movie's production, editing, or acquiring distribution can become a mess because earlier steps were incomplete – even as far back as writing a good script that seasoned movie professionals would feel "deserves to be a movie."

Usually, when you find yourself in a mess it's not really that which composes the mess that is the entirety of the problem. Very often, when in that mess, the real solution is in properly completing something that was done improperly or skipped that is naturally sequentially prior to what turned into a mess. Proper execution of proper completion of essential things in proper sequence is key to smooth-running movie production. Improper sequence can be a major source of messes and psychological and production dispersal akin to falling into quicksand.

CHAPTER TWENTY-THREE:
LOW BUDGET MOVIE PRODUCTION
IS DIFFERENT THAN
LARGE BUDGET STUDIO MOVIE PRODUCTION

Elsewhere in this book, I said that the realities of low budget, micro budget, or no budget movie production resembled something outlawed by the U.S. Constitution because these realities constitute "cruel and unusual punishment." I was only partly joking. Earlier, I pointed out that studio movies typically are shot on a long shooting schedule, often around sixteen weeks or eighty shooting days, which requires a studio director to shoot about 1.5 script pages (about the same amount of on-screen minutes) per day. Most low budget movies are, in sharp contrast, shot on a schedule of somewhere between 15 to 30 days. This means that the low budget director and production is expected to shoot somewhere between three to six script pages (or minutes) of story a day. This is between two to four times as much per day as a studio director, or studio production. This makes some things very different for the low budget director, producer, and the production crew and staff, particularly the first and second assistant directors. Many of the things that I say in this chapter or this section of the book apply directly and intensely to low budget movie production, but do not necessarily apply as directly or at all to larger budget movies.

One of the harshest realities of low budget movie production is the tremendous amount of *proper preparation* that they require and the usual shortage of people, preferably experienced people, to accomplish that proper preparation. If a low budget movie shoots five pages a day, that equals 25 to 30 pages a week, depending upon whether the movie is shooting five or six day weeks. A studio movie would typically shoot about 7.5 pages per week. Normally, a movie should *at least* have the entire week prepped before that week begins shooting. You don't want to be shooting on Monday and know that location for the scene to be shot on Friday has *not* been found and approved. To properly prep an entire low budget movie is a *very major task*. It should be accomplished completely during pre-production but it rarely is handled that way. To properly prep even 25 to 30 pages of script (a week's work) on low budget movies is no joke, particularly for the usual small and largely inexperienced staff of most low budget movies.

When low budget movies are not properly prepped, things go wrong, and as Bill Russell the pro basketball great said, "When things go wrong, (more) things go wrong." Low budget movies do not have extra time or money to deal with things that go wrong. Typically, studio movies have padding in their budgets and shooting schedules. These pads translate to extra money, over budgeting so that money will be available for unforeseen expenses or extra time in the schedule in case the director falls behind schedule. He or she can catch up during the points where the scheduling is purposefully light. Low budget productions are typically stretched to the limit in terms of money and time and have no such pads. When things go wrong on low budget productions, the disasters are not simply absorbed into the production's spare resources. When things go wrong on low budget movies, the director and producer usually get hit *right in the face* with pure, raw, undistilled and uncut hell!

The pads in studio movies are like a safety net. The low budget director or producer is like a tightrope walker working with *no net*. In the first section of this book, I covered the *block it, light it, rehearse it, shoot it, print it* procedure with regard to the director and assistant director's roles.

The producer and virtually everyone in the entire production company needs to understand this process and his or her role in it, as well as how that role changes in the various steps of that process, or shooting a movie. When a producer takes money from investors and promises to use that money to make the movie in which the investors are investing, part of that producer's responsibility is to see that the money is used to the best possible advantage and in the best possible way to make the best possible, most audience-pleasing movie possible so that the movie will have the best possible chance to complete in the worldwide movie marketplace.

In the world of movie making, time is money. Money buys time for pre-production, shooting time, editing time, and mixing time. The producer has a responsibility to be sure that time and money are not wasted. On low budget movies, you usually barely have enough money and time to make the movie, and if time and money are wasted you will *not* have enough money to make the movie, and you will go directly straight to filmmaker hell. On studio movies, lots of time and money are routinely wasted, and it usually does not matter, because they are in a different game, in a different arena, and different rules apply. The producer does *not* have a license to interfere with or undercut or harass the director and it's very counter-productive if the producer does those things and it can cause a lot of wasted time, money, effort, creative energy, physical energy, etc. *but* the producer or line producer does have a very legitimate role in not just backing up and supporting the director but in supervising and guiding the entire production. Sometimes this includes some of the directors, first assistant directors, and second assistant director's actions or inactions.

Two of a low budget producer's major tasks, if well accomplished, will go a long way toward assuring that the movie gets made, and has a shot at success. The first is to make sure that thorough and complete pre-production is accomplished or basically accomplished before shooting begins, and second is to ensure that the *block it, light it, rehearse it, shoot it, print it* procedure runs smoothly and briskly, and time and energy are not wasted because of unnecessary gaps or interruptions or abandonment, or the turning upside down of this process. As I mentioned, a low budget movie typically shoots about 25 setups in a day. As stated, a set up is counted each time the camera is moved and set up for another shot. If you shoot with two cameras, a move would mean two set ups. If a production routinely wastes five minutes between set ups or between the steps of the shooting procedure, that adds up to 125 wasted minutes per day, or over two hours. There are few low budget movies that do not waste at least five minutes between set ups, or between the steps in shooting a shot.

Virtually every script supervisor I worked with had a stopwatch. Script sups have conventional uses for their stopwatches in timing scenes. If I was producing a low budget movie, I would add one very unconventional task to an intern's job. I would have this intern time with a stopwatch how much time elapsed from the moment the director said "cut and print" to the time when the actors for the next shot were on set, and how much time passed from "cut and print" until the director started actually blocking out the actors' positions and moves for the next shot, and how much time the director spent blocking, and how much time was actually spent by the D.P. lighting the shot, and how much time elapsed from the time that the D.P. said the he or she was "lit" until the actors and the director returned to the set and began rehearsing, and how much time was spent rehearsing, and how much time was spent shooting and how much time elapsed between takes, and how much time passed between when the director said print, and the actors in the next shot arrived on set and blocking for the next shot begins. And on and on it would go. I would give this task to an intern and make it their sole job to keep this time log of the steps of shooting. *No* producer that I know of would not have some system of auditing the spending of money during the making of a movie; watching how much money is spent on what. I also know of no producer who currently audits the spending of *time* as I have described previously. Some may even consider it ridiculous. General discussions or admonishments from the producer to the director or assistant directors about the need to speed things up or "get the day" or to not shoot overly long unsustainable days *virtually always are useless*. They usually cause no more efficiency or speed of production. Attempts to influence the director or assistant directors usually need to be based on very specific things to have any positive effect.

Here are examples of the kind of specific, direct, accurate supervision that can work. The producer notices that the time between when the director says "cut and print" and when the actors for the next shot are on set and the director begins blocking the next shot is nine minutes, then twelve minutes, and it is routinely averaging ten minutes. This is way longer than it should take. If the second A.D. has the actors standing by just off set, or if the actors for the next shot are the same actors as are in the current shot, it really should ideally and correctly only take a few minutes for the director to begin blocking the next shot. It is rare for this vital transition to be done that efficiently on low budget movies, but it is an opportunity that's just waiting to be used. In another instance, the producer looking at the intern's log of how long each step of shooting is taking correctly concludes that the production is losing (wasting) at least five minutes between steps in the block it, light it, rehearse it, shoot it process or between takes. This is a common phenomenon – it usually wastes at least two hours each day! When the director says "print" or even "cut" there is often, on low budget movies, what I call a "party time" atmosphere with lots of loud chitchat, big noisy relief among the crew, staff, and bystanders who've been forced to be silent and not move during the take. After the director says "print" the first A.D. needs to quickly, smoothly, politely, even charmingly or humorously, but effectively, *clear the set* of people who should not be on set during blocking. That is followed by moving the actors onto the set for the next shot and then he propels the director into blocking the next shot. The same kind of no b.s. approach is needed between takes or step of this process.

Some directors will resist or balk at being pushed to quickly block the next shot. They need to understand that the point where a director on a low budget movie says "cut and print" is *not a time of rest for the director*! It's not really the end of his or her work cycle. The director's work cycle ends after the next blocking is completed, and the director can rest while the scene is lit. The producer in my example should realize that he or she is losing a couple of hours of shooting time per day because of time lost between "print" and blocking the next shot. He or she should drive this point deeply into the minds of the director, the first and second assistant directors. He or she should emphasize that the second should have the actors for the next shot standing by just off set or on set when the director begins shooting, because the director may print the first take. The producer should also make sure that the director knows that it's part of his or her responsibility to move directly into blocking the next shot right after calling "print" and *not* relax and to see that point as a time for any kind of break.

Typically, a shooting day on a low budget movie has ten to eleven hours planned for shooting time. If two hours of ten hours of shooting time are being wasted, that is twenty percent of the day's shooting time. How much a day of shooting costs can dramatically vary, depending on how much the production is paying actors, crew, staff, and for equipment, locations, food, vehicles, gas, props, set dressing, etc. The cost of the time spent shooting the movie, however, is always a significant part of the movie's budget. The producer should make sure that the director, first and second A.D. understand that they have just enough time and money to make the movie, and they are expected to use time and money to make the movie, but on a low budget, *they have no time or money to waste*. As I've said before, on a low budget movie you will virtually always pay dearly for every minute, every dollar, or every bit of goodwill that you waste. Low budget movies are rarely made with just time and money; they usually require and use a lot of good will.

The next thing that the producer in our example might notice when studying the log of time spent on various steps in shooting is that the D.P. spent half an hour lighting a small easy to light scene. The producer should deliver the news to the D.P. and the first A.D. that the movie's schedule can't stand that kind of indulgence and this picture is the wrong place for a "Rembrandt uber alles" mindset. The D.P. needs to be working to get the movie made, *not* to add to his or her demo reel! If the producer lets people who have obviously wasted time know that the intern is still timing the various steps of shooting so that there will be a clear record of where the day went, it is likely to improve people's behavior, when they see that they can't P.R. or b.s. away the facts.

Stanislavski said that "The general is the enemy of art." I would say that talking to people in generalities when trying to specifically improve or cause efficiency during movie production is virtually always useless and usually results in everyone who is being admonished pointing their finger at someone else, and feeling put upon. In contrast, if you put *specific facts* right in front of people such as, "It took 30 minutes for you (the D.P.) to light that little dinky scene, and you (the A.D.) let him or her take 30 minutes to light scene. Don't do that again – the shooting schedule can't stand that kind of thing!" This type of specific fact-based supervision can have a very positive effect on people's future behavior if the producer notices that the director is taking too long to block and/or rehearse scenes. ("Too long" is an amount of time that is out of proportion to the amount of time available for each set up planned for that day.) The producer should watch the blockings and be sure that the director is *only blocking* during blocking, *not* trying to perfect performances, or engaging in long b.s. discussions about character, psychology, or philosophy. These discussions can be conducted off set when lighting is going on. If the director is taking too long in blocking and rehearsing, it's a sign that the director's "homework" is loose, weak, or absent. It's probably an indication that the director did not fully or successfully prepare (to direct the movie) during pre-production or rehearsals if the producer realizes that is the situation, the producer is well within his or her rights to demand that on the director's next day off, the director engage in further rehearsals of all scenes that shoot in the next week of production, and that the director visit all locations that shoots in the next week of production, and that the director sharpen up his or her homework, storyboards, shot lists, notes, etc. so that the director can accomplish blockings and rehearsals more efficiently and quickly.

Again, the producer does not have a license to try to do the director's job, or to interfere with the director doing the director's job or to be a backseat driver or to harass the director or waste his or her time and energy. The producer's job is largely to support and assist and backup the director, and guide the production.

Sometimes the producer can, however, have a legitimate supervisory role in making sure that *the director does his or her job*, as efficiently as possible, with an awareness of how much time and money are available for the making of the movie. On several movies that I directed, I signed copies of the shooting schedule and budget, which were attached to my directing contract and became part of that documented agreement. I agreed to make the movie, on that budget, on that schedule. It's okay to expect and demand that the director do the assigned job. Understanding the *block it, light it, rehearse it, shoot it, print it* process by which shots are made is also important for crew and staff, because their roles and the actions required or not required of them change as the steps of this process change. Here's an example that illustrates this point. On one movie, we had a makeup lady who was a very good makeup person, but she was brand new to movies. When the A.D. would take actors out of makeup for blocking, she'd argue with the A.D. and basically fight with him, saying "You can't take [the actor], the makeup isn't ready." She was unaware that the actor was *not* going to be filmed. They were just going on set to block out the scene with the director so that the scene could be lit. They did not need to be made up for that step of the process of shooting a shot. Then when the A.D. returned the actor to makeup after blocking, the makeup lady would say, "See, I told ya, you couldn't have him, his makeup wasn't ready."

There is a phenomenon in the movie business where people who are pros and who've been around a bit know what's going on, and how things work. People who are new, and don't know what's going on or how things work, don't want to let people know that they don't know because then people would know that they are *not pros*. A lot of what people who work on movies know is learned by osmosis. They absorb it over time. The movie business is usually not particularly good at explaining things to new people or educating them. Therefore, I suggest *something novel* to anyone making a low budget move with a lot of people new to the business. *Explain things to them! Educate them a bit at the production meetings.*

Here's the next chapter in the saga of the poor uninformed makeup lady. When an actor was brought to the set for blocking, she ran alongside the actor trying to make him up "on the run." When she got to the set, she was told to go back to the makeup room and makeup other actors. So she got the idea the makeup person should not be on set but should be in the makeup room all the time. That is not always true, of course. When the actors are on set during rehearsals and during shooting, the makeup, wardrobe, and hair people should be on set for touchups. Well, during rehearsals, this makeup lady often got called to the set and admonished by the A.D. for not being on set. She was confused. She did not understand that during some steps of the process of making a shot, she needed to be off set, and during other steps of making a shot, she needed to be on set. She did not even understand that there were different steps to the process of making a shot. Why should she understand that? Nobody, including myself (in keeping with movie tradition) bothered to explain it to her. We just expected her to "osmose" it in and "just know" it.

This next point is not that easy to explain or understand, but it's extremely important on low budget filmmaking and it is vital that the director, first and second A.D.'s and producer understand it, have a working, practical awareness of it, and function on set in alignment with it. Here it is: the work cycle of the director does *not* begin with *blocking* and end with "print". Once the first blocking is completed, the real work cycle for the director and all but the lighting crew (once the first blocking is complete, and the scene is lit) is *rehearse it, shoot it, print it, shoot it, print it, block it,* rest. Then repeat that procedure. The work cycle for the lighting crew is *light it, tweak it, break it down, repeat.* Some times, if the director or D.P. screws up, *relight it.* It's vital on low budget movies (and *not* on large budget movies) that the director maintains momentum through rehearsals, shooting, print, and blocking the next scene and *only rests* and breaks momentum when lighting is going on. The A.D.'s and producer need to support and assist propelling the director's work cycle forward.

The job of a movie director, particularly on a low budget, makes enormous physical, mental, and aesthetic demands of that director. It is not fair, wise, efficient, or practical for that director to also be the one that has to push the production and the "production machinery" forward. That is the job of the first A.D., the line producer, and on low budget productions, often the producer behind the scenes.

CHAPTER TWENTY-FOUR:
DON'T JUST WAIT; SIT DOWN AND REST

Standing in line waiting is tiring. Waiting is tiring. Someone I knew who worked on many movies produced by Roger Corman said that a key part of Corman's advice to young directors was to "Sit down as much as you can." There is a periodic time of enforced idleness that every director faces over and over during every shooting day. That is the time when the set is being lit. During that time, the set belongs to the D.P., the A.D. and the lighting crew, and the director is off the set. *It should be a time of physical rest, at the least.*

Just as people overestimate what they can remember without writing it down, people tend to overestimate how much stamina their bodies have. They tend to underestimate how much strength and energy the stress and tension and constant need to make decisions and non-stop mental traffic and physical motion and intense and almost constant demand for communication draws out of a person that is directing a movie. Even if only for a few minutes, there is a need for the director to periodically sit down and *rest*! Not just wait, because waiting is tiring. Resting is refreshing.

I once wrote a script under incredible time pressure; the entire first draft of the script was written in four days. I was working with another writer, Barry Pearson. We'd take turns sitting at the typewriter typing up a first draft script. We were working from a handwritten treatment and some rough draft handwritten script pages, pounding out our ideas that came up as we progressed through the script. Soon, I noticed that if I was sitting typing and Barry was laying on the couch, he came up with all the good ideas, but if he was sitting typing and I was relaxing on the couch, I tended to come up with the best ideas. Why was this? My opinion is that there is a connection between the body being relaxed and not forced to deal with physical demands and *the ability to think productively*. Thus, if the director sits down and rests at least five minutes per setup when lighting is going on, during 25 setups a day that equals over two hours a day that he or she rests during the shooting day. That rest makes a serious difference in what the director's physical and mental condition are likely to be after a week or several of long days of low budget shooting. The director can certainly do work, even important work during these times of physical rest. A P.A. or intern should get the director something to drink if he or she wants it. During these points of rest, the director can talk with actors in detail, answer their questions, go over things shot or yet to be shot with the script supervisor, answer questions that people such as the art department ask, or that others wanted to ask but could not during shooting, or even confer with the producer.

Here's how that process of the director resting and lighting should proceed. The director should always be present when the D.P. makes an estimate of how long it will take to light the next scene. The director should note the time of the making of the estimate and length of the estimate. Example: the D.P. at 2:30 p.m. says the scene will be lit in ten minutes. That means the scene should be lit by 2:40 p.m. Some times when you shoot a master or a two or three-shot, and the next shot is a close-up or over the shoulder (OTS), you will be virtually lit for the next shot, and when you ask the A.D. "How long?" he or she will say "Five" meaning five minutes, or "We're basically lit" or "Momentarily." In these cases, the actors shouldn't leave the set but should sit and rest on set, as should the director, or they should move right into position for the next shot.

If the D.P. estimates ten minutes or longer, the director should leave the set and leave the A.D. in charge of the set. For instance, if the D.P. estimates ten minutes the director has about seven minutes off to rest. After about seven minutes have passed, the director should call the A.D. on the walkie-talkie and ask "How's the D.P. doing?" If the D.P. is on schedule, the director should stay in touch with the "first" by walkie-talkie and return to set just before it's lit with the actors' makeup, wardrobe, hair done, and start rehearsing the next scene.

Producers should realize that directors are human beings with a limited, finite amount of energy, mental capacity, creative energy, and physical stamina, and when these things are exhausted, you can't just drive down to the gas station and have them pump some more creative energy director juice or physical strength into the director. I have seen and experienced personally producers that wasted and destroyed directors' time, energy, physical strength, and creative thought processes in an evil manner. I have seen and experienced producers who were very actively, covertly out to kill the director because they envied the director's ability to create a movie. Never forget that a director's vital energies and time are vital to making a film, but they are a limited vital resource. Wise and positive producers conserve, protect, and encourage the refreshment or replenishing of the director's time and energies, and also recognizes the director's absolute value and irreplaceable function in the making of a movie.

CHAPTER TWENTY-FIVE:
MONEY AND ACCOUNTING

Money is so important to the making of movies that a pure idiot, who knows nothing at all about movies can, if they have money, make a movie, and *many do*. In contrast, a pure cinematic genius that has no money usually can't make a movie until they get money. Finances are of such overwhelming importance in the making of movies, that some times the accounting of where money has been spent, or will be spent, or how much money remains or does not remain to finish the movie and the accounting of that money becomes a task that supercedes the "mere jobs" of doing the things that are actually necessary to make a movie. That's why it is a fatal error to assign any detailed accounting tasks to people who must do things that actually get the movie made. I'm specifically talking about the production manager, line producer, and producer. These people need to be aware of the production's financial condition in detail, and on a very current basis, but if they are burdened with accounting they will likely be "missing in action" right when they are most seriously needed, and the production will often stumble into some sort of disaster because of this very ugly conflict of priorities.

I have a solution to this problem, and I've used it successfully in making movies. Either by going on the Internet or by other means, find an accountant who is "financially OK" (does not need money badly) but is bored with the world of numbers and wants to enter the "glamorous" world of the movie business, complete with beautiful actors, male and female, expensive clothes, cars, jewelry, famous people, exotic and expensive locations, fame, fortune, and sixteen hour days, and freezing your buns off to get a shot. This accountant should want to open the doors to be able to use his or her full creative potential in the future. You give this motivated accountant an associate producer credit, defined by Hollywood as "anyone who will associate with the producer."

These accountants have various systems of accounting. The best, most effective system I ever saw used the budget categories, actors, crew, equipment, location fees, insurance, etc. as the organizational basis for the movie's system of accounting, and final accounting. The young accountant turned associate producer produced a stellar product. The first major task that an accounting of a movie must accomplish is a certified accounting complete with *all receipts and all invoices* that will satisfy an IRS audit and ensure that the movie's investors get all tax benefits to which they are legally entitled. Other major purposes and tasks of this accounting is that it must be able, at any time during the production, to show exactly how much money has been spent or committed to be spent, what upcoming expenses remain and what money remains in the bank to finish the movie. This young associate producer's audit was so perfect, so complete, and so substantiated by *every* perfectly organized receipt and invoice that it was to any potential IRS auditor, like garlic, a cross, and holly water are to vampires. It would repel them if they came near it.

The absolute *worst* accounting system I ever came into contact with was used by the production manager I called "Mr. Take It Apart." This Mr. Big Reputation, who was actually worse than useless and was in many ways a walking pile of rotten dinosaur crap, had an accounting system that not only didn't tell you how much money you had spent and on what at any given point in the production, it ensured that you could not know or figure out how much had been spent. His system relied on invoices or bills coming back into the production office before the expenses could be accounted. It was an extremely complicated, defective system. Some companies took days, weeks, or even a month before sending out bills or invoices. This jerk was constantly running magical, mystical financial projections that showed that I was going over budget. *In actuality, I finished the movie under budget*, but this turkey's projections were constantly scaring the crap out of the movie's money men and although these projections were completely wrong, they impressed the living hell out of the terrified producers, who were busy doing quite a lot to make my life as unpleasant and in jeopardy as they could. So I went into Mr. Big Reputation's office and asked that he show me the accounting he was basing these projections on, because it did not feel like I was going over budget. The feeble crap he pulled out could not verify his claims, and effectively obscured how much had been spent "to date." The complex accounting system he was using had less practical value and usefulness that caveman pencil and paper systems I'd used on micro budget movies and student films.

Here is a word of advice to all the accountants out there that want to get into the glamorous movie business and eventually let their "creative impulses" bloom. Offer your accounting services to low budget movie productions for an associate producer's credit and any money they can spare. Do that two or three times and you will learn a lot about how movies are made, and you will be just one good script, one good director, and a few investors away from becoming a real movie producer. Where can you go from there? That's up to you, but remember that John D. Rockefeller was an accountant before becoming an oil man and mega-rich plutocrat.

CHAPTER TWENTY-SIX:
PRE PRE-PRODUCTION

One of the first actions that should be taken during pre pre-production is to find a "glamour-craving" accountant and turn him or her into one of your production's associate producers, and begin right from the start to put your production's accounting system into place. Pre pre-production is the first phase of pre-production after the script is finished and before a significant number of people have been hired and a tentative start of shooting date has been set. Some of the things that should be done during pre pre-production are:

- A corporation that exists to make the movie should be incorporated, because the liabilities of making a movie are too great to endure without corporate protection.

- A detailed shooting script should be written. The script should be "broken down" scene by scene to reveal all the elements needing to be budgeted.

- A production board shooting schedule should be made either with a physical board and strips or with a computer and software.

The script breakdown should yield a cast list, a location list, a prop list, an art department list of special dressings, if appropriate a costume list, and a special FX and stunts list. A rewrite of the shooting script with attention to production realities should also be completed. The remainder of the three competent and committed people (including the director) that will pledge their "lives, fortunes, and sacred honor" to get the movie made and to be as good as it can be need to be found and attached to the core of the production, along with the accountant/associate producer. The movie needs to be accurately, exactly, and realistically budgeted. Some times a major location for a particular scene just cries out to be found, approved, and acquired by the director and producer during pre pre-production before pre-production begins.

In pre pre-production a decision should be made as to whether the production will "go SAG" (Screen Actors Guild) or not. If the production goes SAG a list of actors with name value who are right for various roles should be made, with the intent of approaching these actors once pre-production proper begins, and trying to cast them or even one of them on a bargain basis. On some productions, storyboarding of some major scenes should begin in pre pre-production, sometimes special FX tests should be done during pre pre-production.

Pre pre-production can go on for a month or months with very little or almost no expense. It is a time to get basic paperwork in order, to get basic planning and mental work done, and to complete the critical process of coalescing a *critical mass* of key people that will form the core of the movie's production staff. It is the time to perfect the script until it's as perfect as you can make it. Once pre-production proper begins, it is a mad dash to the first day of shooting. Before that mad dash begins, some of the more important, more thoughtful tasks that form the foundation for proper pre-production can be easily and more thoroughly and more resiliently be accomplished during the relatively more leisurely and calmer days of pre pre-production than during the more hectic, often chaotic, or even panicked time of pre-production proper. On most low budget movies, pre-production proper usually lasts four to five weeks. Usually, low budget productions cannot afford more prep time than that, and they can't get done the prep that needs to be done with much less time that that. Pre pre-production can last for a month or months before pre-production proper begins. Excellent, stable, pre pre-production need not cost much or anything. I consider it vital to making a low budget movie that can actually compete in the worldwide movie market. Try to get it right. I've found that the way that things begin usually has a lot to do with how they finish up.

CHAPTER TWENTY-SEVEN:
PRAISE IS IMPORTANT

When making a movie, one's attention can get drawn intensely to things that are being done wrong. People can do nine things right or even very well, and they do one thing wrong or incorrectly or fail to do it, and that one thing will draw all the attention. It is vitally important to acknowledge, compliment, and praise people when they do things well or with excellence. If all people hear is criticism, those complaints will soon have little or not positive effect. Well-deserved praise, on the other hand, can build and sustain morale and encourage excellence, even under some of the most trying conditions under which low budget movies are often made.

People will try to please those who praise them, and will try not to displease those that praise them. They will come to despise and resent those who constantly criticize them. Do not ignore things that are well done or excellently done. *Praise them!*

When I was just out of UCLA film school and still breaking into the movie business, I got a job cutting sound FX on a more prestigious, very well-made low budget gangster movie. I had already directed, photographed, and edited one ultra micro budget feature and photographed and edited another. This job was a step up. I cut hundreds of sound effects perfectly right to the exact frame. I staggered into the mixing theater after I had been up all night. I passed Roger Corman in the hallway; he was going the other way to mix another movie. The first thing I heard in the theater was talk about how unprofessional the young SFX editor was and how they could "save" it. The movie had an opening credit sequence with a newsreel montage, and there were some background gunshots that I'd failed to see on the small Movieola screen, and did not cut them. They were more apparent on the screen that on the Movieola editing machine.

Well, I'd almost killed myself working around the clock, and had cut hundreds of excellent SFX's perfectly, but all that mattered was a few missing gunshots in the opening montage. The mixers "looped in" these gunshots to everyone's satisfaction and they were big heroes and I was considered and felt like an unprofessional novice, but I deeply resented the lack of appreciation of all the excellent hard work that I had done. Frankly, it hurt. If I had a machine gun at that point they might not have had to loop in the gunshot SFX – they might have been able to just record them live in that theater.

People work very, very hard at a lot of jobs to get movies made. They deserve and appreciate praise when they do things well. Never forget it, and act accordingly. Some times it's important to keep a "glass half full" attitude rather than to have only a "glass half empty" attitude. Some of what goes on, in *low budget* movie production does resemble "cruel and unusual punishment," but a lot of what goes on in making movies, even most low budget movies, is *fun* and exciting and thrilling and should be experienced as such. When things go well, there is a lot of fun, satisfaction, pleasure, and enjoyment, and not just hard work and tension in making movies. How many people who don't work on movies or TV get paid to join with other like-minded people and go out and "play make-believe" and sell the results of that activity to others whose jobs are a lot less fun than the best jobs in making a movie.

If you're in the movie business, be grateful. There are lots of people who want to be where you are, and if you're making a movie, be thankful to the people that are helping you, especially those who do things that deserve praise!

CHAPTER TWENTY-EIGHT
COMBATTING LEADERS OF THE REVOLUTION –
A PRODUCT'S VALUE COMES FROM CREATION, NOT LABOR ALONE

Although some may differ, and Hollywood caricatures to the contrary, I've learned that a filmmaker with inflated ego doesn't ultimately do very well. It's a Marxist "phallicy" (I'm sure you get the meaning of my spelling) that producers and directors are pigs exploiting the workers. In fact, and particularly if you're making an indie movie, you're a small business person, subsidizing and educating talent, not exploiting. As a smart filmmaker you realize that any product's value comes from bright creative ideas, extensive thought and planning, and not only the glorious labor put forth by those workers who consider that without them, nothing is possible. But that's the good filmmaker I'm talking about.

Some people will obsessively follow authority. Conversely, other people will obsessively rebel against anyone trying to exert control or create something good while using other people's labor. Dear old Karl Marx asserted that all wealth is stolen labor. This is what I called the Marxist phallicy. That was Karl's resentment talking, and you can run into a bit of it in filmmaking from crews. Marx totally missed out on the fact that the ideas behind products often contribute as much or more to the products' value than then labor that makes the products.

Here's an example from my career. One reason my award-winning film *Plague* was such a pleasure to direct was that it had no "leader of the revolution" in the crew or staff. I can't say, however, the same thing about many low budget movies. This phenomenon is so common on film sets that one director I know (and for whom I briefly worked) actually hired a stunt man to pretend to be a grip and disrespectfully pick an argument with this director on the first day of filming. The argument quickly turned into a "fist fight" and down went the stunt man, who would be carried off the set to "the hospital" by two staff people who were in on the ruse. The purpose of this very convincing show was to inoculate the director, the crew, and the production against the bad vibes that a "leader of the revolution" resentment-fomenting type of personality can cause, and to encourage such personalities to lay low, keep their mouths shut, and simply do their jobs. This director could pull it off, I might add. He had a hot temper, serious musculature, and a deserved "macho man" image. When word got around that he punched out grips that gave him trouble (due to the demonstration I just mentioned) he was not bothered by any potential troublemakers.

In contrast, many directors of low budget movies are not as lucky. One shoot on which I was working as an A.D. was shooting extra scenes and narration to put in a movie starring Orson Welles. One member of that crew was a raving, virtually psychotic "leader of the revolution" who became convinced that the producers were going to rip-off the crew and not pay. There was no evidence to support this crazy idea, because the producers were very wealthy, cautious, gentle, and honorable businessmen. Not paying the crew or any legitimate bill was the farthest thing from their minds. The last thing they wanted was to be sued by anyone for non-payment. Well, such things aren't obvious to psychos. The "leader of the revolution" on that shoot eventually stole four days of filmed scenes and put the entire production at risk. He demanded that he and the entire crew be paid before he'd return the film. So they were all paid. He returned the film but he'd caused a lot of stress and disruption and put a lot of creative work at risk. And, it was all unnecessary.

You can recognize this type of personality. They will constantly "bad mouth" the production, the script, the director, the producer, the food, the way the crew is being treated, how much people are being paid, and sometimes the actors. This type of person loves gossip, particularly if they've fabricated it. When they are in full bloom, they will try to block what the production needs at a critical point, as mentioned above, or even convince the crew to walk off the set. I know of two instances of crew walk-offs instigated by such people. While they may have had grievances, if the instigator had not fanned the flames and taken rebellion over the top, there would not have been a walk-off. In one instance, only the camera operator, the director (who actually contributed a lot to the real grievances), and the production manager/producer made up the remaining crew, and they shot the day. In another instance, the walk-off shut the production down, and the movie had a real "fall of Saigon" feeling.

On one production, there was a particularly sneaky reptilian female camera assistant that would invited the crew over to her place to play pool and drink beer after the shoot each day. Later, I found out that she'd use these occasions to bad mouth the production and everything connected to it, including the idea of the movie itself – the very movie that was paying her. She'd constantly make sarcastic putdown jokes about the production and people propelling it, and would encourage others to do so also. She did not succeed in undermining morale on this production, but she sure tried as hard as she could to do that, covertly.

If you are making a low budget movie, you are a small business person. You are an entrepreneur, someone who raises money and uses it to make a product, your movie. You hope to sell that product to people all over the world. You hope to get the investors' money back to them, along with a profit. You are *not* a capitalist, which by definition is someone seeking to make money off *capital*, which is making money off money, not money off a product. You will hear crew say things like "Low budget movies always make money." Or, "If you make it cheap enough, it's got to make money." *Both of those statements are absolutely, extremely, completely, and total false* and so is the mindset that spawns them.

Money invested in low budget movies is *at extreme risk!* Most low budget movies do not get or deserve any real commercial distribution, and very many of them return *zero income* to the investors and production company, and rather than exploit the people that work on them (as leaders of the revolution will claim), most low budget movies actually subsidize the movie business by providing in sports terms a "minor league" system where newcomers can get experience and where new talent can prove itself and rise to higher levels of bigger budget and studio movies. Here's an example. I looked at one D.P.'s resume and he'd been a camera operator for some very famous D.P.'s on some big studio movies. I questioned whether he was right for D.P. on a low budget movie. He blurted out that the didn't put it on his resume but he'd worked on a couple dozen low budget and very low budget movies when he'd started out. "How do you think I learned enough to be able to work for those top D.P.'s on big pictures!" he exclaimed. Now, probably some or all of the investors in some of those low budget productions lost some or all of their investment, and others probably had some or all of their investment tied up for a long time before realizing profits. In reality, those investors were subsidizing the training and development of this aspiring cinematographer's skills until he got to the point where he would be in the position where he could be of use to the studios.

Exploitation is a word you often hear out of the mouths of rabble-rousers infected with very Marxist-derived ideas. You will hear some say that people are being exploited on low budget movies because they work so hard and are paid little or nothing, but the truth is that in many cases, the work done by "green" people is of less value to the production than the value of what they are learning is to them. Thankfully, there now exist some excellent film schools at major universities and technical schools where people can learn. I learned a lot at UCLA film school. I've run into some graduates of these schools, however, who have heavy student loan debts. Many of them have told me that what they learned working on low budget productions was invaluable in pursing a show business career, and usually they learned more on those movies than in four years of college. So who is truly exploiting people, and who is really educating them?

I suggest you fire any "leader of the revolution" as soon as possible after you have evidence of what they're doing, before they do more damage. Many crew people who have an "exploited" mentality will tell you that a certain movie had to have made money simply because it was for sale or rent in a video store, or appeared on cable TV. That's not true. The middle men and distributors (and even sub-distributors) between the production and profits can devour money in ways that make a pack of raging sharks in a feeding frenzy look like English ladies at high tea munching crumpets.

I do not want to leave the discouraging impression that no low budget movies make a profit. I've already provided many example of low budgets that did extremely well, like *Clerks*, *Last House on the Left*, *The Texas Chainsaw Massacre*, *El Mariachi*, *Paranormal Activity*, and many more. When a low budget movie takes off, it can become extraordinarily profitable and launch major careers for those filmmakers. The profits of such movies were much-deserved and the result of excellent coordinated creation, not the result of exploiting people! And it's my guess that very few "leaders of the revolution" were present on any of those productions.

CHAPTER TWENTY-NINE:
THE VARIOUS LAYERS OF FILMMAKER HELL

The lowest and worst level of filmmaker hell is reserved for people that take money from investors and do not even try to make a movie. They run off with the money. If you start trying to raise money for movies you will probably soon hear more than a few of these horror stories. Some are pretty grim.

The next lowest level is for people who take "development" money to develop a production but develop nothing while making a show that they are doing something.

Above them are the people that take money and try to make a movie but can't finish it. They are the people with a useless unfinished movie.

Just above them are the people that finished their movie but it is so bad or so out of touch with what any segment of the viewing public wants to see that even the lowest level, slimiest distributor will not agree to "distribute" the movie and have an opportunity to steal all its profits. (When you operate with that kind of low level distributor, it's a given that their contract is usually a license to steal all the movie's income. I call it "fig leaf" distribution.)

Above the people who made these undistributed and undistributable movies that slime ball fig leaf distributors won't touch are the movies that distributors do distribute, but do not return money to the production. Typically, no money from this type of "distribution" makes its way back to the production company or investors, because of the distributor's expenses.

Above these poor suffering folks are people who made movies that did get real distribution and some money has returned to the production, but have not yet fully repaid their investors. You see, once you repay your investors, you are no longer in filmmaker hell. If it takes a long time to repay them, you are passing through filmmaker purgatory.

Once you are in profit, you are in filmmaker heaven. Highly profitable breakout movies like *The Blair Witch Project* and *Paranormal Activity* have bright beautiful light shining down on them and their filmmakers, who are resting with new financial angels on the highest and most beautiful clouds of filmmaker heaven.

I hope that gives you some idea of how filmmaker hell works, and what it takes to get out of it and rise to greater heights.

CHAPTER THIRTY:
WHEN PEOPLE DON'T CHANGE,
YOU NEED TO CHANGE THEM WITHOUT DELAY

It's true that over a period of time, usually years or decades, people can change who and what they are, but over the time span of the making of a movie (a few weeks or months), *people almost never change*. If the editor you hire can't cut the first scene they try to cut, they probably can't cut the movie, and won't be able to no matter how much you talk to them about editing. You need a new editor immediately! If the D.P. is a ball-busting pain in the ass to the director, that's how he or she will be all through the shoot. If you have a production manager who is like "Mr. Take It Apart" that worked on one of my productions and he screws up the first day of shooting by canceling the director's instructions, then you can expect him to do that in various ways for the whole shoot. That's why you'll need to flush a person like that down the "you're fired" toilet and spray lots of air freshener after the stink left in his or her wake. If someone talked like a "leader of the revolution" you can expect that person to act in line with the talk, usually when the production is most vulnerable and they can do the most damage.

Do not expect people to change just because you speak words to them. Firing people is never pleasant, even with people who richly deserve to be fired, but when people can't do a job or are maliciously harming the production or do things that damage or make production people's jobs much harder, you need to change personnel immediately. When the production is hiring, it will receive many resumes for virtually all jobs. The resumes of the people *not* hired need to be prioritized and kept in a backup file, so that if someone is fired you have a candidate to replace that person, with the "next best" candidate, and next on down. You're now forewarned and can be prepared, so make sure you add this to your pre-production planning.

CHAPTER THIRTY-ONE:
STRATEGIC SCHEDULING

One of the worst jobs of scheduling that I ever saw was on a movie where I was A.D. and second unit director. An inexperienced P.M. would put five pages of script on every single shooting day, without regard to how easy or difficult the scenes were to shoot. It didn't matter if they were action or dialogue to that P.M., and of course he put some of the most difficult scenes to film on our first day of shooting! The director didn't get that day, and was perpetually behind schedule. The director failed to get other days, and was only able to catch up when I turned the second unit into an additional first unit. We caught up and got on schedule the last day of shooting, much to the completion bonder rep's dismay. He was hoping to take over, you see. This example is yet another reason why I believe that the scheduling of a movie should be governed by a *philosophy* and the realities of production.

Here are some of the major points of my general governing philosophy of how to schedule a movie. First, *if possible* (I know all too well that it is not always possible), do not put really important scenes on the first day of shooting or to near, or at the very beginning of shooting or at or near the very end of shooting. Here's what I recommend for the first day of shooting, *if possible*. Get a scene that is near the middle of the script, if that is feasible, or at least not too near the very beginning or ending of the script. Ideally, it should be a scene or group of scenes that require two or more days of shooting in the same location. Then, schedule the first day "light" – meaning half a day or three-quarters of a day actually shooting. Start with the easiest scenes in that location, if at all possible. If the day goes well, be prepared to shoot more than what is scheduled for the first day. If you have scheduled what's really half a day and you shoot three-quarters of a day by getting ahead of schedule and pulling scenes down from the next day and shooting them, *you are ahead of schedule on the first day of shooting!* This is usually a huge morale booster, and can get the production off to a very smooth and momentum-filled start. The same kind of thing can happen if you schedule three-quarters of a day and end up shooting almost a full day. In that manner, you won't have the disappointment that might have resulted if you scheduled a full day and failed to get it. *The director really needs to "get the day" on the first day of shooting.* If the director fails in that attempt, it hurts morale, destroys confidence, and makes the producers and completion bonders instantly nervous. People begin to wonder things like, "If the director can't get the first day of shooting, can the director get the other days of shooting?" They'll wonder if the director can shoot the movie on schedule, or if the production will become a runaway, out-of-control, over-schedule situation.

You see, whether or not the director gets the first day has a lot to do with sane scheduling. There is creative, inspired, excellent scheduling, and in contrast there is insane scheduling.

The end of the first week and the second week of shooting are prime times for shooting the most important scenes in the movie. The crew and cast are not yet burned out and are not "brand new" either. If they start out right, they should be worked into a groove by the third or fourth day of shooting. Near the end of shooting is not a good place to put important scenes, either. At that time, people begin to think about or look for their next job. As the production approaches its end, you get lots of request from actors to shoot their scenes at specific times so that they can go to auditions. They'll say things like, "Can't you finish my scene by 3:00? I have an audition at 4:00." I like to group MOS (without sound) scenes or shots that do not require sync sound and shoot them with a smaller, more mobile crew, sometimes very small, capable of moving in only one vehicle. If you shoot at a place or time of the year when or where rain or snow is likely or possible, and scenes are not specifically designed to be shot in falling rain or snow, *you need to shoot exterior scenes first and have "cover sets" which are interior scenes you can shoot if the exteriors are rained or snowed out.* You do not always have to start shooting on Monday, but sometimes there are advantages to starting then. More stores are open on Monday and Tuesday than on Saturday and Sunday (although that's less true as time goes by), and that makes it easier to complete pre-production. That's why I've started several movies on Wednesday. I've seen and worked on low budget movies that began shooting Friday after noon and then over a weekend, or several weekends in a row. You are usually only charged one day's rent on equipment for a weekend, including that Friday when you rent the equipment. I believe Roger Corman's *Little Shop of Horrors* was shot like that, over one weekend.

Scheduling within the day should also be governed by philosophy and strategy, not by simply slopping the pages onto the shooting schedule or call sheet in any old order. Make the order of scheduling of scenes to be shot work *for the production, for the director, and for the producer, not against them!*

CHAPER THIRTY-TWO:
ORGANIZE YOUR PRODUCTION OFFICE BY PLACE

There is a saying from Shakespeare: "A place for everything, and everything in its place." It is a good idea, particularly in editing rooms, as well as the production and casting offices of low budget movies. Low budget and micro budget movies often have much more turnover of personnel than large budget movies. Low budget and micro budget movies often have interns and P.A.'s working for very low or no money, and if they get an offer of a paying job or better paying job, they will be "gone with the wind" out of that production so quickly they'll leave a pile of work right in the middle of dealing with it. If a production office is organized by *place*, then it is much easier for someone new to come in and take over the work of someone else. Things will be in the places where they are supposed to be, not in some bizarre, idiosyncratic place known only to the person that departed the production.

Not keeping things of a specific type in a specific place leads to "the great production office expeditionary search" where people search all over the office for something that someone else has put somewhere unknown. You won't wonder where that grip's resume is located, or who that P.A. is that lives on La Brea Avenue, if you have a place for everything. You would have the resumes of those people in a box *labeled boldly* "Resumes of crew who have been called" right next to the box "Resumes of crew members yet to be called" and another called "Resumes for interviews." You'll know just where to look.

When a potential crew member is called because he or she has sent in a resume, the person calling writes *on the resume* what happened, such as "Called 2:00 p.m. April 14, not in, left message, his cell phone off." When everyone is trained to this, you'll have a lot less trouble when you need personnel.

D.P.'s send in lots of unsolicited DVD's of their work when they hear that someone is making a movie. So get another few boxes for D.P. sample reels on DVD. Usually, one box should be for DVDs that have not yet been looked at. Keep the D.P.'s resume and other paper info, if any, taped to his or her DVD box. If the D.P. is interviewed, write comments on the resume. If the D.P. is not chosen and takes back his DVD, keep his or her resume, write a description of his or her demo reel on the resume so you can quickly remember who he or she is, and begin building and prioritizing a backup file of D.P.'s in case the one you've chosen turns out to be a turkey or simply doesn't work out and needs to be replaced quickly.

I remember one production office that was about as organized as the aftermath of an explosion at a fireworks stand. A P.A. came galloping through a major and important production meeting that involved the director, producer, P.M., and A.D. He exclaimed, "Remember so-and-so the D.P.? You know where his demo is?" I suggested he try my office, behind the desk. The P.A. galloped off. The rejected D.P. was getting more irate and complaining more and more loudly that he wanted his demo tape back. A few more scared P.A.'s were scurrying around frantically, searching for about fifteen minutes. The D.P. looked like he was about to "go postal" when someone decided to look inside the VCR for the VHS tape everyone wanted to find. Now, if everyone believed in everything in its place, none of this would have happened, but on this production, no one seemed to be able to understand the concept.

Poor suffering actors and want-to-be actors send in head shot pictures and resumes to every production. Bales of them come in, often more than one man can lift, and believe it or not, some actors not called in for auditions will ask for those pictures and resumes back. I don't blame them; they're expensive. So make things easy for yourself and get a box labeled "Not called in to audition" and if an actor comes in wanting their material back, point them to that box and let them look through it.

As soon as word gets out that you are making a movie, you will be hit by an avalanche of music CDs by composers that want to do the music for your movie. Most directors don't want to deal with music in pre-production, and I'm almost always one of them. On some movies, directors do deal with music in pre-production, and it's very appropriate or even necessary in some cases. Most of the time, I get a box and label it "Music" and throw all the music CDs in that box as they come in. when people call in to ask if the director has listened to their music, I instruct staff to say, "The director will listen to the tape during post-production and call back in a couple of months."

Again, if at all possible, a production office should be separate from casting, preferably in different locations. The constant traffic of actors can be very disruptive to a production office. A lot of people and deliveries come in and go out of the production office. A lot of people work there on different things, and some of them quite or get fired or will be periodically "missing in action" running errands or for other reasons. Many things coming in and going out of the office may have to be dealt with on demand. If you do not designate a specific place for *each specific class of important things*, as they pass through the "virtual assembly" line of pre-production and you do not put things and demand that things are put into their proper place, your production office will turn into a mess, or even worse, a messy, time-wasting trap!

CHAPTER THIRTY-THREE:
ANSWERING THE OFFICE PHONE

Whoever answers the phone in the production or casting office, or any other office phone should use a simple procedure:

One: Find out who is calling.

Two: Find out what they are calling about.

Three: Find out to whom the caller wishes to speak.

The person answering the phone should be polite and use friendly, cordial language like "Who may I say is calling?" and "What is this regarding?" The person answering the phone should at the same time be persistent and tenacious, even like a hockey goalie, not passing the call on until the person being called knows who is calling and why, and can take the call or not on the basis of that information. If you call big league talent agents or agencies, or top producers, you will be impressed by how smoothly the person answering the phone finds out who is calling and what the call is about. Their boss will decide whether or not to take the call. You, however, will typically get no information at all about anything from these expert phone handlers. Some phone calls are of enormous importance and the P.M., A.D., director, or producer will want to and need to handle them immediately. Getting the questions "Who is calling?" and "What is this about?" answered should easily reveal how urgent or not each call may be, and in what category of importance (or not) it belongs. Those handling the phones should not give out any information except for common sense exceptions to this general policy.

The person answering should never give out any information unless they know full well whom they are giving it to, and why that person needs to know it. Green P.A.'s and people with weak minds often feel a compulsion to answer every question that is asked, even if they do not know who is asking and why. I remember thoroughly indoctrinating a very bright P.A., a recent college graduate, in this telephone answering procedure, then about two hours later she ran into a meeting and asked breathlessly, "When do we shoot the scene in the park? Someone's on the phone who wants to know." I just looked at her in disappointment and said, "Who's calling and what's it about?" She was embarrassed, and didn't know. She realized what she had failed to do, and she went back to the phone. This kind of over-eager compulsion to answer everyone's questions are not simply annoying and time-wasting, some times it is very harmful. Once, a union called and found out where the production was shooting and some union guys went to the location and slashed the tires of all the production vehicles, including the actors' cars. This successfully intimidated and extorted the producer into hiring some union members.

In another case, a person answering the phone told an unidentified person on the phone that the director was at a small sound studio, mixing the movie. She even gave Mr. Anonymous street by street directions to the place. This sound studio was small. You needed a compass to find it. The caller walked into the studio, verified the director's identity, and served divorce papers on him. A music cutter I worked with was there. He said that the director suffered what could best be described as a suppressed nervous breakdown. This director still very much loved his wife, had *not* cheated on her, and had no idea that she was going to divorce him. He was crushed. He told the editor and mixer to finish the mix without him, then walked out of the studio and never came back.

Movie productions occasionally make and collect enemies, such as actors that are not cast, or people with locations that get messed up. Arguments and disputes arise about how much is owed or paid, or people who resent the fact that they are not part of the glamorous, exciting movie business also sometimes simply want to cause trouble for movie people. There is a saying, "You can't make an omelet without breaking a few eggs." Well, when you make a movie you may collect enemies who, if they get information about the production, can be very creative, imaginative, and persistent in how they go about causing trouble. Making movies, particularly low budget movies, is difficult. It's even more difficult with well-informed enemies who want to cause trouble.

So make sure that people answering the phone persistently and politely find out *who is calling* and *what it is about*. Have them find out whom the caller wants to speak with, then let the intended recipient of the call determine whether or not they want to speak with the caller. Do *not* let them give out information about the production except for rare common sense exceptions.

CHAPTER THIRTY-FOUR:
CALL SHEETS, PROPERTY, RELEASES,
CREW AND ACTORS CONTRACTS,
AND OTHER PAPERWORK

At the end of each day of shooting, "call sheets" that give information about the next day's shooting are typically handed out to the crew and cast. The first and often the only thing that people look at on a call sheet is the time they are called to show up on the set or in makeup, for the next day's shoot. There is a *lot* more information than that on a properly prepared call sheet. I keep a call sheet folded in my pocket when I'm directing or assistant directing. The call sheet states the scenes that are to be shot the next day, the number of pages in these scenes, the cast members in those scenes, a list of props needed for the day's shooting, what extras are needed, the time of sunrise and sunset, the cover set, what vehicles are needed, and any remarks or special instructions. Usually, a map from the Thomas Guide or an Internet map is stapled to the call sheet to show people how to get to the location. (Of course, these days those maps can be found by people with smart phones, but they still should have the paper.)

If an actor asks the director, A.D.'s, producer, or anyone else "What scenes are we shooting tomorrow?" the only safe answer is "We are shooting the scenes on the call sheet." If a foolish A.D. or director or producer answers the above question with something like "We are shooting the scenes in the living room and the kitchen," they run the risk that the call sheet might also feature a scene in the hall and one outside on the patio, and sure enough the actor would know only the lines for the living room and kitchen, but *not* the ones in the hall and on the patio, even though they were very clearly mentioned on the call sheets. You'll hear, "Nobody ever told me we were gonna shoot those scenes!" Drill this into people's heads – Which scenes are we shooting tomorrow? The ones on the call sheets!

Once when I responded to a female actor's question about what we were shooting the next day with my canned response, she told me, "I can't find those scenes. They don't give the page numbers." She meant the pages on the script. I showed her how to find scenes by using scene numbers. Scene 20 was on the call sheet. I opened the script and it was at scene 10. I continued, and flipped the script open wider and wider. Soon I was at Scene 18. I thumbed through page to Scene 19, then "Here's Scene 20." She got the idea that Scene 20 was between Scene 19 and Scene 21. It didn't matter what page it was on.

People need to be comfortable in finding scenes using scene numbers without page numbers. It will make call sheets, shooting schedules, and other production paperwork seem a lot friendlier to them. Signed property releases need to be obtained for all locations before those locations shoot, preferably well before they shoot or are scheduled. Crew and actors and extras need to sign contracts. These and other production documents can be found on Internet sites and specialized stationery stores that cater to movie productions. On one low level production where I was supervising and sometimes making the call sheets, I suspected that nobody was reading the call sheet beyond their personal call time, so in the last section of the call sheet for the next day I put down a *python*. Nobody noticed. The next day I put *a purple python*. Nobody noticed. Then I wrote *twelve pythons,* and after that, *twelve dancing gay pythons. Nobody said a thing.* I concluded that nobody was reading the call sheets, and that was why a lot of people were puzzled about things or asked questions that were answered clearly on the call sheet. Don't let people waste your time – *make them read the call sheet.*

CHAPTER THIRTY-FIVE:
LONG DAYS AND LONGER NIGHTS

When I was at UCLA, I read a pamphlet about Henry Ford, the great automobile manufacturer. I showed the pamphlet to a professor who was an expert on Ford and the 1920s. He'd never heard the story in the pamphlet but he said it might or might not be true. This much is fact: before Ford changed it, the common workday was ten hours, not eight, and the common work week was six days, not five. It is also fact that Ford went to an eight hour day and had three shifts of a total of 24 hours so his factory never shut down, rather than two shifts of ten hours with four hours idle. Ford's major problem was to make enough cars so that everyone in the world who wanted a Ford could own one. Here's the story in question that may or may not be true. According to that pamphlet, Ford did a study to see if there was a common denominator to production accidents that either seriously injured someone or shut down the assembly line, and if there was a common denominator to the making of "lemon" cars that dissatisfied customers. What this study supposedly indicated was that a large number of accidents occurred and lemon cars were made by workers who worked more than eight and nine hours. According to the pamphlet, this "closed the deal" for Ford and caused him to switch from a ten-hour workday to an eight-hour workday.

Whether this story is true or not, I have noticed a drop of energy and efficiency and speed of work of movie crews, casts, A.D.'s, directors, and others after eight or nine hours and an even more serious drop after ten hours of work. Low budget movies typically shoot for around ten or eleven hours and have half an hour or one hour for lunch and half an hour or hour for wrap and a twelve-hour turnaround, usually from the end of wrap to the next day's call time.

It is very important to get the first shot of the day as early as possible, as soon as possible! Hours can be wasted before the first shot is made. This wastes some of the crew and cast's most productive and freshest time. How soon the forward, productive flow of shots and momentum is started can have everything to do with how much gets done that day and how long or overly long a day is. A veteran A.D. once told me to watch the crew after lunch. He said, "Crews slow down after lunch. Watch 'em, they're still digesting their food." It's true. It's usually not until mid or late afternoon that the crew, cast, and director are back to speed after lunch, and then they are not that far from eight hours of work. The A.D. and director should shoot as much as they can as early in the morning portion of the day as they can. This requires a director that has done his or her homework, and who came to the set prepared and ready to shoot a movie and an A.D. that knows what he or she is doing and moves people!

When you see a production that lets hours pass, from call time, before they get the first shot or only gets a few or couple of shots before lunch, you know that production will soon be in *serious* time trouble. Some directors, particularly young and new directors, are scared and thrilled to be directing a movie and their bodies get pumped full of adrenaline, so these people can work around the clock *for a while*. If these directors do not have their homework in good shape, they often try to solve their inefficiency problems with long shooting days or extra-long shooting days that turn into even longer shooting nights. The crew is *not* running on adrenaline. Some of the cast may, but only for a while. Eventually, this long day and longer night "solution" always breaks down one way or another, and there's almost always one kind of hell or another to pay. Once you pass ten hours of work, you start to get noticeably less per hour done.

On really long shooting days, meaning 15, 16, 17, or 18 hour days, the crew may be getting half as much per hour or one-third as much done per hour as they would have done per hour earlier in the day. The law of diminishing returns applies strongly to these kinds of situations. You are burning up the crew and cast, and your own physical energy, goodwill, morale, good humor, and ability to think and act correctly. You are getting less work done per hour and paying out more and more in irreplaceable human resources. I have worked on these ultra-long, virtually around-the-clock shoots and I've also presided over them as a director. They are part of a lot of low budget moviemaking. They are accurately depicted in some of the scenes in the movie *Ed Wood*. They are more horrific than a lot of horror movies. They should be avoided as much as they can, but sometimes they can't be. Nevertheless, they are "cruel and unusual punishment.."

There was a case where a camera operator working a horrifically long day fell asleep driving home and was killed. I once almost fell asleep while driving home on the freeway, after one ultra-long day near the end of a shoot on another movie. On another movie, after an eighteen hour day, the shooting had to wait hours while they rigged a monster to be blown up in front of several cameras, some running in extreme slow motion. It took them a few hours to rig the monster. I laid down on the cement floor and told the A.D. to wake me when the explosives were fully placed and they were ready to shoot the scene. I was so tired I went straight to sleep on the set's cement floor, with people walking and talking all around me.

It would be a lie to deny that some movie crew members get through these long shooting days by using cocaine. That's not a good idea, no matter how good they think they feel. I know of one case of a guy in the art department who was running on cocaine, working around the clock, and he blew out his heart and died. Crews are not as scared or thrilled as directors and usually are not nearly as full of adrenaline, so they go for other chemicals, as well as coffee, energy drinks, and the like.

Start getting shots quickly, as close to call time as you can. Shoot as much as you can as early in the shooting day as you can. The later that you shoot the more human capital it will cost you and the less you will get done for that human capital. Long, overly long, and brutally long, punishing days are not a solution. They are a disaster and should be avoided if at all possible. So how do you avoid them?

By being prepared, really and truly prepared!

You need to be ready, willing, able, and *eager* to start blocking, lighting, rehearsing, and shooting as soon as you hit the set and by having an A.D. who shares this "I'm here to do it" mindset.

CHAPTER THIRTY-SIX:
THE ON AGAIN, OFF AGAIN
TANGO MAMBO CHA CHA CHA

The one thing that no money person ever said to me was, "Don't worry, you are going to make this movie, for sure, so take the next few months to prepare as best you can, and make the best movie that you can." No money person seemed to realize that it was smart to provide some security and peace of mind to the creative people that would actually make the movie that the money person was financing, and the only thing in the universe that could return their money and make them a profit is the movie that these creative people would make.

Money people seem not to realize that ping-ponging the heads of creative people back and forth with "on again, off again" talk and actions and spinning creative people around until they're dizzy with threats and uncertainties only wastes the *valuable, finite, physical, mental*, and *creative energies* that are needed to make the movie, the very vehicle for profit upon which investors money rides. One man on a movie that I was directing and co-producing suddenly, about a week before the first day of shooting, demanded that his girlfriend be cast as the female lead in the movie. That would have been a disaster. It would have frankly destroyed the movie. His girlfriend was a very nice person but she was not a trained or professional actor, and I think she did not even care about acting. Why did this money man want his girlfriend to play the female lead in the movie when she didn't' even care about acting? The money man was friends with a very, very big, ultra-famous studio and corporate executive and movie producer whose wife was a very professional and successful, highly trained actress who had appeared in some mega-sized box office successes. Mr. Money Man thought that because his famous Hollywood producer friend had a wife who had the lead in big movies he could have his girlfriend play the lead in a movie even if she was not a trained or experienced actor and did not even care much about acting. Yes, this is a true story!

He was livid when I refused to cast her. If his girlfriend did not get cast in the lead, he threatened to pull the plug on a movie that my partner and I had worked on for about a year. We had commitments out to people all over town. If the movie "crapped out" a few days before shooting started we would look like world-class flakes. It was a grim, sickening situation. Either we had to put an unqualified person in a lead role and perhaps ruin the movie, or we could have the production shut down days before shooting was scheduled to start.

When I saw *Mulholland Drive*, and the money men gangsters demanded that the director cast a certain actress, and they pulled the plug on the movie, and when the director smashed their car with a golf club and they sent goons after him, I thought, *This is déjà vu; I've lived part of this* (albeit at a lower intensity). Artists under the domination and threat and captivity of money men, or gangsters is the major theme of both *Blue Velvet* and *Mulholland Drive*. Director David Lynch knew what a lot of directors experience, and he put it onscreen.

In my aforementioned situation, my casting assistant and I had discovered a truly excellent young actress to play the lead role. She would later go on to be a bit of a movie star, appearing in movies with people like Tom Cruise, Paul Newman, Cliff Robertson, and she worked with major directors like Martin Scorcese. She had a very strong screen presence. The camera loved her. When she walked into the casting office she looked like many other young women in that place, but when we turned on the camera and she performed her audition, her star potential was so obvious I felt like I could hear the screen shouting, "Cast her! What are you waiting for!?" At the time, she was barely "discovered" and we could get her for union scale.

My partner wanted me to cast the money man's girlfriend. He said, "One actress is the same as the other." Of course, he was contemplating how deep into the garbage pile of dreams gone wrong we would be dumped if the production collapsed on the verge or shooting. Finally, I resolved this dilemma by making a one-take videotape of an audition scene of the real actress with star potential. She "nailed it" and winked to the casting assistant when she left. She knew, and everyone knew, that her ability would show on the tape. After that, I shot 17 takes of Mr. Money Man's girlfriend, and did not try to direct her at all. I just let her flounder around like a beached porpoise. Every take was as bad or worse than the last or next one. We gave that tape to the two brothers who were the money men, and they watched the tape in private. Mr. Money Man did not come out of the viewing room. I think he was too embarrassed to face us. His brother came out looking like a brontosaurus had kicked him in the groin.

"That girl you guys want is quite an actress," he said. "Do you have another role my brother's girlfriend might be right for?" I told him I had just the role, and I did. I cast the girlfriend in a small supporting role, and she worked very hard and behaved very professionally, turning in an okay performance that was at least adequate. At the wrap party, the key grip, who had become the love interest of the movie's leading lady, gave me and the movie's D.P. a combination lecture and critique of how we'd done our jobs. He so offended the D.P. That D.P. never worked with him again. He said to me, "Your homework was a bit lax." He was right; it was. I was still inexperienced when I made that movie, but I felt like shouting at him, "Do you have any f*ing idea how many hours of my time and how much of my energy was spent jumping through b.s. hoops for these money men?" I felt like shouting a lot of things at him, but it was the wrap party and there were more important and happy things to do than educate that key grip into the realities of how movies that provide jobs to people like him actually get made.

One movie that I was directing, not producing, just directing, was financed by two letters of credit, and a Canadian producer was putting up cash. The letters of credit were coming from a foreign sales company and a home video distribution company. There were a total of four front line lawyers involved, and more in the background. One of these "front line" lawyers represented a foreign sales company that would put up a letter of credit. The other lawyer represented a home video distributor that would also put up a letter of credit, and another lawyer represented a big Canadian bank that would actually advance cash on the basis of these two letters of credit, and the Canadian producer of this movie also had a lawyer. All of these legal eagles were supposedly at the top of their profession.

If the intention was to make the deal work and make a movie from which their clients could easily and eventually benefit, then from the lawyers' actions and what they wrote on various documents, you could easily conclude that if brain power was nuclear energy, all of these lawyers together did not have enough of it to turn on a flashlight. If the intention was to shut down the movie, kill it before it was born so that their clients would not endure any risk while covering the lawyer's backsides with lead-plated shields, then they were mentally challenged, highly over-paid, useless turkeys who got in the way of anyone that wanted to do something productive and face the actual risks in making a movie.

Anyway, these four lawyers had managed to grind the financing of the movie to a stop, putting it at a total impasse because what they had written in their various documents so overly protected their clients that they endangered and infringed on what was fair or sane for the other parties to the deal. I was in Toronto. I'd been doing pre-production there for about four weeks, and we were set to start shooting in about a week. The Canadian producer told me that he wasn't sure the movie would get shot because the lawyers could not work out documents that satisfied everyone. The producer had been advancing the money for pre-production out of his own pocket anticipating the finalization of financing and the inflow of the other two parties' money that would cover the cost of making the movie. Now, this Canadian producer was afraid he'd be left on the hook for pre-production expenses for a movie that would collapse just before shooting started, and would not get made. I asked if it was okay if I talked to the lawyers and looked at the documents. He said, "Please do! You are the only one who know all three parties."

That was true. *I had put the deal together*. I brought the home video and foreign sales distributors into the deal and the foreign sales distributor brought in the Canadian producer, who knew of the movies I'd made in Canada. I'd been working for over a year to develop and bring the movie to the point where it was about to become a reality, or a disaster, so I left pre-production to do the over-paid lawyers' jobs for them. I really wanted to make this movie.

I'm not a lawyer, but I have dealt with a lot of contracts and rewritten some. I also speak, read, and write English fluently. In a burst of some of the finest creative writing I've ever done, I rewrote the letters of credit and the other documents so they protected the legitimate interests and rights of each party and did not over-reach and infringe on the legitimate rights of other parties. Before the impasse and before I went to Canada, I had deal memos from the major parties and "strong verbal agreements" from all parties. As Sam Goldwyn said, however, "If you got it on paper, you got a prayer; if not, you got nothin' but air."

I went back to pre-production and got ready to shoot, then began principal photography. At rushes on the second day of shooting, the Canadian producer told me that the letter of credit from the foreign sales company had not yet arrived, and he was still covering with his own cash. The home video company's letter of credit had arrived and was in place just as they'd promised, but the foreign sales company was playing a game of "lead butt" and the mass of their ass was endangering the production. So I called them. They'd distributed one of my movies and I knew them. They were the first place I had taken the script and when they got involved it was the beginning of the entire deal. They'd told me, "Don't worry, the letter of credit will be there." I reminded them that we had already been shooting for two days. I got a "Yeah, yeah, don't worry." So after the first day of the *second* week of shooting, the Canadian producer told me that the foreign sales company's letter of credit still had not arrived and he had given them an ultimatum. If the letter of credit didn't arrive by Friday noon, he said he would go to his money people and raise money against the foreign market and cut the lead butts out of the deal, and take two-thirds of the movie for his investors. He really liked the rushes, and how I was directing. Well, the letter of credit arrived Friday morning about an hour before noon. The Canadian producer had to threaten to "go nuclear" to get the foreign sales company off its butt. At this point, they had been involved with the production for over six months, yet their letter of credit only arrived *after two weeks of shooting* on a movie that had a scheduled four-week production.

This foreign sales company had distributed one of my earlier movies. They knew I'd made a movie that Warner Bros. had distributed and I'd made a number of other movies that had done well in the world market. They knew that I knew how to make a professional, commercially viable movie on a low budget. They knew that the movie was based on a very commercial concept, and they had likely checked the movie's concept and commercial aspects with their clients (people around the world who normally bought their movies). Some of those people had bought my earlier movies, so they knew that there was interest and that they could make sales. In short, the level of risk they were facing with my movie was minimal. The way that they were investing, with a letter of credit, meant that they did not have to come up with cash. The letter of credit would be deducted from the company's credit line at its bank.

I finished shooting the movie before December 31st and immediately the first thing I cut in editing was a promo about ten minutes long. I sent it to the foreign sales company. They took it to the American Film Market in late January and started making sales, and collecting letters of credit. The exact value of the letters of credit, deposits, and other commitments, or interest that were collected from the promo reel alone, I do not know. I was told by an unreliable source that it was between $100,000 and $250,000. Whatever the return from sales and commitments based on the promo actually were, they seriously mitigated the foreign sales company's risk (which I believe was under $200,000), and made it clear that they would ultimately not lose money. Five months after they invested, the finished movie was delivered at the Cannes Film Festival, and many sales were made, letters of credit were issued by foreign buyers, deposits were deposited, and cash purchases were transacted. The movie was no longer a debit to the foreign sales company's credit line. The income they were collecting was boosting their credit line and bank account. My point is that money people often make things a lot harder for creative people than they should be, and they often do it with very little justification.

I was talking with an assistant editor on one of my movies and I told him that the lead actor in the movie had tried to get me fired during the first day of shooting. This was on a movie I'd cowritten, directed, and financed. This was the first and last time that had ever happened to me, but the assistant editor matter of factly said, "So what else is new." He considered it a fairly common occurrence for someone to try to get the director fired or to try to fire the director during the first week of shooting. *I was shocked!* He'd worked on some big studio productions and he told me about some incidents involving fairly famous directors and movies where there had been attempts, in various ways to (metaphorically speaking) stick a knife in the director's back during the first week of shooting, thus putting the production's future in question. It was usually only a temporary hitch, but still, this type of thing is also part of the "on again, off again, tango mambo cha cha cha."

One producer who had produced quite a lot of movies and TV shows told me that when he's on a set and he hears the film running through the camera, then he knows he's making a movie. Until then the wind, or someone's change of mind, can blow everything away or delay everything and force one to start all over. Some times, money people seem to take a perverse pleasure in ping-ponging creative people's heads back and forth with on again, off again antics. They may not be able to actually make a movie themselves but they can sure stop one from being made, by pulling the money out of it. Some times, very unfortunately, the money people and the creative people seem to be on separate teams, playing against each other. It would be a lot more productive and pleasant and enjoyable if the money people and the creative folks were on the same team, both pursuing the same goal of making the best possible movie, on budget, on schedule, and playing only against all obstacles to that goal together, not against each other.

Ted Post told me of how he'd turned own an opportunity to direct the iconic Clint Eastwood movie *Dirty Harry* because he was already committed to another movie that he'd been told was financed. Well, after turning down that chance, he walked into a room for the first meeting on this other movie that he'd been told was financed and one of the producers said, "We got half the money, can you get the other half?" Ted told me he wanted to throw that producer right out the window of a high-rise building. Usually, when someone says that they have half the money for a movie, it really means that they *do not have half* and they want you to raise half so that they can try to raise the other half against your half after you've raised it.

On TV, I saw Sir David Lean, the director of *Lawrence of Arabia* and *Doctor Zhivago* and other acclaimed movies, decry the way he and other filmmakers were jerked around until the very last minute, not knowing whether their movie will be green-lighted or dumped. I was amazed that this b.s. even affected a director as great as David Lean. Kudos to you, Sir David.

Here's one case I know of where a director took bold and effective action, which I much admire, to positively resolve an "on again, off again tango mambo cha cha cha" situation. Las von Trier was in pre-production on his art movie master work *Dancer in the Dark*. At that point, von Trier's movies were financed by co-productions of several European movie companies, and they were ping-ponging back and forth, negotiating and delaying, and the money to shoot the movie was not arriving despite the fact that von Trier was ready to shoot, and in terms of broad general agreement the movie was supposed to be financed. It's my understanding that these co-production parties were simply engaging in the same kind of b.s. games that parties to movie deals often play. The movie that von Trier made previous to *Dancer in the Dark* was *Breaking the Waves*. *L.A. Weekly* called it a masterpiece and von Trier's best movie. I agree. It was also financed via a complicated co-production deal. The video box I have has a list of awards and honors the movie won. They cover the back of the box and including a much-deserved Best Female Actor Oscar nomination for Emily Watson.

Breaking the Waves was a serious success on the art movie circuit, particularly in Europe. There was no valid reason for the money people, the co-production people, to delay. Von Trier, I believe, saw what I and many other moviemakers have experienced. If you are "idle" while these money people diddle around, the production can lose momentum and fall apart – in this case even before shooting would start. Von Trier's solution is something that I admire enormously. *He mortgaged his house and picked up a video camera and began videoing the movie himself.* This is a bold application of "this train is leaving the station, with or without you" principle of financing a movie that I detail in the section of this book about financing.

It worked for von Trier. *Dancer in the Dark* won the Grand Prize and Best Female Actor awards at the Cannes Film Festival, and an Oscar nomination for its lead female actor Bjork, who gave a performance that was perfect. *Dancer in the Dark* was one of the most successful "break out" art movies of its time.

Sometimes in order to get a movie made you have to "grab the bullshit by the horns" and "strike before the iron freezes." A willingness and an ability to do these things is often the difference between people who make movies and people who *almost* make movies.

One of the key things about my movie *Plague* that made it such a successful and smooth-running film to work on was that the money man just raised the money and did his other duties as executive producer and *did not* interfere with the production or creative people. We did not have much time or money to make that movie, but lack of b.s. interference from the money man more than compensated for the very tight burden and schedule. On that movie, the money man and the creative people were on the same team, and that was a big plus!

On the first day of shooting, only $40,000 of the movie's $200,000 budget was in the bank. The money man promised to bust his butt to get the rest in the bank. The morning of the first day of shooting, I took the cinematographer aside and told him the true facts of the movie's financial situation. I said, "If the money man has trouble raising the rest of the money next week or shortly thereafter, you and I may be the whole crew."

He responded, "Count me in, boss."

Positive people with positive attitudes like that can make it a lot more likely that you will make a movie, more so than piles of money in the hands of people who want to play games with promises.

CHAPTER THIRTY-SEVEN:
SOMETIMES IF YOU WANT PEOPLE TO KNOW THINGS AND DO THINGS YOU HAVE TO TELL THEM AND SHOW THEM THOSE THINGS

In addition to the two major production meetings I discussed earlier, small, short, brief production meetings should be held with actors, crew, the art department, props, A.D.'s, staff, special FX, sound people, and others. Tell the people what you want them to do or not to do, and how you want them to do it. They are *not* psychic, even if you're making a paranormal movie! They will not glean your desires, intentions, and instructions out of the air if you don't state them clearly and make sure that they are understood. Here's just one small example.

There is a term that relates to actors positions in relation to the camera. It's called "cheating" and means that the actor will "cheat" their face or body more toward a position where the camera can see more of their face or body than would normally be seen if they were talking to the other actor or actors in real life. If you want to see a good example of "cheating" watch the scene in *Clerks* where Dante's original girlfriend Caitlin returns and they have a long dialogue scene in the video store. You see their faces when you need to because they "cheat" their positions. Many acting coaches or teachers in many acting classes have the actors play their scenes right at the other actor, and never inform their students that if they get a role in a movie they may have to consider the importance of the *camera seeing their face* some times, and the importance of actors positioning their body and face in proper relationship to the camera, not just throwing their performance at the other actor and ignoring the movie's viewers. It does no good to tell an actor to "cheat" if they do *not* know what it means to cheat and you have not explained it to them. This is the kind of thing that should be handled in the meeting with actors.

One occupational hazard that befalls many directors is that when they start directing a movie they believe that they are surrounded by a lot of stupid people, and occasionally they are, but more commonly the director suffers from the fact that the director *can* read the director's mind, and the people around him or her *cannot*, so when things are moving fast and pressure is high people around the director who have *not* been told exactly what to do can seem really stupid to the director, because to the director, what should be done is obvious.

Early in my directing career, there were times when I felt like shouting, "Can't you damn dumbbells just see what should be done and do it?!" Well, they can't and that's one of the reasons that the director's job exists. I felt like shouting, "Do I have to tell you everything?!" As time passed, and I got more experience I realized that, yes, you do have to tell them *everything*. That's why you're the director. It's part of your job!

The demand for clear, easy to understand, and almost impossible to misunderstand communication, about lots of things to lots of people by the director is *enormous*. The demand for almost constant accurate communication is one of the most exhausting things about directing. I've seen struggling directors who can't communicate well and don't communicate well, or very much, just get twisted into a throbbing mass of frustration, because nothing works, nothing is good, nothing is how the director wanted it, etc. Often these directors are lacking in communication because hey lack a clear vision of the movie in their mind or want to be vague to avoid responsibility, and want an easy path to blame others. The people around these types of struggling directors or neophyte directors also get very frustrated because they often don't know what they should do exactly unless *someone tells them*.

The only "someone" who can tell them is a real director with a clear vision of the movie in his or her mind who can and does communicate that vision in terms of clear decisions and instructions that are so ultra-clear that they cannot be misunderstood. When a director communicates clearly and well with the people around him or her, it's amazing how quickly that director becomes so much less stupid in the eyes of his crew and cast, and they become much less stupid in his or her eyes.

CHAPTER THIRTY-EIGHT:
MOMENTUM AND INERTIA,
WINNING AND LOSING

Inertia: Lack of activity; sluggish; that property of matter by virtue of which it tends to remain at rest, if resting, or to move uniformly in a straight line, if moving.

Inert: Having no power of motion or action; lifeless; sluggish.

Momentum: Force of a moving body; impetus (force of motion); the quantity of motion in a body as measured by the product of its mass multiplied by its velocity.

These definitions are largely based on physics, but there is also psychological, spiritual, creative, team or group and individual and leadership inertia and momentum. Two of the major tasks of a movie director and/or producer are often to overcome inertia and/or to maintain momentum. During some days of shooting, inertia seems to dominate and you are basically battling inertia all day. Other days are propelled forward by momentum. Other days of shooting start as days of inertia and become days of momentum, and the reverse also happens.

The creative artists, including the filmmaker, director, producer, screenwriter, actor, and cinematographer, basically are in conflict with reality. Each of them wants to make something new that was not a part of existing reality when their movie project was begun. They want to add their work of art to reality, and they will often find that *reality has its own special kind of inertia*. Earlier in this book I quoted Robert J. Ringer about the importance of acknowledging reality. I'll say it again; acknowledging reality is not the same as surrendering to reality, submitting to reality, being intimidated by reality, or being reality's slave. Sun Tzu, the author of *The Art of War* and a great theoretician on the nature of reality, said "Know yourself and know your enemy and you can be in a hundred battles and never be in danger." Knowing what reality actually is and is not is key to using reality and your creative imagination to defeat existing reality and make something (a work of art) that did not exist as a part of reality before the artist began to create.

Reality tends to move forward and perpetuate and sustain itself, into the future and sustain things as they were. It tends to want to make things as they will be the same as things as they are and things as they were. Reality tends to oppose not only new creation; it also tends to oppose destruction. The military and warriors usually clash with reality from the "other side of the coin" in war. They are trying to put things *out of existence*, to change reality *not to include the enemy any more*. They want to destroy the enemy, its weapons, fortifications, and supplies. The gun and bomb are the inverse of the camera; the gun and bomb are made to destroy something, to put it out of existence, to remove it from reality. The camera is the opposite, made to bring something new into existence. It makes images that are projected for viewing, causing things to exist on an additional level or levels, thus brining about a new reality.

Although the artist is often in conflict with reality and reality's inertia, it is the artist that is the custodian of reality and creating in real time what will be future reality. Wars also do this. The

Trojan war, via *The Iliad* and *The Odyssey*, brought alive the magnificent reality of ancient Greece. The reality of Greece gave birth of democracy, drama, philosophy, science, and forms of math, architecture, and art. The Greeks moved civilization from primitive barbarism toward civilization. The military, the warrior, and the moviemaker have similar conflicts with reality. When I watch the History Channel's depictions of famous battles, they often talk about the weather and the time of sunrise and sunset (items that are also on movie call sheets) and are major concerns of filmmakers as well as generals. Other concerns that the military and the filmmaker share are the delivery of food, the movement of equipment, teamwork, leadership, time, distance, dealing with the unforeseen, planning, strategy, the execution of planning and strategy, morale, chain of command, imagination, and the need to improvise and deal with things as they are, all to achieve a goal.

I once heard a person who knew quite a lot about war talk about the intense naval shelling and aerial bombardment of Japanese positions before amphibious landings, and he said that watching these bombardments, you would think that no human being could survive them, and that all the Japanese would be dead before the Marines went ashore. But when the Marines did go ashore, the Japanese were still very much alive and willing and able to kill Marines. This is how much reality, and the inertia of reality, protects the status quo. It keeps people alive during a hellish shelling and bombardment because they are part of reality's status quo, the way things were, before the assault on existing reality began. Those who would or are embarked on making a movie would do well to notice how seriously the inertia of reality defends the status quo even against tons of high explosives.

The defense of the existing status quo by the inertia of reality is not less determined against the creation of new works of art, particularly new works of art that might challenge existing reality or realities that it is defending. They are like the continued existence of enemy soldiers who are part of reality's composition. *When you make a movie the inertia of reality will oppose you!*

Making a movie is *not* an easy task. Making a successful low budget movie is a major challenge and a major accomplishment, if achieved. Earlier, I discussed how some shooting days begin dominated by inertia, and finish up as days propelled by momentum, and the reverse also happens. One of the most dramatic shooting days in which I ever participated started as a day dominated by inertia, and inertia so strong and grinding that it almost intensified to a point where it could stop production and killed the day, and then it turned into a day where momentum was created by sheer force of will in direct unrelenting, Don Quixote style, opposition to reality and its inertia and then into momentum that raised morale, coalesced a team where before there were individuals ready to accept, defeat, the defeat that the inertia of reality had for them. That team and the momentum that they built then rolled over reality and its inertia like a steamroller.

That day began when the entire movie company – the crew, actors, staff – left Toronto before sunrise and traveled to Hamilton, Ontario (a several hour trip) for a day of exterior filming. It was late December, the air temperature was about twenty degrees. The humidity was thick; both Toronto and Hamilton are near the lake. Condensation forms on the roads and freezes with that kind of temperature and humidity. It made the roads where we planned to do a precision driving car chase and car stunt scenes slick and borderline unsafe.

The day began with lots of inertia. The crew and I were tired. I don't remember exactly what shooting had gone before that, but whatever it was, it had taken its toll. The sluggish definition of inertia really applied to the start of this day. I got a few shots in the morning that were okay, not excellent or special, and by lunch I was not just behind schedule, the head stunt driver and stunt coordinator told me that the road was slick, and he'd slid a bit a few times and almost lost it. That doesn't aid the digestion of your lunch when what's scheduled after lunch is some important precision driving and a dramatically significant car stunt, and then a move to a location next to a canyon for a sequence that culminated with a car going off a cliff and falling one hundred and fifty feet.

Sure enough, it was not long after lunch until I bogged down trying to shoot the car stunt. On one partial rehearsal, a driver somewhat lost control and slid across the road and finished with two wheels in the ditch at the side of the road. It was not major, but it seemed like kind of a bad omen of things to come. I was almost terminally behind schedule at this point. At this time of year in Canada, the sun never gets very high in the sky – it just hangs a bit above the horizon, even at midday. To a movie director like me, it was maddening to shoot a whole day of exteriors as the sun seemed to hang there mocking me as if to say it would set before I made my day. If you fail to get a day that is a big travel day, the consequences can be major. If I failed to get even a few shots at these locations in Hamilton, it would mean that we would have to travel all the way back to Hamilton for those shots, and that would destroy the whole next shooting day, all over a few shots.

Failing to get the day on a big travel day is not the same as missing a few shots when you are going to be back in the same location tomorrow or for a few days. In that case, all you have to do is shoot a few extra shots tomorrow or some time in the next few days. I was looking at going over schedule and over budget, and Canadian movies need to complete principal photography by December 31 for the investors to get their proper tax consideration. Our schedule was butted right up next to New Year's Eve; there was no real margin for error. The conditions of shooting this car stunt were particularly challenging. I called for the cameras to be set up in a farmer's field next to the intersection where the stunt would happen. This field was largely covered with very slick, brittle ice and much of that was frozen over pockets of air. It would shatter under your foot like a pane of glass and your foot would plunge on down to the ground, giving you lots of great chances to twist an ankle. At an air temperature of twenty degrees everyone was wearing lots of clothes and gloves, which slowed everything down. Gloves need to be taken off to do detailed work with the camera for short periods, but they need to be generally worn or you'll lose feeling in your fingers.

While setting up the cameras in this field with ice crunching every time we moved, Lady Rotten Snot, a "leader of the revolution" and second camera assistant made snide comments to other crew members and to me, and provoked a response from me. This was the absolute low point of the day. She thought I was "done for" and that she could safely and happily stick a knife in my back. The inertia of reality sent its little minion to distract me. Crunching ice everywhere, a special nuisance for guys carrying cameras and camera equipment, apparently bone chilling cold, and slick roads, and being behind schedule to near fatal degree were not enough for the troublemaker. Like a circling vulture, she just had to take her shot. After my exchange with her, I realized that I was bouncing off rock bottom. As I watched the stunt drivers' rehearsals go wrong, I realized that I was very close to big trouble at that point. I doubt that even one member of the crew would have bet 10¢ at 100 to 1 odds that I would "get the day." Things were so bad that I knew I needed to do something different and not just follow routine. As I watched the next stunt driver's bad rehearsal, I tried to watch it as a dispassionate observer, not as a participant trapped in the situation with all the distracting emotions that involved. I tried to watch it from a POV emotionally removed from the situation.

I saw that the lead stunt driver was moving too fast in the "run up" to the point just before the stunt. It looked bad because he was slowing down just before the stunt. Earlier, when I discussed shooting action and stunts, I introduced the idea of making things actually safer so that they could be made to look more dangerous. I called the drivers on the walkie talkie and ran across the icy field to the road, crunching and shattering lots of ice, and told them what was wrong and what I wanted to do. The D.P. gave final instructions to the camera operators, and then grabbed a handheld camera and hopped into the lead driver's car. He squashed himself down to be out of view, getting ready to shoot the driver's POV during the stunt. I ran back to the "A" and "B" cameras and gave them instructions, then got in the back of one of the stunt cars and scrunched down out of sight.

The stunt went perfectly. The cars barely missed each other. One car slid across the road and through the intersection just as planned. Suddenly, I had all the shots I needed. This sequence that had caused so much grief was now history. I realized that it was theoretically possible that I could still get my day, but it was only a very slight, physically possible that I could pull it off. I grabbed the first A.D., a personable and somewhat experienced young guy who was always trying hard to be professional. I barked out commands. "Get the picture vehicle and put the camera, extra film, the D.P., the lead actor, the first camera assistant and me in it and we'll drive to the next location and start shooting! You round up the vehicles and the rest of the crew and caravan to the next location!"

I told him I would show him something that he'd never seen before, and that we were going to get the day. I got his agreement on that, and we set about following the axiom of "Dare to struggle, dare to win." We drove to the second location and shot the remaining daylight shots very rapidly, about half a normal day's work in an hour. The last daylight shot was to send a car off a cliff, as I mentioned earlier. We had a very close call when I spotted people at the bottom of the canyon approaching where the car would land, but I managed to avert that looming disaster and we sent the car off the cliff before losing sunlight! Then we shot a few more shots after sunset, and got the day.

My A.D.'s, the crew, and the lead actor had not really been with me when it looked like I would not get the day. It was like they all felt we were on a losing team. When things began to change and it looked like we had a chance to win, however, despite horrific odds, attitudes changed. Morale spiked upward and everyone quit being a part of the inertia of failure that I was struggling against. They all joined in with me and became part of the momentum I'd created and they added to it. The feeling sustained and we all rode the moment forward until we got all the daylight shots. After that, morale and team spirit was very high.

The day had started with inertia very much in control, and it finished with a very strong momentum that basically ended up being sustained for the rest of the shoot. President John Kennedy said, "Victory has a thousand fathers, but defeat is always an orphan." The sometimes successful revolutionary Che Guevera said that without a vanguard, an army is paralyzed and will not move forward, but an army with a moving vanguard will follow that vanguard. The director, the D.P., the A.D.'s, and some times the producer usually form a production's vanguard and move it forward. On the day just discussed, at a key point I was the lone leader of the vanguard, moving everything forward by the force of my will.

Being the only person on a production pushing it forward puts you in direct contact with all the inertia opposing that production and draws energy out of a wide open faucet. Once I pushed a stake into inertia's heart, others filled in my vanguard and soon everyone on the production doing anything important was trying to assist. Once a dragon is mortally wounded, everyone wants to throw a spear and finish it off, and once it's dead everyone wants to put a foot on its chest. If you direct or produce a low budget movie, it is very likely that you or your partners will crash into one of these head-to-head confrontations with inertia, and inertia will either slow the production, crash and stop it, or damage it, or you will break inertia's stranglehold on the production. By defeating it you can create momentum. If you're smart and lucky, you will sustain and ride that momentum to the end of the production and never again allow inertia to get back in control.

I have a unique view of *Ocean's Eleven*, the Steven Soderbergh and George Clooney version. I view the movie as an analogy of how a successful movie gets made. First, you have an idea, then you make a plan, followed by getting a partner who agrees to dream your dream with you and help make that dream a reality. Next, you seek money to finance the making of the dream into reality. Then everyone tells you your plan won't work and they try to crap all over your dream. After that, you get the money, enabling you to recruit a crew and cast that you lead to create an alternative reality that competes with and defeats the existing reality. Then it's up to you to make your reality prevail so that you win, and get paid. That's roughly the plot of *Ocean's Eleven*, and that's the progression of how a lot of successful movies get made. The beginning of Act One in *Ocean's Eleven* deals with various forms of inertia being overcome, and by Act Three the principal actors are pulling off the "caper" and riding the momentum created by their prevailing new reality as they roll toward victory – or at least a kind of victory.

CHAPTER THIRTY-NINE:
COURTESY AND RESPECT FOR OTHERS
WHOSE JOB IS NOT LIKE YOURS
BUT IS EQUALLY ESSENTIAL TO MAKING A MOVIE

Stanislavski believe that good manners were an important part of being a professional artist. Many people do radically different jobs to get a movie made, so it helps to try to understand them from the perspective they bring to their particular job. A gaffer and D.P. that worked on a number of my movies was later nominated as a CNN hero for spectacular good works and invention that dramatically improved the lives of hundreds of thousands of people in Africa. He told me that you could always tell a movie crew and cast when they walked into a restaurant because no other activity would draw together so many people who were so different in type. He was right; this is true of most movies I've worked on. When you make a movie, you will be involved with people doing very different activities than yours. Their job qualifications and activities may be very different than your own. Often, some of them will work while you rest, and then rest while you work. The peak point of intensity of some jobs will occur when you're coasting along easily. You may never have done some of their jobs, or not even be able to do them. Thus you might not have first-hand understanding of the demands of those jobs or their supporting rituals or conventions.

That segment of the mainstream media that feeds on celebrities like biological parasites had a field day once because they got an audiotape of Christian Bale (who played "Batman") on the set of a Terminator movie "going off" at the movie's D.P. because that D.P. moved into Bale's eye line for a second time to adjust a light *during a performance*. The reaction in the media to this audiotape was virtually all anti-Bale, as people questioned what was wrong with him. My reaction was exactly the opposite. The media people were civilians to moviemaking. Though they seemed to think they were exactly right in the situation, they demonstrably knew little about what goes on in the making of a movie. I doubt any of them had ever been on a set, yet they could point a finger with certainty. The truth is, it is common courtesy for crew people to say out of the actor's eye line (where the actor is looking) during takes. It is very hard for me to imagine that a D.P. who had risen to the level of working on a major studio movie did not know this convention thoroughly.

My D.P.s always want to be tweaking (slightly adjusting) lights or the "flags" (flaps on the lights) that partly block a light, to add nuance and detail to the lighting setup. On one movie I was directing a D.P. accidentally tripped over a cable, causing a light to spin during a rehearsal. The A.D. joke, "That's Joe, always tweaking." Most everyone got the joke. For a D.P. to be moving around in a star actor's eye line during a shot, however, is an act of tremendous discourtesy and disrespect. To do it more than once seems to bespeak a real lack of understanding of what actors have to contend with to create a performance, and how they work to do their job. I assume that what set Bale off and infuriated him was that he was "in a moment" and giving a performance that he really liked and felt good, and when his concentration was ruined by movement in his line of vision, he perhaps felt that performance could not be duplicated in another take, and he erupted.

Bale's rant might have been at least partially about ruining something good that might not be replaceable, and the light adjustment was a violation of basic professional courtesy by someone so obsessed with his own craft that he did not extend to others the kind of consideration he would automatically expect as he was doing his own job.

As I've said, the times when a director works the hardest is when he or she is blocking out a scene or shot and setting a shot. Many times when I was busting my brain trying to block out a scene or shot and set a shot nearby, *way too nearby*, crew members, grips, electrics, and sometimes the D.P. are laughing, joking around *not* off the set, they do not know how disrespectful, discourteous, and distracting they are being to the director and what a hindrance they are to the director's concentration, but if someone got in their way when they were setting a light or moving a cable it would be the end of the world to them because they were *working* and someone was in their way! During blocking, no one is truly working to them, and the director is just "dorking around" wasting time, preventing them from doing the "real work" lighting the set. If some director "lost it" and shot a bunch of crew who were breaking that director's concentration during blocking being disrespectful and discourteous assholes at that point when a director has to work hardest and that director grabbed a gun and "terminated" those disrespectful people, and I was on the jury trying that director's case, the defense lawyer would have an ultra-easy task getting me to vote for justifiable homicide.

Mutual respect and courtesy are great lubricants that cause a production to run smoothly and limit wear and tear. Courtesy can go a long way toward assisting a production in getting positive results. Discourtesy can just as easily go a long way in the other direction. Courtesy and respect cost nothing, but they are *very valuable*!

"Wrap" means that shooting is done and it's time to wrap things up. When the director leaves the set for the day, after wrap has been called, the director needs to pass through the area where the crew is wrapping and thank the guys and gals for the day's work, and tell the key crew people who is the staff member overseeing wrap, who they can talk to if any questions or problems arise. Usually, the first A.D. oversees wrap, but the line producer, second or producer sometimes gets that task. The crew's work day is not over until the lighting equipment, camera equipment, costumes, props, and other things are wrapped, and back on appropriate trucks. Sometimes, in a secure location, if you are shooting there the next day you can have a "standing wrap" and leave the camera, lights, and cable all in place.

Personally, I don't think that it's wise for a director to hang around during wrap. At least on a subconscious level, I think most crew would prefer that the director go home, get some sleep, polish their homework, and show up on the set next day prepared and energized to do his or her job efficiently.

When I was doing the A.D.'s job I would sometimes supervise wrap and hang around, talking and joking with the crew during wrap, but I never did that when directing. As Ernest Hemmingway said, "You can't run with the foxes and hunt with the hounds at the same time." It's good for the director to be on a friendly basis with the crew. The crew needs to respect the director, and the director needs to respect the crew. The director and producer are not, however, in the crew and they may have to make decisions that are in the best interest of the movie and the movie's investors that are not always in the best interests of the crew.

CHAPTER FORTY:
PRE-PRODUCTION – WHAT IT IS AND ALL THAT IT IS,
AND WHEN TO START IT OR NOT TO START IT

Pre-production consists of hiring a crew and staff, selecting a lab and making a deal (if you shoot on film), buying film (or videotape), selecting and approving and getting signed property releases on *all locations* for the movie, and designing or building sets if necessary, planning all set dressings and art department tasks and special effects, selecting and hiring your production accountant and lawyer, buying production insurance, casting all the actors for all the roles in the movie, rehearsing the actors, visiting the locations and getting the movie firmly in mind, making appropriate notes and storyboards, and doing all necessary and appropriate homework. That's followed by selecting a camera and lighting and grip equipment company, or a D.P. that has these things, and making an equipment deal. You select a D.P., set up a system to handle petty cash, choose A.D.'s, have two production meetings as previously discussed, and have the prop master collect all necessary props. You also see that all required rewrites are done on the script to perfect it as much as possible.

Before you start pre-production, the movie needs to be accurately budgeted in pre-production and the money to make the movie needs to be raised to make the movie, and that money needs to be under the production company's control in its bank account, not just a promise that investors can back away from. You also need signed contracts with your investors.

By then you can budget the movie, finalize raising the money if it hasn't occurred before pre-production as it should have, and finalize the investors contracts. You'll need to select a completion bonder and make a deal you can live with *only* if you are unfortunate enough to need one or your investors are scared enough to demand one. Avoid completion bonders if at all possible. You'll do whatever tests are required, collect all costumes required, hire the transportation captain and arrange to acquire whatever vehicles the production requires or will require, whenever it will require them.

This is also the time to launch whatever publicity actions are appropriate to your production. You'll make a deal with the Screen Actors Guild and post your bond if you are going to sign SAG contracts. Workmen's comp has to be arranged, production and casting offices have to be selected and rented, and just in case no one's done it yet, you see that the script has been registered with the Writers Guild of America.

And speaking of the script, you'll need to have the script supervisor make up a schedule of days of the story in the script and collaborate with the wardrobe person as to which costumes will be worn on which story day and in which scenes in the script, so that they can work together. The A.D. needs to do a script breakdown and a production shooting schedule so that the A.D. will be on top of what's needed to shoot each scene, and that it will be easy to make accurate call sheets.

I may have left something out but what I've described is basically all the things of which pre–production consists. When you've done those things, you've done pre-production and you are ready to shoot the movie. When you haven't done those things or haven't completed them, you haven't completed pre-production and are not ready to shoot.

A lot of people start shooting before these steps are completed and in place, and many of those unprepared people are shocked when they come to reside in "filmmaker hell." Do not start shooting a movie hoping you will raise more money to complete shooting. Sometimes, rarely, that works. Usually it doesn't, and when it doesn't, it's pure filmmaker hell. *Plague* was a special, complicated circumstance where this rule did not apply, but usually it does. Do not get into a situation where the investors have the right to pull out if they get scared. *They will get scared.* They always do.

Movies are not just made with money. Some money people think they are, but low budget movies are made with a lot of goodwill. When you approach the first day of principal photography, you will have made commitments to a lot of actors, crew, and staff and equipment companies, a lab, etc. These people may have turned down other work to do your movie. If it falls through they are also screwed. If your investors can easily pull out, and basically *screw* all the people with who you have made deals you are a fool. You will very likely get a big knife in the back, and in a way you will deserve it because you will have bought the idea that *only* money matters. You will have turned your back on the value of people and commitments and if the investors pull out and leave you holding the bag, you get to go to all the people and tell them that the movie that they expected to work on and the pay they expected and were counting on to pay the rent and by food will not be materializing and you are not a filmmaker, you like your "investors" are "flakes."

Hollywood and movies always need real investors with the guts to actually invest in movies. It takes a real tolerance for real risk to invest in movies. I've invested in movies myself with both good and bad results, but it is scary, and it's thrilling when it works out in your favor. Hollywood and movies do not need flakes; they will always have more flakes.

Earlier, I mentioned proper sequence. Raising the money to make a movie and securing that money comes before beginning pre-production proper, but not necessarily before pre pre-production which includes detailed budgeting, which can become even more detailed or revised in pre-production proper. From the very beginning of pre-production proper you will be talking to people and making commitments based on your statement that you *are* making a movie, not that you *hope* to make a movie or want to make a movie, or *might* make a movie. If you start pre-production proper without the capability to make a movie you are a flake.

The words *hope* and *might* and raw unfiltered optimism belong in pre-pre-production, not in pre-production proper. Pre-production proper is a realm of brutal reality, unflinching facing of things as they are, not as one hopes or wishes they will be. A production can be productively engaged in pre pre-production for months, six months, a year, or years if financing is not attained and nobody is a flake. This is what pre-pre-production is often for, to get as much done as you properly can before financing is secured.

Again, proper sequence: script – then pre pre-production – then financing – then pre-production proper fully completed – then production (shooting, filming, or videoing) – then editing, post-production, sales, and distribution. I probably need to clarify some things that I've written about *Plague* and my other movies. First, the people doing the on again, off again tango, mambo, cha cha cha were production or distribution companies or their lawyers. I was an employee. They, or the companies they were connected to, should have completed financing and definitive commitment and money or credit transfer far earlier than they did, but they or those they were connected to or those representing them suffered from cowardice.

When I started shooting *Plague* I only had $40,000 in the bank, but if no more money had arrived I would have shot the movie with only that amount and completed filming before December 31st just as I'd promised. I was not joking when I told the D.P. that if no more money came in he and I might be the whole crew. If I'd had to I would have set lights and loaded film magazines for him as well as directing and co-producing rather than not complete filming. If he'd gotten eaten by a polar bear on his way to the set, I'd have loaded the film into the camera and set the F-stop and focus, and shot it myself just as Lars von Trier did when he started shooting *Dancer in the Dark*, and as I had done many times on many movies early in my career.

One point of very intense personal pride for me is that right at the beginning of pre pre-production I asked a couple of really excellent people who'd worked on earlier films with me if they'd help with pre pre-production on deferment until money came in. There was not even a second of hesitation. All said yes, and some of them have gone on to very distinguished movie careers. I did not enter pre-production proper until I knew I could make a movie. I presold the Canadian TV rights and the lab held that presale and promised to do all the lab work to complete the movie. I purchased film stock. I posted the actors union's bond. I had 90 days credit with the equipment company. If no more money had arrived, I would have shot the movie the way indie pioneer moviemakers did, but I would not have been a flake who did not do what he'd promised to do.

Investors have a right to know that the money they invest will be spent on making of the movie, as the budget says that it will be spent, and that they will share in the movie's income and profit (if any) as promised, and they deserve effective legal protections of these important promises, but filmmakers deserve and need to know, before starting pre-production proper that the promised money will be there to make the movie even if the investors get scared when the "fit hits the shan" as it almost certainly will. Real investors deserve a lot of respect and gratitude. Flakes pretending to be investors deserve a lot of pure fiery hell right in the face. Many filmmakers are afraid to "bring things to a head" and press the investors to actually invest, to separate real investors from the ten times (at least) more numerous flakes. You have to have enough real confidence in your movie and its real value to be willing to in a very nice way, very politely, cordially, and professionally slam a potential "investor" or flake against the wall and ask which they are and let them know that if they want to be treated like an investor they have to do the actions of an investor.

If an "investor" says that they will only invest if they have the right to pull out at any time if they want, and you'll have to beg them for each next installment of money you'll need to keep filming, just tell them to pull out right then, pull out of your life and your movie. If they are that scared at the beginning, they will certainly be scared enough to pull out when the film starts rolling and money starts flowing. If you really deep down do not know that your movie is more valuable than the money it would take to make it, then maybe you should not make a movie, and certainly should not start pre-production proper.

If you are not prepared to push potential investors to the point of really investing or to split and stop pretending to invest, then you will be doomed to be jerked around by an endless stream of flakes. It's bad enough to deal with flakes. Don't be one, even with the best of hope and optimistic intentions, and jerk others around, even if "it's not your fault." It all starts with writing or getting the legal right to shoot a script that really deserves to be made into a movie and will give some real investors a good run for their money.

CHAPTER FORTY-ONE:
THE "DISCLAIMER" OVERALL POLICY

I recommend to all of my productions that they have a statement that all cast, crew, and staff sign acknowledging that they have read and understand the production company's "overall basic policy." This policy is designed to provide some legal protection to the production's backside. It includes a warning that the production company does not condone abuse of alcohol during work or travel to and from work and does not condone use of alcohol or illegal drugs by anyone while they are working on the movie, and unauthorized use of alcohol while working on the movie, or use of illegal drugs, along with a warning that doing anything illegal can result in immediate termination from the production. I would also warn that the production does not condone or tolerate sexual harassment and if sexual harassment is proven, that is cause for immediate termination. There should also be a warning to all employees crew and cast that they have the right to refuse to do anything that they feel is unsafe, and they should immediately contact senior staff, the director, or producer about any safety concerns. It should be emphasized that they do have a role and a responsibility in the protection of their own safety. Any other legally advantageous warning that they production's lawyer wants should probably be included, but use common sense.

The fact that employees have signed something indicating that they've read the company's basic policy and agreed to it will *not* protect you from being sued if things go wrong and something bad, or very bad, happens. Nevertheless, if all employees sign a document indicating that they have read and agreed to this policy, it will be harder for anyone suing you to prove negligence or malice. You may be held responsible for what your employees do or fail to do, but if the person suing you or the person causing the suit has signed that document establishing company policy, the lawyer handling the lawsuit will be much more likely to settle for what your insurance offers, rather than "go for the gold" and hold out to make a fortune off your case.

SAG offers hotlines for sexual harassment complaints and for concerns about safety. Actors and crew and staff do have a right to be safe and free of sexual harassment as they do their jobs. Still, it is very easy to get sued. You need to protect yourself up front, even if it's only possible to do so to a small degree. A long time ago, before sexual harassment suits were so plentiful and easy to file, before they offered such lucrative possibilities, I realized that a female grip on a movie I was directing had not been on the set for several days. I asked the key grip is she was sick. I was concerned as to whether we had enough grips for the upcoming night lighting situations. He replied that the female grip was being sexually harassed by someone, and she didn't want to say who or deal with it any more, so she quite and got a job on another production. Not only did I not know this was happening, to this day I don't know who was the perpetrator. If this had happened today in our current environment and the female grip had sued, the plaintiff's lawyer could ask questions like "Did you take steps to protect your employees from this kind of harassment?"

Even if you were not an enabler by inaction, even if you were innocent, if you failed to be proactive or protective in preventing such harassment, a lawyer asking the right accusatory questions could make you look like Jack the Ripper to some members of a jury. There's a saying, "An ounce of prevention is worth a pound of cure." A simple, reasonable, signed document outlining company policy in concrete terms can help you later if accusations arise, whether real or imagined. You might know yourself, but you can't always predict what others in your employ might do. Some productions give crews beer at wrap, and some crews expect it. Many productions don't do that because of accidents that might occur on the way home – they could get sued just like a bar or someone holding a party for providing alcohol to "unlucky" drivers. It's a bit of a damned if you do, damned if you don't situation, but err on the side of caution. There are plenty of predatory attorneys out there. Don't make their jobs easier and more profitable by failing to get a simple document signed by everyone involved with the production that will offer you a bit of protection or mitigation down the line.

CHAPTER FORTY-TWO:
THE ROLE OF THE UNFORSEEN IN MOVIE PRODUCTION

More than once, I've come close to being killed while making a movie. Many people have come close to being killed on movies I have made. Nobody has ever been seriously injured or killed on any of my movies, or on any movie on which I've worked. I've been very *lucky*. I am enormously grateful that this is the case, and a feel very lucky and very blessed that this is the case. When I mention coming *close* to being killed, I'm thinking about feet or seconds, or the decision to do this instead of that. I've mentioned some of these incidents in this book like a metal cable snapping when two cars cross-pulled it taut. It was supposed to pull a dummy out of a car but instead the cable snapped loose and flew across the desert, probably at a few hundred miles per house and just missed some crew members and me by a few feet. That could have killed someone easily. There was the incident pushing the car off a cliff and stopping it seconds before it would have fallen 150 feet on some nature lovers. Once I was about to send two stunt drivers full speed into a tunnel, stopping them seconds before a little old lady and older gentleman in a small car drove out of the tunnel that was supposed to be locked off. I've mentioned almost getting hit by flying metal. All of these incidents were real and potentially fatal by a few seconds or feet.

While writing this book, I took a look at all these incidents in my mind, to determine what they might have had in common. It was *not* carelessness or irresponsibility, or someone trying to take a dangerous shortcut. It had nothing to do with anyone trying to be a wild cowboy. In every case, all these "near misses" had one thing in common – *the unforeseen*. This element is virtually always a major player in low budget moviemaking and with brushes with injury or death. Just because you can't foresee these unforeseen incidents when making a movie, it does not mean that you should ignore the very high probability that unforeseen events and incidents will happen and will likely play a major role in the making of a low budget movie. You need to allow for the fact that the unforeseen is very likely to happen and can even be determinative, and you need to be aware of that and even prepare for it to whatever degree you can.

Those who believe that only what they can foresee is the entire universe of what they need to plan for or be concerned about are just asking to become embroiled in and ensnarled in trouble, messes, quagmires, or tragedies. Once again, my favorite Confucius quote comes into play. You should seek to be the "superior man or woman" because that is the person that prepares for all things as though they will be difficult, and so all things are easy, while the foolish person thinks things will be easy and they can become impossible. Just because you cannot exactly foresee the exact danger that might befall a production does not mean that it is okay to leave anything in a vulnerable condition or situation, and not take action to protect against the unforeseen that might very likely happen.

I'm reminded of a statement by the famous trader and investor Nathan Rothschild, who was probably the most successful money man of all time. He was being criticized and responded that the critic had no idea of how much boldness and caution – both at the same time – that it takes to build and keep a great fortune. Similarly, it takes a lot of simultaneous boldness and caution to make a successful low budget or micro-budget movie. Those who do not in some way prepare for or allow for the unforeseen are likely to be its victim.

Here is a situation in current events that is relevant. When George Bush and members of his administration decided to invade and occupy Iraq, they did not plan for all contingencies, particularly what might happen *after* a successful invasion. One thing that was unforeseen after the occupation of Iraq was that there were numerous huge ammunition dumps or depots in the country. Some were six miles square, with tons and tons of artillery shells. General David Petraeus, who was then a division commander, took Congressman Tom Lantos for a helicopter ride and showed him those huge ammunition assemblies. He told the Congressman, "I do *not* have enough men to guard them. Iraqis sneak in at night and steal artillery shells." Despite this reality Donald Rumsfeld, the Secretary of Defense, for a long time took no real action to stop this. Perhaps he thought that artillery shells with no gun to fire them were not a matter of concern. Nevertheless, the shells were used for explosive charges in Improvised Explosive Devices. What could have been done – if someone had expected the unforeseen to arise – might have been to set aside enough troops to keep weapons from being stolen that were later used to kill so many Americans and Iraqis in car bombs as well as IEDs. Perhaps without these weapons, the Iraqi insurgency might have been severely curtailed before it started.

To be ready to deal with the unforeseen in whatever form it raises its head is something you should prepare for on a production. Apparently, Donald Rumsfeld's method of dealing with the unforeseen was to pretend that it didn't exist, or even deny that it was happening. Actual facts and what is really happening is what matters – the difference between superior and inferior men. It's been reported that during the first Gulf war in the early 1990s, General Colin Powell was told by his staff that it would take 150,000 troops to push Saddam Hussein's army out of Kuwait. Powell asked for and received 400,000 troops, and when foreign troops were added he had 500,000 for a task his staff said would require only 150,000. He was a superior man who believed all things would be difficult and he prepared accordingly. Obviously, the Gulf war was a breeze compared to the occupation of Iraq. The architects of the occupation and invasion of Iraq thought that things were easy, and the invasion was, relatively, but they did not prepare for unforeseen circumstances as Gen. Powell did, and things became difficult and seemingly impossible. Their ideology got in the way, just as any theory you might bring to a film set might hinder situations that arise if you have not prepared a bit for the unforeseen.

Obviously, low budget productions do not have the luxury of overwhelming resources like those brought to bear in the Gulf war, but hard work, thinking things through, and a willingness to find out and face the facts will see you through. I have a very healthy respect for the unforeseen and how important it can be and how necessary it is to deal with and plan for it. When something comes close to killing people on a movie you are making, it tends to get your attention and respect very quickly.

In looking into trying to predict such events, I have studied some of the actions of the famous banking family, the Rothschilds, and how they maintained their enormous fortunes. One recurring theme is present in their triumphs – *superb intelligence gathering*. They spared no ingenuity, inventiveness, effort, or cunning to get and use absolutely accurate, fact-based information about whatever was relevant in the very risky and volatile financial areas in which they operated. Their spectacular success was almost always the result of superior intelligence, investigation, and knowledge of the relevant facts that their competitors lacked, and those competitors paid dearly for their shortcoming. The Rothschilds were not afraid of hard work, thoughtful planning, and careful execution to get the information needed to eliminate the *unforeseen* from being a major player in their affairs. They were rarely the victims of unforeseen circumstances. Lesser, fate-trusting competitors were often blindsided by the unforeseen. Similarly, I have seen many low budget productions plunge headfirst into situations of deep importance and far-reaching consequence without any real research or investigation into how to handle it. I have seen people make decisions that have had heavy consequences not just for a movie production but for people's lives for years to come, just acting off intuition, ideology, or blatantly false information, without any real investigation or effort to collect the actual facts or find the truth and act on the basics of reality alone.

I've seen people do things of very serious consequence in moviemaking that were really stupid because "So-and-So" said this or that and someone wanted to believe what that person said because if it was true, things would be easy. The only problem was that "So-and-So" didn't know anything at all about the things about which they were speaking with "absolute certainty." Some people are like that. The mere fact that they know nothing about something does not at all stop them from speaking things that are false with "absolute certainty." I've seen situations where even a surface preliminary investigation would have revealed that the information upon which a production was acting was false. Sometimes they did not want to know the truth because it mean that to accomplish what they wanted to do would require ten times more effort than if the false information was true.

An examination of the actual facts may require a filmmaker to abandon even cherished *false basic assumptions* and start all over from scratch and develop and test *new* basic assumptions. That can require starting all over from square one and to operate with the increased difficulty of dealing with the real world and anticipating the unforeseen. Taking refuge in the comfort of ideology and ignoring the reality around yourself can lead someone into traveling 100 mph into a brick wall. On any production, you must investigate, research, find the truth, deal with facts, and pay attention only to fact-based suggestions. Try to eliminate the unforeseen but never disregard its potential importance. Try to have ways of dealing with any unexpected situation or danger, and you're much less likely to become a victim.

Every year, a number of people are paralyzed from the neck down by jumping headfirst into bodies of water without knowing how deep it is until their head hits the bottom. They are victims of the unforeseen. Metaphorically speaking, I have seen filmmakers that failed to investigate, find the truth, and plan ahead or be aware of the unforeseen and its power, do things that are very similar to someone breaking their neck with an unthinking dive.

Don't become a victim of the unforeseen. Investigate, research, have plans, find out the truth, and rise above the unforeseen. Do not dive headfirst into filmmaker hell. I have watched many uninformed or misinformed, out of touch with reality people do just that. Don't follow them.

CHAPTER FORTY-THREE:
DISPUTES

If you have two or more people with the same or very similar basic assumptions who basically agree on what the facts of the situation are and these people are open to logic, reason, and common sense, it is usually fairly easy to resolve disputes among them by focusing on the facts of the situation and working toward a solution of the dispute. In contrast, however, where you have people that have very different assumptions and disagree about the basic facts or ignore facts that they don't like or can't see, facts that don't support some ideology or ideological point of view that has them hypnotized, you have a very different situation.

Often when people have a dispute it is not the thing that is being disputed that is actually causing the dispute. It may be an underlying conflict of basic assumptions, or view of the facts, or a different view of what the facts are, or even a desire to get their own way or prove they are right (even when they are very wrong), or to show who is boss and outranks everyone to indulge their own prejudice. To resolve some disputes you need to look not just at the dispute but the factors underlying that dispute. Those factors may be irresolvable because one of both of the parties will not surrender to logic or reason. One producer I worked with wrote into my contract that any dispute between the director and the producers (the money men) would be automatically resolved in the producers' favor, always. This producer understandably did not have any confidence in his own ability to win any argument with logic or facts. Instead, he resorted to his version of the Golden Rule – The man with the gold makes the rules. His idea was that he outranked everyone and was right because he was paying for making the movie. He wanted his way even if he was really wrong and did not have a logical or common sense leg to stand on. He was also fighting an old battle with another director that was long gone. Although I appreciated the fact that he gave me the money to make the movie when nobody else would, I sharply resented that clause in my contract during the production. That is simply not how someone who developed the project from a stack of blank paper all the way into a movie should be treated. For what it's worth, that movie was eventually distributed by Warner Bros. and the movie he and his brother invested in after mine was a project from Hollywood that starred an Oscar-winning actor. It was so bad it never got distributed. Even the projectionist couldn't watch it. Can anyone say "karma"?

At the opposite end of the spectrum is the best producer I ever worked with. We worked by mutual agreement and were always able to resolve disagreements via logic. I had confidence that if we disagreed and I was right, I could convince him with facts and logic, and he basically felt the same way. If we disagreed and he was right he could use facts and logic to convince me. I was interviewed by a film magazine and they asked me who had the higher rank, the director or producer. I said, "It depends, but on projects I wrote or co-wrote and was directing, I usually was credited as one of the producers to assert that nobody outranked me, where that was possible." Often, the producer can theoretically fire the director and sometimes the producer works for the director, but what I emphasized to that magazine was that if you are working with a good producer or the producer is working with a good director, it never gets to a mano-a-mano impasse showdown. Whoever is right can convince the other reasonable party of their correctness, and they will each respect the other's job.

When you are putting together the core of a movie's staff, the three component committed people at the center of the production you need to get people whose basic assumptions are similar and align. Try to get people who agree that facts, reality, and logic matter. Try to avoid people that are so blinded by ideology that they cannot see or ignore facts that don't match their fixed ideas. You need people that will and can change basic assumptions if those assumptions are logically proven to be false. Avoid people that just want their own way, just because they do. Some people can never admit they are wrong. They can't learn or change, are "always right" and will not help your production. Check out people's opinions about what movies they like, what filmmakers they respect, and their goals. How do they feel about the paying audience? How do they feel about the investors' money?

In short, you need the three component, committed, compatible, complimentary people I've previously mentioned, who can work together as the core of a team based on reason and logic and common sense, who have an excellent knowledge of movies and will work hard to resolve disputes. If a dispute arises anyway, I always try to focus on the *facts* of the dispute, and get the contenders to do the same. I try to avoid infantile cravings to get one's own way, and try not to personalize disputes if at all possible. Personality attacks of the "This is what's wrong with you" variety must be avoided whenever possible. Disputes within a production and with people outside the production are often a part of moviemaking, but not always. Usually, you can resolve upsets smoothly if you are dealing with people of goodwill who have positive intentions and are not psycho. Unfortunately, that's not always possible in the movie business.

I'm of the opinion that the real, never-ending battles in moviemaking arise between people who have made movies and who know how to make movies and people who have never made a movie and don't know how movies are actually made. The latter get in the way of real moviemakers and make trouble. They often make the lives of the real filmmakers hard as hell. So try to weed those people out going in, and less troubles will arise.

PART FOUR

FINANCING MOVIES:
BUDGETING, ACCOUNTING,
A DEFINITION OF LOW BUDGET,
RETURNING MONEY AND PROFITS TO INVESTORS
AND OTHER FINANCIAL NECESSITIES AND REALITIES

CHAPTER FORTY-FOUR:
NOBODY SHOULD EVER INVEST ANY MONEY IN ANY MOVIE, PARTICULARLY A LOW BUDGET MOVIE, UNLESS THEY CAN AFFORD TO LOSE ALL OR PART OF THAT MONEY, OR HAVE IT TIED UP FOR A LONG OR VERY LONG TIME

It is true that some low budget movies have been very profitable for some investors and when a low budget movie does hit it big, the profit potential can be enormous, because of the relatively mall amount of money that needs to be recovered before they go into profit. Nevertheless, no one should ever invest money in a movie unless they can completely afford to lose it. Investing in movies is *very risky*. I've invested my own money. Some times it worked out and sometimes I lost my own money as well as that of investors. It is *not* pleasant when money does not come back. Some investors in some of my movies have been well rewarded financially and some have not. When someone invests in your movie, they will be part of your life for a while, some times a long while. People are real. Investors are real people. *Investors' money needs to be enormously respected*. It can be tied up for a long time, so they're taking quite a chance with you.

Robert Rodriguez earned the $8,000 that he used to make *El Mariachi* by checking into a clinic where a drug company tested new unproven drugs on him. Kevin Smith financed *Clerks* with credit cards, and he remarked on the DVD commentary on *Clerks II* that if *Clerks* had not been a hit, at the time he was making *Clerks II* over ten years later, he would still have been paying off his credit card debit from the first movie. *I do not recommend* using credit card debt to finance a movie, but it's hard to condemn it when you see the amount of student loan debt that many young people are now routinely burdened with when they graduate from college and you weight the value of a college education versus the value of making an independent feature-length movie as a learning experience and a career-advancing opportunity. It's hard to categorically rule out debt as a way of financing a movie. If you use debt, you need to think about paying off that debt before you incur it, just in case your movie is not like the one in several thousand odds that *Clerks* won in becoming a big hit.

Read the chapter title again, and keep that in mind when you're dealing with investors.

t was very interesting to listen to the commentary on the DVD of the multi-Oscar-winning Best Picture of the year movie *Crash*. Paul Haggis, that movie's director, co-producer, and co-writer, said that one of the first things that they did with the script when it was finished was to get the script to the much-admired and acclaimed actor Don Cheadle and offer him a role as producer as well as actor, because Haggis knew Cheadle *would pull in a cast*. This is a prime example of the use of what I call *script plus*. Paul Haggis is one of the very top screenwriters in Hollywood. His script for *Million Dollar Baby* was nominated for an Oscar for Best Screenplay, and won Best Picture of the Year before *Crash*. His script for *Letters From Iwo Jima* was also nominated. Haggis has a long and distinguished, much admired television career as well, as a screenwriter, story editor, and producer on popular TV shows.

When Haggis went out to finance *Crash*, his screenplay was turned down by "everyone" much in the same way scripts for many other successful movies were rejected. I don't know whom exactly Haggis pitched *Crash* to while trying to independently raise $7,000,000 to make the movie. (One million went to financing fees and six million went into making the movie.) I also do not know how much of the stellar cast was committed to the movie before financing and how many joined after it was financed. When you look at *Crash*'s cast and how much many of its star actors have been paid to be in big studio movies, one pitch that could have been made is the list of top stars involved in the project. It would have been reasonable to project that with all those movie stars and name actors, the movie could easily earn back its money from DVD sales, cable TV, and foreign sales.

However *Crash* was financed, very successful TV writer-producer Haggis reached out to a highly-respected actor to *pull in a cast* (who would know it was a quality project because Cheadle was involved, and perhaps they wanted to work with him as well). Getting Cheadle involved was one of Haggis's first actions to get the script made into boost a movie. That's *script plus*. He did not rely only upon the quality of his screenplay. When you add *script plus*, the script becomes a *project*, not just a screenplay. On the DVD commentary of *Reservoir Dogs* Quentin Tarantino, when describing how the movie was financed, pointed out that when Harvey Keitel committed to the script, it was not instantly financed, but Keitel's commitment gave the project *credibility* in the eyes of Hollywood players. That is again, *script plus*. Once Tarantino and his producing partner Lawrence Bender had name actor Keitel, a man with a long and respected track record and box office value, they were no longer in the same league as the thousands of other guys and gals running around town waving a script in the air and hoping someone would finance their wonderful words typed on white paper.

Even the greatest, very well-written words are often not enough to impress people with money and convince them to finance your movie. Those words can, however impress actors whose names have value, or even "bankability." An excellent script may not be recognized by money people but it very often is instantly recognized by actors. Good scripts can impress and attach actors to the project and give it *script plus* punch.

Here's another very different example of *script plus*. I had written a screenplay about a very specific type of telepathic monster. A foreign sales company that had distributed one of my earlier movies was interested in the script and brought a Canadian producer into the deal. The Canadian producer put up some pre-production money. We used that money to make a small scale model of the monster out of clay. A lawyer who was a friend of an associate of mine wanted to be a producer. He liked the project from reading an early draft of the at that point sketchy and flawed script. He told me hc could get a meeting with a very famous and powerful female executive who was a long-time friend of this lawyer. I saw that a very makable and sweet deal was possible if we could sell this executive and bring the home video company into the deal. The financial risk could be split between the foreign distributor, the home video company, and the Canadian producer. Each of the three could protect and recover their investment from the territory or market of their expertise, and they could share in profits from the other two partner's areas. I knew that if we got the home video company into the deal it would solidify the whole deal. It would lower the amount of money that the Canadian producer and the foreign sales company would have to risk, and it would boost their confidence to see this solid well-known home video company also believing in the project, and putting their money into it.

We got the meeting with the executive and her assistant, who had read the script. The executive hadn't read it. The assistant was "iffy" about the script. He didn't like it that much and asked questions like "How's this or that going to work?" He wanted to know if I was sure that these things would turn out as I explained. To be fair to him, the script was weak at that point and not that polished. Later, another writer improved it enormously. Anyway, the meeting droned on, touching on various bases, and it looked like it was heading for a non-conclusive stalemate. I did not have a lot of chemistry with either executive. Then I said, "I'd like to show you something." We had the model of the monster in a shoebox. I put that on the table, let a little anticipation build, and then I pulled the monster out of the box and set it on the table. The assistant shut up, which improved the meeting a lot. The female executive looked at the monster model, smiled, and her face lit up. She did not take her eyes off the monster. After a long pause, she began to talk with us again. Reading the look on her face, my guess is that she was thinking "free movie" when seeing that monster mockup. At the time there were about 40,000 video stores in North America. She knew how much profit her company made on each video that they sold, and she knew that with that monster and its picture on the video box, her company could sell at least one tape to almost every video stores that had a decent horror movie section. She knew that even if the movie was weak the monster would sell enough videos to more than cover her company's investment. I think that she also saw that if we made a model of the monster at that early stage, we knew what was important and would get the on-set monster right.

She was correct, if that's what she was indeed thinking. Her company did sell at least one video to almost every stores in North America that had a sold horror movie section. The tone of the meeting changed dramatically after she'd looked over the monster model. There was no more talk about whether or not they would invest. The talk shifted to *how* they would invest, what they would gct, etc. The assistant saw that his boss was sold. He stopped sniping and making objections and began talking about various possible mechanics of the deal. The executive said, "Have the foreign sales company call me. We'll work things out." And they did.

The fact that we had a *script plus* in the form of the model monster closed the deal. If we'd just had a script, I doubt that the meeting would have ended with a deal.

This was all another example of *script plus*. The model monster was something physical and tangible, something you could *show* people. It spoke for itself. It was not just the ideas or opinions that we had about it. For a lot of people, a script is just a lot of words on paper, leading to opinions or criticisms. In reality, a script is something that exists in the writer's and reader's minds alone. It is much more a part of the "ether" than the physical world. When I said, "I'd like to show you something" and brought the model out of the shoebox "lair" I moved the meeting from ideas and objections into the world of *physical reality*, where real movies are made, not just talked about. This illustrates the difference in a script and *script plus*. This quality pulls the project out of the purely mental realm.

Let me make a couple of points about the script in question before I move on. The early draft that I wrote was weak, unperfected, and deficient in some aspects but it had a very good concept, one that gave it excellent commercial potential for a low budget movie. This less than excellent script was the one we used to make the deal that financed the movie, however. By the time we shot the movie, though, the script was excellent, particularly for a low budget movie, thanks to another writer's improvements. I then touched up some of what he wrote while doing the shooting script. Then during rehearsals, the dialogue was fine-tuned even more. By the time we shot the script, it was as good as or better than almost every low budget movie I had seen to that point except for excellent "break out" low budget movies like *Night of the Living Dead*.

It is a paradox that usually a movie's script and its concept are most often the *single most important element in determining and influencing a movie's probability of success*. In contrast, with low budget movies in particular, the script is usually *not* the most important element that causes a movie to be financed.

On another movie, my business partner and I had struggled for a while, very energetically and with a lot of activity to finance *Starship Invasions*, which at that time was titled *Legion of the Winged Serpent*. It looked like we'd come to a dead end. We had both tried everything that we could think of to finance the movie. We'd approached over one hundred people or companies, and all we had to show for it was two very "iffy" flakes that said they could fund the movie. My suspicion is that they were actually out to try to steal the project from us, and thought they could contractually entangle us so that if they did come up with the money they would ruin it by amateur meddling during production or pre-production. My business partner wanted to take their deal and sign a contract with them, but I said no. He asked what else we could do. I said, "Every day we are going to sit in your apartment (our "office" at the time, basically a room with a mattress for a bed and a telephone), from 9:00 in the morning until 5:00 in the evening until one of us comes up with another idea of how to finance this movie, and if we agree it's good, we'll try it. So we sat there and read and reread *Variety*.

Then one day in the mail came a pamphlet from the Canadian government that listed every film production company in Canada, virtually every filmmaker in the country. These companies made industrial films, educational films, TV commercials, TV shows, and movies. I spent about half an hour berating the government bureaucrats and griping about how useless they were. I asked my partner how many written pictorial presentation booklets we had. He counted them up. He'd been diligent in retrieving each presentation and script every time the project was rejected. We had over eighty presentations. I said, "We will go through this booklet and we'll pick the eight strongest prospects and send them each a presentation and cover letter pitching the project and we'll send just the cover letter to every other company in the booklet."

There were over 300 companies and filmmakers listed. We would hit them all with either a presentation and cover letter or simply a letter. The company that eventually funded the movie was sent a presentation because my partner thought that they were a good prospect. I didn't think they were, but he knew something about that company so I went along with his instinct. A day or so after they received our package, we had an early morning meeting with a toothless, feeble distributor. When that meeting ended my business partner checked his answering service and sure enough, the "hunch" company had left a message asking us to call. My partner reached the lead "money man" at the company, who invited us to come straight over and talk.

The money man loved the presentation, which included a letter of commitment from the agent of actor Robert Vaughn and lots of drawings of proposed costumes, the special makeup that would determine the look of the aliens, designs for UFOs, storyboard type drawings of various important shots and scenes, and special FX shots. It also included information on how much money various sci-fi movies had made. That was over a year and a half before the debut of *Close Encounters of the Third Kind* was released and about a year before *Star Wars* was released. No one in Toronto at that point knew anything about these movies or the success any new sci-fi movie might have. We showed the money man our 16mm UFO test film. It looked very impressive. I had funded a very inventive special FX man with a few hundred dollars that I'd earned driving a cab between movies. The money man was stunned the first time he saw the test film. He thought it looked great.

"Did you have a crane holding the UFO?" he asked.

I explained that we had a tiny two-inch in diameter UFO model on a piece of moving glass right in front of the camera. I had operated the camera myself while crawling around in mud in a vacant field, shooting through the special FX device. The money man asked if he could watch the UFO test again, so we projected it a second time. After that, he literally started jumping up and down around the viewing theater!

"Wow, wow, wow!" he exclaimed. "This is great! Making a movie is like having an asshole. Everyone has one, but this is *special*!"

We finished the meeting and the money man kept the UFO test to show to his brother, who was his business partner. When my business partner and I walked out of the building, we were both silent for a while, then we looked at each other, smiled, and broke out laughing. *We knew we had a deal!* Despite the serious bumps in the road we'd endured, we had a deal. We made the movie, Warner Bros. distributed it in theaters, and NBC showed it in prime time! We never would have made the movie without *script plus*. The money men did not even like the script. It was weak and in some ways defective, but again, it had an excellent concept with superb commercial potential.

When Burt Reynolds was one of the biggest movie starts in the world, screenwriter Steve Shagan gave him a script that became a movie that starred French beauty Catherine Deneuve called *Hustle*. Burt liked the script and told Shagan, "I'll get this made." Shagan explained that it had been "everywhere" and been turned down all over. Reynolds responded it, "It might have been everywhere, but it hasn't been anywhere with me attached." Reynolds was right. A studio financed Robert Aldrich, a top director, to direct it. This was once again *script plus* with a major star actor. Reynolds got a script made that had been turned down by "everyone."

Sam Raimi made an approximately 40-minute 8mm movie called *Evil in the Forest* and used that as a demo to convince investors to finance his first professional feature length, enormously successful cult classic horror movie *The Evil Dead*. That was a major serious use of *script plus*.

One distributor that distributed two of my movies was also making a sci-fi movie that starred one of the cast members of the original *Star Trek* TV series. Part of the movie was to be shot on a planetarium's very realistic and convincing looking moonscape. I asked the executive that actually sold the company's movies to foreign territories if the script was any good. He said it was "a piece of crap." And he was right; I learned that as soon as I saw the finished movie. That executive told me that even before the movie was shot he had deals in progress all over the world that were less than half an inch from closing at a top-notch sale price, just based on the *Star Trek* actor's name and some promotional stills of people in astronaut costumes on the moonscape. He was positive that the movie would make money, and again he was right. Despite the "piece of crap" script the movie sold virtually every territory in the world at a good price for a low budget movie. It also sold extremely well in the home video market, and was a profitable movie. Why did they make a movie from such a bad script with an undistinguished director? It had *great script plus!*

One real filmmaker who was a partner in a distribution company I worked with on a movie greatly admired and enjoyed my film. When I later sent him a script (with no *script plus*), out of professional courtesy he told me the truth. He explained that his company was not even reading scripts that had nothing but a director attached. They were looking for scripts with name actors attached and some money attached as well. They would only read the script if it was a *project*, not just a script. He didn't give me some excuse about the script. As this example illustrates, sending only scripts that have no script plus to low budget distributors is virtually always completely useless. Most of these low budget distributors do *not have enough cash to finance an entire movie alone*. They will almost never take a chance solely on a script. Executives and producers or money men in the movie business usually have had the experience of reading a script that did *not* impress and then seeing that script become a very successful movie, and they have also had the experience that runs in the opposite direction, reading and admiring a script that is then turned into a mediocre or lackluster failed or barely successful movie.

I had an experience like that. I read the scripts for *Basic Instinct* and *The Last Boy Scout* well before either movie was released. Just reading the script for *Basic Instinct* did not impress me. After watching the movie many times, however, I recognized that the script was one of the most important elements of the movie. It was a great script. I didn't recognize that until I saw the completed movie. And when I read the script of *The Last Boy Scout* I thought it was one of the best I'd ever read, and that included Oscar winning and nominated screenplays at the Academy of Motion Picture Arts and Sciences library. When I saw *The Last Boy Scout* movie, though, I was very disappointed. It was a very unimpressive movie. There were things about its production that I did not like at all, and there were things about the production of *Basic Instinct* that I thought were absolutely perfect, but the difference in the two productions was only part of the overall story – I had simply misjudged both those scripts with regard to movie potential despite being a screenwriter, producer, director, and editor who had studied a lot of scripts and movies.

I can only try to imagine how an executive who has never written a script or made a movie truly feels about their own ability to judge the quality or success potential of a movie by simply reading the screenplay. Many executives cannot even judge a movie's prospects for success or failure by watching the finished movie! Here is a story I was told by someone with a lot of credibility that was in a position to actually know the truth of the situation. The story centers on George Lucas's enormously successful classic masterpiece *American Graffiti*. Apparently, the studio funded the movie on a very low budget based on Francis Ford Coppola's participation as executive producer. According to the story I heard, Coppola walked into the screening from where *American Graffiti* was about to be shown for the first time to studio executives and said, "I hope this is good. I haven't seen a frame of it."

Immediately, some execs got nervous and worried. When the movie finished screening, some of them began griping and threatening to sue Coppola because he had not closely supervised the making of the movie and had let Lucas make the movie he wanted to make. Coppola apparently called their bluff and took out his checkbook and said, "You don't like this movie, and you don't think it has value, I'll buy it back from you right here and now for what it cost." Only one executive in the group believed strongly in the movie, which went on to become a huge hit. Some people even consider it to be Lucas's best movie. The other executives backed down. If Coppola thought it was good and was willing to buy it, they reasoned, suddenly they were not interested in selling it. How confident do you think people can be in their own judgment if they thought *American Graffiti* was worthless? They are *not* confident enough to finance a movie based on just a script!

This is not a one of a kind isolated incident. Wes Craven, the writer and director of *Nightmare on Elm Street*, which launched ten "Freddy Krueger" movies, said on a DVD commentary that after the screening of the first rough cut of the movie, the head of the distribution company that financed the filming turned to him and said, "Well, do you think there's a movie in there somewhere?" He was totally unimpressed by a movie that would turn into a huge chunk of gold at the box office, he had no foresight that the movie and its villain would propel his company from being a small-time distributor of low budget horror movies into being virtually a major studio that would produce the *Lord of the Rings* trilogy, make a ton of money, and get a herd of Oscar nominations while winning several Oscars.

This executive was apparently blind to the classic horror movie value of *Nightmare on Elm Street* and its superbly commercial assets, but he was light years ahead of many other distributors in Hollywood. He had financed the movie when everyone else had turned the script down. According to Craven's commentary, he was told the script wasn't scary. Wow, I would love to see those old reader reports! How much confidence do you think someone that turned down

Nightmare on Elm Street's script down would have in their own ability to judge the value of a movie that would result from just a script alone, with no apparent *script plus*? None.

Here's another incident that involves a very commercial, highly successful cult classic horror movie masterpiece. Sam Raimi commented that when *The Evil Dead* opened in New York, he went to a theater in a classy part of the city, and after the movie finished, the audience seemed confused, even numb. The movie had exceeded the existing boundaries of horrific gore that audiences were used to at the time, and as Raimi emerged from the theater, the distributor said, "We're going to have to do a *lot* of re-editing before the movie goes into wide release.

Raimi, his partner and distributor then went to another less classy theater in a much less classy area of the city. The movie had just ended and the people coming out of the theater were gushing about how great is was. All or some of the evening's shows had been sold out. Raimi and his companions watched the movie again with an audience that totally "got" the movie and loved it, and the distributor said, "Maybe we'll hold off on re-editing." On the DVD commentary, Raimi said that was the fastest change of an editing plan he ever saw.

Many very powerful and highly-positioned people in the movie business cannot even recognize the value of a very valuable movie even by looking at the finished film. Nevertheless, I've seen many screenwriters shower such people, and others of lesser stature, with scripts in numbers like a hailstorm, then walk away surprised and wounded when the scripts bounce back into their mailbox (if they're returned at all). There are cases where a movie gets made because someone in power falls in love with a script and makes the movie just because of the script, as in the Reynolds example. The situation does happen, but very rarely. Much more often, it requires *script plus* to get a movie made. Many development people and script readers play ping-pong with screenwriters' minds and spin their heads around like roulette wheels. That's why I always advise screenwriters and filmmakers to take their scripts to people who have the power to say *yes*, whenever possible. The legendary movie producer Alexander Korda said that whenever he asked a bank for money he would always ask for a million dollars or more, because he wanted to be sure he was talking to someone who had the power to say *yes*. He was very successful; do you want to be anything less?

CHAPTER FORTY-SIX:
GETTING MONEY FROM PEOPLE THAT DEPEND ON
AND PROFIT FROM MOVIES BEING MADE

On one movie that I co-wrote, directed, and co-produced, one largely financed with private investors money, I went to the head of a Canadian TV station and network and offered to presell him the Canadian TV rights to the movie if he'd pay the movie's lab bill. He agreed and put the agreement in writing. I took that agreement to the owner of Toronto's largest movie lab, who'd done the lab work on my movies, and had profited handsomely from that work. He also said yes. The private money came in slowly over a period of time, even during filming, but when I had this lab deal in place I knew that if I shot the movie I could finish it. That helped.

Previously, I talked about how I financed a movie with a Canadian producer, a foreign sales and a home video company, each providing a low risk portion of the movie's budget. It is always worthwhile to approach people for financing that will benefit if the movie is made. Sometimes the approach works, sometimes it doesn't, but if you don't get them this time you may well get them next time. They will remember you if you say you will make a movie and you actually go out and *do it*.

CHAPTER FORTY-SEVEN:
IF YOU JUMP THROUGH HOOPS, TRY TO MAKE SURE
THERE REALLY IS MONEY ON THE OTHER SIDE

There are many people out there on the fringes of showbiz that pretend to have money for movies or half the money to make a movie. Some of them delight in manipulating moviemakers to impress money people they may know. Sometimes, their money people are so far removed from participating in their ideas they barely know these manipulators exist. Thus it's very valid to seriously question any self-proclaimed money source, and qualify them before you jump through any of their hoops. Get them to provide evidence of who they are and why you should take them seriously. It's extremely worthwhile to "push back." If you actually have a *real project* you have a right to know if someone who is representing him or herself as an investor or financier or producer is real, or is a flake. The fringes of the movie business in Hollywood and other places have more "flakes" than a blizzard, so know whom you are dealing with and whether claims of money are real before you jump as soon as they put a hoop in front of you. Say something like, "If we do those things, will you finance the movie?" Or even more bluntly, "Do you have the money to finance this movie?" You can ask, "Are you really ready to take the risks that investing in a movie involve?" Don't hit them too hard, too soon. It's like catching a fish. First, you have to hook them, but eventually you have to reel them in.

Usually, when people ask to see a budget (and you definitely need a budget), all they really look at is how much the principals, like you who are intent on making the movie, plan to take as salaries. Real investors will often show the budget to someone they can access in the movie business, to verify if the movie can be made for the stated figure, and if the salaries are reasonable. Real, qualified, potential investors respect questions like those above as a sign of your professionalism when you qualify them, while flakes resent having their "integrity" challenged, and they will flinch away when you try to qualify them. Real investors will try to qualify you and your project, and they should accept that you will do the same with them.

CHAPTER FORTY-EIGHT:
PITCH YOUR MOVIE TO PEOPLE WHO CAN FINANCE ALL OR PART OF IT; IF NOT THIS TIME, THEN MAYBE THE NEXT

Here's a story you might appreciate. When I was making movies in Canada, you had to finish a Canadian movie by December 31 for the investors to get their tax write-off in that tax year. Most Canadian moviemakers I knew would set out trying to finance a movie early in the year, and if it wasn't financed by summer they were worried, and as the leaves began falling and the air turned cold in the fall, if they had not financed their movie they would usually become resigned to the bitter reality that they would not make a movie that year. That was my situation one year, after having made a movie every year for five years in a row. In October, I was thinking of going back to Los Angeles before the bitter Canadian winter set in. One Sunday night, I got a call from a "money-raiser" executive producer who had put one investor for a very small amount of money into one of my least successful movies. His tax shelter mechanics had clashed with the tax shelter specifics of the main investors' shelter on *Starship Invasions*, so he didn't invest in it, although he'd been thoroughly pitched and had been interested.

The first thing that he did was to ask me if I could start making a movie immediately and finish principal photography before December 31st. I answered *Yes!* Although it was theoretically possible, I doubt that at that time many or any other moviemakers in Toronto would have given him that answer, but I told him to come right over and we'd write up and sign a contract. "Right now," I said. "Tonight. Come over here as soon as you hang up the phone."

When you are financing a movie, it's important to strike before the iron freezes. While I was waiting, I wrote out some points that needed to be in the contract. When he arrived, I put two pieces of paper in the typewriter with a carbon paper between the sheets, then repeated each point or clause we discussed and negotiated verbally. When we were in agreement, I typed that point up. In about an hour or so, we each had a signed contract to finance and make a movie. When this money-raising executive producer left, I called my business and writing partner and we began to plan in detail how we could make the movie.

What resulted was the most positive and rewarding moviemaking experience I have yet had. The movie went on to win Best Picture and Best Screenplay at the second most prestigious festival of sci-fi, horror, and fantasy films in the world. The film was a good experience for all who were involved in it. Why did this money man executive producer call me up in October so anxious to make a movie? The movie producer whose movies he usually invested in had been caught embezzling large amounts of money and had killed himself. The movie that the money man had planned to put his investors' money in was suddenly cancelled shortly before it was scheduled to start filming because of the discovery of the thievery and the death of its producer.

The money man executive producer *knew me* because I pitched him on other earlier movies in which he did not invest. He'd seen me say I was going to make a movie, and then go out and actually make that movie. Some times, it's harder for people to invest in your movie when they have just met you, and easier for them to invest when you have pitched them about financing earlier and been turned down, yet you make your film despite their rejection. Sometimes, when you are "making the rounds" pitching people, trying to get them to finance your movie, you may not known it but you may not just be trying to finance one lone movie. You may also be planting seeds that will sprout and bloom later with another project.

CHAPTER FORTY-NINE:
THIS TRAIN IS LEAVING ONE WAY OR ANOTHER, WITH OR WITHOUT YOU, SO GET ON AND RIDE OR STAND THERE AND WATCH IT ROLL OUT OF SIGHT

When you are pitching someone, trying to get them to invest in or finance your movie, if they get the impression that if they say no they can "kill" the project and it will only get made if they say yes, you are in a very bad, disadvantageous position. Many people with money get a perverse satisfaction out of killing a creative person's dream, or a positive satisfaction out of making that dream live and be part of reality. If a money person feels that he or she can turn down a movie project and suffer no risk because if they turn it down it will never get made, and they will never have to face the prospect that they made the wrong decision, then there is a lot of pressure not to take a risk. On the other hand, if they feel that if they turn the movie down someone else will finance it, or someone is about to finance it, turning it down is not without risk. What if someone else finances the project and it becomes a hit that makes money? If it becomes a famous movie and they missed out on "riding" it they won't be happy.

One of the things that can make people want something is to see that other people want it. One of the best ways to sell a script is to get two or more people who are thinking about buying it. One of them will be driven by fear that another person will buy it, make it into a hit movie, and they will be kicking themselves for letting it slip through its fingers. One of the best ways to get a decent distribution deal is to get two or more distributors interested in distributing the movie. Nothing moves a distributors' hand more quickly toward signing a decent and fair distribution contract (if such a thing exists) than the fear that someone else might make the movie, distribute it successfully, and make a lot of money while the distributor in front of you has to sit and watch "the one that got away." The business part of the movie business often *runs on greed and fear*.

Low budget movie projects frequently have a hard time generating greed, although some do, but the fear of "the one that got away' is often more effective and appropriate in making a potential investor look seriously at a project, and many times it requires an appeal to both greed and fear to get an investor to face the very serious risk of investing in a low budget movie. If you say "This movie is going to get made one way or another, whether you invest or not," you'd better be able to make it stick. You'd better be able to turn it into reality. If you don't, many people will consider you a flake. If you promise that you'll make a script into a movie many times and it doesn't happen, most people will cease to take you seriously, and they may not be wrong in doing so.

If you say it and mean it and are willing to do what is necessary to make your statement come true, that can be a strong sales tool if used correctly by the right person with the right potential investor. To say to someone this train (your movie) is leaving the station, you can get on and ride, or you can watch it move down the track toward the rising sun without you, it's your choice," that can bring things to a head and dispense with a good deal of dithering around. What you say needs to be true, though; lies usually don't work.

Someone who knew a lot about guns and killing people told me once, "Never point a gun at anyone unless you are willing to kill them." He also said, "Never point an unloaded gun at anyone." His logic applies to the use of the "leaving train" statement in getting a movie financed. If you're serious about what you're doing, people notice.

CHAPTER FIFTY:
BUDGETING AND ACCOUNTING

Here is a list of major and minor budget categories and subcategories on a standard movie budget.

Story: Story purchase, title purchase, writer(s), typist, copying expenses, research expenses

Producer: Producer salary and expenses, per diem (if applicable), producer's assistant(s), associate producer's compensation, co-producer's compensation, executive producer's compensation (including financial finder's fees if appropriate), producer's secretary

Director: Director's salary, expenses, per diem (if appropriate), assistants to the director

Cast: List the cast of the movie's characters, and how many days they are scheduled to work, "buy outs" (if appropriate), pension H.O.W. contributions, money for name actors (stars if appropriate), money set aside in case of overtime, money for fittings, rehearsals, etc. (You can get the daily or weekly costs of SAG actors by calling the Screen Actors Guild.)

Extras: Figure out how many extras you will need and how much you are going to have to pay them.

Stunts: Equipment and people.

Animal wranglers and animals: As appropriate.

Stunt adjustments: Pay to actors if they do their own stunts.

Production staff salaries: Production manager (how many weeks at how much a week), unit manager, 1st assistant director, 2nd assistant director, secretaries, script clerk, choreographer (if needed), casting director and staff, first aid, technical advisor(s)

Camera crew: Cinematographer or Director of Photography, camera operator(s), 1st asst. camera person or "focus puller", 2nd camera asst. or "loader", still person, camera crew overtime

Sound department: Sound recordist, sound recorder (Nagra), boom person

Wardrobe department: Wardrobe, wardrobe purchases, cleaning and repairs, assistant(s)

Makeup and hair department: Head makeup, assistant makeup, head hair, assistant(s)

Grip department: Key grip, additional grip(s), extra labor

Prop department: Prop master, assistant(s), prop purchase, prop rental, props damage

Art department: production designer, art director, set dresser, art department production assistant(s), greens person, extra labor, sketch artist

Electrical department: Gaffer, "best" person, electric(s), wind machine operator, generator operator, rental lights and cable, other electrical equipment, generator and fuel

Special effects: On-set pyrotechnics, prosthetics, other on-set special FX and assistant(s)

Construction: Carpenters, painters

Security: Guards for sets and equipment, and cast and crew (if appropriate)

Transportation: Transportation captain, driver(s), automobiles, pilots, helicopters, planes

Camera equipment rentals and purchases: Expendable purchases, equipment purchases, camera car rental, camera crane rental, camera truck or van rental, camera and related equipment rental

Editing, post-production and laboratory: Editor, assistant(s), pay multiplied by number of weeks expected to work, editing room, supplies and equipment for film or video editing as appropriate, negative cutter

Purchase of stock: Film raw stock (number of feet times price per foot), video or DVD (as appropriate), film developing (number of feet times price per foot), work print (number of feet times price per foot)

Note about shooting ratio – 35mm movie film moves through a movie camera or projector at 90 feet per minute. 16mm movie film moves through a movie camera or projector at 36 feet per minute. A 35mm 90 minute movie is 8,100 feet long. If a director shot only 8,100 feet of film and the final movie was 8,100 feet long or 90 minutes, the director would have a shooting ratio of one to one. The only director I know of who may have accomplished a one to one shooting ratio is Andy Warhol. Some of his apparent one to one shooting ratio movies were professionally distributed. The shooting ratio is the amount of film exposed divided by the length of the final movie. *It is not the number of takes the director uses!* If the director shoots only one take on the master of a scene, the front of the shot with the slate on it while camera and sound are moving to "speed" and before the director callas action are not useable as is the end of the shot after the director says "Cut" until the camera is stopped. If the director shoots only one take and only masters on an entire movie this loss of the beginning and end of a shot will alone give the director a shooting ratio of about 1.2 or 1.3 to 1. I almost did this myself on a professionally distributed movie. Its ratio was about 1.5 to 1.

If a director shoots a master (only one take), two close-ups (only one take), and a two-shot (only one take) to cover a scene, the director will probably have exposed about five times as much film as the length of the final scene. This director has taken only one take from four different angles. A shooting ratio of 5 to 1 usually does not entitle a director to 4 or 5 takes.

Make sure you actually budget enough film for the director to shoot the movie!

10 to 1 is not a really high shooting ratio. I shot a movie that won major awards and was successfully distributed in theaters and worldwide in several media, at a shooting ratio of 5 to 1. The owner of the lab told me that my movie was the only movie of any quality that he remembered that shot the movie with only 40,000 feet of 35mm film. One editing assistant that worked on one of my movies had earlier worked with one of the very top editors in the world on *Aliens*. This editor had also worked for Stanley Kubrick and had a special editing system to keep track of enormous quantities of film. Kubrick's movies and *Aliens* (shot by Jim Cameron) had each exposed over a million feet of film; in some cases, millions of feet of film. On *Aliens*, Jim Cameron and his D.P. Jordan Cronenweth routinely had four cameras rolling at once. Try shooting a few takes with four cameras and see what it does to your shooting ratio.

In the commentary of one of the *Blade* movies, the D.P. said he always liked to have three or four cameras rolling on a shot and had used as many as seven. Studio movies now use an enormous amount of movie film. Low budget movies do not have that option! Shooting on video reduces the crushing pressure of shooting ratio on directors making low budget movies, but shooting on video also has its negative as well as positive aspects.

And now back to budget items…

Sound: Print sounds, sound effects recording or purchase
Foley: Foley artist(s) and theater

Music: Composer, synthesizer, singers or musicians, music studio, arranger, music rights purchase

Sound mix: How many hours times how much an hour

Answer print: The final color-corrected composite print with sound and picture (how much a foot times the length of the movie), main and end titles, stock footage, optical effects, video transfers

Financials: Workman's comp, Social Security, pension plan contributions

Travel: Bus, rentals, gas, oil, air or train fares

Lodging: Hotels or motels

Food: Meals, snacks, coffee, soft drinks, water, ice, catering

Location: Location manager and scouts, location fees, damage repair, per diems, permits, "gratuities"

Studio rentals: If studios are used in shooting, portable dressing rooms and toilets if appropriate
Office rentals
Tests

Production vehicles rental: Vehicles used in movie, vehicles used in production

Advertising: Publicity stills, developing, painting, trailer, poster, *Variety* or *Hollywood Reporter* ads

Insurance: Taxes, director insurance, negative insurance (against damage of the actual physical negative from which the movie is printed), life insurance, miscellaneous insurance, liability insurance (many locations will not allow filming unless you have at least one million dollars in liability insurance)

City, state tax: Incorporation costs

Legal fees: Financial finders fees, completion bond (if it absolutely cannot be avoided)

Miscellaneous: Contingency (most completion bonders want to see a ten to seven percent contingency and they are just being realistic, five percent contingency is tight, less than five percent contingency is just wishing and hoping)

If you don't have a contingency, the first time you spend one cent for anything that's not in the budget, and you can't not avoid spending money on something that is in the budget of comparable value, *you are over-budget*!

The list of categories and items I've listed may look fairly complete and it sort of is, but there are stationery stores, websites, and software packages that have even more complete and detailed budgets than what I listed. It is amazing but an unavoidable fact of low budget filmmaking life that you can make a budget that you think is very complete and exact, and as soon as you go out and start to actually make a movie, unavoidably, unbudgeted for, unexpected, and absolutely necessary expenses appear. These unexpected expenses create a need for a serious appropriate allotment of money to the miscellaneous and contingency sections of the budget.

And now for accounting. Again, there are software and websites with accounting systems, but the best accounting system I ever saw used on any of my movies was a very simple system used by a young accountant turned associate producer. He took the budgets major categories and assigned them a number, and each item or subcategory a number (of the category to which it belonged) and a letter, and he organized the receipts, invoices, purchases, and obligations of the production into these categories. His accounting was only a day or two behind the actual production, and it was very detailed, very accurate, and very useful. He could say things like, "You have budgeted for this category $1,000. As of two days ago you had spent or committed to spend $742." Any accounting system for a movie needs to be able to verify for a production, as close to present time as possible, how much money has been spent or committed and how much is left, so that the facts are available to see whether the production is aligned with or diverged from the budget. It also has to satisfy the Internal Revenue Service so your investors can get proper tax treatment and the production can also get proper tax treatment should the movie go into profit.

Here's how to handle petty cash. The P.M. dispenses petty cash to P.A.'s, department heads, and other personnel. When they bring him receipts he gives them more money for the amount of receipts. Ideally, the receipts should be stapled to a piece of paper with a short handwritten notation next to each receipt stating what the receipt is for and the person's initial and an amount in a column and a running total down and up and down the page and a total at the bottom of the page signed by the person spending the petty cash.

All invoices should have a notation on the invoice or attached to it indicating what the invoice is for, in terms of the production. Save, save, save all receipts and contracts, all property releases, all invoices, all paper documentation of all things. In our present, b.s. plentiful culture, pity anyone that cannot producer the proper piece of paper to prove even the most obvious truth when it is demanded by a bureaucratic turkey (who had never made a single useful thing in their entire life but now has the authority and power of the government behind him or her, who delights in his or her power over people that actually do things, or by a lawyer who is more reptilian than a herd of rattlesnakes). Keep all your paper, and keep it organized. Keep it so obvious that it will act like insect repellent should some "number worshipper" legal bandit government official decide to look at your paper verification of the truth.

Remember, just because what you say is true, that is no defense unless you have the paper to prove it is true. You can be accused of money laundering or taking all the money raised as personal income, with all the tax obligations that entails, if you cannot prove it with paper, in a neatly organized fashion, in a way that even a moron can understand. It's like the young child being trained on the potty – The job's not done until the paperwork's done. You should plan for the proper completion of your movie's paperwork at the very beginning of pre pre-production. How you begin will determine how you end!

CHAPTER FIFTY-ONE:
DEFINITIONS OF LOW BUDGET

The Screen Actors Guild (SAG) defines low budget as one of $2.5 million or less. It also has a more extreme low budget category for movies budgets of $600,000 and under. Many would consider anything under $100,000 as micro budget. Here are some budgets of low and micro budget movies that reached breakout success:

Paranormal Activity - $15,000
Once - $100,000
Clerks - $35,000
El Mariachi - $8,000
Night of the Living Dead (1968) - $114, 000
Martin - $100,000
The Evil Dead – $350,000 (estimated)
She's Gotta Have It - $100,000
Sex, Lies, and Videotape - $1.2 million

I made a movie for $23,000 that received professional theatrical (in theaters) distribution and I made others for much less than $23,000. To a degree, low budget is in the eye of the beholder. Many people that are accustomed to studio productions and budgets would consider the $6 million true budget of *Crash* to be low budget. Given its stars, it was that indeed. The movie viewing public does *not* care how much a movie costs. They only care about how much it pleases, satisfies, interests, and entertains them, in calculating how "good" that movie is and how willing they will be to pay to see it.

CHAPTER FIFTY-TWO:
CONTRACTS, DEAL MEMOS, LETTERS OF INTENT, PROPERTY RELEASES, INVESTORS, INSURANCE – ALL THE THINGS YOU NEED TO GET IN WRITING

Legendary movie producer Sam Goldwyn said, "If you get it on paper, you got a prayer. If not, you got nothing but air." He also said that a verbal contract "isn't worth the paper it's written on." Verbal contracts are theoretically legal, but just try to enforce one. *Get it in writing! Get it signed! Who owns the script? Get it in writing!* Don't try to build a house on a piece of land you don't own. Don't waste time trying to finance a movie where the ownership of the script is unclear or in dispute or potentially in dispute. You need signed contracts with actors, extras, crew, and others. You need signed property releases on locations. If a name actor says he or she likes your script and wants to be in your movie, *get a letter of intent that is signed*. If someone says he or she will invest equipment, money, lab services, or other things, and a full contract is not appropriate, get a written *deal memo* about anything important. *Get it in writing!* Do that with all important agreements.

Get it on paper and save the paper. Be sure you can find the proper paper whenever you might need it. Investment contracts are particularly important and need to be approved by and/or drawn up by lawyers. You need to be as honest as possible with investors and potential investors. It's true that some low budget movies have made an enormous amount of money compared to their costs. There is profit potential in low budget movies. Some "home runs" have been hit and others will be hit. There is, however, also a lot of risk and it needs to be made clear to potential investors that just because after the movie is made they see it in a video store or on cable TV or even in a theater that does *not* automatically mean that money is pouring back to the production company. There are many middle people between the money that a movie earns and the production company that made the movie. Sometimes the vicious hunger for this money that the movie earns causes these middle people to grab and "chew" on that money and swallow it in a way that would embarrass the living you know what out of a school of sharks in a feeding frenzy and make them look like an bunch of old English ladies sipping tea and nibbling on crumpets. Just because a movie is shown in some market doesn't necessarily mean that lots or even some of that money always gets back to the production company and even if it does, it can take a seriously long amount of time!

Beware of deals with your actors that obligate you to pay them money or more money if the movie is shown in a market or media. The distributor may show the movie in that market or media without your knowledge, or with your unknown consent. Distribution contracts have a lot of fine print and legalese, in case you have never seen one. You may be obligated to instantly pay the actors because of showing in a market from which you may receive little or no money to pay the actors and whoops, here comes the actors union acting like you are a combination of Jack the Ripper, Charles Manson, and Ted Bundy. Make sure that all the realities of movie investing dealing with returning money (expenses) are written into the contracts that investors sign. Explain them verbally to the investors clearly, but also put them in writing in the contracts that are signed.

If someone invests in your movie, they will likely be in your life for a long or perhaps very long time. It is best to start the relationship on a foundation of honesty and understanding and keep it on that basis as much as is possible! You need movie production insurance, and there are insurance companies that do offer bare bones essential insurance packages to low budget productions. Things can happen during the making of a movie. People can die or be horribly injured. The potential for liability is enormous. You need insurance if you don't want to risk your entire future. Many locations will not let you shoot there if you lack insurance of a certain amount and type. They usually want proof of insurance in writing.

Again, regarding everything of any importance, remember Sam Goldwyn's statements. "If you get it on paper, you got a prayer. If not, you got nothing but air." And, "a verbal contract isn't worth the paper it's written on."

PART FIVE

SELLING INDEPENDENT LOW BUDGET
AND MICRO-BUDGET MOVIES
AND GETTING THEM MADE!

CHAPTER FIFTY-THREE:
GETTING YOUR MOVIE DISTRIBUTED AND RECOGNIZED, GETTING MONEY AND PROFITS BACK TO YOUR INVESTORS AND ADVANCING YOUR MOVIE CAREER

George S. Kaufman, the much honored playwright and screenwriter of several of the Marx Brothers' best movies, reportedly once told a young aspiring playwright whose play he'd read, "The trouble with your play's ending is its beginning." This illustrates a central theme in this book, which is that how a thing begins very often has absolutely everything to do with how that thing ends. A movie's *concept*, particularly with a low budget movie, often has more to do with whether that movie has a chance at commercial distribution than any other factor. Here's a portion of a chapter from another book of mine about screenwriting that illustrates my point.

"THE DESIRE TO SEE" AND A SCRIPT OR MOVIE'S CONCEPT AND CONCEPTUALIZATION

Several times I've written or co-written, directed, and or produced or co-produced movies that had no distributor involved in the movie's financing or production. When you complete a movie, with no distributor attached, the next step is to *get a distributor*. The first question a distributor asks when you tell them that you've made a movie and are looking for a distributor is virtually always "Who's in it?" They are asking whether or not the movie has any actors whose name will help a distributor sell the movie. The next question is virtually always "What's it about?" The distributor is not asking for a summary of the movie's story. He or she is asking for the movie's concept. The distributor wants to know about the movie's genre and its commercial content. Most of all the distributor wants to know if he or she can reduce the movie to an image or two and a few lines of copy or a few words that will grab the attention of buyers and convince some significant segment of the public to pay money to view the movie. When Arnold Schwarzenegger was one of the highest paid movie stars in the world it was reported that he would only agree to do a movie after seeing a "mock up" of its advertising campaign. This is actually very smart and probably contributed to the high amount of audience appeal of many of the movies in which he chose to star.

When you complete a movie, you are very often in some very important ways, right where you started, face to face with the movies concept. Michael Crichton the author, screenwriter, and producer of *Jurassic Park*, was among the most financially successful writers of all time. His books, movies, TV shows and related products have probably earned well over a billion dollars (more likely several billion dollars) in gross income. About three decades ago I saw him being interviewed on TV. When he was asked about how he came up with the ideas for his books, his response was slow, thoughtful, exceptionally frank and enlightening. He said that when he was in college he took a class in creative writing. He soon realized, that in his creative writing class of about thirty people there were people who could create more human, more believable, more complex and more interesting characters than he would ever be able to create and there were other people who could write better dialogue and create more complex and involved plots than he could and there were also people who could write with a more accomplished literary style

256

than he would ever be able to write. He asked himself how he could ever have a career as a creative writer in the face of these facts.

My answer to that question is to look at the *concepts* of Crichton's books and movies. *Jurassic Park* is one of the most commercial movie *concepts* ever. The very concept of *Jurassic Park* provokes an instant, intense "desire to see" in a very large part of the movie viewing public. *They want to see the dinosaurs. They want to visit Jurassic Park.* Crichton is a master of concepts and *conceptualization.* He became an enormously successful creative writer not by mastering the things that were being taught in his creative writing class, but by mastering something that was far more important than what was being taught in his creative writing class.

A few years ago another writer and myself were looking at a trade paper's notices of movies that were about to go into production. My fellow screenwriter read the notice for *Bruce Almighty.* It included the movies *concept* and a description if a few of its key scenes and its cast. We both laughed, and agreed "that's a great concept." The movie lived up to its concept and was a huge hit. It stood out even when reduced to a couple of written paragraphs. Some concepts are so strong that they are basically "pure gold." The posters for *Jaws* with the image of the shark, with its mouth open, and the sharp shark's teeth showing virtually shouts "If you want to see a scary action adventure movie, *this is it!*" The movie *Saw* and its sequels have been enormously successful. Saw was reportedly made for $1.2 million, and grossed over $100 million in U.S. theatres. The concept of *Saw* is simple, direct, horrific and a superb concept for a cutting edge, hard core, torture, "horrorificsimo" horror movie. The idea of someone chained and destined for certain death unless they saw off their own limb is a *horrific* idea. It's a horrifying image, and a horrifying situation. It is virtually guaranteed to excite a "desire to see" in *avid horror movie fans,* especially in the season of Halloween. It is a great concept for its specific genre and subgenre.

Borat is a great comic concept. If you are at all interested in comedy, and you hear a one paragraph summary of *Borat* or see a few images, or hear a few key lines of dialog from *Borat* you know it's a "must see" movie. *Titanic* has a great concept; two young lovers from different worlds on a doomed ship; love that triumphs over death itself. It resonates with the same kind of emotional power as Shakespeare's classic story of doomed love, *Romeo and Juliet. Wedding Crashers* is an excellent concept for a romantic comedy, "date movie." *Wedding Crashers* starts out as kind of a male fantasy, two young cynical bachelor divorce lawyers crash weddings with false identities and con many romantically vulnerable beautiful women into having sex with them. *Wedding Crashers* then morphs into a more female oriented romantic movie as each of these cynical lying slimy "sex machine" divorce lawyers falls in love with their respective female soul mates. *Wedding Crashers* appeals to males and females making it a great date movie. The two wedding crashers false identity scam is cynically funny when it worked and even funnier when they are almost discovered and ultimately it supplies some serious drama and suspense when "things go really wrong."

Casablanca is a perfect concept for a World War II propaganda movie, and a love story. The purpose of WWII propaganda movies was to inspire members of the audience to sacrifice and to contribute to the common "war effort." Humphrey Bogart's character Rick, sacrifices his chance to be with Ingrid Bergman's character so he can give "his all" to the war effort. He makes this sacrifice after the movie shows Bogart's and Bergman's characters love for each other in strong and emotionally involving detail. How could any "red blooded" American in the world war two movie audience do less? *Casablanca* also has an evil Nazi hovering over all. The evil Nazis threatening to torture and kill anyone who gets in his way. He's a reminder to the audience of what everyone's life would be like if the Nazis win World War II. *Casablanca is not just some kind of accidental great movie. It's a great movie that grew out of a highly polished and perfected and well-aligned concept!*

A movie's concept is not simply its story, or a condensed summary of its story. When the great writer, director, producer Stanley Kubrick began writing the screenplay for *Dr. Strangelove* he was working with the novel, *Red Alert*, which was a suspense thriller about an accidental nuclear war between Russia and the USA. Kubrick and the writer(s) he was working with were writing the script in a "deadly serious" tone. They were throwing away their best ideas because they were "funny" and not right for a suspense thriller. At some point, Kubrick realized that the *story* of an accidental nuclear war launched by a crazy general had a lot more potential as a ruthlessly irreverent *black comedy* than as a suspense thriller. Kubrick and his fellow screenwriter(s), retrieved their rejected hilarious ideas and *reconceptualized Dr. Strangelove*, as one of the most horrifically biting satirical movies ever made. Their *comic* concept allowed Kubrick and his fellow writers to explore and expose the actual absurdity and insanity of the "mutually assured nuclear destruction", which was the real actual defense strategy of the cold war. Irreverent comedy allowed a deeper look at this reality with more impact than their original suspense thriller concept would have allowed. Kubrick's reconceptualization opened the door for *Dr. Strangelove* to become a virtually unique masterpiece. The events of the *story* of *Dr. Strangelove* either as a *suspense thriller* or a *black comedy* would have been very similar or the same, but they are two very different ways of conceptualizing the story. These two concepts are radically separate.

Again, a movie's concept is not just a summary of its story. The famous movie critic, Roger Ebert, pointed out that the story of legendary art film writer, director Ingmar Bergman's art movie masterpiece *Jungfrukällan* (*The Virgin Spring*)**,** is basically the same as the story of the low budget exploitation bloody horror movie, *Last House on the Left***,** which was written and directed by horror movie master Wes Craven. Craven is best known for *Scream*, its sequels, *A Nightmare on Elm Street***,** and the other Freddy Kruger movies.

Last House on the Left was also produced by Sean Cunningham, best known for *Friday the 13th* and its sequels. *The Virgin Spring* is set in the Middle Ages. It tells the story of a young girl who goes into the woods to pick berries and is brutally raped and murdered by a band of thugs. Later, these thugs, by chance, arrive at the murdered girl's house and are given hospitality by her father and mother. Her father, played by Max Von Sydow, discovers evidence that the thugs have murdered his beloved, innocent daughter and he slaughters the thugs. Later, he finds his daughter's body in the woods and buries her. He laments, "How can God allow such evil to happen?" and questions whether God exists. A spring of water bubbles up from his daughter's grave and he takes it as a sign from God. Critics all over the world have written very, very much about the profound philosophical implications of *The Virgin Spring* and Bergman's greatness as a dramatist. *The Virgin Spring* is an archetypal 1960's "art movie."

Last House on the Left tells the story of two teenage girls who go to the city to attend a rock music concert and end up being raped and murdered by a band of escaped criminals. These criminals end up at the house of the parents of one of the girls who they've murdered. As in T*he Virgin Spring,* the girl's father discovers evidence of their crime, and he and the girl's mother slaughter the murdering rapist criminals in pure 1970's low budget, horror movie blood and guts style, "to the max" and with great "gusto".

The same story can be conceptualized as an art movie about the nature of evil and mans relationship to God or as a blood and guts horror movie about blood and guts and horror. T*he Virgin Spring* was an enormously successful art movie, and *Last House on the Left* was an enormously successful low budget "cult classic" horror movie. It was made for a budget of about $70,000. It launched Wes Craven's and Sean Cunningham's careers. Each of these movies belongs to very different genre's and subgenre's and despite the similarity of their stories each movie's concept aligns exactly and with great gusto to its genre or subgenres basic "desire to see." The basic "desire to see" of the art movie genre is a "desire to see something that will cause one to think and which will enrich one intellectually and can cause one to continue to think and discuss the movie long after viewing it." The basic "desire to see" of a "blood and guts" horror movie is to see blood and guts and something horrifying.

Meet the Parents and *Meet the Fockers* are based on comic concepts that are funny and also have considerable depth. The situation of a young man who's deeply in love meeting his fiancé's parents is ripe with both dramatic and comic potential. When you add to that basic situation; a compulsive desire on the part of that young man to impress his father in law to be and you also add that the young man has a chronic tendency to tell little white social lies to ingratiate himself and the prospective father in law to be is a fiercely suspicious absolute truth fiend, retired CIA spy catcher who really feels nobody is good enough for *his* daughter, you have a super charged concept for a romantic comedy. Then the screenwriters add to that basic concept a kind of governing rule that "everything that can go wrong does go wrong" and you have a great concept. The sequel, *Meet the Fockers*, follows a very similar pattern and is also a "solid gold" concept!

The concept at the heart of the Frank Capra classic *It's a Wonderful Life* is to show the value of one good person's life, and how the world or a small town would be different if that one good person had not lived. It's a concept that cuts deeply on an emotional level and engages almost everyone who sees it. *Finding Nemo* is a great concept for a children's movie. A "child like" cute little animated fish gets lost in the big dangerous ocean. The impulse to find a lost child and the impulse of a lost child to return to its family have enormous emotional strength. *Finding Nemo* appeals deeply to "desires to see" at the root of its genre. *Happy Feet* is also a great concept for a children's movie. What is cuter that dancing penguins?

The multi-Oscar winning movie *Crash* is an "independent American art movie." Its basic concept of showing the inter connection and interrelationship of the lives of people from different social strata in Los Angeles is a great *art movie* concept. It is a thoughtful and discussion provoking movie that is about *things that people think about but don't talk about*. *Crash* shows characters that appear to be or are "bad" people that take good or heroic actions, and characters that appear to be good people do bad things. The movie's view of good and evil has a large grey area that aligns very much with the world view of much of its thoughtful intellectual "target audience."

Some may feel that its unjust or wrong for movie distributors to rely so strongly on a surface examination of a movie's concept when deciding whether a movie is worth distributing or not. Whether it's fair or just or not is a matter of opinion that belongs outside this book. However the importance of a movie's concept to whether or not it will be distributed and the importance of a scripts concept as to whether or not it will sell or be made into a movie is a reality! It is a reality that is based on and connected to another reality; *how people choose which movies they will pay money to see.* Whether on DVD, TV or in movie theatres large segments of the movie viewing public base their decisions of which movie(s) they want to see on a brief exposure to the movies *concept*, either from a TV commercial, or "trailer" or newspaper or internet add or promo, or brief word of mouth comment about the movie.

One point that's important to make is that the vast majority of successful movies have concepts that can meet a distributor's needs. These successful movies, almost uniformly can be reduced to a few words, sentences, or an image that can grab the attention of a significant segment of the movie viewing public, and cause them to pay to see these successful movies. The classic Western *High Noon* was a great concept for a Western; at a specific time, in a specific place, in the streets of a small town one "good guy" will shoot it out with a group of vengeful outlaw "bad guys." That concept aligns directly with some of the Western genres most deeply-rooted *"desire to see"* a violent life and death "black and white" conflict between pure good and pure evil, with the outcome decided by skill in the use of the gun. Its very concept is about duty, integrity, physical courage, honor and the importance of, and often isolation of the lone individual, and the nature of *dramatic decision. High Noon* is almost the ultimate "a man's gotta do what a man's gotta do" movie. Other classic westerns with great concepts that were also about one individual's skill with a gun and courage, are *Shane* and *Rio Bravo* and *Stagecoach*.

Night of the Living Dead and *The Evil Dead* are both mega cult classic horror movies. *Night of the Living Dead*'s story concept is that recently dead people have come back to life as flesh eating zombies who surround a farm house that seven people have turned into a barricaded mini–fortress. The people trapped in the isolated farmhouse conflict with each other as to what course of action is best. The conflict is resonant with and reminiscent of the social conflicts of the 1960s, when the movie was made. *Night of the Living Dead*'s concept is clear, clean, penetrating, and sharply focused not just as a horror movie but as George Romero said "a horror movie with something more." Romero, the director, and co-screenwriter of *Night of the Living Dead*, has made many successful horror movies and is a master of the horror movie genre. His is a masterful filmmaker and screenwriter. In my opinion, *Night of the Living Dead* is Romero's best movie and it's certainly his most classic and most widely viewed. Its success is partly caused by its excellent concept, and conceptualization.

Sam Raimi's first movie, *The Evil Dead*, is also based on a supremely excellent *concept*. The basic story concept of The Evil Dead is that four young people go to an isolated cabin for a break. The cabin turns out to be haunted by a disembodied evil spirit. At first, the evil spirit animates objects and even animates the trees in the forest to attack and rape one girl. The evil spirit then takes possession of each of the people in the cabin one at a time in sequence, turning one after another into "gore" ridden puss spitting demonic monsters while the remaining horrified cabin dwells battle each friend turned monster until the last one is captured by the evil spirit. This a great concept for a *fangoria-a-go-go, gore uber alles* horror movie. The isolation from civilization and safety, the horrific demonic images, the power of the disembodied spirit and the inability of mere humans to combat it, the H.P. Lovecraft feel and homage, are all part of this ultra cult classic movie's powerful *concept* which appeals very strongly to the "desires to see" of a significant segment of the horror movie audience.

Citizen Kane's concept is like a highly polished, and exquisitely cut diamond. The entire movie, with all its elegance, immense detail, and absolutely inspired and virtuoso genius in several directions, boils down to the mystery surrounding, the meaning of Kane's last words "rosebud". Solving the mystery of the significance of "Rosebud" and the meaning of Kane's life, and curiosity about how the mega-rich and mega-powerful actually live are at the heart of this supremely acclaimed ultra classic movie's artistically masterful concept.

The concept of *E.T.* grabs most viewer's heartstrings by subconsciously reminding them of the death of their first pet, and the vanquishing of their childhood imaginary friend(s) by the cruel adult world of reality. *E.T.* is also about "going home." It shares this part of its concept with *Rambo* and *The Odyssey* which are both also about going home.

Star Wars is an epic concept of an exhilarating battle between good and evil, heroism and tyranny set against an amazingly grand space opera background. It's a great concept for a heroic epic.
Alien has a concept that combines isolation and danger. Being trapped in a spaceship is in itself scary, but being trap with vile terrifying murderous super insect monster that will wipeout human life on earth if not stopped is a mega concept.

The devil invades and takes over the body of a young girl, and priests battle the devil for the girl's soul. That is the simple and superb concept of *The Exorcist*.

I use the word *conceptualization* to express two specific meanings. The first is *the perfecting of the movie's concept by polishing the script, focusing it, qualifying it, enhancing it, and developing it*. The second definition is *the process of using a concept as a kind of DNA code to grow and unify an entire script or movie and all its parts, large and small*. Let's compare some of the clear, clean, focused, unified, biting "desire to see" satisfying concepts of the successful and very successful movies mentioned earlier with some conspicuously unsuccessful movies. Again, for a database of conspicuously unsuccessful movies lets look at the bottom level of movies that barely get distribution or fail to get any distribution at all. Let's also look at scripts that don't get made into movies and don't deserve to be made into movies.

If you look at a number of these unsuccessful movies, and their advertising campaigns, and read some of these scripts, as I have, you'll find that almost none of them have attention grabbing strongly interesting *original clear, well perfected concepts*. This is in strong contrast with the concepts of very many successful and very successful movies. These unsuccessful movies usually don't grow out of and are often not unified by a clear effective *concept*. Often the best way to describe these movies and scripts level of *conceptualization* is "malfunction." Many of these low level movies and scripts do not seem to be organically unified and the product of one concept. Often they are more like the body of Frankenstein's monster; an arm from here, a leg from over there, a head from someplace else, and all the parts are put together with the seams obviously showing. In contrast most, successful and very successful movies appear to have grown in an organically unified way into a unified whole governed by a single effective concept, or at least to be unified by a single concept.

Most of these very unsuccessful movies and scripts are written by a method I call "kindergarten finger painting self expression uber alles." In this method of screenwriting the screenwriter just splatters the page with whatever comes into his or her mind and seems "good" at the time. This method does not involve much if any "skull busting" conceptualization but it has serious limits and liabilities, and is very different from a method of screenwriting that involves serious effective conceptualization. However, it must be said that for some writers in some case the "kindergarten finger painting self-expression uber alles" method of screenwriting can and does work, but for many it does not.

The most successful screenwriter with whom I ever worked was a master of conceptualization. I will call him Mr. "What's this movie about?" because he would repeatedly and relentlessly ask "What's this movie about?" when reacting to a script or story idea, and when developing a concept or outlining a potential script. Eventually he sold a lot of scripts to major movie studios and a few of them were made into movies. He made a lot of money as a screenwriter and became a successful practicing master of the craft.

When I contrast "Mr. what's this movie about?" and his high level of success with other screenwriters I've known, and whose scripts I've read, who in my opinion have talent but have failed to achieve real screenwriting success, I'm usually struck by how *unexceptional* many of the concepts of their scripts are. Many of these unsuccessful scripts (which will never be made into movies or sold) show talent, and have good things on them. What they virtually all lack is an excellent interest grabbing, unique or original *concept.* I know several screenwriters who decided to write a script on a concept or story line after only a few minutes or hours of thinking about the story, and very little or no real conceptualization. These less than successful (but in my opinion often talented) screenwriters would often end up spending a lot of time writing and rewriting their scripts. Their rewriting was often patchwork and did not involve any real conceptualization or reconceptualization. They'd then spend a lot of time photocopying their scripts, and getting their scripts to more and more producers, or so-called producers or want-to-be producers, or "b.s. slinging flakes" and then more patchwork rewrites, and often jumping through more hoops, meetings, phone calls, etc. to no positive result. In a couple of cases I saw these unconceptualized scripts made into undistributable movies with very bad results.

This process of investing only a tiny percentage of time and energy into qualifying and perfecting a concept is a common trait of screenwriters I've known who, despite talent, experienced and endless gauntlet of rejection and frustration as a response to their scripts or movies. In contrast "Mr. what's this movie about?" spent a lot of time and invested a lot of thought in qualifying perfecting and often rejecting concepts and a huge amount of time and mental energy in very harsh demanding "industrial strength" *conceptualization* before actually writing his scripts. He experienced, in contrast, a lot of financial rewards and success from his screenwriting. "Mr. what's this movie about?" was friends with a well-known studio executive. At one point that studio executive told "Mr. what's this movie about?" many of the concepts that he and the studio were developing. "Mr. what's this movie about?" did not tell me any of the executive's concept's but he said that the executive did not even have to tell him which of the studio's concepts were for TV and which were for movies. "Mr. what's this movie about?" said that there is something special about a concept that's actually worth making into a movie, and *you can feel it when you hear the concept.*

He was right! Low budget movies face an additional challenge. In order for them to compete or even have any chance of competing against the avalanche of big budget studio-produced and studio distributed or large independently produced and distributed movies they almost always must deliver something that some significant segment of the movie-viewing audience desires to see but is *not* being delivered to them by larger budget movies from major studios or large independents. The success of the many runaway success independent movies like *Clerks* that I have mentioned rested not just on the fact that the movies were excellent. Each of them also delivered to some significant segment of the movie-viewing public that something they desired to see that was not being delivered otherwise.

Major studio movies are now largely aimed at the lowest common denominator of the worldwide market. A high percentage of studio movies are currently based on comic book superheroes, old TV shows, video games, or are sequels. Many romantic comedies are thinly-veiled copies of similar movies that made money, or are star actor or director's pet projects. This means that there are significant pockets of the movie-viewing public that are not likely to be interested. Studios have low budget arms like Sony Classics that make and distribute lower budget fare like *Juno* and *Sideways* that appeal to pockets of viewers who might not be that fond of major budget blockbusters. Those viewers are a "happy hunting ground" for low budget filmmakers.

Your movie's basic concept may well determine whether or not your movie has a chance of getting real distribution or not, even before the script is written and before one scene is shot. This is a fact that low budget filmmakers need to face head-on without flinching or kidding around. There are herds of people running around with video cameras making what they think are movies, but far too many non-movies are shot on video that have no concept, no interesting story, no professional quality script, and in many cases no real actors, just people in front of the camera. They have no real cinematographer, just someone pointing a camera under some lights. They have no real director, no real editor, and they unsurprisingly do not end up with a real movie. The only thing these non-movies have in common is a camera. They lack virtually everything else.

It is not the fact that they were shot on video or a low budget, with unknown actors, that makes these non-movies. Spike Lee's *Bamboozled* was shot on prosumer video cameras and was a real movie, as was *Center of the World* and Lars von Trier's *Dancer in the Dark*, which won the Grand Prize and Best Actress awards at the Cannes Film Festival and an Oscar nomination for its lead actress, Bjork. Robert Rodriguez shot *Once Upon A Time In Mexico* on video, and other great independent films like *28 Days* and *Once* were also shot that way, as was *Paranormal Activity*, the great movie success story of 2009. With so much being shot on video, distributors have less prejudice, but they do have a dislike for amateurish filmmaking because audiences can't stand it. Non-movies may be easy to make, but they are usually impossible to sell.

For a competent cinematographer the look of a video image is not a problem. For a competent director, even in low budget, unknown actors are not what dooms non-movies. The finances available do not doom the project. The ultimate downfall of any failed low budget film is *lack of distribution*. Low budget movies that please an audience can get distributed and breakout! Lack of distribution is almost always a reflection of lack of concept, story, script that are really worth making into a movie or lack of genre-specific commercial content.

A studio executive working with Kevin Smith on *Mall Rats* (Smith's second movie) said *Clerks* wasn't a real movie. I suppose that was because *Clerks* wasn't shot on 35mm color stock with professional, name actors like *Mall Rats*. Well, *Clerks* remains Smiths' best movie, a $35,000 wonder with a million dollar script, good acting in its most important roles, very good directing, adequate cinematography, and excellent editing. Those are the elements that make a "real movie" and guess which of those two movies was a bigger hit?

One of your main tasks in making a low budget independent movie, particularly if shot on video with no name actors, is to somehow separate your movie from the heaving, relentless sea of "shot on video with credit cards" non-movies out there. You will have to show your movie to professional no-nonsense, cash register next to their brain, often literally cigar-chomping distributors, and you will have to show them that some significant segment of the movie viewing audience will be willing to *pay to see your movie*. Your movie will have to show the distributor something that can be sold to someone. Your movie can be a serious drama like *Faces* or *Breathless*, or cutting-edge sci-fi like *Alphaville*, or ultra-horror like *The Evil Dead*, or a comedy like *Clerks*, or an action comedy like *El Mariachi*. Just because you are running a camera with people in front of it doesn't mean you're making a movie that distributors and a paying audience will want to see. Remember Jean Luc Godard's statement that "Movies will not truly be an art form until the cost of making a movie approximates the cost of paints and canvas or the cost of pencil and paper." That statement carries with it a not so pleasant corollary. As it gets cheaper and cheaper to make movies, more and more people who have not done the work necessary to actually become artists or real professional storytellers, but who want to be artists or to be considered to be artists, or to pretend to be artists will make non-movies that are crap. They will make these non-movies simply because they can get their hands on a camera. At this time, they have made lots of bad films, mostly shot on video, that often logjams the flow of low budget and micro-budget movies trying to make their way to the movie going public. Do not contribute to this sea of crap! Do not let it swallow up your movie or your ambitions!

Every single breakout movie I've studied, no matter what its budget size, whether it had name actors or unknowns, or was shot on 35mm, 16mm, black and white, color, or video, always had a good to excellent or superb concept, story, and script, as well as good acting, directing, and editing. As I've discussed, a script is often not enough to get a movie financed. You need *script plus* to get a movie financed. What I'm about to tell you might seem to contradict that. It does not, but it does present a paradox. Almost always, the are clear determinative factors in whether a low budget independent movie gets real commercial distribution. These factors also determine how successful that movie will be. They are: its originality and understanding of its audience's "desire to see" and the excellence or lack thereof, the artistic quality and commercial potential and audience appeal to at least to some significant segment of the movie-viewing public, or lack of these things in the movie's concept, story, and script. These things are what will usually determine whether or not a low budget independent movie has a chance to see commercial success.

If you want to have a good career as a movie director or producer, you need to make good scripts into good movies. You may need to write the scripts yourself. You many need to guide other writers, or find the scripts in the open market. You might partner with another writer to turn out a screenplay. Rich and interesting material can be found in novels, plays, short stories, magazine, or newspaper articles. If you look at the careers of successful directors or producers you will see that the movies that made the careers of those filmmakers all had good or excellent concepts, stories, and scripts. You need to develop a feel for what those things mean with regard to successful films. Even if you don't write scripts, you need to become an expert on screenwriting, scene writing, judging an audience's reactions, and commercial concepts. You should also know the history of successful stage plays and other forms of dramatic writing.

Ted Post told me stories of how he worked with Clint Eastwood as an actor, before Eastwood began to direct. He said Eastwood would go over the script dialogue line by line and the script itself word by word, sentence by sentence, implied shot by implied shot. Ted said he had never worked with anyone that went over scripts in such detail. Accordingly, Eastwood's movie *The Outlaw Josey Wales* has one of the best scripts every written. The dialogue in that script is polished to perfection and features recurring phrases much the way Eastwood and Ted Post's *Magnum Force* (screenplay by John Milius), had lines like "A man's got to know his limitations" and "This is a .44 magnum, the most powerful handgun in the world. It can take your head clean off. You've got to ask yourself one question, Do I feel lucky?" On the DVD commentary of *Magnum Force*, which I strongly recommend to screenwriters, directors, and producers, and actors, John Milius comments on how Eastwood's notes for script changes were always valuable and useful, always concerned with making the script better. If you look at the development and continuation and ascendancy of Eastwood's career one thing that marks it, beside his tremendous screen presence and charisma is *excellent scripts* whose concepts and stories attract and satisfy audiences, and scripts that are very perfected and polished. *Million Dollar Baby* and *Letters from Iwo Jima* were nominated for Best Screenplay Oscars. At age 78, Eastwood make two Oscar quality movies in one year, *Gran Torino* and *The Changeling*. Simply making two good movies in one year is a major accomplishment for anyone, at any age. Both those films came from great scripts.

Actors become movie stars partly because of their screen presence, charisma, and audience appeal. They have an ability to get an audience to identify with them, and of course they often have great physical beauty, but there is almost always one other factor. Star actors play a role that captures an audience's imagination and interests them in a movie or movies that audiences enjoy. These roles are written by screenwriters who know their craft. Actors, movie stars, directors, and producers involved with movies that audiences enjoy see their careers grow and blossom. Actors, movie stars, directors, and producers involved with movies that audiences do not enjoy see their careers decline. The factor of being involved with enjoyable movies or not is separate from the skill of the people involved in the productions. An actor, director, or producer can individually do an excellent job, yet if they are involved with a movie that audiences do not enjoy, it can harm a career.

Whether an audience enjoys a movie or not usually depends greatly on a movie's concept, story, and script. A movie camera, a movie editing machine (or computer using a program like Final Cut Pro) are very seductive tools. They are fun to use, like toys. Writing a professional script can be fun when it's going well, too, but it's usually a lot of *very hard work*. Facing a blank page is usually *not* fun and can be scary, boring, frustrating, tedious, and even disheartening. Professional screenwriting is very difficult. It can be fun, but it's hard work.

In contrast, running a camera is fun. That's one more reason why there are so many more movies being made than there are good scripts that can be made into good movies!

Before you write a script, or have another writer write one, or before you select a script to make into a movie, think long and hard about the potential movie's concept and story. Imagine yourself on the phone with a distributor *after* the movie is made and you only have a couple of sentences, after the distributor has asked "What's this movie about?" to explain the movie's concept and convince that distributor that they can interest the movie-viewing public or some significant segment of same with a few words or images that they should pay good money to see your movie. Many concepts are not worth making into movies or writing into scripts! Many concepts that seem great may have already been made into a recent movie, so you have to know history and the marketplace, too.

One thing that is clear about breakout movies is that they are virtually never copies of earlier, recent movies. They are original, or at least seem original! Their concepts are fresh or they are a new take on an old concept that has been temporarily forgotten by older audience members, or never been seen by younger audience members. All distributors, metaphorically speaking, basically draw their money from the same well, the movie-going public. What makes your movie distributable is not a contract or a distributor saying yes. The fact that is has commercial value to a financially significant segment of moviegoers gives it commercial value. When your movie will please and satisfy that audience, you have a winner.

If a distributor says yes – and some will even put up a cash advance – that is like reading your grade on a test and being thrilled at what you see. Confucius's statement about preparation comes into play yet again, with the movie's concept, story, and script serving as the previous preparation that will get the movie distributed if the early preparation is sufficient and the movie is well-made. Here are the basic mechanics of how to make a distribution deal. I've done this process many times. First, you get a list of distributors. The first level of this list should be composed of distributors that are likely to distribute low budget independent movies, who had advertised in the film festival issues of *Varity* and *The Hollywood Reporter*. These issues come out before large events like the Cannes Film Festival and the American Film Market. They have ads from distributors and list contacts at those companies. These are the first distributors you should approach if you've made a low budget independent movie. If they are taking out ads in the "trades" they are active, and have some cash flow. You want a distributor that is solvent enough to pay you if your movie makes money, and one that has a high enough profile to sell your movie, if they say yes, they do want to distribute it. You can buy these pre-festival issues even if you do not subscribe to the trades. Those who live in Los Angeles can also do a lot of research at the Margaret Herrick Library of the Academy of Motion Picture Arts and Sciences, but many university libraries that have film schools also have subscriptions to the trades. Try the top level distributors first. If you strike out there, you can get long lists of distributors from websites like www.filmfestivals.com.

The way you approach a distributor is very simple and straightforward. You call the company's contact person and tell them that you've made a movie and are looking for a distributor. They will ask questions like "Who's in it?" and the other standard questions I've previously discussed. You can lie about things like a movie's budget, as long as your movie looks more expensive than it really was to shoot, so keep in mind the size of the advance you want. It is much easier to get a $100,000 advance from a distributor if he or she believe that your movie cost $300,000 to produce instead of the $75,000 it actually cost. One distributor who distributed a movie of mine multiplied his movie's budgets by a factor of ten when he spoke to the trade papers, and the reporters and buyers "swallowed it whole." I was making a movie for him for $175,000 and reading the trade papers at lunch – that's where I saw what he was claiming it cost to make the movie. Too bad I couldn't get him to multiply my salary by ten! There it was in black and white in the industry's "bibles." I knew how much my movie was costing, and every single movie this distributor had listed in production or pre-production had its budget multiplied by ten. This gentleman told me, "If you see it in print, you know it's a lie." He had an unusually realistic point of view toward life and the movie business, and had very realistic and successful methods of dealing with both.

I have never had a problem getting distributors to look at movies I've made. I have never had to do much selling to get a contact person at a distribution company to view my movies when I told them I was looking for a distributor. If you have a shot on video movie, however, and the contact person has just finishing watching a dozen "shot on video, no names" movies that didn't match up to the not-filmmakers glowing descriptions, you may not find it very easy to get the contact person to view your movie. If in good faith and with enough conviction, you can assert that your movie is worth seeing and has value, that it will appeal to a significant segment of the movie-going public, from my experience I would say you're likely to have distributors say yes to looking at your film. No one wants to be the person that turned down a movie that some other distributor picks up and turns into a big hit that makes a lot of money. It is part of the job of even the person on the lowest rung of a distribution company to have someone look at new product.

Distributors are in business to *make money*. They distribute movies to make money. That means they need to acquire movies for distribution, so someone has to view movies that come in, that are available to be acquired. Making independent movies and getting them distributed is certainly an area where the phrase "Many are called but few are chosen" in Matthew 22:14 applies to business. Personally, I've been very fortunate in this regard. Every professional movie I've made has been distributed, usually in many markets. One of my student films was even distributed professionally. I have had contact people at major studios view my movies. In some cases, these were movies that did not have name actors. When you call a distributor and tell the person on the phone that you've made a movie and are looking for a distributor, you are *not* asking for some special extraordinary favor. You are simply asking them and helping them to do a vital part of their job. Some of my movies that were made for only a few hundred thousand dollars were viewed at major studios. The distribution of *Starship Invasions* by Warner Bros. was managed when the movie's money men producers screened it for the head of Warner Bros. Canada, who recommended it to the head of Warners in Burbank, and a print was shipped to "Hollywood" and viewed, then the distribution deal for the U.S. and Canada was made and signed. The movie basically sold itself with one screening at the Warner Bros. studio.

Again, locating distributors that advertise in trade papers and elsewhere and getting them to view your movie should not be a problem if you are diligent and confident of your movie's value, and you stay assertive and even aggressive if necessary. Once you get a distributor or merely someone at a distribution company to view your movie, it has to stand on its own two feet and create an audience with that distributor and/or employee. You may hear lots of stories from independent moviemakers about how difficult it is to get distribution. Well, if you make a movie that has no appeal to the public or a significant segment of the movie going public, then it is very likely not only going to be difficult to find distribution, it will probably be impossible to get any real commercial distribution for that movie.

One professor at UCLA told me that the mindset of a movie distributor was that "All the money in the world secretly belonged to that distributor" and you should be willing to give that distributor your movie for free, and pay his or her expenses and work for nothing to help that distributor get his or her money back for he or she alone to enjoy. This is not the mindset of all distributors but it does come pretty close to the actual mentality of some of them. Some people have told me that distributors have a cash register in place of a brain, but this isn't really a warranted remark. Many distributors are very smart and have very highly developed artistic sensibilities. I've worked for and with distributors, been in their homes, and talked with them about many movies. I've seen their art collections and discussed their appreciation for great movies. What usually differentiates distributors from moviemakers is their intense contact with the public and their no nonsense realization of what the public's taste is and is *not*. Movie distributors are not just in touch with the reality of the public, they constantly smash into it headfirst every time they sell or try to sell a movie to the public or a sub-distributor that is even more directly in contact with the public.

Movie distributors cannot afford to be out of touch with reality. Those that are out of touch with reality do not usually stay in business long enough to matter. In contrast, being out of touch with reality is not just an occupational hazard for screenwriters and some moviemakers, for many it is an absolutely sacred way of life. This is also usually true to a lesser degree for some directors and actors. Speaking metaphorically again, if you put a large bar of gold in an intersection and put a movie distributor on the corner of that intersection and make sure that the distributor saw that bar of gold, you can be almost certain that distributor would venture out into traffic, even heavy traffic, to take possession of that gold! You can guess what any distributor would do if they saw a pile of crap.

You want distribution? Make a movie that is perceived to be a bar of gold. Make a movie that screams to a distributor's business sense that a significant segment of the movie going public will pay to see it! If you get one distributor who wants to distribute your movie, do everything that you can to get another one, also. If you get two, do everything you can to get three or more. It is very difficult to get a real distribution advance unless you have at least two or more distributors that seriously want to distribute the movie. The best story that I ever heard about a moviemaker getting a distribution advance involves Ivan Reitman's breakout low budget independent movie *Meatballs* that starred Bill Murray and launched his career as a movie star after he'd been a TV star on *Saturday Night Live*. Here's the story that I heard from a reliable source. I cannot vouch for every detail but I'm virtually sure that it's basic premise is true. Reitman made *Meatballs* in Canada for about $800,000 (listed on the Internet Movie Database as an estimated $1.6 million Canadian). Anyway you look at it, a movie like that was low budget. Reitman reportedly sold the movie for a $12 million advance against a percentage of future profits. I cannot vouch with certainty for those exact figures but the basic premise of the story, that he made the movie for under a million and sold it to a studio for an advance several times the size of its budget, is almost certainly true.

It's impossible for me to imagine that kind of advance was made unless more than one, and probably several distributors wanted the movie, and wanted it seriously. My guess is that every distributor that saw the movie wanted it badly. They saw a giant-sized bar of gold! Distributors want to distribute movies that will make money for them, but even more they do *not* want movies to slip through their hands and make a lot of money for one of their competitors. You want to instigate a bidding war over your movie, if you can. You do *not* want to give your movie for free to the first distributor that admires it. If you have accomplished the difficult task of actually making a movie that has real and perceived value, you want to collect everything you can get, for yourself and your investors. The kind of success that Ivan Reitman had in getting an advance for *Meatballs* is very rare, but it has happened, it continues to happen, and it *can* happen for you. I do not know the exact numerical details of the advances, distribution deals, and income paid to the producers of the top independent movies I've discussed in this book. I'm sure that many of them are at least in the same league as Reitman was with *Meatballs*, though. If the opportunity for that kind of success comes to you, grab it and take full advantage. Be a pig! You deserve that kind of payoff and so do your investors! Remember, however, that kind of success is only one highly valuable, audience-pleasing movie away from yourself or any other existing or potential moviemaker.

Here is how movie distributors or their staff watch movies that are seeking distribution that are lined up for them to view. When I was working for a large independent distributor editing the movie I made for him we used his projection room as an editing room and post-production office. During lunch hour, he'd reclaim his projection room and watch movies that were seeking distribution. We'd eat lunch and watch them with him. It was very, very educational. These movies were on 35mm film. A 35mm projection reel is normally about 20 minutes long. The distributor would watch the first five or ten minutes of a movie. If it did not catch his interest, he'd tell the projectionist to switch to the second reel about 20 minutes into the movie. If the first few minutes of that reel did not catch his interest, he'd jump to the next reel and so on. He'd say, "You don't have to eat an entire cake to know if that cake is any good." He felt he didn't have to watch the whole movie to know if he wanted to distribute it. I was told later by an editor that watched my movie that the distributor picked up and successfully distributed in theaters and to foreign countries that the distributor watched *all* of my movie, which was a rarity for that distributor, who was a former director and very complimentary to me about my direction of that movie. He entered it in a major film festival where it won two major awards.

Sometimes these lunch hour viewing sessions got downright brutal! I still remember when a movie was being screened, and the movie was made by a real close friend of mine, and it had some commercial potential and its maker and I were dearly hoping that the distributor would pick it up and do the kind of stellar bang-up job that he had done with a similar movie years earlier. Early in the movie, there were several overly long self-indulgent unnecessary shots of a vintage car driving around, delaying access to the movie's story, commercial content, and boring the viewer. The distributor remarked, "You know they're gonna show that car as much as they can. They paid $100 to rent it." We all laughed, because it was so true. The moviemakers were so proud of this vintage car, they bored the audience with their indulgence and delayed the onset of valuable commercial content. As soon as the distributor made that remark, I knew that the movie was in trouble with regard to this distributor acquiring it, because the distributor was beginning to have disdain for the makers of the movie.

Still, the movie had an *excellent* title and commercial content. If it had been edited and made with more of an eye to what the audience actually wanted to see, and if the story was unfolded at a more brisk pace, it might have had a bit of a chance, but its pace, its lack of consideration for the viewer antagonized the distributor and by the latter part of the screening the distributor was openly and comically mocking the movie and lots of his barbed comments were funny in a very black comedy way and cuttingly *true*. I stopped eating my lunch halfway through the screening. It was grim. After the screening, my friend called me, wanting to know how the screening went. He asked cheerily, full of enthusiasm and anticipation and hope. It was my unpleasant task to warn him that the distributor would pass on the movie. I could hear in his voice that he was crushed. He could feel his hopes and dreams for this movie and his immediate future in movie production "going down the drain" which is exactly what happened.

A little more understanding of the movie audience and a bit more understanding of what they *desired to see* and a bit more consideration of that audience and his movie could have been a hit. It could have launched him on a career as a moviemaker, and sustained him, instead of disappointing him. He had an excellent concept, a perfect title, but the movie lacked an understanding of the audience's *desire to see*.

Another brutal incident I recall is the viewing of a movie that had an overly long, boring, inept and annoying opening title sequence. It so antagonized the distributor that he switched to the next movie without watching any other reel. That moviemaker did not even make it through his piece of crap opening title sequence before the distributor passed on the movie. The distributor's reasoning was that if the opening title sequence was this bad, why waste time watching the rest of the movie that was made by the same moviemaker? It was likely just as bad or worse.

If you ate a piece of icing off the top of a cake and it made you vomit, would you eat the rest of the cake?

In William Shakespeare's time, about 500 years ago before movies and TV, cheap tickets were sold to "groundlings" – audience members that would stand on the ground around the stage. They had no seats. Typically, these playgoers would bring bags of rotten fruit with them to the plays. If the play did not capture their attention in the first few minutes, they'd start making rude noises and comments. If it continued to fail to amuse them, they would throw their rotten fruit at the actors. They were intent on getting some entertainment one way or another. That's why Shakespeare's plays open with attention-grabbing scenes, such as the witches in "Macbeth" and the ghost in "Hamlet."

Things have not really changed much in five centuries. Most TV shows and news broadcasts open with some attention-grabbing bit before going to the first commercial. In truth, things have not changed all that much in 2,500 years. If you read the best plays of ancient Greece, the very beginnings of drama and comedy in the West, you will see that these plays move quickly to grab the attention of the audience and pull viewers' attention into the world of the play. The play's *concept* is quickly presented to the audience to "hook" them into the drama or comedy of the story.

No script reader owes your script their attention and no movie viewer owes his or her attention to your movie, and no distributor or employee of a distribution company owes their attention to your movie, no matter how much blood, sweat, and tears or how many months or years of your life it took to make the movie, or how much that movie carries your most cherished dreams and hopes or your immediate future or the money of your family, friends, or credit card companies. Your script or your movie has to reach out and *grab* the reader or viewer and pull them into the imaginary world you created and make them care about the characters that inhabit it. You want them to care what happens to those people and what the outcome of the story will be. You are not a college professor lecturing a captive audience. You are a storyteller and/or a story *seller*. You have to take the responsibility and satisfy an audience. You have to make them want to see the rest of the movie once they watch its first few minutes. If you don't, it's very easy for a distributor to simply say, "I pass on this movie." Nowadays, many movies seeking distribution are viewed on DVD with exactly the same philosophy and method of operations as the distributor that I worked for used in his 35mm projection room. The distributor, contact person, or employee of the distribution company that watches the DVD of a movie seeking distribution will likely pay close attention to the first few minutes of the movie. A lot of good movies, even some of Hitchcock's best movies, use the opening credit sequence to set a movie's mood, expose its main themes, and even begin to introduce its concept and pull the viewer into its world. If the first few minutes of the movie impress the distributor, or his or her employee, they will likely continue to watch attentively, particularly as long as they entertain the idea that it is possible that they might want to acquire the movie for distribution, particularly if it has valuable name actors or a saleable concept. If the movie lacks these assets or loses the distributor's employee's attention they will likely fast forward through the movie, and will only stop for something that interests them. It is disheartening but they may take or make phone calls while watching the movie. They may do other tasks while "watching" the movie. I was not joking or talking lightly when I said your movie has to *reach out and grab their attention and hold it. Your movie has to be able to create its own audience!*

One associate of mine who was a very successful screenwriter and very good moviemaker did everything possible to get his movies seen in screening rooms with audience, *not* by distributors alone with a video while taking calls. He told me of all the potential distractions he foresaw competing with his movie if the distributor viewed it alone. I told him, quoting Jack Nicholson in *Chinatown*, "When you're right, you're right, and you're right." You can invite distributors to screenings and often they don't show up. They are busy. They have their own schedule; looking

271

at unacquired movies is at the bottom of their "to do" list. Usually, I just send them a print or a video and hope that they watch it under half-decent circumstances. The truth is that the result will be determined by the movie's value. If it's there, some distributor will see it. If not, nobody will see it.

If you can get your movie entered into *any* film festival, do it! This is particularly true for major festivals. Distributors and their scouts watch movies at these festivals very closely. They view the movies that are to some degree "pre-qualified" and a positive reaction at these festival screenings or the winning of an award can bolster a distributor's confidence and desire to acquire a movie for distribution. Successful screenings and winning awards at major film festivals played major roles in causing stellar distribution for *Clerks*, *El Mariachi*, and *Sex, Lies, and Videotape*. *Crash* was acquired for distribution after it was screened at the Toronto Film Festival.

When a distributor or distribution company employee is watching a DVD of a movie seeking distribution, often they slip into what I call "defensive viewing." They are watching the movie to be sure that they are *not* passing on a movie that they will regret not distributing. Your movie may be assumed to be guilty of being a worthless piece of crap unless and until it proves itself innocent of that charge. The movie viewing audience and distributors are ready to reward moviemakers that deliver what people desire to see, even in a low budget movie, and they are equally ready to shun movies that do not deliver.

Before you sign any distribution contract with any distributor, unless that distributor offers you a huge cash advance, you should ask the distributor for the name and phone number of at least one producer whose movie that they have distributed who is happy with the distribution that this distributor has done with their movie, and feels they have been paid fairly with regard to their share of the movie's income. If the distributor gives you even one such producer's name and phone number and you call up that producer and he or she verifies that they were treated well, you know immediately that you are dealing with a distributor who is in the top five or ten percent of all distributors, and may well be in an even higher bracket. If, on the other hand, the distributor gives you a song and dance about why they can't give you the name of even one producer that feels the distributor did a good job distributing their movie, and that they have paid them fairly, then you know you are in the "Twilight Zone" of serious jeopardy and you need to behave accordingly no matter how much the distributor tells you that he or she loves your movie and is going to do wonderful things with it but just can't come up with any signing cash advance because of the "expenses" that they will incur distributing your wonderful movie.

When you sign a distribution deal, always make sure that expenses come off the top, not from the producer's share. It can make a big different. Here is how that works. Suppose a movie has an income of $50,000 and expenses of $20,000 and the distributor's share is 33-1/3%. If the movie's expenses come off the top, the $20,000 of expense is subtracted from the $50,000 of income and that leaves $30,000. 33-1/3% goes to the distributor. This is $10,000. The producer or production company gets the remaining $20,000. In contrast, if the expenses come from the producer's share, the distributor takes 33-1/3% of the entire $50,000 income or about $16,600, a lot more than $10,000, and the producer pays the $20,000 in expenses from the remaining $33,400, leaving the producer with about $13,400, a lot less than $20,000 if expenses were taken off the top and it's actually less than the distributor would get in this example.

Now let's take a look at what happens if there is $50,000 of income and $50,000 of expenses, something that can easily happen. The distributor takes his or her 33–1/3%, about $16,600 and the producer or production company gets *zero money* and the producer still owes the distributor $16,600 in "expenses." *Try explaining this lovely situation to the investors.* The movie has made money for someone, including the distributor, but not for the investors, and the movie's been shown and their friends have seen it in theaters, but no money for them, and more money needs to be made to pay expenses before the investors see a dime. Whether a movie's expenses come of the top (as they should) or out of the producer's share becomes of vital importance if the movie is distributed theatrically, because movie theater distribution incurs a lot of expenses and if those expenses are recouped from the producer's share, they cannot only eat up the income from the theaters, they can even eat up income from other backup markets, like DVDs and TV, or foreign, and leave you with a movie that has been distributed all over the world in many markets and very little or no money has come back to the production company and the movie's investors.

Try explaining that little gem to movie investors that falsely believe that a movie has to make some money if it's shown anywhere in any market under any circumstances. "Where's their share?" they'll ask. If you can't hand over that share you "must be stealing" from them. After all, the movie was shown on cable or in Hong Kong, and they found a copy in a video store. "It had to make *some* money." Obviously, you must be stealing their share.

Accountants have been working very diligently for over a hundred years to enrich distributors, and develop and find and create ways to legally and sneakily steal from producers and production companies and their investors. Recovering the distributor's expenses from the producer's share of the movie's income is only one of their best tricks. It is bad enough that the producer has to pay the distributor's expenses, but it's less lethal if these expenses come off the top. The distributor does not pay the producer's expenses unless the producer can force the distributor to pay an upfront cash advance that covers the cost of making the movie. This rarely happens but it does happen, and if you ever get in a situation where two or more distributors want your movie badly, push them and push them hard to come up with a cash advance that pays for your movie's production expenses (the cost of making the movie) because the distributor will certainly make your movie pay for his or her distribution expenses. Just make sure they are off the top, *not* out of your share! You don't want to end up paying the distributor's expenses forever and owing that distributor more and more as more income rolls in and more "expenses" are incurred.

Here's a summary and recap of the mechanics of how one gets distribution for a movie.

First: Before you make the movie be very, very sure your movie has a good or excellent concept that will appeal to some significant segment of the paying movie viewing public.

Second: When the movie is completed, make a list of distributors who do, who have, and who might distribute low budget independently made movies. The top layer of this list should be composed, at least mostly, of distributors that have advertised in industry trade papers large film festival issues recently.

Third: You call up contact people at these distribution companies, you get them interested in your movie, and you get them to view your movie at a screening or on a DVD, or if you are fortunate enough, at a film festival.

Fourth: You interest as many distributors as possible in distributing your movie.

Fifth: You get as large a cash advance as possible. In movie distribution, "Money talks and b.s. walks." A cash advance is wroth a lot more than promises about all the wonderful things the distributor will do with your movie.

Sixth: If you can make a distribution deal, hopefully signing with a distributor that has provided you with the name of at least one producer whose movie they have distributed who feels that the distributor did a good job and paid them fairly, and you get expenses "off the top" and other prudent protections in your contract.

Personal friendship with a distributor will not get your movie distributed by that distributor. After I'd worked with a distributor, and I'd made two movies that he'd distributed with excellent results, he turned down a movie that I made later, simply because he didn't think he could make money distributing it. "It wasn't personal; it was just business." Movies get made "because someone knows someone" but that rarely happens with distribution. Also, there is no magic distributor out there hiding in the weeds! If your movie doesn't appeal to some segment of the movie-viewing public, no distributor can make money with it and none will want it. The idea that if you make a movie cheaply enough it's going to make some money and thus be profitable is completely and utterly *false*. False a-go-go, false uber alles. There are lots of very cheap movies out there that will never make a penny, and don't deserve to make a penny.

I saw a gentleman make two flawed movies with his own money. He non-wrote, barely directed, and produced them. He showed them to distributor after distributor. He recut them and showed them some more. He always believed that somewhere out there hiding somewhere was a distributor that could take his flawed movies and sell them to a few markets. His "movies" were not only very unprofessional – they totally lacked any awareness at all of the audience and what the audience desired to see. This gentleman had once worked as a sub-distributor and had sold some very bad movies that he felt were a lot worse than his own. Maybe they were "worse" but they were targeted at a very specific segment of the movie-viewing public. They hit that target. This gentleman never seemed to realize that there is an audience, and the audience *matters*! When he was writing his scripts, I'd tell him, the audience will not like this or that or, do this or that and the audience will react positively to it. He acted like this was sacrilege. He'd say, "This is how I want to do it." He said, "To hell with the audience" and through numerous distributors the audience said to hell with him and his movies. From Sophocles to Picasso, the task of the artist or the storyteller, whether dramatic or comic, is to make a creative product that attracts, pleases, and satisfies others, to make an artistic, dramatic, or comic product that others *value*, and that the artists themselves also value. Those who make movies that they don't value but they think the public will like are like prostitutes and their labors usually go afoul. Those who make movies *only* for themselves usually end up alone in an "Oh, solo mio" trap and ignored, often aggressively ignored.

Those cavemen that sat around campfires and told tales of the hunt and made their stories interesting and involving for cave people audiences became successful storytellers. Those who didn't entertain got to go out in the cold and gather firewood. The same is true of early oral storytellers like Homer, and the early Greek playwrights. It's the same with Shakespeare and those of later times. It is true of early silent filmmakers like Charlie Chaplin, Buster Keaton, and D.W. Griffith, and it remains true with current TV shows and movies.

That's why some movies get distribution and many do not. The reason that the vast majority of low budget independently made movies have not gotten and will not get any real commercial distribution is that very many of them are not based on concepts that are good enough or have stories, or scripts that are good enough to attract, please and satisfy some significant segment of the movie-viewing audience. *Their concepts, stories, and scripts did not really deserve to be made into movies!* Their makers did not take the very beginning of the movie-making process seriously enough. They did not work hard enough at the very beginning of the moviemaking process to get a good or great concept, so for them this process had an unhappy ending.

Here is a distribution plan that I've wanted to try out in reality for a very long time but I have never had a chance to try it. Here's how it would work. You put money right into the movie's budget for a "test marketing" theatrical opening or limited release. You hire a distributor or film booker as a consultant to open your movie in a few theaters in some small, out-of-the-way (limited TV advertising required) market and you create the movie's TV ads trailer newspaper ads, poster, etc. With the film booker's help you open, "test" the movie in this "out of the way" market. You have the audience members express how they felt about the movie in writing on cards, and if your movie attracts, pleases, and satisfies that audience, if the numbers "make sense" you are in a very strong position when you deal with distributors. You not only have a movie of value, you have a movie of proven value. This open test marketing of your movie yourself could be used as a first move in the gambit of getting a distributor, or as a backup of last resort if no distributors initially offers a deal you like.

I have never tried this plan, but I have wanted to many times.

I have seen people running around trying to finance a movie, or after they have "sold" a movie waving distribution contract say, "I've got distribution." Well, b.s. They usually have only a piece of paper. Many distribution contracts are just licenses for the distributor to legally steal the movie's income. No piece of paper forces a distributor to distribute a movie. If the movie falters and the public doesn't like it, the distributor will drop it, and sell it short in backup markets to recover expenses.

It is the movie's *value to the movie-viewing public* that causes it to be distributed, or lack of value that prevents its distribution. There are those who recognize that they are essentially working *for* the audience, and they attract, please, and satisfy that audience, and also please and satisfy themselves, in that process, and they are rewarded, sometimes enormously, with money and also with even more valuable intangibles. Those who ignore the audience or fail to make movies that the audience values are ignored by the audience!

It would not really be very fair, or productive, or even useful or helpful for me to simply exhort you as a reader to come up with a good concept, story, and script without pointing to some path to accomplish these vital tasks! Therefore, I wrote another book entitled *Become A Screenwriter Who Writes Scripts That Are Made Into Successful Movies: A Step-By-Step Handbook and Course*. That book is the result of over 32 years of on and off research. It is unlike any other book I've seen about screenwriting, dramatic writing, or script. It is primarily intended for screenwriters, writer/directors, and writer/producers and those who want to be screenwriters, and it does contain a learn it yourself course, as the title states. The book is also intended to be of use and interest to directors, producers, script readers, actors development and movie production executives, and even movie reviewers, critics, and teachers of screenwriting and creative writing. The book is set up so that much of it can also easily be read by those that do *not* intend to write scripts, but whose success as directors, producers, actors, etc. depends on their ability to judge and develop and perfect, and often to "fix" scenes or scripts.

There was a time when I thought that a script was just something that you had to have to get the money to make a movie. I learned that hard way how vital and absolutely essential a good, excellent, superb script is to a movie's success, and that is what launched me on a long, long journey of study of the scripts of successful and very successful movies of very different types. I found the common denominators of these very different successful and very successful movies, and I also found the contrasting common denominators of unsuccessful scripts and movies. My screenwriting book deals with the subjects of concepts, conceptualization, what composes the stories of successful movies and their real, recurring, identical dramatic structure. It also identifies, dissects, and analyzes what I call the *emotionally involving game* which is at the very heart of the vast majority of artistically and financially successful movies. This emotionally involving game is based on a *unifying physical emotionally repulsive evil goal*, which is like the DNA nucleus of very many successful movies and dynamic audience-involving dramas. The book also has a matter of fact quantifiable, measurable definition of the term *successful movie*. It has a detailed analysis of very many very successful movies. It deals with the vital subject of movie genres, and has very many things in it that are very helpful and very practical, not just for screenwriters or aspiring screenwriters. Much of the book is of vital use to directors and producers who are seeking to make movies that will get distributed widely, and will not go undistributed!

CHAPTER FIFTY-FOUR:
CASTING FOR AND WITHOUT DOLLARS
IN ORDER TO GET MOVIES MADE AND DISTRIBUTED

If you acknowledge reality, it automatically works for you. If you fail to acknowledge reality it automatically works against you. – Robert J. Ringer

The other extremely vital factor besides concept, story, and script in determining a movie's prospects for wide successful distribution is the quality of the cast or lack thereof, and the presence of name or star actors or their absence. As I said earlier, the first question a distributor almost always asks about a movie is "Who's in it?" They ask that question even before they ask "What's it about?" This chapter contains some information about using casting to finance movies as well as to get them distributed because using casting to finance movies and get them distributed are really two sides of the same coin. The successful use of casting to finance a movie will also provoke or directly cause a movie's distribution in most cases. Many people that make low budget movies automatically assume that top level movie stars are out of their reach because of lack of money. Usually that's true, but sometimes a great script can get star actors that money alone can't buy.

Hector Babenco, the director of the much honored Brazilian movie masterpiece *Pixote*, sent William Hurt, who was then a very hot top level movie star, the script for *Kiss of the Spider Woman*. Hurt read it and said yes, he wanted to do it. He loved the script and his character. Babenco told him, "Here's the bad news." Babenco couldn't pay Hurt. Hurt responded that there was no way he'd turn it down. The part had Oscar written all over it. Hurt asked for and got a room in a first class hotel, and made the movie. He gave the performance of his life, in the role of his career, and won an Oscar in a movie whose budget had no money for stars, but whose script was not just an Oscar-nominated script. Its script, in my opinion, is a world class masterpiece of surrealist dramatic literature.

If you have a good script, with good roles for actors, you may have something that some name actors and some movie starts value more than just money. If you don't have a good script I advise you *not* to make a movie until you do have a good, excellent, or superb script. The budget of *Pulp Fiction* was reportedly to be around $6 million. Bruce Willis routinely received much more than that per movie. The superb (and later, Oscar-winning) quality script of *Pulp Fiction* and Willis's admiration of Tarantino's earlier movie *Reservoir Dogs* and Harvey Keitel's performance in that movie induced Willis to play a lead role in *Pulp Fiction* for a fraction of his normal actor's salary. Similarly, I heard from a reliable source that Brad Pitt wanted to play a role in *Sideways*, a lower budget studio independent movie, whose budget was a faction of Pitt's normal salary. A script is vital not just because it is the movie's blueprint, highly determinative of the movie's overall quality and potential, but also because it is a major attraction to actors, name actors, and even star actors.

A letter of intent from an actor or an actor's agent is not a binding contract, like a "deal memo" or a formal detailed contract. A letter of intent from a name actor, however, can be very valuable when you are working to finance a movie. That name actor will be of value when you are seeking distribution, and when the movie is being distributed and sold. The fact that I had a letter of intent from Robert Vaughn and his agent was very useful in financing *Starship Invasions*. It might be useful to take a look at my basic strategy and basic assumptions regarding the origin of that movie (which was originally entitled *Legion of the Winged Serpent*) to see how its financing and production and distribution occurred by Warner Bros., and how casting was a factor throughout this process.

The origin of my concept for *Starship Invasions* came from watching Roger Corman's movie *Death Race 2000*. I had already made several very low budget movies that had received professional distribution before I wrote the first draft of that script. When I saw Corman's movie at the Younge Theater in Toronto, an old-time movie palace with thousands of seats and a huge multi-level balcony. It filled all those seats full show after show, and had a block-long line of people outside the theater waiting to buy tickets. I was inspired! Watching a movie that drew people so strongly shook up my thinking. At that point, I was deciding which of my ideas for movies I would turn into my next script and attempt to make into a movie. I went through the various story concepts that I had, trying to identify the one with the best potential to draw the kinds of crowds that *Death Race 2000* drew. One concept clearly stood out, about a scientist investigating legitimate evidence that UFOs are extraterrestrial spacecraft. The scientist gets drawn into a space opera war between good aliens and bad aliens. I took out a Bic pen and a stack of the cheapest possible yellow paper and I wrote *Legion of the Winged Serpent*. During production, the movie was called *Alien Encounter*, but when Warner Bros. released it, they change the title to *Starship Invasions*. The script was written a few days or weeks at the most, and it was written years before there was any publicity about either *Star Wars* or *Close Encounters of the Third Kind*. I had no knowledge of either movie when I wrote my script.

Here was my strategy. I'd heard that *Death Race 2000* cost under $500,000 to make. It starred David Carradine and Sylvester Stallone (pre-*Rocky*). I had also read that network TV was buying movies to show in prime time for $500,000 and up. I theorized that if I could make *Legion of the Winged Serpent* for about $500,000 and have a major TV name actor as its star, then the movie would have a great shot at being a success in theaters like *Death Race 2000*. My backup plan was the strong probability of a network TV sale that could cover all or most of the movie's production costs. (At that time, David Carradine was not a movie star, but he had been a TV star in the series *Kung Fu*.) To me at that point, $500,000 seemed like a huge budget. The largest I'd worked with had been $50,000, and I'd just made a movie made in 35mm color for $23,000 that had played in a major theater in Toronto and taken in more money in one weekend than it cost to make. So after I made a special FX test that showed that the movie's UFO effects could be done with effective quality on the $500,000 budget, I went to Hollywood to get a letter of intent from a name TV star.

I called Lorne Greene's agent, Darren McGavin's agent, and Robert Vaughn's agent. Greene and McGavin's agents didn't want to read an unfinanced script from a producer/director seeking a letter of intent. Robert Vaughn's agent, quite generously, did read the script and passed it on to Vaughn, and wrote a letter of intent once I committed to Vaughn for the movie's lead role. When I returned to Toronto with that letter of intent I thought that I would finance the movie easily in a matter of weeks, months at the most. Only a few years before, Robert Vaughn had been a very big TV star on the hit show *The Man From U.N.C.L.E.*, a James Bond type super-spy program that ran very successfully for years. Sadly, I found that even with the UFO special FX test and the letter of intent it was not nearly as easy to finance the movie as I had originally thought. This was still before there was any publicity about or awareness of either *Star Wars* or *Close Encounters of the Third Kind*. In fact, one distributor that my partner and I approached told us that sci-fi movies never made any money, except for *2001: A Space Odyssey* and that was because Stanley Kubrick was a genius. Since I wasn't, according to that distributor, my project didn't count. Over a year later, after *Star Wars* was released, this "genius" distributor took a movie he was distributing called *Car Hops* (about young girls in skimpy costumes roller skating around waitressing to parked cars) and retitled it *Star Hops* to capitalize on one word from George Lucas's blockbuster sci-fi hit. He also tried to "sci-fi up" the ad campaign.

Some people lead, some are ahead of the pack, and some people simply follow whatever it is that makes money. It was only some time later that I realized that the vast majority of people and companies that rejected our project at that time did not necessarily do so for the reasons they stated. The vast majority, maybe all of them actually, simply did *not* have the financial strength to finance a movie! Later, when the money men who eventually did finance the movie were considering whether or not to invest, one of them opened a presentation to the Robert Vaughn letter of intent and asked, "What are the odds that Robert Vaughn will actually be in the movie if we finance it?"

I replied, "Very good. He and his agent have read the script. He wants to do the movie. We have a verbal agreement on his price. If there isn't an irresolvable scheduling conflict, he'll be in the movie."

"Are you sure?" he asked.

I then told him, "The agent's phone number is on the letter. Call him up and verify it yourself."

And the money man did. *That letter of intent was one very important tool in financing that movie.* It's always nice when you actually have the goods, not just b.s., and can call people's bluff.

After *Starship* was financed, my business partner (who was one of the producers) told me that we could squeeze the budget's contingency and tighten up some budget categories and have enough money to buy a second major name actor to strengthen the movie's cast and name appeal. He wanted an actor whose name would be strong in the foreign market to compliment Vaughn's strength in the U.S. and on TV. First, we went to Lee Van Cleef's agent because Van Cleef had a strong foreign appeal from being in "spaghetti Westerns" like *The Good, The Bad, And The Ugly*. His agent was not flexible and would not lower Van Cleef's price, because we only needed him for one week. Then we thought of Christopher Lee, and we called his agent. He was reasonable, and open to reading the script and our presentation and Robert Vaughn's letter of intent, and a viewing of our UFO test helped convince him. He recommended the movie to Mr. Lee, and we made a firm offer for an amount of money that worked for them and was within our budget. We added some very strong complimentary star power and a very accomplished and charismatic actor was added to the cast after the movie was already financed! I'm sure that it helped us with the movie's distributor, Warner Bros.

Attempting to get a letter of intent from a name or star actor before a movie is financed is a different activity from making a "firm offer" and attempting to cast a name or star actor after a movie is financed. Both can be very important casting actions that can help cause a movie's financing and distribution. Asking for a letter of intent is asking for a favor. Making a firm offer is doing business.

On another movie that I co-wrote and directed, the producers made a deal for Oscar winner Jose Ferrer to be in one scene, shot in half a day to add name value to a low budget horror movie. The movie played in theaters and was very widely distributed in home video release.

A star actor is said to be "bankable" when their name alone can finance a movie. There are probably not many more than a dozen (if that many) actors in Hollywood at any time that are so strongly bankable that their name alone can "green light" or finance a movie. The only bankable movie star that I ever got to read an unfinanced script was Paul Newman. My writing partner and I decided that Paul Newman was our ideal choice for a script we'd written called *Treasure*. It was written before *The Deep* came out and it never got made, largely because *The Deep* premiered right when we were trying to get *Treasure* financed. Here's how we reached Newman. You can find out who an actor's agent is and their phone number by checking with online databases like the Internet Movie Database Pro version at http://pro.imdb.com but back then the best method was one still applicable, by calling the Screen Actors Guild (check www.sag.org for the phone number). I called Newman's agent and asked if he would read our script. The agent asked if I had the money to pay Newman if he liked the script. I replied very honestly, "No, but if Paul Newman likes the script and wants to do the movie, I can get the money to pay him and make the movie." (Newman was *very* bankable at the time, after *Butch Cassidy and the Sundance Kid* and *The Sting*.) The agent was very upfront. He said, "OK, send the script. Paul has a reader. The reader knows exactly what interests Paul and what he likes. It'll take her about two months to get to your script. She has a big backlog, but if she likes it she'll give it to Paul. It'll take him about a month to read it."

I thanked the agent and sent the script to him. A few months later, we got the script back with a *very* nice letter from Paul Newman making some very specific nice comments about aspects of the script, indicating that he actually had read the script but had decided to pass, and he thanked us for letting him have a look at the screenplay. It was the nicest rejection letter I ever got. You really can't ask for more than that in a rejection. One of the biggest, most bankable movie stars in Hollywood was willing to open his doors to all the screenwriters in the world to receive scripts. If our script had been better, been more along the lines of what he was looking for, it could have become a major movie starring Paul Newman

Sometimes movie stars that are bankable are more willing to read (or have their readers read) unfinanced scripts than stars or name actors whose names are valuable but are not bankable. Many agents will not read unfinanced scripts or pass them on to their clients, or bother them with giving out letters of intent. They only want to read scripts if they are attached to a firm offer. They are in the business of doing business not doing favors for moviemakers struggling to finance their movies. Bankable stars and their agents sometimes have a different attitude. Sometimes they are looking for material that excites them and interests them. Most bankable stars have at least a few scripts regularly sent to them with firm "pay or play" offers (almost like checks attached to them, sometimes very large checks). Routinely, these bankable stars often turn down some of these financed movies or cash offers. Bankable actors have the luxury of searching for material, not just hoping for someone to give them a job and pay them. If you have a great script that is *perfect* for a bankable movie star, it may be just what he or she is looking for, and if he or she likes it, *they can get it made into a movie.*

I know of a case where a screenwriter's script had been turned down by over fifty companies and the screenwriter's wife got the script to the secretary of one of the most bankable actor/directors in the world. The secretary liked the script as did the actor/director and his producing partner, and they not only made it into a movie, the film had two sequels.

Sending scripts to production company development people or readers is OK but I view it like buying a lottery ticket. It's OK – if it pays off, it's great, but it's not something that you can count on or on which you want to stake your hopes or future. I'm sure that there are cases where a screenwriter sent a script to a production company's development or script department and a reader loved it, passed it on to the boss, and a decision was made purely on the basis of "love of script" and the movie got made and distributed. I do not personally know, however, of a single case where this happened! I'm not saying don't send scripts to development departments or people or readers. I'm simply saying that no matter how much these people posture and pretend to have power, and how much they hypnotize many writers into "script and reader's report uber alles psychosis" don't ever expect anything positive from them. If it does happen, great, it's like winning the lottery. The most successful screenwriter I ever knew who was also an ardent and *very* insightful student of the realities of Hollywood told me, "Movies get made because someone really badly, seriously wants that particular movie made, and is willing to fight to get it made, then fights until it is made." He went on to say that I had to fight to get my movies made independently while others fight inside of the studio system.

What he said matched my experience exactly. What did *not* match my experience at all is what many screenwriters and would be screenwriters believe in, which I call the "Tooth Fairy reader's report" method. If I had simply submitted my script for *Starship Invasions* to Warner Bros. script department, there is *no* chance that they would have on their own made and distributed the movie, yet when I did the producer's job and made the movie, they distributed it. In most cases where a script deserves to get made into a movie, and the movie does get made, it is simply because *someone does the producer's job and gets the movie made!* In most cases, movies do *not* get made, simply because nobody does the producers' job and nobody gets the script made into a movie.

Actors only get paid if movies get made and they act in them. Development people get paid whether they say no to writers or pass the script onto their bosses. Development people can never say yes. Actors can be on your side if you're trying to get a movie made. Development people usually are not. If the script of *Reservoir Dogs* had been sent to a dozen development departments its superb writing likely would have been recognized and admired but I doubt that it would have been made into a movie because of pursuing that route. Getting that script to Harvey Keitel gave it a major push toward becoming a movie. It happened in a roundabout way. Lawrence Bender, Quentin Tarantino's producing partner, was in an acting class, and the wife of his acting teacher got the script to Keitel. When Keitel got involved, it change the project from a $30,000 micro-budget that Tarantino was going to shoot with his friends, and got the budget bumped up to $1.5 million. I am very much in favor of getting excellent scripts to bankable star actors, stars, and name actors as part of the process of financing movies and propelling them into wide distribution.

The writers I know that subscribe to the development Tooth Fairy approach of hoping to get a movie made have experienced endless frustration. I also know some writers that have played the "pitching" game and have gotten development deals to write development deal scripts and have made a lot of money doing that. Only one writer I know, though, ever had a development deal script made into a movie, and he also had some great concepts that got gobbled up and lost in the studio system. If these development people are so smart and so powerful, why did "everyone" turn down *Crash* and *A Nightmare On Elm Street*, and why did fifty companies turn down *Every Which Way But Loose*?

Directly after signing a contract for the financing of a movie that I co-wrote, co-produced, and directed, I was meeting with the movie's casting person going through the Academy Players Directory trying to come up with a name actor or actors that our $200,000 production could afford. Suddenly, she blurted out "Bette Davis!" This was near the end of Bette Davis's career and life. At first, we derided and dismissed the suggestion. Then I thought about it a bit. Bette Davis had been in *Whatever Happened To Baby Jane?* and *Hush Hush, Sweet Charlotte*. Both movies had a definite horror flavor as did our movie. She would have been perfect for one role in our movie. I checked the schedule. I could shoot her part in a week. Again, I squeezed the contingency in the budget and looked at paying Bette Davis in cash and finishing the movie in debt and then I decided that if I actually got Bette Davis I was virtually sure I could raise more money to pay her. I called her agent in Hollywood from Toronto. He was a grand old gentleman whose roots ran deep into the history of the Golden Age of Hollywood studios. Even from just talking to him on the phone, his class and charm were impressive. When I asked him how long it would take him to read a script if I sent it to him (we were working under extreme time pressure), he said that if the script was attached to a firm offer, it usually took about an hour and a half to read it! Wow, great! I couldn't ask for better. But just when I was entertaining the idea of working with an actual Hollywood screen legend, reality spoiled the party. He asked about scheduling. When were we going to shoot?

It turned out there was a direct absolute conflict. She was shooting a supporting role in a studio movie in another part of the world exactly when we planned to shoot, and we had to finish principal photography before December 31st due to shooting in Canada. So there was no way to work things out. What had looked like might be a close encounter with a Hollywood legend was only an encounter with her agent. In true agent style, he tried to sell me another senior actress (an Oscar winner) that he represented, but I told him that unlike Bette Davis, that actress would not give me the clout I would need to get her paid.

Here is my scale of *actors' bankability and name value.*

At the top are actors who are *bankable.* Their name can presell the movie, get studios to say yes, quickly raise large amounts of independent money. These are the very few, big stars whose name along can actually finance movies. Who is bankable and who is not changes constantly and is very dependent on how an actor's last movie or last few movies did or did not do at the box office, who is hot and who is not.

One notch down are actors that are stars, but are not instantly bankable. Their name alone cannot by itself instantly finance a movie, but they are stars, and they give a project or a movie credibility and contribute strongly to its appeal and value. Harvey Keitel in *Reservoir Dogs* was that kind of star, particularly in the world of independent movies. Robert Vaughn and Christopher Lee were each that kind of star on *Starship Invasions.* Actors like this strongly help to get movies financed and distributed.

The next notch down is what I'll call *name actors*. They usually do not help that much in the struggle to get the movie financed, but in some genres of film they can. Their real value often comes in making the distributor's job a bit easier. If a distributor can put a name actor's name on the DVD box and list some of the famous or well-liked movies in which they appeared it can add substance to the movie's commercial appeal in the DVD market.

The next notch down is working actors of no real name value.

Below that is *unknown actors*. These actors' acting and all other actors acting in movies may contribute a lot of value to the movie through their performance but their mere name does not. The unknown actors in *Clerks* contributed enormous value to that movie. Their names did not. The same is true of the unknown actors in *The Passion of the Christ*.

The next notched down is *actors that have negative name value*. These are actors that have been in so many bad movies and even movies that are spectacularly bad, that their names are like flashing a warning light to potential movie viewers saying, "Don't go there, this one is a real piece of crap!"

One female actor that is the "queen of negative name value" is an excellent actress, a really good actress. She has appeared in some very big, excellent movies and acted with some of the very biggest movie stars and has been directed by some very top directors. Even now, with the right script, the right role, the right director, I'm sure she could give an Oscar caliber performance. Here's how she managed to destroy the value of her name to the point where her name now has negative value. A long time ago, when her acting career was still functioning well, she gave a talk to a group of "aspiring artists" and her main theme was that movie executives spent too much time worrying about the deal when they should simply "get the product!" I assume that by that she meant just make, fund, every movie project that was put in front of them, no matter how much risk it entailed for them. The reason that movie executives (the people with money to make movies) and distributors care about the deal and the project's potential to draw paying audiences is that they don't want to gamble with their own existence in the movie business. They want to protect themselves from excessive risk, so that if they're wrong they are not destroyed and out of business. This actress was, back then, kind of a star, at least a very strong movie name. She really didn't know, however, what the executives should do; she only knew what she wanted them to do. I believe she saw moviemaking as an "arena of the arts" where she and other artists could practice their craft and the money people should simply be patrons.

That's not how the movie business worked then, or now.

That actress seems to have destroyed her career despite considerable talent by applying her "get the product" mantra to her work. She said yes to every awful script that was thrown her way with a check attached. She made a string of low-level truly awful movies and her name on a movie became like a warning that her latest movie would be even more terrible than the last. While any actor from time to time will be in a turkey or even a bomb. When an actor appears in a relentless string of bad films, that's a descending spiral and that actor is an accomplice to audience abuse. Soon, only the scripts that actor will be offered are worse and worse pieces of crap, and the actor's name value will become negative. There are some names you are better off not having in your movie!

I know for a fact that when this actress's name was mentioned in casting discussions, people would make faces and shout out things like "No! No! Not her!" None of these people every criticized her acting; they all knew she was good. They never criticized her performance in terrible movies. What they balked at, and looked like they might puke over, was the string of very bad movies in which she had appeared, making her name a kiss of death to a project.

One would-be movie director very proudly showed me several scripts, each of which had letters of intent attached from actors whose names had no value or negative value. The fact he didn't realize was that those actors would do *any* movie that paid double or triple SAG scale or $5,000 a week. You could have sent them a photocopy of the phonebook and if a decent check was attached, they'd perform it. Some of the actors had started out with names of value, some were related to famous actors, but *all* the dozen letters he had were of the "kiss of death" variety. Did I tell him the truth? Hell no! I just said, "That's pretty interesting. Good luck." If I'd told him the truth he'd have blamed the messenger (me). I let reality smack him hard right in the face, so that he could recognize the truth and learn from it.

One screenwriter associate of mine would often ask me very hopefully and confidently, even assertively, about some actor's name being strong enough to finance a movie. He'd want or expect me to agree and say it had value. When I told him the truth, he'd argue. These actors' names were virtually always completely worthless as far as financing or helping to finance a movie. When I diplomatically and tried to tell him the facts, he would not be convinced. He'd say something like, "But he's been on a soap opera for ten years." He'd swallowed a lot of bad information by the boyfriend of a working actress who was not a name. He believed her name was much bigger and could get a movie financed. That was absolute b.s.

My associate was completely unrealistic about how truly difficult it is to raise money for a movie, and how very high-powered an actor's name value has to be, to be of any value at all in the real world where real movies are actually really funded, financed, and made and distributed to paying viewers. He thought that it was much easier to finance and make a movie than it actually was, probably because he had never successfully gotten a movie financed. I had financed many movies, and it was always very difficult. Even when we had real star names attached, it was often very hard. It sometimes takes a lot of money to make some movies. Distribution companies, privates investors, and production companies do *not* have the kind of money necessary to make some movies just laying around waiting to be spent. Distributors have money because they live in the real world. If the public does not know who an actors is, that actor's name has no value at all.

There is a rule about the value of name and star actors, and no name and non-star actors, and it's virtually always true. *If you have to explain to a distributor, producer, movie buyer, TV executive, foreign distributor, or production executive who the actor is, then that name is almost always worthless as far as financing a movie.* The distributor or movie buyer will correctly reason that if they don't know who this actor is, then the public to whom they sell their movies (less knowledgeable than Hollywood people) will also not know who this actor is and thus the actor's name will be worthless in selling the movie to the public.

My associate's errors in assessing the value of the names he had in mind was provoked and sustained by people speaking a lot of pleasant-sounding untruth. My associate had also never had some of the harsh and disappointing learning experiences that I'd had. When I returned to Toronto with the letter of intent from Robert Vaughn and his agent, I thought that in a matter of weeks I'd have the movie financed. It took over six months, a time which now seems relatively short. We had a lot of other *script plus* combined with that letter of intent to finance the movie. We showed the letter and our other assets to over 100 companies supposedly in the business of making and selling movies, and none of them jumped up and took out a checkbook to finance our movie, probably because their checking accounts were overdrawn or empty. At that point, Robert Vaughn was a major TV star and everyone knew who he was. The movie's invested money would have been protected by his name. At the least, we could probably have gotten a network TV sale. But even with a star name, it was not easy to move money into a movie in the real world.

There is another incident that also illustrates this point. I was working to finance a *Road Warrior* type movie. I got a letter of intent from a bona fide female "B" movie star. People knew her name. She's starred in movies. She'd done a pictorial in *Playboy* magazine and that issue sold more magazines than any issue until Joan Collins of TV's *Dynasty* fame did her pictorial. This movie star eventually had her own line of videos of action movies – she was a star and had fans! When you said her name to people, they not only knew who she was, most of the men probably remembered a picture of her beautiful body. Again, I thought a letter of intent from her would quickly and easily get my movie financed. It called for her to be paid $100,000. I figured a distributor would put up $300,000 or more and I could pay the actress and use the rest of the money to make the movie. Well, I got a meeting with a distributor that distributed a lot of movies and participated in a lot of productions. My business partner and I sat across the desk from a hardcore Grade A "cigar chomper" distributor executive producer (who had inherited the distribution of *Starship Invasions* about five years after it was made), and we were told that even by selling "third string" territories and markets – the leftovers of distribution – my earlier movie was still taking in about $100,000 a year.

With that vote of confidence, we proudly showed him our letter of intent and he responded that the female movie star was a name, but he would not pay her more than $5,000 a week. My dreams of easy financing crumbled. As we talked more, it became clear that the chance of him or any other distributor putting up $300,000 or more to make our movie with that "movie star" was about as likely as flapping our arms and flying to Mars. It was a large dose of painful learning. It is not easy to finance movies! $300,000 in an action movie starring this actress at that time would have been relatively safe. The video and foreign markets would have been strong, but there were no takers.

Here is a description of what happened in another meeting where another large bit of painful learning occurred. My business partner producer and I were in a meeting with the head of production of the largest independent moviemaker in Hollywood at that time (since departed). We had three scripts. We talked briefly with the executive and told him what each script was about. He said, "OK, you guys got a three picture deal. We'll make all three movies. Call me tomorrow, we'll work out the details."

We left there with a supposed three-picture deal. My partner was sure it was real, thought we'd struck a deal, hit a gusher. At that point, I'd made seven movies and it all seemed a bit too easy. It was too good to be true. Well, the next day my business partner called up this "head of production" to work out the details and the executive didn't take the call. My partner called repeatedly that day and left a message each time. He did this same routine for a week. His calls were never returned. My partner was furious. He wanted to bust into the company offices and give that head of production some "physical therapy." At one point, he even contemplated taking a pistol and using it in various ways until the executive made good on his verbal deal. I pointed out that it's difficult to make movies, but it would be much more difficult to make them from jail. Slowly and reluctantly, he got the point. Finally, I decided to make a joke out of it all and laugh off this cruel asshole's infuriating behavior. I told my business partner, "Look, before we went into that office, we were probably the only people in Hollywood who didn't have a three-picture deal and now we're just like everyone else. Our three-picture deal isn't worth three specs of flying flea crap."

Lots of people in Hollywood lie, and they lie a lot, easily and convincingly. I could write another book about the lies I've heard. There was a guy who was going to make 90 movies financed by the King of Rorartunga and a financial genius with an insurance scheme to finance over 100 movies whose address turned out to be an answering service on La Brea Avenue. We found him answering phones and taking messages at 3:00 a.m., and the financial genius was working on a billion dollar scheme to put paper dots in oil being shipped in oil tankers. There are herds of others like that, all equally goofy. There are more flakes in Hollywood than in a Canadian blizzard. There is a saying that money talks and b.s. walks. Well, in Hollywood b.s. also talks. At the lower levels of the business the bullshitters never stop talking and b.s.ing. If you believe them its your fault and you own the results you get from your association. Many people on the fringes of show business (particularly aspiring screenwriters) live in a world composed of rumor They don't know what to believe about "so-and-so said" and have a hard time sorting out the truth.

Everyone that believes b.s. is responsible for all the bad results that come from believing something that is false. Anyone that does not detect and identify b.s. for what it is, false, is responsible for their actions or inactions. Robert J. Ringer's axiom that if you acknowledge reality it automatically works for you should be kept in mind in dealing with Hollywood. Whether or not an actor's name is strong enough to move or cause the movement of money into a production is not just a matter of opinion, it's based on facts. Similarly, the movement of money into financing a movie is a physical fact. Whether it occurs or not is a physical fact that occurs in the physical world of reality as strong as where the sun rises in the morning. Almost always, the only way any movie worth anything gets financed is because of facts.

If a dozen people in a room argue about the room temperature with great certainty, those who are wrong will not change the temperature. All the b.s.ers in Hollywood can't change the facts about the business, no matter how much they talk about being best buddies with the king of Roratunga. Let me give you an example of someone that was enormously successful in the movie business and did the best job of casting for and with dollars that I've ever seen and basically only cared about a few facts that were very important for him. I worked for a very successful distributor who distributed two of my movies. He entered each of them in a film festival and awards competition. They together won three major prizes. He sold my $200,000 movie to Japan for $90,000, almost half the budget, in one sale. He sold it to late night television for $75,000. The buyer that bought it said that it was the only movie he could remember buying for that slot that had no names. (If we'd gotten Bette Davis we'd have gotten more money.) He sold my movies all over the world. This distributor told me about the casts of the movies that he produced. He was very proud of how little money he spent on the casts of his movies and how much value these casts added to his movies in the marketplace, as well as how much the movies earned. The most successful of the movies that he produced sold to virtually every significant market and territory in the world, for good prices. They played in theaters and then sold to network TV, often to prime time network TV, for good money. They did well in cable and syndication. They had modest budgets and they earned a lot of profits.

Here is how he cast those movies. He would run the name of various actors under consideration past the foreign buyers who had actually bought his movies and distributed them around the world. He also checked possible name and star actors with TV buyers that had bought his movies in the past and might buy them in the future. He was not at all interested in opinions or talk. He was only interested in two central facts: (a) could or would this or that actor's name help or cause the movement of money or letters of credit into his bank account, and (b) how much did this or that actor cost.

He told me about some of the detailed research that he did. He was justifiably proud of it. The value of many actors was often kind of an anomaly. Determining their value did not always surrender easily to guesswork or even logic. Here's one case that stood out. On one of his movie posters I saw the name of an actor that played a major role in the classic TV show *Gilligan's Island*. At that point, the show had been off American TV screens for decades. I asked him if the name was the actor from the show and he said yes. That actor hadn't appeared in anything, TV or movies, for decades, and if you mentioned his name in Hollywood the most likely reaction would have been, "Is he still alive?" The distributor smiled proudly and told me why that ancient actor was in the movie and his name was on the poster. In one very important and valuable market about ten years earlier they'd begun showing reruns of *Gilligan's Island*, and its popularity had grown until it was one of the most popular TV shows in that market. This actor who was now a senior citizen was a big TV star in that market. The distributor, who was also the producer of that movie, had been told of this by the major buyer of that territory and he'd hired that actor for a couple of days for a few thousand dollars and the main buyer for that major territory was overjoyed that the actor was in the movie he'd bought. He paid top price. On another poster was an actress who'd starred in one of Stanley Kubrick's most provocative movies. At that point, Hollywood was no longer hiring her, but her name still had value in many markets around the world, and to TV buyers, so the distributor hired her for a week at a small price and added significantly to the movie's cast name value. There were several other actors' names on the posters who were not getting many offers to work for one reason or another but had name value in the foreign or TV markets. The male lead actor in one of his more successful movies was an alumnus on a TV series and starred in a movie directed by Haskell Wexler (one of my favorite movies) and had more recently received an Oscar nomination for his excellent acting in Tarantino's *Jackie Brown*. The distributor/producer hired this actor when Hollywood was ignoring him. He got the actor for a bargain price, and the movie sold in *every* market in the world and did well in U.S. theaters and sold to network TV prime time, I believe for more than it cost to make. This leading man could carry the movie, his name helped everywhere, so why pay more for someone else who was over-priced just because everyone currently wanted that actor? This actor also had a small cameo in *Mulholland Drive* and added some class to an early scene in that great movie. Using him in what became this distributor's signature movie was very good and effective casting, and proved very profitable.

I'm not suggesting that this type of ultra-researched method is the way that all movies should be cast, or even that it's the way that most independent low budget movies should or could be cast, but it's light years better than the rumor-based method of finding actors for movies used by many beginners in Hollywood. You cannot always do this type of research but you can do research, particularly with all the Internet sites devoted to the movie business these days. *Look at the facts!* Draw your own conclusions based on facts. Ignore all the rumor and b.s. – if you know the facts, you'll know what is b.s. If someone tells you that a no name or barely recognized actor's name is strong enough to get a movie financed, restrain yourself from laughing and just ask the person telling you this to name one movie that the actor's name got financed. If they can name a movie, ask for the name of the movie's producer and that person's phone number. If that doesn't send them scurrying for the bushes and you actually get a phone number, call that producer and discover the truth. Ask anyone touting a no name actor why there aren't producers swarming all over this actor, signing him or her up to projects so they'll get financed.

There are no shortage of producers that want to finance their movies, so why aren't they all lining up to sign up this no name or negative name actor? Then tell your friend to stay away from the fringes of the movie business and quit spreading crap that could be put to better use in a fertilizer factory.

There are a few more points about the producer/distributor for whom I worked. He not only acknowledged reality ala Robert J. Ringer, he saluted it, understood it, put a saddle on it, and rode it to the bank. The method not only worked for him, it was as if he'd bought reality's mortgage and it was paying him rent. A very successful screenwriter had also earlier in his career worked as an editor for this distributor/producer and he knew him well. He said of this distributor/producer that "He never loses money. He checks things out so thoroughly and sets things up so carefully and looks at things from so many angles, and has so many contingencies figured out that if he goes into a deal or makes a move he's got it figured out so that, "If there's a nuclear war he breaks even and if there's not a nuclear war, he makes a profit."

This distributor was at the top of the independent distribution and production pyramid. You can contrast his method of seeking out, understanding and acknowledging reality with the ignoring of reality, denying of reality, attempting to escape reality, hiding from reality, and failing to acknowledge reality that is the way of life for so many unsuccessful screenwriters or would-be screenwriters, and so many unsuccessful or would-be moviemakers, and you virtually cannot help but notice how strongly reality not only works against them, it often basically grabs them and smashes them or pounds them into pulp, or sentences them to a kind of Chinese water torture of drip, drip, drip, rejection, rejection, rejection death by a thousand rejections.

Would-be screenwriters or unsuccessful screenwriters that run around Hollywood throwing scripts at everyone and everything that moves, then wonder why their scripts never get made into movies, but never spend ten seconds looking at unpleasant facts, and never really try to diligently discover and understand and acknowledge reality, and would-be moviemakers that never get their movies made or who make undistributable movies that distributors won't even attempt to steal, never look at, discover, or study and acknowledged reality, are like folks standing in the path of Godzilla on an enclosed dance floor – they'll be stepped on hard many times.

An ounce of research, an ounce of facts, an ounce of reality is worth a lot more than several tons of hope and positive thinking. When people fail to acknowledge reality and it works against them, it becomes more of an enemy than reality basically is to some degree for everyone. The job of the moviemaker is to acknowledge reality, get it working for them to help get the movie made and then grab reality by the throat and get it to do what you need it to do to get your movie made and to cause the movie to be successful. Failure to acknowledge reality has a way of putting one at war with reality, and reality has a way of winning that war.

Let me conclude about my strategy and basic assumptions when I set out to make *Starship Invasions*. First, I thought that if I cast a TV star in the lead, the movie's investment would be protected by a prime time TV sale. *Starship* cost about $800,000 and sold to network TV for about that much. My basic assumption proved true. I thought that the UFO theme and space alien theme would cause theatrical distribution and foreign sales and they did. The final movie pretty much hit the targets and goals that I set up when the project was originally conceptualized, and a strategy was planned. Robert Rodriguez's basic assumption and strategy when he decided to make *El Mariachi* was that he'd made a ten-minute student film for about $1,000 and the theorized that he could make an approximate 80-minute feature-length movie for about $8,000. That basic assumption turned out to be true. His second assumption and point of strategy was that the feature-length movie that he could make for $8,000 would be worth more than $8,000 to the Spanish language video market. That assumption and point of strategy also was very true. *El Mariachi* exceeded its original targets enormously.

It's important to have end targets and end goals and strategic plan of how to get to those end targets and end goals right at the very beginning of a movie project. A movie may exceed or fall short of its targets or goals, but those targets and goals and the plan contained in or derived form its strategy give it a clear direction and point the way forward, to get it made and distributed, and basically call for steps of action to be taken.

There is a method of trying to finance a movie that I've seen tried a lot in efforts to try to get movies made. I've never seen it work but that does not stop people from doing it. I call it the talk, talk, talk, agree, agree, agree method. It goes like this. Some people who have a script usually get together and talk, talk, talk about making a movie, and agree, agree, agree to make the movie, but nobody writes anything down, no plan or strategy is formed or put into a series of sequenced steps of key actions. Things that need to be done and nailed down are floating loose and are sometimes left to flap around. No record is made of who will do what. There's no attention to the physical actions that need to be taken or how the end result will be reached or how things will get done, or which things need to get done to make the movie. It's amazing to me how people feel comfortable doing things in this way, doomed to produce no result, but they do, and they do it a lot. There is a corollary to this talk, talk, talk, agree, agree, agree method that I've seen happen during production. I've seen art department meetings and special FX department meetings, and even A.D. and P.M. meetings that follow this method. The key and flawed feature of these unproductive meetings when they go wrong and are useless or largely useless is that *nothing is written down*. Who will do what is not written down. Actions are not put in to sequence or even given prime importance. How things will get done is not worked out. These kind of meetings and methods of trying to finance movies have a kind of "belief in magic and unreality" aspect to them. It's kind of like there's some kind of belief that if you talk about something and agree about it enough, it will magically happen without people actually having to do the things in proper order in the real world that need to happen to get a scene ready to shoot or to finance and make a movie.

I've seen art departments and special FX departments have an hour or longer meeting and then when you arrive on set half the stuff you need to shoot the scene isn't there. Why? You'll hear, "Nobody told me to do this or that." Or you might hear, "I didn't know it was my job to do this or that." It's the same thing in trying to finance movies. What I have seen work in financing movies is one finds an "angel" with money, and convinces that person to invest, and one nails the project's foundation down securely and then put one layer of *script plus* on top of it, and then another layer of *script plus* on that, and another, until the project looks really attractive, and instead of an angel, or in conjunction with an angel, one gets industry participation and makes the deal as attractive and as protected as possible and then when it's time for money to actually move, probably someone will balk or get cold feet and you'll have to put things back together, and if it's not all firmly nailed down. If it floats loose it will flap and fall apart, and then as you approach shooting usually some form of on-again, off-again mambo tango cha cha cha will happen and if you weather and handle that and start shooting for a while and spend some money and stay on schedule, you'll finally know that you are making a movie.

It's back to Confucius' saying again about the wise superior person believing all things will be difficult and preparing for all things as though they will be difficult and for that prepared person, all things will be easy. In making movies, people that think it will be easy to finance and make movies and that it can be accomplished with talk, talk, talk, agree, agree, agree grossly underestimate what it actually takes to move money into a movie and make it. A step by step approach to doing things in the real world is essential! On *Starship*, once the script was done I signed up a special FX person, we made a UFO special FX test, promo and without that there never would have been a movie. That UFO test and promo was done in the real world. It could be shown to people in the real world it was not just words, words, words. It was the same with my model monster movie. And on *Starship* the next step was a letter of intent from a TV star, something in writing. That was followed by a physical presentation booklet to copy and show the investor, and a list of people to pitch. We set up appointments and pitched them one by one by the dozen, and eventually by the hundreds.

There is one other axiom of Robert J. Ringer's that I found of enormous value in the process of financing movies. Ringer calls it the maintenance of a long-term positive attitude by adopting a short-term negative or skeptical attitude. Here's how it works, and it does work. Ringer was essentially a real estate salesperson and he would sell very large and expensive buildings. His job was to find a building that was for sale and find a real qualified buyer and put the buyer and seller together and shepherd the deal through to completion and he would get a small percentage as a commission when the deal closed. The small percentage of these very expensive buildings was a significant amount of money. What Ringer found was that a lot of people that called themselves buyers were not really that. They did not have the money to buy one of the buildings. What they were actually doing was collecting lists of buildings that were for sale and taking those lists to people who might be buyers or buyer's agents. He also found that many people who represent themselves as sellers were not really anxious to sell their building. They just wanted to know how much they could sell the building for if they did indeed decide to sell it.

So Ringer found himself in many situations where he was avidly pitching supposed buyers and sellers where there really was no chance to make a deal. Going into those situations, he really had no way of knowing who was for real and who was just an agent or second or third layer agent, or just playing a game. Ringer found it very depressing to enthusiastically pitch dozens and dozens of people where there was no real chance of making a deal and he never knew whether or not there was a chance to make a deal or not. He found that it sapped his energy and his ability to do his job and to be effective at his job.

Then he decided to acknowledge reality. He decided to cheerfully adopt a short term negative or skeptical mental point of view. He considered that each situation he pitched would probably not work out and faced the fact that most of the time he probably had no real chance even before he pitched them. So he invested no emotion in hoping that the deal would work out. He also adopted equally strong long-term positive mental attitudes based on acknowledging the positive reality that some of the buildings truly were for sale, and some of buyers were for real, and he was a very good real estate sales person and if he did his job well enough, diligently enough and aggressively enough, and did not allow himself to de depressed by short-term setbacks, he would make sales and be successful in the long-term.

The first year Ringer put this method into practice, his income skyrocketed.

Raising money for movies often but not always parallels Ringer's situation. On one movie, I pitched two people and they both invested. I had the movie financed and did not have to pitch anyone else. On another movie, I did not even consider that I'd started trying to raise money until I'd been turned down at least a dozen times. Ringer's method of short-term assumption of negative results, and long-term assumption of positive results works *only* if you are really acknowledging reality when you assumed that the facts support a long-term positive outcome. It only works if you are as good at your job as Ringer. If you have a good and valid project and you assume that if you keep going someone will recognize it and you'll make the movie, you are just acknowledging a positive reality if the above facts are really true and you are doing things correctly. I have seen people who adopt and propound a method that is the opposite of Ringer's short-term negative and long-term positive assumptions, and I have often observed that method produce crushingly bad results.

I have seen people invest all their emotion and hopes and "positive mental attitude" and "certainty" in each and every single situation and even believe that by a sort of magical voodoo thinking that if they even entertain any thought of the possibility that each situation might not work out they were causing it to fail with their "negative thoughts." Time after time, I watched reality step in and cause these short-term single shot situations to fail and after that happened even once or a few times, these people get really crushed and gave up. They "crapped out" before they find out what the long-term situation could bring.

I recommend Ringer's method in raising money for good and valid movie projects. I've used it, and it works. I have not seen what I call positive mental attitude uber alles situations in opposition to reality work at all, and I've seen it cause some bad results. I have seen this method that's the opposite of Ringer's fall in one bloody splash after another.

This brings us to the vital subject of *basic assumptions*. Since these can cause the success or failure of anything and everything and methods of doing things are likely to only be as good as the basic assumptions upon which they sit I have to deal with that subject before this very pivotal chapter can begin to conclude. If someone believes that it will be easy to finance a movies that is a basic assumption. If someone believes that you always have to shoot a master on every scene, that is a basic assumption. If someone believes that the only thing that matters in a movie is its written dialogue and its actor's performance, that is a basis assumption. If someone believes that you have to take the audience's desire to see and likely reactions into consideration when writing and directing a movie that is a basic assumption. When someone believes that you only need to take the writers intentions, desires, and words into consideration when writing and directing a movie that is a basic assumption. When someone believes only the director's desires to see, ideas, and tastes matter, not the audience's or writer's, that is a basic assumption.

Some basic assumptions align with reality very sharply and work very well and almost always produce good or very good results when they are connected to talent and hard work. I call these basic assumptions that are true and are based on facts. Some basic assumptions do not align with reality or facts and do not work and even when connected to some talent and hard work usually do *not* produce good results and very often produce bad or very bad results. I call these *false basic assumptions*. If someone has talent and works hard, over a period of time they should produce some positive results. If they do not, one very likely cause of bad results or no good results despite talent and hard work is false basic assumptions. These basic assumptions contradict facts or reality, or just don't work in the real world.

When people enter a field like screenwriting or moviemaking, directing, producing, or acting, they are new to that field and often very susceptible to grabbing onto anything said to them by someone of authority, or with status, or stature, or by something they read in a book that has prestige or authority. These newcomers are often very impressionable and will grab onto a sentence, an idea, a paragraph, and make it one of their basic assumptions. There is a line in the great Western movie *Red Sun* that "Men need ideas to live by." Well, some of them sure do, and some of them become virtual slaves commanded by an idea or a phrase. I saw one would-be director shoot scene after scene in a destructive, awful way simply because he'd become a mental slave to a b.s. statement made by a college professor who had never made a movie. I saw a screenwriter virtually cancel out his chances for success for decades because he believed that one should never rewrite because of something told to him or he'd read that was based on a misleading, wrong, misinterpretation of the actual facts.

I've seen people refuse to prepare and study and learn because their basic assumption is that real artists are inspired and express themselves and preparation and learning is not necessary for real artists. I've watched people with some talent who would work very hard and who had achieved considerable success in other fields just pour themselves down the drain as screenwriters or movie makers because of false basic assumptions. One of the most amazing things that I have observed over decades of moviemaking and screenwriting and working on movies and studying movies and teaching people and trying to teach people is the degree to which people will cling to a very destructive false basic assumption that has not worked does not work, and will not work, and has caused repeated failure. In some cases, the more it fails the harder some people will work to prove that it's really true and correct.

People will not just go over the cliff holding on tightly to their false basic assumption that took them over that cliff. They will not just go over the cliff several times, they will go over the same cliff because of the same damned false basic assumption and not notice how unworkable it is. The two screenwriters I knew that were most successful, and with whom I worked both had basic assumptions that were in sharp alignment with reality and the facts. They both had a striking lack of what I would call false basic assumptions, or unworkable basic assumptions. The very successful distributor/producer that I mentioned earlier who virtually never lost money, whose movies were always profitable, had basic assumptions that did not just align with facts and reality, they were derived from facts and reality, and they really worked! They were tested and checked.

So what's the cure for false basic assumptions?

Notice whether one is failing or succeeding. If one is not producing positive results despite talent and hard work, examine one's basic assumptions honestly, objectively like an outside observer and look at the relevant facts and acquire a knowledge of reality in the situation and of what actually works! Form new basic assumptions based on what works, and align with the facts and reality, and test them in action. If they work they're true. If they don't, they're not! It's that simple.

I'm going to draw a distinction between a writer's point of view and a writer's goal and a producer's goal, and I am also going to illustrate and present a producer's basic job description, by way of an example.

"The one that got away" always has a certain kind of fascination. Here's what happened to the most "makeable" movie project that I ever saw that got *destroyed*. This project was just begging to be produced and made into a movie. It had a great title, an excellent concept, a good script that easily could have been made even better. One of the script's writers knew at least three, probably more "movie stars" or very strong name type actors who could have given letters of intent to be in the movie, and the script and movie was just dripping with opportunities for *commercial content*, strong "bar of gold" take it to the bank type commercial content. Two writers owned the script. The original writer wrote it first as a porno script, and the second writer rewrote it into a good low budget real movie. It was kind of a murder mystery erotic thriller with strong dramatic content and a very commercial premise and ambience.

Well, here's what happened. The writers sold the script for a tiny amount of money to people that they hoped would make it into a movie. That hasn't happened. The writers got no turnaround clause in their sale contract. It is almost impossible to resurrect the script because you'd almost have to get an affidavit from everyone who was ever involved with it (and there are many) that they no longer have any claim on the project because if it ever got close to being shot, the likelihood that someone would file some sort of lawsuit, or make scary noises and scare off the investors, is possible enough to scare away any producer away from going out on a limb with the movie. One liability the project always had was that its core was never solid and nailed down. It never had a solid, unmoving foundation upon with layers of *script plus* could be placed.

Here's the screenwriter's point of view. The screenwriter wants to sell their script get paid and have someone else make their script into a movie that is at least as good as their script, hopefully even better than the script, but certainly not worse. Period. End of story. That's the screenwriter's point of view and goal.

The producer's goal, the producer's point of view, and the producer's job description is very different. The producer's basic job description is to do whatever is necessary (within the law) to finance and make the movie and then to get it distributed and get the investors' money back and get them some profits. That's the producer's job - to get the money to make the movie, get the movie made, get the movie distributed, get the investors' money back, and get the investors some profits. If that movie's core had been solidly nailed down (prior to or instead of the script being sold) to form a foundation upon which a *script plus* could have been added, and if a director with a record of making low budget movies on budget was attached to the project with letters of intent from the name or star actors, and visual representations of the movie's "bar of gold" commercial content were added the presentation of the project could have been extremely effective. A very sweet 50/50 deal could have been constructed with a foreign sales company and a home video company, and even possibly a theatrical and TV distributor. There was a lot for a producer to work with on this project.

This script had serious psychological depth, and a possible lead actor that could have really played the nuance of that psychological depth that could have been enhanced and bonded with philosophical resonance. I think the movie could have been a breakout movie, but almost certainly a commercial success.

This book is not primarily aimed at screenwriters. It is primarily aimed at directors, producers, and those who would take on those roles. There is, however, one segment of screenwriters for whom this book is very much intended. I'll call that segment of the screenwriting population *dissatisfied screenwriters*. This would include screenwriters who've written scripts that they believe are better than some of the movies at their video store or that they see on TV or in the theaters, but they have not had much if any luck in selling their scripts or if they have sold scripts they haven't been made into movies or if they have been made into movies they feel that the evil, illiterate, rotten, stupid, overly glorified S.O.B. director ruined their great script. That should encompass a big chunk of the Writers Guild members and writers who aren't happy writing for TV.

I'm thinking about writers that want to take more control of their work and what happens to it by becoming writer/directors or writer/producers or writer/director/producers. I'm also presenting this to actors who want to create their own work by becoming actor/writers, actor/producers, actor/directors, or actor/writer/directors, and create and propel their own careers.

I was a member of the Writers Guild of America, west for a while. I went to a lot of Writers Guild events, saw speakers, panel discussions, and strike meetings, and walked the picket lines a lot in a major strike, and talked with a lot of writers. In almost all of these events there were two almost religious themes:

One – The director is the devil, the vile, evil, stupid, director is stealing the writer's credit and glory and ruining the writer's scripts, and

Two – The writer is being repeatedly crucified, or sacrificed on the altar of the movie business.

At one event the multi-Oscar-winning very great screenwriter Waldo Salt said that the hated auteur theory was just a conspiracy to raise the pay of directors in relationship to the pay of writers, and he got a huge cheer from the writers in the audience for that particular conspiracy theory. At one strike meeting when the strike committee reported and started their report by revealing that parking spaces on the studio lot had again been denied for writers a writer (one of several thousand gathered in the auditorium yelled loudly "Strike!"). At first the writers laughed then some began to chant, "Strike! Strike! Strike!" Soon they were all chanting.

My general impression was that a lot of these working writers who write most of the TV shows and movies we all watch are mad as hell about the status of the writer and what often happens to their work and the level of power that writers have or don't have in the movie business, and how that contrasts to how they think things should be, *but they are going to take it some more because the money's so good!*

There's a kind of joking phrase that the real golden rule is "The man with the gold makes the rules." Money certainly has a lot of power in the movie business. That fact is very eloquently depicted in the great movie *Mulholland Drive* when it shows what happens when a director clashes with money people and there's a real power play. I would say that there is a corollary to this kind of sour golden rule. I call it "the rule of the gold." Briefly stated, "The amount of power a type of job or person such as producer, director, writer will have is directly proportional to the amount of money for which they are taking responsibility, and how much it would cost to redo their work, and not necessarily how important or determinative their contribution is to making a good or bad movie or a successful or unsuccessful movie.

The amount of power that a job or person has is determined by the realities of the medium of movies, and those realities of the medium were clearly present and obvious as far back as the day of the nickelodeon. The cost of redoing a writer's work is just the salary paid the writer, the cost of some paper, and maybe some typing. The cost of redoing the director's work is usually substantial. Whatever it cost to shoot what's being redone, the director essentially takes responsibility for the entire amount of the movie's budget. When the movie's shot and the money is gone all you have to show for it is the movie the director made. Both the director and producer essentially take responsibility for the entire cost of the movie. Even producers who hate directors and want to see them dead don't want them to die on their movie. "The damned S.O.B. has the whole movie in his (or her) f*ing head."

The amount of power that screenwriters have or lack is not determined because of the "auteur theory" or any other ideas that people have or don't have in their heads. It's determined by how much money they are or are not taking responsibility for, and the realities of the medium of movies, not by ideas, not be how things should be! Power is determined by how things are!

In the theater the playwright has total power, because in the theater the playwright is the whole show. In TV, writers have much more power than in movies. I would argue that is because of the realities of that medium. TV is basically theater with changing real backgrounds. With most, not all, TV shows you can turn up the volume and go into the next room and listen to the dialogue and follow the show. Most TV is theater with changing real backgrounds. The stories of most TV shows are told largely in dialogue, not always, but very often. Robert Rodriguez said that he was very glad that he'd withdrawn from the Writers Guild because they'd succeeded in making the writer the least important person on a movie, when the writer should be the most important person on the movie.

Joe Esterzhas, one of the most successful screenwriters of all time, said that most screenwriters just go around asking to be victims. All the shouting about how things should be will not change how things are, because things are the way that they are, because of very real and powerful realities, not just some ideas in people's minds, like the "auteur theory." Many screenwriters see movies just as their scripts. They are not! Many screenwriters do not see or value movies the way paying audiences or viewers do. Most screenwriters have never made a movie, and many of them have an *absolutely false* idea of what the director's job actually is on a movie, and what the director actually does and needs to do, and how movies actually get made, and have no understanding at all of the language, grammar, or medium of motion pictures!

Most screenwriters forget that motion pictures at the beginning drew audiences based on motion pictures, pictures of motion with no writer involvement at all. Personally, I believe that screenwriters who are just screenwriters do not as a group deserve any more power than they have. Star writers are a different story. Many screenwriters who are the biggest "weeping willows" who bellyache the most about how badly writers are treated and how awful directors are do not have the slightest idea of what the medium the art form of motion pictures actually is. They could profit a lot from having a movie camera glued to their eye for a while and an editing machine glued to their hands for a while.

I think if screenwriters want more power and more control they need to take more responsibility and become writer/directors or writer/producers, and not endlessly cry about how things should be and flounder around wallowing in the self-rightness of the divine right of the writer to always be right. If you're that much smarter than the evil, stupid, directors pick up a camera and prove it, nobody's stopping you.

Almost anyone can learn to drive a car, but everyone that drives a car is not qualified to drive a race car in a NASCAR race. Anyone who would try to drive a race car in a race but who has not mastered the mechanics of driving a car would be a fool, and would likely end up splattered all over the race track!

Not having learned and mastered the mechanics of directing a movie does not always deter future splatterees from splattering themselves onto movie sets and movie screens. On the very enlightening DVD commentary on *Who's Afraid Of Virginia Woolf?* Legendary cinematographer Haskell Wexler quite eloquently talked about what happens when people assume that just because a screenwriter wrote a script and knows the script that automatically qualifies them to direct the movie. Wexler goes over in detail things that directors need to know and do and deal with and he makes the obvious but much ignored point that directing the movie is a job, and a craft and it has its parts and aspects that need to be learned and understood if someone is really going to do that job and practice that craft.

Can writers learn to be directors? Are you kidding? There are bozos out there with video cameras who don't know the difference between a screenplay and foreplay but they are doing the mechanics of directing properly, because they *learned them!* Yes, writers can be directors if they realize that there are things about the director's job to learn, and that need to be learned and don't delude themselves that some underwritten b.s. non-job description of a director's job (written by a writer who hates directors) is actually all that a director does, or does not do. Can a writer drive a car? Yes, if they learn how to do it. It's the same with directing. If a writer wants to learn how to direct, I recommend this book and the learn it yourself course that is now only one small chapter away.

Here is one final comment about casting that may be of use some time. Sir David Lean, the director of *Lawrence of Arabia*, *The Bridge Over the River Kwai*, and *Ryan's Daughter*, talked in an interview about "casting against the grain." He said he cast a sensitive actor, Peter O'Toole, in *Lawrence of Arabia* and that was "casting against the grain." He said that if he'd cast an action actor to play a man of action, that would have been casting that was too "on point" and would have been boring. In *Ryan's Daughter*, he cast an "action actor" – Robert Mitchum – to play the role of a sensitive man, and he felt that if he'd cast a sensitive actor in that role it too would have been boring, so again he cast the opposite. If this casting against the grain is not done right by someone who knows what they are doing and knows the range of the actor they cast, then this can cause casting someone that is wrong for the part and can result in a disaster. This casting against the grain can also apply to choosing directors for movies, or scripts. Here is one example. I read the original script for *Alien*. It was a straight down the middle "B" horror movie, monster in a spaceship movie, with a male protagonist, and lots of "B" movie dialogue. Ridley Scott, who at that time was basically an "arty" British TV commercial director whose only previous movie was the very out of touch with the mass audience "arty" picture, *The Duelists*

Scott used the script only as a rough blueprint. He cast Sigourney Weaver – a woman as the movie's protagonist. Scott improvised a great deal of the movie's dialogue and its ultra-realistic very natural non "B" movie spectacular attention to detail and spectacle lifted it above the "B" movie "Ten Little Indians" basics of its material and its original script. This casting "against the grain" of an arty, classy cutting edge director with a "B" movie script worked very well on *Alien* and produced a much better and more interesting and successful result than using a "B" movie director with a "B" movie script.

In contrast, Roman Polanski said that some people are afraid of obvious casting, but he likes obvious casting.

PART SIX

THE ROLE OF A STORYTELLER IN A CULTURE

"The arts put man at the center of the universe, whether he belongs there or not."
- Kurt Vonnegut

CHAPTER FIFTY-FIVE:
THE ROLE OF THE PROFESSIONAL STORYTELLER
AND THE PROFESSIONAL STORY SELLER,
WRITER, DIRECTOR, PRODUCER

Storytellers are vitally important in a culture. Commonly known stories bind people together, give them "words to live by" and aesthetic lenses through which to view their experience and put it into context to try to understand. Much cultural information and learning is passed on through stories. Many of the world's most sacred and influential religious books contain stories, some directly intended for teaching. Myths and legends that were central to early religions and methods by which early people tried to understand their world and their place in it were simply stories.

Stories are one thing that separates humans from animals. Someone might in the future decode whale and porpoise talk and discover they are telling stories, but for the moment, humans seem alone in the use of stories. Public opinion is shaped, changed, and some would say controlled by stories. Stories can fuel the desire for war or peace as well. One of the greatest movies ever made, *Casablanca*, is basically a very effective piece of war propaganda. *Dr. Strangelove* probably did more to cause people to think sanely about the reality of the possibility and results of nuclear war that all the learned treatises on the subject written previous to the release of Stanly Kubrick's masterpiece. The identity of a culture's heroes and villains and the society's values are presented and changed in the stories it embraces. In addition, people need and crave entertainment and good stories can be so good they become timeless. Stories presented in dramatic form have had enormous power over those that view them ever since ancient Greek drama was invented 2,500 years ago.

The screenwriter is the source, the prime mover, the "fountainhead" of stories in movies, but in the *visual* medium of movies the director is also very often a major player in a movie's storytelling. Some directors are storytellers also. I call producers story sellers because that describes their job very accurately. They sell investors to finance the movie, then sell the movie to the public. There has never been as much opportunity for, or demand for storyteller as there is now in our rapidly-changing technology-oriented, entertainment demanding culture.

Deep down, cultures know that storytellers are a *very* important profession to a culture. Many cultures have tried to censor or control them. A culture only allows its very best storyteller to successfully make a profession out of this vital activity and make a living from it. Some of a culture's smartest and most talent people will be drawn to this profession of storyteller, or story seller. The competition for who will have those jobs is intense. Many, many scripts are written. Many fewer are made into movies. Many movies are made, not so many are distributed, and even fewer are really successful.

On the other hand, technology is now such that virtually anyone that can write a great script and if they can write one that can be shot on a low budget can go out and make a great movie from that script. *Paranormal Activity* cost $15,000. *El Mariachi* cost $8,000.

Napoleon said, "Imagination rules the world." It is now easier and more exciting to share one's imagination through stories in movies than it has ever been. There is a massive and ever-growing, increasingly segmented movie audience out there that wants to be entertained and engaged by movie stories. The means of delivery of finished movies to viewers are getting easier and easier. Only storytellers, screenwriters, directors, story sellers, and producers can supply these viewers.

A culture will amply reward those that master the profession of storyteller, and ignore those who try to practice storytelling but are unprofessionally inept. For this reason, you must practice your movie storytelling and continue to perfect it not just in the beginning, but also throughout your career.

PART SEVEN

A LEARN-IT-YOURSELF COURSE TO BECOME
A MOVIE DIRECTOR AND/OR MOVIE PRODUCER

PREFACE

Much thought, filmmaking experience, and unofficial teaching went into the creation of this course. If you do the course exactly as written, in the exact sequence laid out, you can expect the best possible results, based on your own level of talent, experience, knowledge, skill, hard work, discipline, and inspiration. If you don't do the course as outlined, you cannot hope to expect the best possible results.

This course if done anywhere near properly is at the very least more substantial and should be more valuable than a two-year associate degree course in moviemaking at a technical school. If done thoroughly it is easily on a par with or superior to a bachelor's degree from a major film school. (I have a bachelor's degree in filmmaking and have taken some of UCLA's graduate courses in screenwriting.)

This course has the potential to be the equivalent of a masters degrees in both screenwriting and directing or producing movies, and to propel one who properly completes it and who has talent and other necessary attributes directly into a career in the movie business. It is not easy but it is doable and is set up starting with easy steps that gradually increase in difficulty. It does not promise to make you a moviemaker in one weekend.

Stanley Kubrick made two movies and three shorts before he made a good movie, and he was a genius. Polanski, Rodriguez, Spielberg, Sam Raimi and many others made many short movies before they became professional moviemakers. People don't expect to become doctors, lawyers, accountants, teachers, auto mechanics, or members of other serious professions in a weekend seminar. Screenwriting, directing, and producing movies are professions at least as difficult as the ones mentioned above. This course may take years to do. That's not because I'm mean and nasty but because the jobs it is designed to prepare you to do are difficult but potentially very rewarding jobs. As I said in the preface, this book and its course has not been dumbed down to please a wide audience, but it will yield results for those who do not shy away from hard work and pursue it diligently.

So, good luck.

"Luck is not chance; it's toil. Fortune's expensive smile is earned." -- Emily Dickinson, poet

It is useful to keep a written record of all steps and actions done or written in this course in a computer file, a written notebook, or a combination of both. One of the major purposes of this course is to allow you to make the mistakes that beginners make quickly, cheaply, somewhat less painfully and less embarrassingly that most filmmakers do when starting out, and to allow you to make your mistakes in private! Some people like Orson Welles with *Citizen Kane* or Kevin Smith with *Clerks* or George Romero with *Night of the Living Dead* burst onto the moviemaking scene as full-blown geniuses, and their first movie is their best, or at least one of their best movies. This is not always how artists or moviemakers develop, however. A long time ago, I read a book with a title something like *Excerpts from the Worst Parts of Early Drafts of Unknown Works by Very Great Writers*. These pages came from novels, plays, short stories and were truly awful even though written by the greatest of writers and Nobel Prize winners whose works are studied in literature courses at the very best college and universities. These writers did not start at the top and instantly display genius, but they sure had a capacity to grow, learn, and improve in the extreme. Similarly, anyone seeing Stanley Kubrick's first two films before seeing his subsequent masterpieces should be encouraged if their own first movies (short or feature-length) are not so great. Anyone seeing Roman Polanski's first, worst short films before his six masterpieces will be encouraged if their own early short films are not instant masterpieces.

What matters about this course is how much it helps you and how good you are when you complete it. It also matters how good you become after completing it, not how good you are when you do the first few steps of the course. The first part is the same for directors and producers. Then it diverges and becomes different, depending on which job you decide to concentrate on at the time. Of course, since much of a producer's real job is to support the director, it will help a producer to have some basic directing experience.

To reiterate, I encourage you to make your mistakes quickly, cheaply, easily, and in private, not on a set with 40 actors, crew, and staff watching, or even worse, on the screen with an audience watching in a movie theater. What's important is to not worry about potential mistakes; everyone makes plenty of them. You simply need to continue through the course and improve as you go forward. So go ahead and get started now. And have fun!

PART ONE:
THE BEGINNING -
BECOMING A STUDENT MOVIEMAKER AND ENDING
JUST BEING AN AUDIENCE MEMBER

SECTION ONE:
BEGINNING OF PRACTICE

STEP ONE - Acquire the use of or buy a movie camera (film or video) any type that captures moving images, along with a compatible editing system that allows those images to be placed next to each other and edited into a montage, then sequences, and ultimately into a movie. *Do not go forward in this course until you have accomplished this step.* This course is based on study and practice. Before you can practice making movies you need to be able to use real tools in the real world.

STEP TWO - Use your movie camera to make a short film of any kind you want, as long as involves some editing. Do all the editing yourself.

Make the best short movie you can. The point at this time is to *use the camera and the editing system to make a short movie.* If it has sound, that's fine, but not mandatory. The movie you make can be a day in the life of your pet cat, your brother's birthday party, or any other documentary you wish, even your own fictional sci-fi or horror gem, comedy or drama, it doesn't matter, it can be about anything you want. Just make the movie!

Do not go forward in this course until you have accomplished this step. These steps are laid out in a specific order for specific reasons. Later steps will not be as effective if they are done or started before earlier steps are fully completed.

STEP THREE - Show your movie to at least one person. *Congratulations!* You are now a moviemaker; no matter how bad or good your movie is, you made it. Whether anyone else likes it or not, no matter what anyone might think is wrong with it, you took the action in the reality of the physical world to make a movie. You are light years ahead of people who want to be movie directors or producers yet have "made dreams their master" and never picked up a camera or operated an editing device. You're not just a talker now - you've done something. The task that remains ahead of you, which hopefully the rest of this book will help you to achieve, is to become the very best moviemaker that you can be, and to become a successful moviemaker.

I see four basic phases that go into the accomplishment of virtually any task. The first is simply *to start.*

The second phase is to work diligently, regularly, and persistently, and to constantly make significant progress. Do that and in a while you will be at the front door of phase three.

Phase three of this course is intended to go well past the midpoint of the task to where what remains to be done is significantly smaller than what has already been done, so that completion of the task not only looks possible but likely or inevitable.

Phase four is to analyze and list the steps and details that need to be accomplished to complete the task. Put them in the best, most effective order and do them in the best order, which may change as you make progress, until all the steps are done and the full task is complete.

You have done step one. You have started. Your task now is to work on this course diligently, regularly and persistently, and to constantly make progress.

SECTION TWO:
STUDY A SUCCESSFUL MOVIE

STEP FOUR - I define a successful movie as any of the following:

(1) A movie that makes a very large amount of money (profits) proportional to its budget.

(2) A movie that receives serious major critical acclaim such as at the Oscars, the Golden Globes, Independent Spirit awards, major film festival awards, critic's association's awards, and stellar reviews from major critics, or markedly advances or launches the career of its screenwriter and makers.

(3) A low budget movie that breaks out financially, critically or both, and launches its screenwriters and makers careers.

(4) A movie that becomes a classic, whether it was well received or not when it was originally released.

Here are some examples of each of these four categories of successful movies.

1. <u>Financially successful</u>: *Jaws, Star Wars, Titanic, Something About Mary, Saw.*

2. <u>Critically successful</u>: *Crash, Being John Malkovich, American Beauty, Gods and Monsters, Dancer In The Dark, The Pianist.*

3. <u>Low budget break out</u>: *Once, Clerks, El Mariachi, Momento, She's gotta Have It, Sex Lies And Videotape, Night Of The Living Dead, The Evil Dead, Texas Chainsaw Massacre, (Godard's) Breathless, Roger And Me, Paranormal Activity.*

4. <u>Classics</u>: *Casablanca, Citizen Kane, It's A Wonderful Life, Sunset Blvd., Little Shop Of Horrors, Marx Bros comedies, Charlie Chaplin's best comedies, and plays like Hamlet, Macbeth, Othello, Oedipus Rex, Antigone.*

This book is largely about movies whose success can be measured and quantified. It is *not* about my favorite movies or movies that I consider to be "art" or "good" or movies that I think the reader should like. This book is concerned with the common characteristics and common denominators of "successful movies" - the common characteristics that successful movies share but unsuccessful movies *conspicuously lack!*

What are those common characteristics and common denominators of very different but very measurably successful movies? What would you say are the common characteristics and common denominators of the screenplays and movies of *Star Wars, Titanic, Something About Mary, Saw, Crash, Being John Malkovich, American Beauty, Gods and Monsters, Dancer In The Dark, The Pianist, Once, Clerks, El Mariachi, Momento, She's Gotta Have It, Sex Lies And Videotape, Night Of The Living Dead, The Evil Dead, Texas Chainsaw Massacre, (Godard's)*

Breathless, Casablanca, Citizen Kane, It's A Wonderful Life, Sunset Blvd., Little Shop Of Horrors, Marx Bros. comedies, Charlie Chaplin's best comedies, and plays like Hamlet, Macbeth, Othello, Oedipus Rex, Antigone. I discuss a lot of it in this book and course, but you can also read my book about screenwriting and find out more.

STEP FIVE - Read the following lists of various types of successful movies. The purpose of including these lists, at this point, is to add some more *substance* to the term *successful movie.* Not all of the movies on these lists fit even one definition of successful movies in this book, but there are only a very few that do not. Almost all the movies on these lists fit one or more definitions of successful movies in this book and very many of these movies are very successful. These lists are intended to help the reader form his or her *own database* of movies that are successful or very successful and are admired by the reader and are relevant to the script or scripts which the reader may be writing or will write, and the movies that the reader is making or plans to make.

There is no implication by including these lists that the author feels or is promoting the idea that the movie that is fifteen in one of these lists is *better* than the movie that is at position fifty. Almost anyone who reads these lists is likely to disagree with or be surprised by some of the positions, omissions, and inclusions. Deciding which movies are best is not the purpose of these lists. I've included the lists of the "one hundred funniest comedies" and sixty of the "scariest one hundred horror movies" to help aspiring filmmakers in those genres form their own relevant databases. Many very successful movies in these genres are often absent from other lists.

Out of necessity, I formed a list, of my own, of most successful low budget breakout movies. It's the first list I know of about these types of movies. I consider these movies to be a very important and dynamic part of the history of movies and the present activity of movie making. This type of movie is likely to play an even more important role in the future of movies, and may be of special interest to readers who want to go out and make their movie "by whatever means necessary."

Consider this quote from legendary political leader and writer Benjamin Disraeli. "The more extensive a man's (or woman's) knowledge of *what has been done* the greater will be his (or her) power of *knowing what to do."*

This is the American Film Institute's list of 100 greatest movies produced during the first 100 years of American filmmaking.

1. Citizen Kane (1941)
2. Casablanca (1942)
3. The Godfather (1972)
4. Gone With the Wind (1939)
5. Lawrence of Arabia (1962)
6. The Wizard of Oz (1939)
7. The Graduate (1967)
8. On the Waterfront (1954)
9. Schindler's List (1993)

308

10. Singin' in the Rain (1952)
11. It's a Wonderful Life (1946)
12. Sunset Blvd. (1950)
13. The Bridge on the River Kwai (1957)
14. Some like it Hot (1959)
15. Star Wars (1977)
16. All About Eve (1950)
17. The African Queen (1951)
18. Psycho (1960)
19. Chinatown (1974)
20. One Flew Over the Cuckoo's Nest (1975)
21. The Grapes of Wrath (1940)
22. 2001: A Space Odyssey (1968)
23. The Maltese Falcon (1941)
24. Raging Bull (1980)
25. E.T. The Extra-Terrestrial (1982)
26. Dr. Strangelove (1964)
27. Bonnie and Clyde (1967)
28. Apocalypse Now (1979)
29. Mr. Smith Goes to Washington (1939)
30. The Treasure of the Sierra Madre (1948)
31. Annie Hall (1977)
32. The Godfather Part II (1974)
33. High Noon (1952)
34. To Kill a Mockingbird (1962)
35. It Happened One Night (1934)
36. Midnight Cowboy (1969)
37. The Best Years of Our Lives (1946)
38. Double Indemnity (1944)
39. Doctor Zhivago (1965.
40. North by Northwest (1959)
41. West Side Story (1961)
42. Rear Window (1954)
43. King Kong (1933)
44. The Birth of a Nation (1915)
45. A Streetcar Named Desire (1951)
46. A Clockwork Orange (1971)
47. Taxi Driver (1976)
48. Jaws (1975)
49. Snow White and the Seven Dwarfs (1937)
50. Butch Cassidy and the Sundance Kid (1969)
51. The Philadelphia Story (1940)
52. From Here to Eternity (1953)
53. Amadeus (1984)
54. All Quiet on the Western Front (1930)
55. The Sound of Music (1965)

56. M.A.S.H. (1970)
57. The Third Man (1949)
58. Fantasia (1940)
59. Rebel Without a Cause (1955)
60. Raiders of the Lost Ark (1981)
61. Vertigo (1958)
62. Tootsie (1982)
63. Stagecoach (1939)
64. Close Encounters of the Third Kind (1977)
65. The Silence of the Lambs (1991)
66. Network (1976)
67. The Manchurian Candidate (1962)
68. An American in Paris (1951)
69. Shane (1953)
70. The French Connection (1971)
71. Forrest Gump (1994)
72. Ben Hur (1959)
73. Wuthering Heights (1939)
74. The Gold Rush (1925)
75. Dances With Wolves (1990)
76. City Lights (1931)
77. American Graffiti (1973)
78. Rocky (1976)
79. The Deer Hunter (1978)
80. The Wild Bunch (1969)
81. Modern Times (1936)
82. Giant (1956)
83. Platoon (1986)
84. Fargo (1996)
85. Duck Soup (1933)
86. Mutiny on the Bounty (1935)
87. Frankenstein (1931)
88. Easy Rider (1969)
89. Patton (1970)
90. The Jazz Singer (1927)
91. My Fair Lady (1964)
92. A Place in the Sun (1951)
93. The Apartment (1960)
94. GoodFellas (1990)
95. Pulp Fiction (1994)
96. The Searchers (1956)
97. Bringing Up Baby (1938)
98. Unforgiven (1992)
99. Guess Who's Coming to Dinner (1967)
100. Yankee Doodle Dandy (1942)

The following are all-time box office champs in the United States as of May 2010. (Source: Internet Movie Database.) The numbers given represent millions in gross receipts.

1. Avatar (2009) $748M
2. Titanic (1997) $601M
3. The Dark Knight (2008) $533M
4. Star Wars: Episode IV - A New Hope (1977) $461M
5. Shrek 2 (2004) $436M
6. E.T.: The Extra-Terrestrial (1982) $435M
7. Star Wars: Episode I - The Phantom Menace (1999) $431M
8. Pirates of the Caribbean: Dead Man's Chest (2006) $423M
9. Spider-Man (2002) $404M
10. Transformers: Revenge of the Fallen (2009) $402M
11. Star Wars: Episode III - Revenge of the Sith (2005) $380M
12. The Lord of the Rings: The Return of the King (2003) $377M
13. Spider-Man 2 (2004) $373M
14. The Passion of the Christ (2004) $370M
15. Jurassic Park (1993) $357M
16. The Lord of the Rings: The Two Towers (2002) $340M
17. Finding Nemo (2003) $340M
18. Spider-Man 3 (2007) $337M
19. Alice in Wonderland (2010) $332M
20. Forrest Gump (1994) $330M
21. The Lion King (1994) $328M
22. Shrek the Third (2007) $321M
23. Transformers (2007) $319M
24. Iron Man (2008) $318M
25. Harry Potter and the Sorcerer's Stone (2001) $318M
26. Indiana Jones and the Kingdom of the Crystal Skull (2008) $317M
27. The Lord of the Rings: The Fellowship of the Ring (2001) $314M
28. Star Wars: Episode II - Attack of the Clones (2002) $311M
29. Pirates of the Caribbean: At World's End (2007) $309M
30. Star Wars: Episode VI - Return of the Jedi (1983) $309M
31. Independence Day (1996) $306M
32. Pirates of the Caribbean: The Curse of the Black Pearl (2003) $305M
33. Harry Potter and the Half-Blood Prince (2009) $302M
34. New Moon (2009) $297M
35. The Sixth Sense (1999) $294M
36. Up (2009) $293M
37. Harry Potter and the Order of the Phoenix (2007) $292M
38. The Chronicles of Narnia: The Lion, the Witch and the Wardrobe (2005) $292M
39. Star Wars: Episode V - The Empire Strikes Back (1980) $290M
40. Harry Potter and the Goblet of Fire (2005) $290M
41. Home Alone (1990) $286M
42. The Matrix Reloaded (2003) $281M
43. Meet the Fockers (2004) $279M

44. The Hangover (2009) $277M
45. Shrek (2001) $268M
46. Harry Potter and the Chamber of Secrets (2002) $262M
47. The Incredibles (2004) $261M
48. How the Grinch Stole Christmas (2000) $260M
49. Jaws (1975) $260M
50. Star Trek (2009) $258M

The following movies are 1994 rankings by *Entertainment Weekly* in a top 100 by total viewers in all media.

1. E.T. The Extra Terrestrial
2. Gone With the Wind
3. 101 Dalmatians
4. Star Wars
5. Fantasia
6. Jaws
7. The Jungle Book
8. Beverly Hills Cop
9. The Sound of Music
10. Aladdin
11. Home Alone
12. Ghost
13. Ghostbusters
14. Pretty Woman
15. Back to the Future
16. Top Gun
17. Beauty and the Beast
18. The Sting
19. Raiders of the Lost Ark
20. Three Men and a Baby
21. Return of the Jedi
22. Sister Act
23. Home Alone 2
24. Fatal Attraction
25. The Godfather
26. Batman
27. "Crocodile" Dundee
28. The Empire Strikes Back
29. Pinocchio
30. The Silence of the Lambs
31. Who Framed Roger Rabbit?
32. The Exorcist
33. Teenage Mutant Ninja Turtles
34. Basic Instinct
35. Bambi

36. Father of the Bride
37. Beverly Hills Cop II
38. National Lampoon's Animal House
39. A Few Good Men
40. Tootsie
41. Big
42. Sleeping Beauty
43. Grease
44. Terminator 2
45. Wayne's World
46. A League of Their Own
47. Coming to America
48. Dances With Wolves
49. Lethal Weapon
50. Die Hard
51. Dirty Dancing
52. The Terminator
53. City Slickers
54. Dr. Zhivago
55. Cocoon
56. The Ten Commandments
57. Unforgiven
58. Rainman
59. Close Encounters of the Third Kind
60. Honey, I Shrunk The Kids
61. Thelma & Louise
62. A Fish Called Wanda
63. 48 Hrs.
64. Lethal Weapon 2
65. Robin Hood: Prince of Thieves
66. The Bodyguard
67. Parenthood
68. The Wizard of Oz
69. Indecent Proposal
70. Rocky
71. Fried Green Tomatoes
72. Look Who's Talking
73. Total Recall
74. 9 ½ Weeks
75. Mary Poppins
76. Indiana Jones and the Last Crusade
77. The Hunt for Red October
78. Good Morning, Vietnam
79. When Harry Met Sally
80. Kindergarten Cop
81. Alice in Wonderland

82. Smokey and the Bandit
83. Beethoven
84. Gremlins
85. Indiana Jones and the Temple of Doom
86. The Karate Kid
87. Lady and the Tramp
88. Scent of a Woman
89. Superman
90. Rambo: First Blood Part II
91. American Graffiti
92. Peter Pan
93. The Hand That Rocks the Cradle
94. Batman Returns
95. Stand By Me
96. Moonstruck
97. Ben-Hur
98. Casablanca
99. My Cousin Vinny
100. Blazing Saddles

The following movies represent the All-Time USA Box office as of January 2010 from the Internet Movie Database. (See http://www.imdb.com/boxoffice/alltimegross for a more up to date listing of even more films.)

1. Titanic (1997) $600,779,824
2. The Dark Knight (2008) $533,316,061
3. Star Wars (1977) $460,935,665
4. Shrek 2 (2004) $436,471,036
5. E.T.: The Extra-Terrestrial (1982) $434,949,459
6. Star Wars: Episode I - The Phantom Menace (1999) $431,065,444
7. Pirates of the Caribbean: Dead Man's Chest (2006) $423,032,628
8. Spider-Man (2002) $403,706,375
9. Transformers: Revenge of the Fallen (2009) $402,076,689
10. Star Wars: Episode III - Revenge of the Sith (2005) $380,262,555
11. The Lord of the Rings: The Return of the King (2003) $377,019,252
12. Spider-Man 2 (2004) $373,377,893
13. The Passion of the Christ (2004) $370,270,943
14. Avatar (2009) $360,209,452
15. Jurassic Park (1993) $356,784,000
16. The Lord of the Rings: The Two Towers (2002) $310,478,898
17. Finding Nemo (2003) $339,714,367
18. Spider-Man 3 (2007) $336,530,303
19. Forrest Gump (1994) $329,691,196
20. The Lion King (1994) $328,423,001
21. Shrek the Third (2007) $320,706,665
22. Transformers (2007) $318,759,914

23. Iron Man (2008) $318,298,180
24. Harry Potter and the Sorcerer's Stone (2001) $317,557,891
25. Indiana Jones and the Kingdom of the Crystal Skull (2008) $317,011,114
26. The Lord of the Rings: The Fellowship of the Ring (2001) $313,837,577
27. Star Wars: Episode II - Attack of the Clones (2002) $310,675,583
28. Pirates of the Caribbean: At World's End (2007) $309,404,152
29. Star Wars: Episode VI - Return of the Jedi (1983) $309,125,409
30. Independence Day (1996) $306,124,059
31. Pirates of the Caribbean: The Curse of the Black Pearl (2003) $305,388,685
32. Harry Potter and the Half-Blood Prince (2009) $301,956,980
33. The Sixth Sense (1999) $293,501,675
34. Up (2009) $292,979,556
35. Harry Potter and the Order of the Phoenix (2007) $292,000,866
36. The Chronicles of Narnia: The Lion, the Witch and the Wardrobe (2005) $291,709,845
37. Star Wars: Episode V - The Empire Strikes Back (1980) $290,158,751
38. Harry Potter and the Goblet of Fire (2005) $289,994,397
39. New Moon (2009) $288,269,091
40. Home Alone (1990) $285,761,243
41. The Matrix Reloaded (2003) $281,492,479
42. Meet the Fockers (2004) $279,167,575
43. The Hangover (2009) $277,313,371
44. Shrek (2001) $267,652,016
45. Harry Potter and the Chamber of Secrets (2002) $261,970,615
46. The Incredibles (2004) $261,437,578
47. How the Grinch Stole Christmas (2000) $260,031,035
48. Jaws (1975) $260,000,000
49. Star Trek (2009) $257,704,099
50. I Am Legend (2007) $256,386,216
51. Monsters, Inc. (2001) $255,870,172
52. Batman (1989) $251,188,924
53. Night at the Museum (2006) $250,863,268
54. Men in Black (1997) $250,147,615
55. Harry Potter and the Prisoner of Azkaban (2004) $249,358,727
56. Toy Story 2 (1999) $245,823,397
57. Cars (2006) $244,052,771
58. Bruce Almighty (2003) $242,589,580
59. Raiders of the Lost Ark (1981) $242,374,454
60. Twister (1996) $241,688,385
61. My Big Fat Greek Wedding (2002) $241,437,427
62. Ghost Busters (1984) $238,600,000
63. Beverly Hills Cop (1984) $234,760,500
64. X-Men: The Last Stand (2006) $234,360,014
65. War of the Worlds (2005) $234,277,056
66. Cast Away (2000) $233,630,478
67. The Lost World: Jurassic Park (1997) $229,074,524
68. Signs (2002) $227,965,690

69. Hancock (2008) $227,946,274
70. The Bourne Ultimatum (2007) $227,225,045
71. Rush Hour 2 (2001) $226,138,454
72. WALL·E (2008) $223,806,889
73. National Treasure: Book of Secrets (2007) $219,961,501
74. Mrs. Doubtfire (1993) $219,200,000
75. King Kong (2005) $218,051,260
76. Ghost (1990) $217,631,306
77. The Da Vinci Code (2006) $217,536,138
78. Aladdin (1992) $217,350,219
79. Alvin and the Chipmunks (2007) $217,326,336
80. Saving Private Ryan (1998) $216,119,491
81. Mission: Impossible II (2000) $215,397,307
82. Kung Fu Panda (2008) $215,395,021
83. X2 (2003) $214,948,780
84. Austin Powers in Goldmember (2002) $213,079,163
85. Back to the Future (1985) $210,609,762
86. 300 (2006) $210,592,590
87. The Blind Side (2009) $209,300,187
88. Wedding Crashers (2005) $209,218,368
89. Charlie and the Chocolate Factory (2005) $206,456,431
90. Ratatouille (2007) $206,435,493
91. Austin Powers: The Spy Who Shagged Me (1999) $205,399,422
92. Batman Begins (2005) $205,343,774
93. Terminator 2: Judgment Day (1991) $204,843,350
94. The Exorcist (1973) $204,565,000
95. The Mummy Returns (2001) $202,007,640
96. Armageddon (1998/I) $201,573,391
97. Superman Returns (2006) $200,069,408
98. Gone with the Wind (1939) $198,655,278
99. Pearl Harbor (2001) $198,539,855
100. Monsters vs. Aliens (2009) $198,332,128

The following movies are Best Picture Oscar winners.

2008 Slumdog Millionaire
2007 No Country For Old Men
2006 The Departed
2005 Crash
2004 Million Dollar Baby
2003 Lord of the Rings
2002 Chicago
2001 A Beautiful Mind
2000 Gladiator
1999 American Beauty
1998 Shakespeare in Love

1997 Titanic
1996 The English Patient
1995 Braveheart
1994 Forrest Gump
1993 Schindler's List
1992 Unforgiven
1991 Silence of the Lambs
1990 Dances With Wolves
1989 Driving Miss Daisy
1988 Rainman
1987 The Last Emperor
1986 Platoon
1985 Out of Africa
1984 Amadeus
1983 Terms of Endearment
1982 Gandhi
1981 Chariots of Fire
1980 Ordinary People
1979 Kramer vs. Kramer
1978 Deer Hunter
1977 Annie Hall
1976 Rocky
1975 One Flew Over the Cuckoo's Nest
1974 The Godfather, Part II
1973 The Sting
1972 The Godfather
1971 The French Connection
1970 Patton
1969 Midnight Cowboy
1968 Oliver
1967 In the Heat of the Night
1966 A Man For All Seasons
1965 The Sound of Music
1964 My Fair Lady
1963 Tom Jones
1962 Lawrence of Arabia
1961 West Side Story
1960 The Apartment
1959 Ben Hur
1958 Gigi
1957 The Bridge on the River Kwai
1956 Around the World in 80 Days
1955 Marty
1954 On the Waterfront
1953 From Here to Eternity
1952 The Greatest Show on Earth

1951 An American in Paris
1950 All about Eve
1949 All the King's Men
1948 Hamlet
1947 Gentlemen's Agreement
1946 The Best Years of Our Lives
1945 The Lost Weekend
1944 Going My Way
1943 Casablanca
1942 Mrs. Miniver
1941 How Green Was My Valley
1940 Rebecca
1939 Gone With the Wind
1938 You Can't Take it With You
1937 The Life of Emile Zola
1936 The Great Ziegfield
1935 Mutiny on the Bounty
1934 It Happened One Night
1933 Cavalcade
1932 Grand Hotel
1931 Cimarron
1930 All Quiet on the Western Front
1928/29 Broadway Melody
1927/28 Wings

The following are the American Film Institute's Top One Hundred Funniest Movies.

1. Some Like It Hot (1959)
2. Tootsie (1982)
3. Dr. Strangelove (1964)
4. Annie Hall (1977)
5. Duck Soup (1933)
6. Blazing Saddles (1974)
7. M*A*S*H (1970)
8. It Happened One Night (1934)
9. The Graduate (1967)
10. Airplane! (1980)
11. The Producers (1968)
12. A Night At The Opera (1935)
13. Young Frankenstein (1974)
14. Bringing Up Baby (1938)
15. The Philadelphia Story (1940)
16. Singin' In The Rain (1952)
17. The Odd Couple (1968)
18. The General (1927)
19. His Girl Friday (1940)

20. The Apartment (1960)
21. A Fish Called Wanda (1988)
22. Adam's Rib (1949)
23. When Harry Met Sally... (1989)
24. Born Yesterday (1950)
25. The Gold Rush (1925)
26. Being There (1979)
27. There's Something About Mary (1998)
28. Ghostbusters (1984)
29. This Is Spinal Tap (1984)
30. Arsenic And Old Lace (1944)
31. Raising Arizona (1987)
32. The Thin Man (1934)
33. Modern Times (1936)
34. Groundhog Day (1993)
35. Harvey (1950)
36. National Lampoon's Animal House (1978)
37. The Great Dictator (1940)
38. City Lights (1931)
39. Sullivan's Travels (1941)
40. It's A Mad Mad Mad Mad World (1963)
41. Moonstruck (1987)
42. Big (1988)
43. American Graffiti (1973)
44. My Man Godfrey (1936)
45. Harold And Maude (1972)
46. Manhattan (1979)
47. Shampoo (1975)
48. A Shot In The Dark (1964)
49. To Be Or Not To Be (1942)
50. Cat Ballou (1965)
51. The Seven Year Itch (1955)
52. Ninotchka (1939)
53. Arthur (1981)
54. The Miracle Of Morgan's Creek (1944)
55. The Lady Eve (1941)
56. Abbott And Costello Meet Frankenstein (1948)
57. Diner (1982)
58. It's A Gift (1934)
59. A Day At The Races (1937)
60. Topper (1937)
61. What's Up, Doc? (1972)
62. Sherlock, Jr. (1924)
63. Beverly Hills Cop (1984)
64. Broadcast News (1987)
65. Horse Feathers (1932)

66. Take The Money And Run (1969)
67. Mrs. Doubtfire (1993)
68. The Awful Truth (1937)
69. Bananas (1971)
70. Mr. Deeds Goes To Town (1936)
71. Caddyshack (1980)
72. Mr. Blandings Builds His Dream House (1948)
73. Monkey Business (1931)
74. 9 To 5 (1980)
75. She Done Him Wrong (1933)
76. Victor/Victoria (1982)
77. The Palm Beach Story (1942)
78. Road To Morocco (1942)
79. The Freshman (1925)
80. Sleeper (1973)
81. The Navigator (1924)
82. Private Benjamin (1980)
83. Father Of The Bride (1950)
84. Lost In America (1985)
85. Dinner At Eight (1933)
86. City Slickers (1991)
87. Fast Times At Ridgemont High (1982)
88. Beetlejuice (1988)
89. The Jerk (1979)
90. Woman Of The Year (1942)
91. The Heartbreak Kid (1972)
92. Ball Of Fire (1941)
93. Fargo (1996)
94. Auntie Mame (1958)
95. Silver Streak (1976)
96. Sons Of The Desert (1933)
97. Bull Durham (1988)
98. The Court Jester (1956)
99. The Nutty Professor (1963)
100. Good Morning, Vietnam (1987)

Here are sixty of the One Hundred Scariest Horror Movies per a TV show with that title.

1. Jaws
2. Alien
3. The Exorcist
4. Psycho
5. The Texas Chainsaw Massacre
6. The Shining
7. Silence of the Lambs
8. Carrie

9. Night of the Living Dead
10. Wait Until Dark
11. Audition
12. Misery
13. Scream
14. Halloween
15. Freaks
16. Omen
17. Nightmare on Elm Street
18. The Haunting
19. Hellraiser
20. The Ring
21. Jacob's Ladder
22. Don't Look Now
23. Rosemary's Baby
24. Susparia
25. Phantasm
26. Seven
27. Frankenstein
28. When a Stranger Calls
29. The Serpent and the Rainbow
30. The Blair Witch Project
31. Friday the Thirteenth
32. Pet Cemetery
33. The Fly
34. Hitcher
35. Aliens
36. Cape Fear
37. House on Haunted Hill
38. Peeping Tom
39. Dawn of the Dead (the Romero original)
40. Black Sunday
41. The Hills Have Eyes
42. American Werewolf
43. It's Alive
44. The Game
45. Wicker Man (the original)
46. Sentinel
47. Nosaferatu
48. The Thing
49. Diabolique
50. Last House on the Left
51. Deadzone
52. Phantom of the Opera
53. Demons
54. Changeling

55. Vanishing
56. Single White Female
57. House of Wax
58. Cujo
59. Fatal Attraction
60. Beyond

The following are fifty of the most successful *low budget breakout movies*. I formulated this list because I couldn't find any list of this type already in existence. I consider this type of low budget break out movie making to be a type of movie making that's very important, vital, and dynamic, and often cutting edge and revolutionary in a very positive and influential way. It probably *is* or *is not* of serious interest depending on various readers' orientation and career situation, and future plans. The criteria I used in selecting and positioning the low budget breakout movies in this list was as follows:

(1) The lowness of the budget. I gave more credit *the lower the budget.* The lowest budget I found was $2,500.00 for *A Polish Vampire in Burbank* which was shot on 8mm film and transferred to video and had a very profitable and successful release in video and on cable TV. The next lowest budget was David Cronenberg's *Stereo* for $5,000.00 shot in 35mm b/w. It launched Cronenberg's unique and highly acclaimed career. The next lowest was Robert Rodriquez's *El Mariachi* shot for $8,000.00 in 16mm color. All of these moviemakers deserve *huge* credit for making viable successful *"breakout"* movies on these micro budgets.

(2) How much money or profits the movie earned in relation to the size of its budget.

(3) How much critical acclaim, awards, stellar reviews, etc. they received.

(5) Did the movie become a classic or cult classic?

(5) Did the movie spawn sequels? If so, how many and how successful?

(6) How much did the movie advance and/or propel its screenwriter's or maker's careers?

(7) How *"important"* and successful and influential did the movie's writers' or makers become eventually?
(8) How much influence did the breakout movie have on moviemaking overall or "the history of cinema"?

Here's the list of low budget breakout movies.

1. El Mariachi. (shot for $8,000.00 in 16mm color by Robert Rodriquez. Also photographed and written by Rodriquez, it has spawned two sequels **Desperado** and **Once Upon a Time in Mexico.** In my opinion, although Rodriquez has made a lot of movies with great directing cinematography editing and much more production value than **El Mariachi**), it is still, in my opinion, the best **most original *script* Rodriquez has yet filmed.**)

2. **Clerks** (written, directed and co-edited by Kevin Smith **Clerks** was made for $35,000.00 in 16mm b/w. It's a $35,000.00 movie with a **million dollar plus script. Clerks** is one of the best scripts and best comedies of the 1990's. It has propelled Kevin Smith's entire career and spawned a cartoon series and one sequel **Clerks II**).

3. **Breathless** (Jean Luc Goddard's original). (In the 1950's movies were dominated by Hollywood studios. Some saw most of these studio movies as stagnant, stogy, boxed in and compose of "boxy" stale images. Two young movie critics in Paris were writing for a "cinema" magazine, **Cashier Du Cinema**, and they were writing and talking the talk of *"cinematic revolution"*. Their names were Jean Lu Goddard and Francois Truffaut. Truffaut wrote a treatment for gangster movie, **Breathless**. Goddard decided to walk the walk of *cinematic revolution*. He stole the petty cash of his employer **Cashiers Du Cinema**, and used the money to begin filming **Breathless** with Truffaut acting as his assistant. When the owners and management discovered Goddard's "revolutionary action", some would say *crime*, and confronted Goddard, he confronted them in response. Goddard gave them two choices; they could prosecute him for his *crime* and loose all the money he'd spent on the movie, or they could raise money to finish the movie and participate in its possible profits, and do something real about *cinematic revolution* instead of just writing and talking about it. They chose to raise the money needed to finish filming and complete **Breathless** on a microscopic budget. **Breathless** was almost instantly a huge hit in Paris. Lines of people outside theaters waiting to see it in its first run movie theatre extended around city blocks for miles. **Breathless** eventually played profitable and very successfully in "art house" movie theatres all over the world. The enormous success of **Breathless** launched and propelled Goddard's career and provoked the writing financing and making of Truffaut's first movie **The 400 Blows**, which was nominated for an Oscar for best screenplay and was probably the best movie of the entire French new wave movement which **Breathless** started. **Breathless** re-wrote and redefined the grammar of movies and "cinematic storytelling". Many techniques that were revolutionary in **Breathless** are now common and accepted in recent movies like the Oscar winning **Traffic**, or the TV shows **CSI Miami**. or in music videos. Godard and Truffaut influenced many, many, movie makers all over the world. Quentin Tarintino has accurately credited Goddard as an influence in his screenwriting and moviemaking, and cites **Breathless** as a movie he much admires and he also named a production company after another of Goddard's movies **A Band Apart**. **Pulp Fiction** has some strong "homages" and references to Goddard. **Grab a treatment, grab the money, grab a camera, and a "game" cinematographer, grab some actors and start filming and keep going until the movies finished. Make a movie that breaks many of the most accepted cinematic rules of the day and is a huge hit when released and continues to influence moviemakers and movies for generations,** *that's a low budget break out movie.* **Breathless is a classic, and its also a major league "low budget** *breakout* **movie."**

4. **Faces**. (I've heard that **Faces** was an actual "no budget" movie. John Cassavetes used 16mm b/w film to film his script, and cast some very, very, talented unemployed or under employed actors he knew. **Faces** was nominated for a best screenplay Oscar in 1968. In the commentary in **Knocked Up** Judd Adaptow remarks on how John Cassavetes way of making movies influences the most cutting edge hippest movies like **Knocked Up**. Inspired improvisation has played a key role in many of Martin Scorcese's most acclaimed movies. The pedigree of that kind of improvisation leads straight back to **Faces**.

5. **The Texas Chainsaw Massacre**. (Shot in Texas in the 1970's, Stephen King calls this movie one of the most terrifying best horror movies ever made. It earned a tremendous amount of money compared to its budget, and has spawned a sequel and remake).

6. **Night of the Living Dead**. (In the 1960's George Romero was a young film maker making TV commercials in Pittsburgh. He wrote the script for **Night of the Living Dead** with John Russo. Romero joined with two other local film production companies and their principles and directed, photographed and edited **Night of the Living Dead** for $108,000.00 in 35mm b/w, and it played on the "B" movie theatre circuit in 1968, but like the zombies in the movie it *did not die*. In the 1970's it came back stronger and stronger in midnight screenings in major cities all over the world and in the 1980's as video store sprouted their horror section virtually always had copies of **Night of the Living Dead**. It still sells briskly in DVD, especially around Halloween, and is one of the most ultra cult classic horror movies ever. Wes Craven , "the master of horror" has said that after viewing **Night of the living Dead** he thought "George Romero has made a political statement and a horror movie can go as high as you can take it and reach as deep as you can take it as long as you scare the sh.. out of the audience". Many regarded it as one of the most metaphoric insightful works of art of the 1960's).

7. **The Blair Witch Project.**

8. **Halloween.**

9. **Easy Rider.**

10. **She's Gotta Have It** (Spike Lee's first movie; shot in 16mm b/w for $100,000.00. He's made many more polished movies with much higher production values and major star actors but…has he ever filmed a more original more interesting more entertaining comic script, or a better script? The movie was a serious financial success and critically acclaimed hit and launched Lee's career).

(This list continues shortly; it contains more than fifty more low budget breakout movies.)

A word on low budget breakout movies: *One thing that struck me about the ten low budget breakout movies listed here and the more than fifty listed later is that these movies all have very strong screenplays and original effective concepts.* Many of these movies were made with tiny budgets and slim resources compare to studio movies. In some cases it seems far better for a moviemaker to have an excellent or great script and tiny resources than to have huge resources and a bad or stale script, or ineffective concept. If Spike Lee, Jean Luc Goddard, Robert Rodriquez, Kevin Smith, John Cassavetes, and George Romero had waited around for someone with money and power to *like* their scripts and pay them a lot of money for it and put up a lot of money to "make it right" with the very best big star actors *they might all be still waiting to make their first movie.*

The list of low budget breakout movies continues.

11. *Sex, Lies, and Videotape*
12. *Little Shop of Horrors*
13. *Greetings*
14. *Knife in the Water*
15. *Chien Andalou*
16. *Los Olivdados.*
17. *Friday the 13th*
18. *The Evil Dead*
19. *Once*
20. *Momento*
21. *Goin' Down the Road*
22. *Roger and Me.*
23. *The Reanimator*
24. *Breaking The Waves*
25. *Last House on the Left*
26. *Superfly*
27. *Medium Cool*
28. *Secrets and Lies*
29. *Hollywood Blvd.*
30. *The Gods Must Be Crazy*
31. *Martin*
32. *Kentucky Fried Movie*
33. *Phantasm*
34. *A Polish Vampire in Burbank*
35. *Saw*
36. *Targets*
37. *Killer's Kiss*
38. *Stereo.*
39. *Crimes of the Future*
40. *The Parasite Murders*
41. *Rabid*
42. *Detour*
43. *Bowling for Columbine*
44. *David and Lisa*
45. *Down By Law*
46. *Pink Flamingos*
47. *The Hills Have Eyes*
48. *Meatballs*
49. *Pixote*
50. *Nightmare on Elm Street*
51. *Gone In Sixty Seconds*
52. *Mean Streets*
53. *Stud Sweetback's Bad Ass Song*
54. *Schlock*
55. *Crazies*
56. *Dirty Movie*

57. *Simon in the Desert*
58. *Eraserhead*
59. *Blue Velvet*
60. *Kiss of the Spider Woman*
61. *Coffee and Cigarettes*
62. *Paranormal Activity*

STEP SIX - Go back and look through those movie lists and possibly think of other more recent movies like *300*, or *Borat*, or *Juno*, or *Crank*, or *Superbad*, or *Knocked Up*, or *Gran Torino*, or *The Changeling*, or *Inglorious Bastards* that are not on the lists but are very financially and critically successful. Select one movie that you admire that was a serious hit and also critically acclaimed. Select one from which you know you can learn.

STEP SEVEN - Watch the movie that you have selected at least forty (40) times or more, beginning to end at regular speed. Here's why that is valuable. First, this method of watching a good movie that you admire repeatedly has been used by many successful directors to become a director or to become a better one. William Wellman, the much-admired, Oscar-winning studio director and screenwriter, who directed *Wings* in the silent era about aerial combat in World War I, had a career that spanned the Golden Era of studio-made movies. He learned to direct by watching a movie repeatedly. Another director who learned that way is Orson Welles, who studied John Ford's and D.W. Griffith's movies. The great Japanese director Akira Kurosawa was an established veteran director before he made *Seven Samurai*, but he reportedly watched John Ford's movie *Stagecoach* over forty times as part of preparation for directing *Seven Samurai*. Steven Spielberg supposedly watched *Lawrence of Arabia* and *Bridge Over the River Kwai* over and over during the making of *Close Encounters of the Third Kind*, learning from the great director David Lean.

I have heard stories about French New Wave directors, former movie critics like Truffaut and Godard, studying movies many times to prepare to direct their first movies, but I won't repeat stories here because I'm not sure they are accurate. When I was a film student at UCLA I heard of this method of learning to become a director and so I watched the James Bond movies *Goldfinger* and *Thunderball* over forty times each. I also watched *Rosemary's Baby, Who's Afraid of Virginia Woolf* more than fifty times each when I was a film student. Watching these movies repeatedly greatly changed the way that I saw a movie and how much I absorbed from watching it, even if I only viewed it once.

When I ask you to watch a movie forty times or more, I'm only asking you to do something that many people who directed professional movies have done many times. This course is composed of *study and practice*. The practice part began with Step Two (making a short movie). The study part of this course begins here with watching and studying one movie forty or more times. I have watched very many movies very many times, particularly while learning how to direct, and while doing research on this book and my other book. Remember, choose a movie you admire, one that you can learn from, that was financially successful and critically acclaimed.

Watching a movie forty times should move you away from the world of the movie viewer, the audience member that watches a movie to be entertained, into the world of the student of movies who studies them to see how professional films are composed and how moviemakers use the "grammar of cinema" and the tools of moviemaking to make their movies work, and cause them to be successful.

One would-be director that was having a terrible time trying to direct a movie asked for my help. I told him to watch *Psycho* forty times. After he'd watched it only seven times, he called me and said, "This is painful!" I replied that it might be, but not nearly as painful as what awaited him because he started shooting a movie before he had properly prepared himself to be a director. He has the *false basic assumption* that the only reason to watch a movie was to enjoy it, to be entertained. He also had another *false basic assumption* that watching movies for enjoyment and to be entertained was enough study to be a director. Watching *Psycho* repeatedly was painful, so he quit. I said, no pain, no gain.

He learned the hard way what real pain is as he plunged into filmmaker hell as punishment for the sin of unpreparedness.

Professional bodybuilders know that it is not just the number of weightlifting repetitions that will cause their muscles to grow, but more specifically it is the number of weightlifting repetitions they perform *after* a muscle has been exhausted and pain is screaming to them that they should stop. When they don't stop, that will cause that muscle to grow the most! I think this is a relevant corollary to watching a movie over and over. The number of times you watch it *after it has ceased to entertain you, after it has stopped being pleasurable to watch*, is even more important. When you force yourself to watch a movie after it no longer entertains you (if you do it long enough) your mind will abhor a vacuum and will begin to study the movie and you will start to see and notice and understand things that you did not see or notice or understand when the movie entertained you. You should begin to leave the world of the amateur viewer, audience member, and begin to move as you learn into the world of the student that is no longer seeking to be entertained but who is instead seeking and learning how to make a professional movie.

Learn how to be successful from a successful movie made by a successful moviemaker that went before you. Watch the movie that you selected forty times or more and study it. Learn from it. See where the director places the camera and where the director places the camera again after each cut. Learn to watch the movie shot by shot, and watch whether the director moves the camera or not, and where and why the director movies the camera. Watch the lighting and the actors and their acting and their performances, and the composition of shots, and study the movie's script and its story. Study everything you can in the movie and learn as much as you can from this one movie.

Do not skimp or cheat on this step. If you do you only cheat yourself. As I have said repeatedly, becoming a movie director requires *study* and *practice* and also requires hard work. It is not just fun. *Do Step Seven!* Watch the movie you selected at least forty times and study it and learn form it. If you actually correctly do this step it should move you dramatically and dynamically toward your goal of becoming a movie director and/or producer.

Do not move farther into this course until you have fully and completely finished Step Seven!

SECTION THREE:
MAKING BETTER MOVIES

STEP EIGHT - Make a second short movie. It must be at least ten minutes long. You must operate the camera and edit the movie yourself. You must write a script for it. It must be a drama or comedy, or horror, sci-fi, Western, or musical - any movie type that involves actors. Here is all you need to know about script format at this point. Dialogue is written like this, with the name of the character that is talking in the center of the page, and the dialogue that they are saying indented, and the location and interior or exterior and day or night at the top of the scene.

1. INT. HOUSE - DAY

                    JOE
         Hi, Sally.

                    SALLY
         Hi, Joe.

Action is written near the margins.

2. EXT. STREET - DAY

GODZILLA walks down the street roaring and stepping on cars and houses.

3. INT. HOUSE - DAY

JOE goes to the window.

                    JOE
         Godzilla is doing his thing again.

                    SALLY
         Yeah, he's a rude bastard.

You can put in things like CLOSEUP ON: XYZ or WIDE SHOT, or CAMERA MOVES WITH if those directions help you, but don't overdo it. Later, I will have much to say about script format.

This second movie must also have sound of some sort. It does not necessarily have to be "sync sound." The only other requirement for this movie is that it must be better (by your own judgment) than your first movie. Make this movie in accordance with the specifications set forth above.

STEP NINE - When this movie is finished, gather a few people together as an audience and show it to them. When you have done this, congratulations! Again, you are no longer just a first-time director. You are becoming a better movie director, so keep up the progress.

STEP TEN - Decide in which movie genre or genres you wish to work, and which you are most likely to pick as the genre(s) of your first feature-length movie. Obviously, this prediction can change as time passes and reality develops and the unforeseen may happen, but with what you know now and with the awareness that things can change, decide on genre and write down your decision.

STEP ELEVEN - Select five movies that you admire from the genre(s) you favor that you think you can learn from, which have also been financially successful and critically acclaimed. Watch these movies at least ten times each and study them as much as you can. Learn as much as you can about the genre of the movies while watching.

STEP TWELVE - *Make your next short movie.* It must have sync sound. This time, you do not have to operate the camera yourself or edit it yourself if you have someone else to do those jobs and you don't want to do them yourself. Again, write a script for the movie and make an effort to use "real" actors or people who are aspiring to be real (professional) actors. This movie must be in the genre(s) in which you intend to work. If you have great ideas for short movies that are not in the genre(s) you picked, make them also, apart from this movie. You can do that as a part of Step Twelve, or in a later step. To complete Step Twelve, at least one short movie that you make must be in the genre(s) in which you intend to work, and must meet the specifications stated above.

STEP THIRTEEN - When this movie is completed, show it a few times to audiences of several people.

STEP FOURTEEN - There are websites where people post short movies, like the most prominent one, YouTube, but don't settle for the obvious. Find other websites and watch a lot of short movies made by other people, preferably people who are not just entertaining themselves but aspire to be serious filmmakers.

STEP FIFTEEN - Watch your latest movie and compare it to the movies that you see posted on the Internet. Make a judgment. Is your movie good enough that you feel proud of it compared to these other movies? Would you be happy to post it so that it could be viewed next to movies made by other people? Here's a hint of how amazing some of the movies can be. In December 2009, Fede Alvarez of Uruguay made a short sci fi film about giant robots destroying Montevideo, the capital of his country. Supposedly, the entire short cost only $700 to make. After it received endless "hits" on YouTube, Alvarez was signed by Ghost House Pictures in Hollywood to develop and direct an original genre film based on his short movie. Sam Raimi was one of the people who met with Alvarez to work out the deal. If the answer to your questions about your movie is "No" then redo Step Twelve. Make another movie that meets Step Twelve's requirements and again compare it to short movies that are posted on the Net and if you think it compares favorably with other folks' movies and you're proud of it, post it. You don't have to match the quality of Alvarez's movie, just make one of quality. Repeat Step Twelve as many times as necessary until you have a short that matches the step's qualifications and you are proud of it and feel it compares favorably with other similar movies you've seen. Then post it on the Web.

STEP SIXTEEN - Go through the lists of successful movies again and select at least ten movies that you personally admire that are very successful. Without regard to genre, I am talking about movies that made a huge amount of money and/or received tremendous critical acclaim and/or became major classics or cult classics, and/or broke out big time and launched major directors' careers. When you have a list of at least ten very successful movies that you admire, watch each of these movies at least five times, and study and learn from them and form your own opinion as to what it was exactly that made each of these movies so successful and write down your own conclusions on what made each one of these movies so successful.

STEP SEVENTEEN - Here are some exercises. I warn you – some of them are work and some may seem silly, but you will feel a lot sillier if you try to learn some of these things on a set with money being spent every minute and 40 professional people are watching your every move.

(a) Get your camera and go out and shoot some shots of people and things with a wide angle lens shoot things and people who are close to the camera with the wide angle lens, and things and people who are far from the camera with the wide angle lens. Shoot people who move past the wide angle lens and shoot people and things that come into frame and move away from the lens and camera. Repeat these exercises with the camera at low and very low angles, then chest or waist-high, then eye level, then high angle, then very high angle. Shoot interior and exterior. You should notice the type of aesthetic effect that this wide angle lens causes, when used in various ways from various angles. For example, a wide angle lens makes interior rooms look much larger. It can make people or things moving toward or away from the camera seem to move more rapidly. Play with it and have fun.

Repeat these exercises until you feel comfortable that you know the effects a wide angle lens causes when used in various ways, covering various things and people moving in various ways and shot from various vantage points, low angle, high angle. Cover it all until you can recognize shots in professional movies that were shot with a wide angle lens.

Then repeat the exercises with a normal, neutral, non-telephoto lens until you are confident that you understand its aesthetic effect or lack of effect, when used in various ways, and you can recognize the use of this type of lens in professional movies and TV shows.

Next, repeat the exercises with a telephoto lens until you have the same final recognition abilities as stated in the two above exercises.

Now go repeat the exercises using a wide angle lens, a neutral lens, and a telephoto lens in rotation, one after the other. Shoot the same people or things from the same angle covering the same type of motion, with different lenses.

Do this again in situations that have lots of light and also situations that have little light. You should be able to see a marked difference in "depth of field" in these three types of lenses. Do this until you are sure you understand depth of field

Reread Chapter Seven of this book about the Director and the Motion Picture Camera.

Repeat all the above exercises until you feel you understand the effects of lenses, light, low or high, and depth of field, and you can easily recognize the use of various lenses and the aesthetic effects each type of lens creates, and the aesthetic effects different vantage points or camera positions create. If you invest a few weekends or days doing these exercises thoroughly, you will probably be very glad you did when you direct your first professional movie.

I know of people that tried to director movies who were afraid to touch a movie camera. They were scared of a movie camera like it was a rattlesnake. I've encountered others who thought the camera belonged to the Director of Photography. It only *partly* does. It is also a director's tool and the director should feel confident and comfortable using a camera to tell a story, including using various lenses and camera angles to cause various aesthetic effects, and if the director can do these things, that director can speak the same "language" of moviemaking to the D.P. The director does not need to interfere with the D.P. doing the D.P.'s job but will be able to direct the D.P. when doing the director's job.

The above exercises can all be done in one day, and could easily be done in a weekend, and if done properly and thoroughly they should remove a good deal of ignorance and uncertainty from a beginning director's world. Doing this exercise properly should be fun and is easy. It is enormously worthwhile, and the more time and practice you invest in it, the more you get out of it. Knowing how to use a movie camera and lenses is a key part of becoming a professional director.

(b) Reread Chapter Five about picturization, blocking, and composition. Get a copy of *Citizen Kane* and move to the scene in that movie where the young Charles Foster Kane is removed from his mother and father by a banker, Mr. Thatcher. The scene begins with young Charles throwing snowballs at a sign on his mother's house. There is a point in that scene a couple of shots in, where a long (in time) shot begins with Kane throwing a snowball. He's seen through a window. The camera pulls back and we see Kane's mother, father, and the banker. The shot continues as dialogue unfolds and they move forward to a table in another part of the house. The camera moves back in front of them. Kane's mother signs over Kane and her silver mine to the banker in exchange for a specified constant income. The scene then goes outside to where Kane is playing and the camera follows, and the scene ends on a shot of "Rosebud" - Kane's sled - whose meaning is the movie's "Macguffin" - that thing main characters in the movie are after. Watch this scene from beginning to end at least ten times.

Get a copy of The Five Fundamentals of Play Directing and read the sections in that book about blocking, picturization, and composition. The book has blockings and picturizations and diagrams and stick figure illustrations of various blockings and picturizations of famous plays, directed by top theater directors, and analysis of same. There is absolutely no substitute for reading and studying the sections of that book, so do it!

I have seen would-be directors to whom I have given the important parts of that book fail to read and study what I gave them and then go out and crash and burn in the fires of filmmaker hell. Do not join them!

Get three large dolls that can stand up and a smaller one, or get three large plastic cups (the largest kind offered by fast food places) and a smaller one. Roll up some paper into four balls several inches in diameter. Turn the cups upside down and tape the paper balls on top of the bottom of the cups. The small cup is young Kane. Draw his face on the paper ball. On the paper balls of the larger cups, draw the faces of Kane's mother, his father, and the banker. Watch the scene again. Get a large flat surface like a table and put a TV screen at one end of that surface and put your *Citizen Kane* rough character representations in front of the TV. Get a small box only a few inches long on each side. A Bigelow tea box is about the right size - it represents the movie camera.

Now, play the scene and stop it often. Move the representations of the characters and camera in that scene the way that Welles moved the actors and camera when he shot that scene. Do this from the beginning of the scene to the end of the scene several times. This scene is one of the most classic and virtuoso examples of blocking and picturization in all of the history of cinema and it is full of meaning and symbolism caused by its picturization, which supports the scene's dialogue and its meaning. Little Kane is in the background out in the snow playing. He can be seen through the window while the people in the foreground, his mother, the banker, his father, and money decide his future. Several times, the scene uses the kind of "triangle composition" that the Five Fundamentals of Play Directing discusses. So does *Close Encounters of the Third Kind* and *Jaws*. Do you think Spielberg might have studied this scene?

Kane's mother is in the center of the composition of much of this scene, and the banker is on one side, and Kane's father is on the other. They are each arguing for opposite actions regarding Kane's future. The mother in the center decides Kane's fate. I'm not going to over-analyze the scene and its picturization for you, but you should be able to see the use of picturization to create and support meaning. When you have gone through this scene several times and moved the character representations and the "camera" the way that Welles did with his direction, when you feel you understand his picturization in this scene, move on to a scene a bit farther into the movie. This scene is inside Kane's office at his newspaper. It is preceded by a montage of Kane as a boy, clashing with Mr. Thatcher the banker. The montage features lots of front pages of newspapers with a headline of Spanish galleons off the Jersey coast. When the newspaper is lowered it shows Kane fully grown (played by Orson Welles) sitting at his desk. Mr. Thatcher is holding the newspaper and standing. He's trying to lecture Kane like Kane was still a little boy. It's not working at one key point and Kane faces Thatcher and tells him off. Kane is asserting himself as an independent adult. There is much excellent blocking and picturization in this scene. It ends with Kane saying that yes, he's losing a million dollars year with his newspaper, and at that rate he'll have to stop in 60 years.

Repeat what you did with the "actors" and camera representations and watching the scene in sections and moving them in the same patterns as Welles. Do this many times until you have confidence that you understand Welles' use of blocking and picturization to create and support meaning in this scene. You are learning from an absolute master of blocking. Do *not* cheat yourself. Do this many times. Learn lots from Welles, it's free!

Get a copy of Steven Spielberg's movie *Jaws*. There is an exterior scene well into the movie that comes after Richard Dreyfuss and Roy Scheider have gone out onto the ocean at night. Dreyfuss goes scuba diving on a wrecked sunken boat. He pulls a shark's tooth out of the boat and drops it when he sees horrifying faces of dead people. The scene you need to study comes right after this, and involves Dreyfuss' character and Roy Scheider's character pleading with the mayor of their town to close the beaches and take actions to kill the shark. The scene begins on a small hill and moves forward toward the camera as it moves back. Part of the scene takes place with a vandalized billboard in the background.

Make representations of the characters and camera and do with this scene what you did with the scenes in *Citizen Kane*. Repeat it many times until you understand Spielberg's blocking and use of picturization in the scene. Again, learn from a master!

Now repeat the same exercise with the end scene of *Casablanca*, the one at the airport. Don't forget the camera. Repeat it many times until you understand director Michael Curtiz's use of picturization, blocking, and composition and his use of the camera movements to provide directorial comments. Do this and the previous exercises in Step Seventeen thoroughly before you move past this point.

(c) Here's an actual blocking and picturization practice.

1. Select a dozen substantial scenes from very successful movies that were directed by very successful directors that you admire, and from whom you wish to learn. Get a commitment from some actors, want-to-be actors, friends, and movie enthusiasts that want to be in front of a camera. Get some experience blocking and creating picturizations with real people. You can tell these people that if they help you complete these blocking exercises you will use them in short movies. You will do four short movie exercises to fully complete this section of this course, and you can also truly tell them that participating in these blocking exercises will be good experience for them if they want to pursue a career in moviemaking.

Now get a video camera. Take out the cups with the paper ball heads. (You saved them, didn't you?) This is the last time you'll need them. *They are a good way to learn blocking quickly* while imitating the best directors, a step in bridging from just watching movies to actually moving and controlling people and a camera, or cameras. Move these representations of actors and camera through all twelve substantial scenes you have selected. Do this several times with each scene paralleling the movement of the actual actors and camera moved through as directed by these pro directors in the scenes from professional movies.

2. Take the video camera and some actors and move them through the actions and dialogue, not necessarily word for word. The actors can improvise and don't need to know the exact lines, or you can read the exact lines. The actors need to move at least roughly as the actors did in the two scenes in *Citizen Kane*, the one scene from *Jaws*, and the ending scene in *Casablanca*. Videotape these four scenes with blocking and picturization.

3. Take two of the twelve scenes you've selected and with your actors work out your own blocking to shoot the scene with the *observational* method or telling a story as written in Chapter Eight. (Reread Chapter Eight before doing this.).

Take two other scenes of your twelve selected scenes and work out your own blocking and shoot them in the directorial comment method, using a motion picture camera to tell a story (your video camera is sufficient for this exercise).

Take two other of your twelve scenes and shoot them in the "looking good" or "cinematic poetry" method of using the motion picture camera to tell a story.

Take two other of your twelve selected scenes and shoot them by the montage method of using a movie camera to tell a story.

(d) *Control of blocking and shooting scenes by different effective professional methods.* (Reread Chapter Nine about the five common methods of shooting a scene.) Before continuing with the actual physical exercises, let me tell you a story that will illustrate their potential value. An associate of mine is friends with a producer that worked with Steven Spielberg at the beginning of Spielberg's professional career when Spielberg was directing a TV episode. The producer noticed that they were behind schedule and would not finish on time because too many shots remained to be shot. He pointed this out to Spielberg, who thought a while then devised a single shot that covered all of what remained of the scene, negating the need for several other setups, and they finished the day on schedule. This producer considered Spielberg a genius because he could do that.

Spielberg *is* a genius. You can see that by looking at his movies, but what he did can also be done by a properly-trained and experienced movie director that can think on his or her feet and who knows how to tell a story with a movie camera, as well as how to shoot a scene in any one of the five basic ways that a scene can commonly be shot, and is not trapped and isolated by the idea that the only way to shoot a scene is the master and coverage method. I have no doubt that Spielberg did a stellar job in the situation just mentioned, probably better than almost any other director then working in television would have done, and earned the producer's judgment that he was a genius, but I suspect that at least part of the reason that the TV producer was so impressed was that *most* of the TV directors he was working with were not qualified movie directors, could not tell a story with a movie camera, and really were only a bit more than traffic directors who knew only how to shoot scenes by the master and coverage method, and how to keep shots *visually interesting* while the dialogue told the story of the TV episode. Being little more than a traffic cop with actors, keeping shots visually interesting while coming up with shots that cover a lot of pages, being someone who can set his or her shots, and get the day. If the script says wide shot, master, close-up, shoot it that way, not giving the D.P. detailed instructions or directing the lead actors too much, and God forbid ever changing the script, is a pretty good way to keep and job and keep working as a TV director. Be minimal.

You may find yourself in some kind of situation that in some way resembles the one described, in which young Spielberg found himself.

Hopefully, the previous and following exercises will help you develop the skills to deal with such a situation, or some other unforeseen situation

1. Take two of your twelve scenes and your actors and block out and shoot those scenes by the master and coverage method of shooting a scene and edit them. *Always shoot a master before shooting coverage unless for some very rare reason that's obviously wrong or virtually impossible.* If you shoot coverage before shooting the master, it's called "jumping a master" as well as "oh what a tangled web we weave." Avoid it at all costs.

Here's some advice for the future. When you make a feature movie, it's very likely that someone on the crew will suggest "Why don't we shoot everything in this room that's facing this way from every scene in the script in this room. This would mean shooting part of scene 21, part of scene 45, part of scene 71 without blocking out and shooting masters of the scene. It's what I call "the TV trap" because it is sometimes done on TV series. David Chase refers to it on a DVD commentary on *The Sopranos* but TV shows have major league heavy duty industrial strength script supervisors. It may work in TV in that kind of personnel situation, but even in TV Chase said it was very difficult. I have never seen this kind of thing done successfully on a low budget movie. Usually, it degenerates into a confused mess with the actors, director, and D.P. confused as hell and begging for mercy and just hoping to get back to a clean scene where they can shoot a master and then coverage. The very best cinematographer I ever worked with quickly squashed this suggestion from a crew member and said "No! If I shoot the master then coverage I know where my key light is in the scene. I know the whole lighting scheme, if we just shoot pieces of scenes I don't know where the hell I am, and if we have to relight in the same location that's easy. We can do it quickly, but if we get confused we can chase our own tail for hours."

Boy, was he ever right. This desire of the crew for shooting everything facing a certain way from five different scenes is a spasm of Marxist thinking - "The only thing that matters is crew labor." On low budget movies it never works. Bat it down! Stomp on it! Smash it! Throw it off the set from the whole movie. *Shoot whole scenes*, by whatever method you choose. If you shoot pieces of scenes, everyone will get confused and the set will go crazy and turn into a mess. Whoever suggests this shot every bit of every scene facing a certain way is likely at least a potential "professional leader of the revolution" to a greater or lesser degree.

Take two other scenes and shoot them by the shooting in sequential method, and edit them.

Take two more scenes and shoot them by the montage method, and edit them.

Take two more scenes and shoot them by the "get it all in one shot" method.

Take two more scenes and shoot them by the documentaryesque method, and edit them.

2. Select one very substantial scene and shoot it by the master and coverage method, the shooting in sequential units method, the montage method, the "get it all in one shot" method, and the documentary style method.

The purpose of the exercises you have just done is to develop skill and judgment so that you can choose which method of shooting a scene is best for a scene or a movie or which method you prefer, or which method best deals with your actual immediate situation during shooting.

3. There are two common actor's positions, blockings, or compositions that can be very useful in shooting dialogue. One is to have some valid motivation for both actors in a two actor scene to be looking forward toward the camera, not looking at each other. They can be moving or stationary and they can be next to each other or one can be in the foreground and the other in the background. This method is used very well in *Clerks* and *Lawrence of Arabia*. You will see variations on it in other movies. For instance, where one character is looking out a window and

the camera is in front of both actors and one actor is behind the one that is looking out the window, or the camera is tracking back in front of the two actors walking forward while talking is also a common variation.

Setting up a scene so that two actors are both looking forward (toward the camera) at something in the movie that's not in the shot is another common variation on this method of shooting dialogue. Shoot some dialogue by all of the methods mentioned above and add some of your own variations on this method if you can.

Actors do not always need to look at each other, as they are often taught in acting class by teachers that don't seem to know that there is such a thing as a motion picture camera and actors' faces need to be seen by that camera if the audience or viewer is to see the actor's performances. Another common method of shooting dialogue is where both actors' faces can be seen at the same time is to have one actor in the foreground with their head pointing sideways in profile looking off to the side and to have that look motivated in some way; the actor is "thinking" and doesn't want to "face" the other actor, etc. The second actor is in the background looking forward toward the camera and maybe at the other actor. Spielberg uses this composition blocking in *Raiders of the Lost Ark* and it is used extremely well in an excellent John Wayne movie, *Wake of the Red Witch*, and many other movies.

The other common methods of shooting dialogue is a two-shot in profile with the two actors facing each other, or reverse close-ups or medium shots on each actor shot over the shoulder (O.T.S.). Shoot some dialogue using these methods.

There are other very inventive and very many methods of shooting dialogue.

STEP EIGHTEEN - Watch the first 15 minutes of *Blue Velvet*, David Lynch's great movie, with the sound off. Watch Fritz Lang's *Metropolis* and don't read its title cards. Watch Hitchcock's *Read Window, Psycho, Vertigo,* and *The Birds* with the sound off. You should pretty much be able to follow these movies without dialogue, because their images tell the stories and push the stories forward.

STEP NINETEEN - Write a script for a ten-minute or longer movie with a story that is told entirely in images. *No dialogue!* Write this script in detail. It is a shooting script written shot to shot. Incorporate what you've learned about lenses, camera angles, the four methods of telling a story with a movie camera, observational directorial comment, "looking good," and montage, and the five common methods of shooting a scene, master and coverage, shooting in sequential units, montage, "get it all in one shot," and documentaryesque styles. Put it all together. Use what you have learned. This movie is an exercise. It doesn't have to be a masterpiece. It should be fun, so have fun with it!

STEP TWENTY - Do it! Shoot the script!

STEP TWENTY-ONE - Edit the movie and show it to several groups of several people and see if they can follow the movie's story. Post it on the Internet. If it's not good enough to post, do it again until it is good enough to post.

STEP TWENTY-TWO - Watch *Casablanca*. Shut your eyes whenever there is dialogue and just listen to the dialogue. Do the same thing with *The Maltese Falcon, Knocked Up, Superbad, Clerks, Jay and Silent Bob Strike Back, Chasing Amy,* and *Coffee and Cigarettes*. Do it with Quentin Tarantino's movies, *Reservoir Dogs, Pulp Fiction, True Romance,* and *Jackie Brown.*

STEP TWENTY-THREE - Write a script that is *all* dialogue, wall-to-wall dialogue. I go into this subject in more depth and explanation in my book about screenwriting but here I will just say that after a detailed study of scripts like *Chinatown, Clerks, Jackie Brown, The Hustler, Who's Afraid of Virginia Woolf,* and many others I've found that a lot of the actors' speeches in truly excellent scripts are *only one line long!*

1. To be clear, not *all* the speeches are one line long (although in *Chinatown* and *Clerks* most are). Some are two and three lines long, but a lot or even most in some scripts are only one line.

2. Some excellent scripts in some places have longer speeches, and in some cases even have one or a few very long speeches.

3. They have a lot of speeches that are one line long and usually, only one line, is the most common length of an actor's speech.

If you are looking for single, definitive, most common denominators that separate truly excellent professional and Oscar-winning scripts from the amateur, unprofessional, doomed never to be made into a movie, don't deserve to be made into a movie, scripts and non-scripts, that fly around Hollywood like swarms of locusts, this matter of professional scripts, excellent scripts, scripts that cry out to be made into very successful movies having a lot of dialogue that's one line long and bad unprofessional scripts that are doomed never to be made into movies not having much dialogue that is one line long, and having a lot of overly long over-written and often grossly and grotesquely overly long over-written dialogue is a serious common denominator that sharply separates these two groups.

In my screenwriting book I go into much more detail about this "one line long factor" and why its so I important particularly when dealing with star actors and when dealing with actors in low budget movies.

STEP TWENTY-FOUR - Shoot that script and edit the movie.

STEP TWENTY-FIVE - Show that movie to several audiences several times and post your movie on the Internet. Again, with the sound off, watch the first 15 minutes of *Blue Velvet, Metropolis, Rear Window, Psycho, Vertigo,* and *The Birds.*

STEP TWENTY-SIX - Again, write a shooting script with a story for a movie that is at least ten minutes long and is composed only of images, no dialogue, shoot it, edit the movie, and show it to several groups of several people, and post it on the Internet. Watch *Casablanca, The Maltese Falcon, Knocked Up, Superbad, Clerks, Jay and Silent Bob Strike Back, Chasing Amy,* and *Coffee and Cigarettes* and shut your eyes and just listen to the dialogue when there is dialogue in these movies. Write a script that's all dialogue. Shoot it, edit it, show it to audiences, and post it on the Web.

STEP TWENTY-SEVEN - Write a treatment for a movie that is over ten minutes long that has a story and that will be all dialogue. Take your actors into an audio or videotaped rehearsal where you allow the actors to improvise, based on the treatment. You guide and organize these improvisations into a rough script. Shoot the movie allowing the actors to improvise from the improvisation-based script. Edit it. Show it to several audiences of several people, and post it on the Internet.

The intended result of this part of the course is for the student to be comfortable using a movie camera and lenses to tell a story effectively, and to be familiar with and able to use various methods to tell a story with a movie camera and to be able to use various common methods of shooting scenes and to be able and comfortable telling a story with images, or with dialogue, and to be able to guide and use improvisation.

If you have attained these results move forward in the course. If you haven't, repeat the recent steps in this course as needed, until you get the above stated result.

SECTION FIVE:
MORE THINGS IN HEAVEN AND EARTH -
BE PREPARED FOR UNEXPECTED OPPORTUNITIES

STEP TWENTY-EIGHT - Make a documentary about anything that is at least five minutes long. Make a TV commercial about anything that is at least three minutes long. Make a TV commercial about anything that is one and one-half minutes long and also has a thirty second version. Make an educational or instructional video or film that's at least ten minutes long. Make a music video for any piece of music.

SECTION SIX:
THE JOB'S NOT DONE UNTIL
THE PAPERWORK'S DONE

STEP TWENTY-NINE - Write a review of a movie you've recently seen and make your best efforts to get it published in a local newspaper, school paper, or on the Internet. Write an essay about a classic movie, and use your best efforts to get it published in a film magazine or journal. Read at least two dozen reviews written by prestigious critics of movies that you have seen. Write another review of a just-released movie and use your best efforts to get it published. Go to the library regularly and spend long sections of time looking at art books with pictures of paintings and sculptures by famous and great artists. Do this until you are familiar with the major famous artists and sculptors and their great and famous works of art. Do the same thing with books of pictures of architecture, books of photography, and photographic art. Develop your eye for art, beauty, form, images, and places. Also listen to music and develop your knowledge and appreciation for music that causes emotion.

STEP THIRTY - Decide in which genre(s) your first feature movie will most likely reside. Unforeseen future events can change one's plans, but that is not a reason to have no plans. Select the most likely genre(s) of your first feature length movie.

STEP THIRTY-ONE - Select two very financially successful and critically acclaimed movies form that genre(s) and watch them each over forty times. You need to become an expert in the genre in which you are working if you are to be a successful, professional moviemaker. Select at least a dozen successful movies from that genre and watch them at least two times each. Successful moviemakers are experts in the genres in which they work. Do this step for real. Take it seriously. Soon you will be putting what you learn in this section into real competitive *succeed* or *fail* professional competition.

SECTION EIGHT:
SHOW TIME, AWARD-WINNING MOVIE OF EXCELLENCE TIME

STEP THIRTY-TWO - The standards of this course shift dramatically and steeply upward at this point. "Good enough" is no longer adequate. Only excellence is good enough because you are about to break into the cold cruel reality-based world of professional movie-making and leave behind the soft comfortable forgiving world of student filmmaking and being a student. If you have done the steps of this course you have accomplished a lot, and you have moved from being an audience member or movie viewer to be a serious student and a movie maker. You are about to begin another major leap. Congratulations!

You are going to make a "calling card" movie that is at least ten minutes long, but it can be longer. This needs to be a movie of stellar excellence. The exercises to learn the basics are over. This needs to be a movie that you would show to a potential investor who you are trying to convince to fund or invest in your first feature film. It needs to be a movie that you will proudly enter in awards competitions, or have shown at appropriate film festivals. It needs to be a movie that provokes job offers.

The world of professional moviemaking is extremely competitive. There's a song in the great, ultra-cult movie classic *Hollywood Blvd.* directed by Joe Dante and produced by Roger Corman. It has a line in it about Hollywood being a rough and rocky road that's sides are littered with those who couldn't carry the heavy load. It's no joke! You need to make a movie that can compete very strongly with the very best.

The only job you need to do on this movie is either director, or producer. This is the point where this course diverges and breaks into two separate directions, one for directors, one for producers. If you want someone else to write the script, operate the camera, or edit the movie, you only need to direct or produce. You are a moviemaker. Now you need to become a professional moviemaker. You no longer need to be a student "one-man band" doing all the jobs yourself, but you can if you want to.

Make a stellar calling card movie that is at least ten minutes long, either direct or produce it or direct and produce it, and do or don't do any other jobs on the movie you want to do or don't want to do. When the movie is done if it meets the necessary standards of excellence enter it in awards competitions, film festivals, and show it to people. Use it to advance your career in any and every way possible. If the first movie you make for this step does not meet the high quality needed for a calling card movie, make another one, and if necessary, another, until you have a movie of strong excellence that can open doors for you or at least stop them from being slammed in your face. When you have successfully completed this step, congratulations! You have completed Part One of this course and are moving into the world of professional moviemaking.

In terms of the four steps of getting a task done, you have completed Step Two and are doing Step Three as you move forward from here. It should be clear to you that you *can* complete this course if you have gotten this far.

PART TWO:
THE MIDDLE -
SCRIPT AND PROFESSIONAL WORK

STEP THIRTY-THREE - Get a copy of my other book, *Become A Screenwriter: An Analysis of the Common Denominator of the Scripts of Financially successful and Critically Acclaimed Movies and the Contrasting Common Denominators of Unsuccessful Scripts.* This book can be read and used two different ways. One way is to read the book is to use its workbook to write a script as you read the book. This way of using the book is intended for screenwriters or those that want to be screenwriters and have an idea for a script. The other way to read the book is to skip the workbook and read the other sections of the book to learn about successful scripts, and successful screenwriting. This way of reading the book is intended for writers who have not had an idea for a script, or those who are not, and don't want to be, writers but whose careers or lack of careers depend upon getting possession of and the legal rights to shoot *good scripts*; directors, producers, actor, and others.

Use the book in one of two ways: (1) to write your own script, a script that you strongly believe deserves to be made into a movie because you strongly believe, based on evidence and facts that it will please and attract and satisfy some significant segment of the movie-viewing public; or (2) use the book to set standards and specify qualities to use to search for or to work with writers to create such a script, which you would get the legal right to make into a movie.

The end of Part Two of this course is to have a script that meets the above description in your possession, and to have the legal right to make it into a movie, whether you wrote it or got it by other means. You need to have a burning desire to shoot it and confidence, based on facts and rational analysis that it will be successful. So get my screenwriting book and either start writing or start searching.

STEP THIRTY-FOUR - While you are either writing or searching in your quest for a script that deserves to be made into a movie, and that you can make into a movie, do the following actions.

1. Work on a professional movie for at least two weeks. You can work as an unpaid intern, a paid or unpaid production assistant, a crew or staff member, an extra, any job. You need to develop a professional mindset. Working on professional movies is the best way to do that.

2. Read Part Eight - Pathway Into the Movie Biz - and Part Nine - Aim Higher - of this book if you have not yet done so.

3. Select at least one director that you strongly admire and study that director's movies. Read reviews of that director's movies if DVDs with commentaries by that director are available, listen to them. Study that director's work and movies in depth.

4. *See lots of movies.* If you need a part-time job, working at a video store is a good way to make this easier.

5. Read many scripts and plays and watch lots of movies with English subtitles on the screen so you can read the dialogue as in a script.

6. Watch a lot of low budget "breakout" movies.

7. Show your calling card movie to people in the movie business. Meet people in the movie business. Get to know people in the movie business.

When you have a script in your possession and have the legal right to make it into a movie and you are strongly confident based on logic, facts, sane analysis, that if that script is made into a movie it will attract and appeal to some significant segment of the movie-viewing public and have completed the other steps listed, you have completed Part Two of this course.

Congratulations!

PART THREE:
THE END -
MAKE A SUCCESSFUL MOVIE

Reread this book. Find and bond with at least two other competent committed people, find whatever resources financial or otherwise necessary to make your script into a successful professional feature length movie, and use the information in this book to make a feature length movie that receives professional distribution, returns all investors money and makes at least one cent profit, when you have done that, congratulations! You have successfully completed this course.

This is Step Four in completing a task. Write out what needs to be done to complete the task, put the steps in order, do them, and complete the task.

Let me summarize and emphasize what a director actually does to conclude this course. Even a minimal director controls what is on the movie screen and the soundtrack, and that matters to paying customers. While the assistant director is in charge of the set and controls the set, the directors controls the actors performances, line delivery, and position and movement, and the position and movement of the movie camera. He also controls the image on the screen and the viewer's attention. The director controls what will be seen or not seen and how much of it and how it will be seen. The director controls image after image, shot after shot, on the movie screen. The director also controls what will be heard on the soundtrack. The editor controls and is in charge of post-production, but the director controls the flow of images and the connection of images into a meaningful montage. Often, the editor makes big contributions in this area, but an editor cannot cut footage that doesn't exist, or "does not cut." Even directors who don't enter the cutting room often control this flow of images and montage. On *Plague* I wrote, storyboarded, and shot a long involved car chase sequence. When I finished shooting December 31st in Toronto, I left the movie's footage in the hands of a world-class editor, Ron Wisman, and I went back to Los Angeles to thaw out. When Ron had a rough cut, I came back and watched the movie. It was cut beautifully, in contrast to many rough cuts that are stomach-wrenching messes.

The cut car chase matched my storyboard almost exactly. Ron had made a few cuts that made it better, but the basic image flow, and montage was in my storyboard. Ron controlled post-production start to finish. But I, the director, determined the image flow, the montage that the viewer would see to a very large degree, not just when I shot shots, but even before I filmed. My storyboard made from images in my mind determined these things. The editor made the cuts, splices precise to the best possible frame, and added things the director missed and polished the picture, like writing an even more polished script, but without correctly shot footage an editor is in trouble. The director controls whether you're going to see an actor's face or see it close up when you need to see it or not see it when you need to see it, whether action or dialogue will seem real and effective, or fake.

Usually, the screenwriter supplies the movie's story, and supplies or refines its concept, its plot, its structure, its characters and usually most or all of its dialogue. It's easy for actors and/or the director to "fix" or perfect dialogue, but structure, plot, story, concept, theme are a far different matter and can sometimes be beyond even the fixing abilities of the editor. Both the writer and director are so important to the making of a movie that trying to dismiss either's contribution to a movie is ridiculous. Nevertheless, it happens all the time because of ideology disconnected from the real world and because of greedy, craven self-interest.

A movie is many things to different people. To the screenwriter, it's likely to be concept, story, plot, character, dialogue, themes, and other things. To the cinematographer, it's usually images. To the audience it's all the above, as images on a movie screen or TV screen, and sounds on a soundtrack. If these all work, a movie forms a window into an interesting and entertaining world for the audience or viewer. As many directors and all editors know, however, a movie is also something else very physical. A movie frame is about one inch square, with 24 of those square pictures passing through an editing machine or a projector every second, 90 feet per minute. A finished movie is about two miles long, one picture after another. A feature film is made up of about 100,000 one-inch squares, all put into position by the director and editor after being created by the director and cinematographer.

Good luck with that!

PART FOUR:
PATHWAYS INTO THE MOVIE BIZ

"Military science is probably right about the contemptibility of man and the vastness of the universe… still I deny that contemptibility, and I get you to deny it through the creation and appreciation of art."
- Kurt Vonnegut

There's a book that's in a lot of libraries. It's called *Breaking In: How Twenty Directors Got Their Start* by Nicholas Jarecki. It's published by Broadway Books, a division of Random House. It was published in 2001. Get a copy and read it as background to this chapters. It has interviews with these twenty directors and covers their educational backgrounds, their entry level jobs that got them into the movie biz, and how they became movie directors and how in most cases they became hot at least hot in 2001. They are a diverse and interesting group of directors. The book is well worth reading if you are working to break into the movie biz, or are trying to work in the movie biz prior to making your first movie.

There are very many routes and paths into the movie biz. There is the screenwriting route, the director of music videos route, the director of cable TV commercials and then bigger budget commercials. There is the film school and advanced studies route. There is the movie critic route. There is the unpaid intern to P.A. to third A.D. to second or first A.D. route. There is the "get a bunch of friends and associates together and make a low budget break out independent movie route." There is the posting short movies on the Internet or to impress someone and get a job route. There is the raise money co-producer or executive producer to producer route. There is the crew, grip or electric route to D.P. and then to director. There is the actor route or extra to actor, and actor to director, or writer or writer/director, or producer route.

John Wayne was an assistant prop person before becoming an actor and John Ford was a prop person for Allan Dwan before becoming a director. Roger Corman started as a producer, and then became a director also. When I graduated from UCLA film school, I called over 300 film and movie companies before I got even one job interview. After I showed my student film to a couple of companies, one of them offered to buy my student film for distribution. The film cost about $90 to make. They bought the distribution rights for $75. I thought that was pretty good; nobody else sold their student film for commercial distribution. That company hired me to make a feature length movie shot in 16mm b/w. They paid me $50 to write, photograph, direct, edit, cut the sound and sound FX, cut the negative and mix it. This process took me three weeks. I earned a bit under $17 a week on my first professional movie job as a director, cinematographer, and editor.

Then I hit the big time. That company hired me at $50 a week as a P.A. and all-purpose filmmaking assistant. My salary had tripled! Almost every day I was working with film or on films. I did lots of editing and assistant camera work for the owner of the company, who was the company's chief cinematographer. He liked to smoke pot when he shot film (something I do not recommend). After about an hour he had trouble with focus. After two hours, I had the camera. I was no longer an assistant. Soon I was shooting, directing, and editing 16mm films. I was editing and doing sound FX on 35mm features and also doing jobs like art department P.A. and still photographer, assistant camera on drive-in movies often shot over a weekend or two. About six to nine months after my first job interview I was up to my ears in movie work often doing two full-time jobs at the same time working from early in the morning to well after midnight.

There is a fine line between getting into the movie biz and advancing, fitting in, and not getting into the movie biz at all. If I had stopped calling movie and film companies after a mere 200 calls, I might never have gotten my first job. If I had not been willing to work for less than $17 a week I might never have gotten my first job. If I hadn't been willing to work for $50 a week and do very labor-intensive jobs I might not have gotten my second job. I did a lot of film work, got a lot of hands-on film experience. I advanced the process of learning I'd begun in film school.

Time passed. The world turned. I saved my money and made a 16mm b/w feature "art" film intended for distribution on college campuses. It was called *Diary of a Living Target*. It's not on my resume because it only had a few screenings on college campuses and never really got professional distribution. I showed it to a movie distributor, theater owner, who had just also become a movie producer. He didn't like the art movie's political point of view and disagreed with its premise, but he said that it showed that I could handle film, and make a movie. He asked if I could make a 35mm color feature for $50,000. I said "Sure!" I'd previously sent him a script I'd written in ten days. He liked it and said that it had "a certain dramatic validity." He bought it and hired me to direct and edit it. Then he distributed it profitably.

For a period of about six years I directed, wrote or co-wrote, and often also produced or co-produced a movie a year, and did camera work and editing between movies. One piece of advice that I would give people starting out in the movie biz and trying to make their way into the movie biz and trying to advance is to *work with people wherever possible who do what they say they will do!* This holds true even to very small details. If they stay they'll call tomorrow at 3:00 and they don't, it's usually a warning signal. If they say they'll do something (even small) and they don't it's another warning. If people don't do what they say they will do, nothing positive will come from trying to work with or for them. If you don't know if a person is b.s. or OK, ask them to *do* something. If they do what they say they will do repeatedly they're probably or maybe OK. If they don't, they are likely b.s. and can easily be a "black hole" that will eat and sap your time and energy.

As you enter the movie biz at whatever level, you will meet and get to know people. They are a resource. Lawrence Bender, the producer of *Reservoir Dogs* and Tarantino's partner, was taking an acting class when they were working to finance *Reservoir Dogs*. Bender gave the movie's script to someone in the acting class who read it, and loved it to and sent to someone in New York that read it and also loved it and got it to Harvey Keitel, and that put the project on a path to becoming a movie. You have to plan and execute or improvise you own individual entry into the movie biz. Everyone is different and there are many paths that lead to where you want to go.

There is a saying "Be nice to the people you meet on the way up because they're the same people you'll meet on the way down." Few careers do not have downs as well as ups. Beware of people that tell you that they can see that you have no talent or won't make it in the movie biz. When

Burt Reynolds and Clint Eastwood were $75 a week contract actors at Universal Studios a "genius" called them in and fired them both. He fired Clint Eastwood because his Adam's apple was too big, and Reynolds because he couldn't act. The story goes that Reynolds and Eastwood left the studio and walked about a block and Reynolds said, "I'm in a lot better situation than you.

"How's that?" Eastwood replied.

"I can always learn to act. You're gonna have a helluva time trying to swallow that Adam's apple."

I will confess that when I was casting a low budget horror movie I "passed" on one actress who became a major movie star, and on another one that eventually won an Oscar for Best Female Actor. The lady I cast became a TV movie star.

The strongest story I ever heard of this type was of a big time music agent that represented country music stars. A young singer auditioned for him but he turned down the chance to represent him because the singer insisted on making "strange motions" when singing. The agent told the singer, "Kid, you're handsome as hell, you got a great voice, but you gotta learn to just stand there and sing your song and stop all this crazy jumpin' around. You'll scare the audience." That young singer was Elvis Presley.

Beware of falling into the trap of wallowing in and consoling yourself after disappointments with mantras about all that is wrong with Hollywood and how things should be. Sure, lots of things are very wrong with Hollywood and virtually everywhere else, too. Your job is to deal with reality, turn it to your advantage, and make your movies and make them successful and build your power, and advance your career. When something really is wrong with Hollywood, there usually is a potential, and unseen opportunity behind that wrongness. Henry Ford said, "Don't find fault, find a remedy, anybody can complain." Here's an example. In the 1980s, studios were not making movies about African-Americans and movies had not really dealt with smart middle class hip artistic African-Americans. Spike Lee could have complained how no studio would make his script into a movie. Instead, he made *She's Gotta Have It* himself. It served an audience that studios had ignored. It was a huge success, and launched his career. The same kind of thing is true of Godard and *Breathless*, and John Cassavetes and *Faces*, and Robert Rodriguez and *El Mariachi*, and Kevin Smith and *Clerks*, Steven Soderbergh with *Sex, Lies, and Videotape*, and George Romero and *Night of the Living Dead*, and Sam Raimi and *The Evil Dead*. Behind wrongness there is often a hidden opportunity if one does not fall into the *trap* of complaining, but instead *finds a remedy*.

In a way, the same kind of thing applies to Harvey Weinstein and Miramax. *Shakespeare in Love Pulp Fiction, The English Patient*, and *Good Will Hunting*, some of Miramax's biggest hits and Oscar winners, were movie studio developed or contracted movies, but when it came time to make them, some studios and some executives got stupid and decided to jerk around the filmmakers attached to these projects. They said they'd only make *Shakespeare in Love* if Julia Roberts was in it, and she didn't want to do it. So Mr. Weinstein took the project with Gwyneth Paltrow, who was perfect for the part and won an Oscar, as did the movie. Something wrong in

Hollywood opened an opportunity and he grabbed it and ran with it and the Oscars and money fell on Miramax. Other geniuses decided *Pulp Fiction* should not have dirty talk or violence or John Travolta, right before shooting was about to start, again something wrong in Hollywood. The old on again, off again dance to jerk the creative folks' heads around, again resulting in an Oscar-winning big hit that fell out of stupid studios' hands and Mr. Weinstein and Miramax caught the Oscars and big hit's money. The same kind of thing happened with *The English Patient* and *Good Will Hunting*.

When something's wrong in Hollywood – and lots is – follow Henry Ford's advice. Don't waste time complaining. Find a remedy, look for the opportunity on the other side of that wrongness. There usually is an opportunity there caused by the wrongness, but many people never see it because they are too busy complaining.

PART FIVE:
AIM HIGHER

"Our purpose is to make mankind aware of itself, in all its
complexity, and to dream its dreams."
- Kurt Vonnegut

In 1917, when World War I had slaughtered hundreds of thousands of soldiers in single battles and there seem to be no end in sight to the horrific carnage of that war, the legendary moviemaker D.W. Griffith made a silent movie, *Intolerance*. Most critics and film historians rank it as the very best silent movie ever made, and more than a few consider it the greatest movie of all time. Griffith's purpose in making *Intolerance* with his own movie money was to end World War I, and he depicts the end of war at the end of the film. He wanted to end intolerance and cause humans to stop their cruelty to one another and abandon war as a fact of life and death and recognize what he saw as their universal brotherhood. Griffith once told his fellow filmmakers, "People around the world will see the movies you make here, and they will understand them." He saw movies as a new universal language that could travel across borders and from culture to culture. He thought that they could bring about a level of human understanding that would make warfare and petty hatreds and cruelties obsolete.

He was either a long way ahead of his time or a major idealist. Silent movies actually were a kind of universal language of the image, much more than talking pictures. *Intolerance* fell short of Griffith's target, though. It did not end World War I or bring about universal brotherhood, but it was a very great movie and by far, without doubt it was the greatest movie that had been made up to that point, and one of the most spectacular ever made. It was about three hours in length, a historical and modern epic with major philosophical and social themes. In contrast, most movies of that time were ten-minute "one-reelers."

The legendary French movie director, screenwriter, producer, movie critic and cinematic theorist Francois Truffaut, in his great movie *Day for Night* (a film about making movies), said "When you start out to make a movie you start out to make a *great movie*, then as the realities of making the movie befall you (Shakespeare's "slings and arrows of outrageous fortune) you will be happy just to make a good movie, then as you go farther into the process you'll be happy just making a movie, and by the end, you'll be happy if you just live through the making of the movie."

What he meant was what I call the effect of the "inertia of reality" which is a kind of gravity pull that reality has on the moviemaker as he or she pushes forward trying to bring a vision into existence and into reality, with reality opposing and trying to squash or scrape away one's dreams and hopes, and pull down the brighter part of that vision. People who shoot rifles with telescopic sights at targets that are great distances away, over a mile or more adjust their sighting mechanism to allow for the effect the gravity and wind will have on even a supersonic bullet traveling a long distance. This slight adjustment in the sighting mechanism causes the rifle to "aim higher" so that when gravity pulls the bullet down or wind pushes it aside, over its path, it will still hit its target.

When you conceptualize a movie, or when you decide on a course of action in the movie biz, if you aim right at a low target you may accomplish it or even exceed it, but you may also be pulled down a notch or so just below it. I've watched screenwriters or moviemakers that "just want to get a movie made" repeatedly *almost* get movies made. If their target had been to make a good movie, or a great movie, they probably would have at least gotten a movie made even if contact with reality pulled them down a notch or two. Some of these people thought that the way to accomplish their goal was to lower objectives to "just getting a movie made" they would have had better prospects if they'd raised their goal at least to writing or making "the best damned movie they could."

When I originally conceptualized the script that eventually became *Starship Invasions*, I conceptualized it as a low budget (about $500,000) "exploitation movie" like Roger Corman's *Death Race 2000*, a "B" movie that was proud and happy to be what it was, not a movie that set out to be a great movie. When my movie was finished and screened, the movie's cinematographer said to me, "That movie will sell a lot of popcorn." My goal was to make a movie that would draw a lot of people into theaters, like Corman's movie had. I watched *Starship Invasions* in a full theater on Younge Street in Toronto. It did draw people to the theaters, and did indeed sell a lot of popcorn! *Starship* was mildly successful when Warner Bros. released it. After the TV and foreign sales it was profitable for the money men, but it was not a breakout movie. Its script had been weak and unperfected.

Compared to the other Canadian movies that were being made or not being made at that time, though, it was a spectacular success. It suffered, however, in comparison to *Star Wars* and *Close Encounters of the Third Kind*, both of which had similar subject matter. My budget was around $800,000, while I've seen the budget of *Star Wars* reported at around $12,000,000 and *Close Encounters* at about $30,000,000.

The real difference between those mega-successful movies and mine begins with their conceptualization. Both George Lucas and Steven Spielberg were setting out to make the best movie of that type that had ever been made. They wanted to exceed any other movie that had come before in the sci–fi genre. They each already had the experience I was seeking of drawing lots of people to theaters. Lucas's *American Graffiti* and Spielberg's *Jaws* had both filled up lots of movie theaters. They raised their sights to much higher goals with their sci-fi movies, which were very high goals indeed. Lucas aimed particularly high with his story fashioned around the story structure laid out in Joseph Campbell's *The Hero with a Thousand Faces*, which examines the great religions, myths, and legends of the Earth. He was not simply aiming at the big leagues but looking to stand tall among storytelling giants.

Both of those movies, from their concepts to the finished films, had very strong thematic depth and enormous detail, and a very strong connection to and understanding of the movie audience's "desire to see." Before *Starship*, I thought that scripts were simply something you had to have to get the money to make the movie, and once you had the money you could do what worked and use or change the script and work it all out in making the movie. During *Starship*'s editing and when it failed to break out I began to realize how truly important the script is to a movie's success, and potential to break out. I began a long journey of study of the scripts of successful and breakout movies, and a process of outlining the successful common denominators of successful movie scripts and the contrasting common denominators of unsuccessful and surprisingly unsuccessful movies. What I found is in my book about screenwriting.

The very beginning of the process of writing a script, when a movie is conceptualized, is of *vital importance*. What kind of movie will it be? What will be its "DNA code"? How deep will it go? What are its ambitions? At this point of the very beginning of the beginning of writing a script or starting a project is usually when creative energies and inspirations are most dynamic and easiest to provoke and that is when the screenwriter or moviemaker decides which direction to take and not to take. There are exceptions, but scripts and movies usually don't rise much above their original conceptualization.

So aim higher! As the character of Orson Welles said in the movie *Ed Wood*: "Visions are worth fighting for. Why spend your life making someone else's dreams?" I'm going to end this book by paraphrasing the great poem *If* by Rudyard Kipling. Here's my take on it, with regard to making it in the movie biz.

If you can keep your head when all about you are losing their and blaming it on you
If you can trust yourself when all folks doubt you, but make allowance for their doubting, too
If you can wait and not be tired by waiting, or being lied about, don't deal in lies
Or being hated, don't give way to hating, and yet don't look too good, nor talk too wise
If you can dream and not make dreams your master,
If you can think and not make thoughts your aim
If you can meet with triumph and disaster
And treat those two impostors just the same
If you can bear to hear the truth you've spoken twisted by knaves to make a trap for fools
Or watch things you gave your life to, broken, and stop and build again with worn-out tools
If you can make a heap of all your winnings, and risk it on one turn or pitch and toss
And lose, and start again at your beginnings, and never breath a word about your loss
If you can force your heart and nerve and sinew to serve your turn long after they are gone
And so hold on when there is nothing in you except the will which says to them,
"Hold on!"
If you can talk with crowds and keep your virtue, or walk with kings
Nor lose the common touch
If neither foes nor loving friends can hurt you
If all men count with you but none too much
If you can fill the unforgiving minute with sixty second's worth of distance run...

You should be able to apply for a job as a superhero, and if that doesn't work out, try being a movie director and/or producer, and if you're properly prepared you can go as far as your imagination and talent will take you.

Good luck, and all the best.

Ed Hunt: Awards & Recognition

On the pages that follow, you will find the following:

1) Internet Movie Database (IMDb) listing for the 1979 winners at the Sitges – Catalonian International Film Festival.

2) Letter to distributor Brandon Chase regarding the Sitges win for "Plague" for Best Picture and Best Screenplay.

3) Sitges award in Spanish signed by the Committee.

4) Flyer in Spanish from the Sitges screening.

5) Golden Scroll of Merit Award from the Academy of Science Fiction, Fantasy, and Horror Films in Hollywood for the documentary "UFOs Are Real"

6) *TV Guide* full page listing for a national showing of "UFOs Are Real" on the Fox Network.

7) Movie poster for Warner Bros. feature film *Starship Invasions* written, directed, and produced by Ed Hunt

8) Picture grosses week ending report of February 22, 1978 from *Variety* magazine with *Starship Invasions* at #16 out of the Top 50 films

9) Sketch of monster and storyboard sequence from Ed Hunt film *The Brain*

Search [ ] All [ ] Go | Advanced Search

IMDb Resume New! | Company Directory | People Directory | In Production | STARmeter | Box Office | News | Message Boards

Home > Events > Festivals > Sitges - Catalonian International Film Festival > 1979

Event
Main Details
Overview
Discuss

Sitges - Catalonian International Film Festival

Date: October 6 - October 13 1979   **Location:** Sitges, Catalonia, Spain

www.cinemasitges.com

Award History
2009 2008 2007 2006
2005 2004 2003 2002
2001 2000 1999 1998
1997 1996 1995 1994
1993 1992 1991 1990
1989 1988 1987 1986
1985 1984 1983 1982
1981 1980 1979 1978
1977 1976 1975 1974
1973 1972 1971

Events Charts
All Events
Awards
Festivals
Calendar

Awards for 1979

Medalla Sitges en Oro de Ley

Best Director

WINNER

 Panna a netvor: Juraj Herz

Medalla Sitges en Plata de Ley

Best Actor

WINNER

Der Mörder: Gerhard Olschewski

Best Actress

WINNER

 Jennifer: Lisa Pelikan

Best Screenplay

WINNER

 Plague: Barry Pearson, Ed Hunt

Best Cinematography

WINNER

 The Comeback: Peter Jessop

Best Special Effects

WINNER

Thirst: Conrad Rothmann

Best Short Film

WINNER

Fantabiblical: Guido Manuli

Prize of the International Critics' Jury

WINNER

 Plague: Ed Hunt

PLAGUE WINS AWARDS
BEST PICTURE
BEST SCREENPLAY

Mr. Brandon Chase
The GROUP 1
9220 Sunset Boulevard
Los Angeles, Calif.90069

Dear Brandon,

I am pleased to confirm that, as it appears from the enclosed photo-
copy of a page of the specialized magazine CINEINFORM, the prizes
obtained by "PLAGUE" in the last Sitges Film Festival, were two and
exactly:

- Prize for the best film, say first prize;
- Prize for the best screenplay.

This will naturally be of great help for the possible sale of the
picture to Spain and other territories, and I have already informed
Cuevas and other Spanish Distributors.

FESTIVAL INTERNACIONAL DE CINE FANTASTICO Y DE TERROR

competitiva seccion por la FIAPF

San Isidro, 12 - SITGES (España) - Telefono 894 12 88 - Cables FANTASFILM - V. Sitges - Telex 51383

PREMIO INTERNACIONAL DE LA CRITICA

Teniendo en cuenta el débil nivel de los films seleccionados
y el hecho de que algunos de ellos no pertenecen a la temática
terror-fantastico, el Jurado destaca tres producciones —LA BELLA
Y LA BESTIA, THIRTS y PLAGUE— y atribuye por mayoría su premio
a

PLAGUE (Estados Unidos)

por la seriedad del tema, que pone de relieve la importancia actual del cine de ciencia-ficción.

FESTIVAL INTERNACIONAL DE CINE FANTASTICO Y DE TERROR

ACTA DEL JURADO INTERNACIONAL
****

CLAVEL MEDALLA DE PLATA al mejor guión, por mayoría, a Barry
Pearson y Ed Hunt por su labor en la película "PLAGUE".

FESTIVAL INTERNACIONAL DE CINE FANTASTICO Y DE TERROR

ACTA DEL JURADO INTERNACIONAL
****

Reunido el Jurado Internacional del XII FESTIVAL INTERNACIO-
NAL DE CINE FANTASTICO Y DE TERROR, de Sitges, en el Salón
de Actos del Gran Casino de Barcelona, bajo la presidencia
de Camille Keaton y con la asistencia de todos sus miembros,
señores Wilhelm Petersen (Alemania Federal); Eduardo Ruiz Sa-
viñón (Méjico) y los españoles Ricardo Muñoz Suay y Manuel Es-
teba Gallego, actuando como secretario con voz y sin voto Fernando Montejano, acuerdan conceder el siguiente palmarés:

CLAVEL MEDALLA DE PLATA al mejor realizador de cortometra-
jes, por mayoría, a Manuli Guido, por su película "FANTABIBLI-
CAL".

CLAVEL MEDALLA DE PLATA a los mejores efectos especiales,
por mayoría, a Conrad C. Rothmann, por su trabajo en la película "THIRST".

CLAVEL MEDALLA DE PLATA a la mejor fotografía, por mayoría,
a Peter Jessop, por su trabajo en la película "THE COMEBACK".

CLAVEL MEDALLA DE PLATA al mejor guión, por mayoría, a Barry
Pearson y Ed Hunt por su labor en la película "PLAGUE".

CLAVEL MEDALLA DE PLATA a la mejor actriz, por unanimidad,
a Lisa Pelikan, por su trabajo en la película "JENNIFER".

CLAVEL MEDALLA DE PLATA al mejor actor, por mayoría, a Ger-
had Olschewki, por su trabajo en la película "DER MÖRDER".

Y CLAVEL MEDALLA DE ORO al mejor realizador de largometrajes,
por unanimidad, a Juraj Herz, por su labor en la película "LA
BELLA Y LA BESTIA".

Por mayoría de votos, el Jurado concede, asimismo, una MENCION
ESPECIAL al film "VIAJE CONTRA EL TIEMPO", de Jindrich Polak.

Por ultimo, el Jurado, sugiere al Comité Ejecutivo que el próx-
imo año ponga a disposición del público un premio facultativo
que sería concedido por votación popular.

Lo que declaran a las 14,30 horas del día 13 de Octubre de
Mil novecientos setenta y nueve.

CAMILLE KEATON - PRESIDENTE

RUIZ SAVIÑAN   Wilhelm PETERSEN

RICARDO MUÑOZ SUAY

                                              MANUEL ESTEBA
FERNANDO MONTEJANO

ESTADOS UNIDOS   presentó a concurso

" P L A G U E "

P R E M I O .... AL MEJOR GUION
P R E M I O ..... MEJOR PELICULA del JURADO INTER DE LA CRITICA

Director... Ed Hunt	Intérpretes.. Daniel Pilon
Guión ..... Ed Hunt n Pearson	" .. Kate Reid
Fotografía. Mark Irwin	" .. Celine Lomez
Productora. Group 1	" .. Michael J. Reynolds
Versión ... Inglesa	Duración .. 90 mínutos

S I N O P S I S

Un virus mortal procedente de unos experimentos realizados
en unos laboratorios de investigaciones comerciales contagiará la
atmosfera y a unos gorriones que construyeron su nido dentro de la
tuberia de escape. Al morir uno de los gorriones y ser enterrado
por un niño, este morirá entre espantosos calambres. Otro viadante
trata de ayudar a otro de los gorriones... El virus se va extendien-
do por la ciudad. Los medicos intervienen aislando en cuarentena a
posibles contagiados. Uno de ellos, una joven huye asustada al ver
morir a un aislado y todo lo que va tocando es contagiado producien-
do la muerte. Entretanto, uno de los medicos, encerrado en el labo-
ratorio y aconsejado por entidades mundiales, consigue hallar el
anti-virus en un momento dramático para la ciudad ....

The Academy of Science Fiction
Fantasy and Horror Films

Golden Scroll
Award of Merit

to

Ed Hunt

UFO's Are Real

for

Outstanding Achievement

Dr. Donald A. Reed

Dr. Donald A. Reed
President

Date: _1980_

After 30 years of government cover up... the truth is revealed!

"It seemed to move toward us, then partially away, then return, then depart."
JIMMY CARTER, President

"I believe that these extraterrestrial vehicles and their crews are visiting this planet from other planets."
GORDON COOPER, Astronaut

"...highly secret government UFO investigations are going on that we don't know about."
BARRY GOLDWATER, Senator

"...the Army grabbed [one] and would not let us have it for cursory examination."
J. EDGAR HOOVER, former FBI Chief

We dare you not to believe after you've seen...

UFO'S ARE REAL.

8PM FOX 11

We know they are there- advanced beyond our imagination.

Why have they come?

"STARSHIP INVASIONS"

ROBERT VAUGHN

CHRISTOPHER LEE

Music by GIL MELLE • Executive Producers EARL A. GLICK & NORMAN GLICK
Produced by NORMAN GLICK, ED HUNT & KEN GORD • Written & Directed by ED HUNT
A HAL ROACH Studios Presentation

50 Top-Grossing Films

(WEEK ENDING FEBRUARY 15)

Compiled by Standard Data Corp., N.Y.

TITLE	DSTR	THIS WEEK $	RANK	LAST WEEK $	RANK	TOTALS CITIES	FIRST RUN	SHOW CASE	ROAD SHOW	THE-ATRES	WEEKS ON CHART	TOTAL TO DATE $
THE BETSY	AA	1,339,400	1		1	18	11	122		133	1	1,339,400
CLOSE ENCOUNTERS THIRD KIND	COL	1,276,332	2	1,489,164	2	20	11	90		101	13	25,725,321
THE GOODBYE GIRL	WB	1,095,106	3	528,211	6	20	18	116		134	11	8,368,148
SATURDAY NIGHT FEVER	PAR	1,091,907	4	982,675	2	20	13	104		117	9	16,907,987
COMA	UA	993,900	5	275,000	11	14	9	50		59	2	1,249,629
HIGH ANXIETY	FOX	922,549	6	659,500	5	13	15	49		64	8	2,635,329
THE ONE AND ONLY	PAN	830,397	7	941,550	3	19	18	65		83	2	1,817,385
TURNING-POINT	FOX	522,711	8	720,987	4	17	16	55		71	13	5,656,013
CANDLESHOE	BV	391,900	9			12	6	50		56	1	394,100
SEMI-TOUGH	UA	340,850	10	228,600	12	12	10	73		83	13	7,593,546
ADVENTURES WILDERNESS FAMILY	PIE	336,109	11	320,170	10	2		49		49	22	6,791,039
OTHER SIDE OF THE MOUNTAIN II	U	330,000	12			12	4	41		45	1	330,000
STAR WARS	FOX	311,172	13	323,469	9	19	17	12		29	38	59,995,911
LATE GREAT PLANET EARTH	PIE	242,991	14	484,245	7	5		66		66	5	1,032,659
JULIA	FOX	199,383	15	218,102	13	13	13	10		23	19	4,313,071
STARSHIP INVASIONS	WB	173,476	16			1		66		66	5	355,616
ACROSS THE GREAT DIVIDE	PIE	156,783	17	342,615	8	4		47		47	11	1,682,216
BLUE COLLAR	U	154,000	18			3	6			6	1	154,000
THE BOYS IN COMPANY C	COL	151,000	19	166,935	15	3	3	6		9	2	317,935
SHORT EYES	FL	122,500	20	45,000	31	3	2	18		20	18	1,147,661
THE GAUNTLET	WB	110,717	21	144,248	17	12	7	22		29	8	5,924,949
HERO AINT NOTHIN BUT SANDWICH	NW	87,700	22	45,500	30	3	4	5		9	2	125,390
BEYOND AND BACK	SUN	80,500	23	201,100	14	2	2	13		15	3	303,600
WHICH WAY IS UP	U	79,200	24	154,900	16	9	8	6		14	15	5,3??,694
THE LACEMAKER	NY	67,000	25	34,400	38	3	2	15		17	15	411,697
ONE GOD	WR	66,100	26	103,100,020	20	6	8	10		18	19	17,545,840

Production Material from the feature film *The Brain*

Now somewhat of a cult classic, this 1988 film from Shapiro-Glickehnaus was sold thanks to a good script and a great monster mockup. When the movie was pitched the financier was interested, but when she saw a model of what the brain would look like, in a box right before her eyes, she loved it and made a deal. The way this movie came together is an early example of the *Script Plus* concept in this book.

The monster, a giant brain with mind controlling thought and hallucinatory powers, is master-minded by the mad Dr. Blake, who runs a TV show called "Independent Thinkers." The only thing between the villain and world domination is brilliant but troubled high school student Jim Majelewski and his girlfriend, Janet.

Following a sketch that shows the fully-grown "The Brain" to scale, you will see pages of the storyboards for a scene from the movie that can be viewed on YouTube at http://www.youtube.com/watch?v=X-JdEPjjVU8.

The scene itself begins at 3:39 in the posted clip of 9:41 in length.

As you'll see if you compare the scene from the movie with the pages in the book, quite often the script and storyboards don't match what makes it onto the screen, but in this case it's pretty darn close, and we hope you enjoy the movie. After all, as this book went to press you could see the entire film in parts on YouTube.

Best of luck in your own filmmaking adventures!

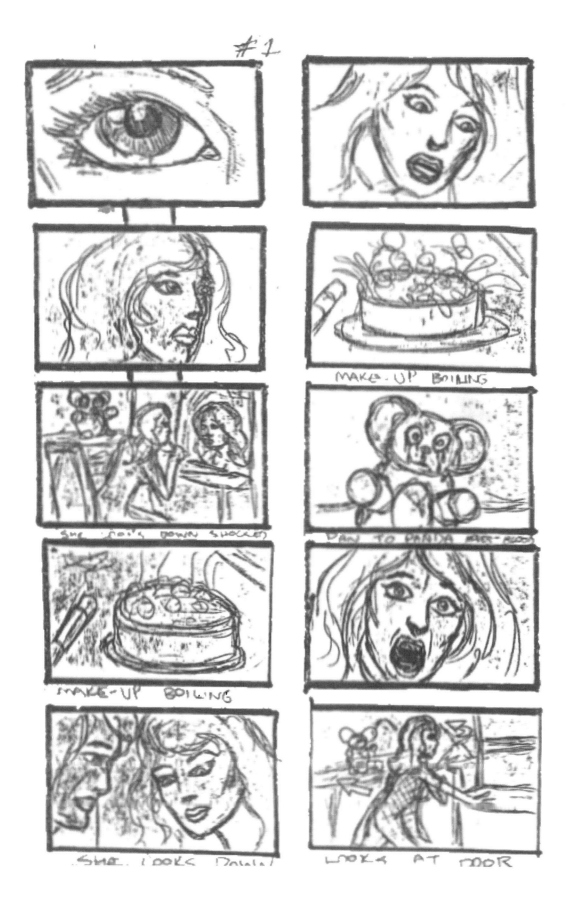

DOOR SLAMMING SHUT

GRABS BECKY

BECKY GRABS SCISSORS

SLAM

" SHE STABS CLAW

SHE BREAKS FREE

CLAW JUMPS FROM TV

SHE BACKS AWAY

HAND PROTRUDES

BACK AGAINST WALL

TENTACLES BUSTS THRU WALL

TENTACLE BUST OUT AROUND NECK

BLOOD GUSHES OUT

WALLS CLOSING IN

HER REACTION

HER POV OF THE TENTACLES

THINGS GET CLOSER

TENTACLES GRAB FEET

SCREAMS FOR MOTHER

BRAIN PULSATING

MIRROR

MIRROR W GIRL.

TENTACLE W SCISSORS

BRAIN SUPERIMPOSING

DOOR OPENS

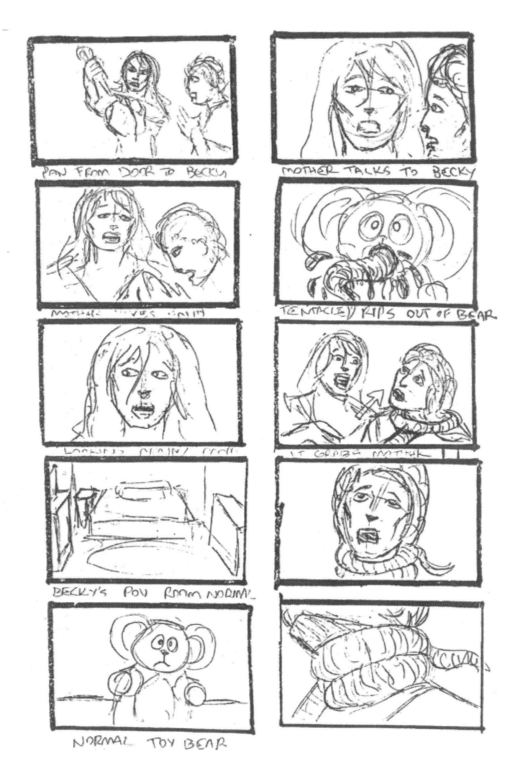

PAN FROM DOOR TO BECKY

MOTHER TALKS TO BECKY

MOTHER [...] YES [...]

TENTACLE) RIPS OUT OF BEAR

LOOKING [...]

IT GRABS MOTHER

BECKY'S POV FROM NORMAL

NORMAL TOY BEAR

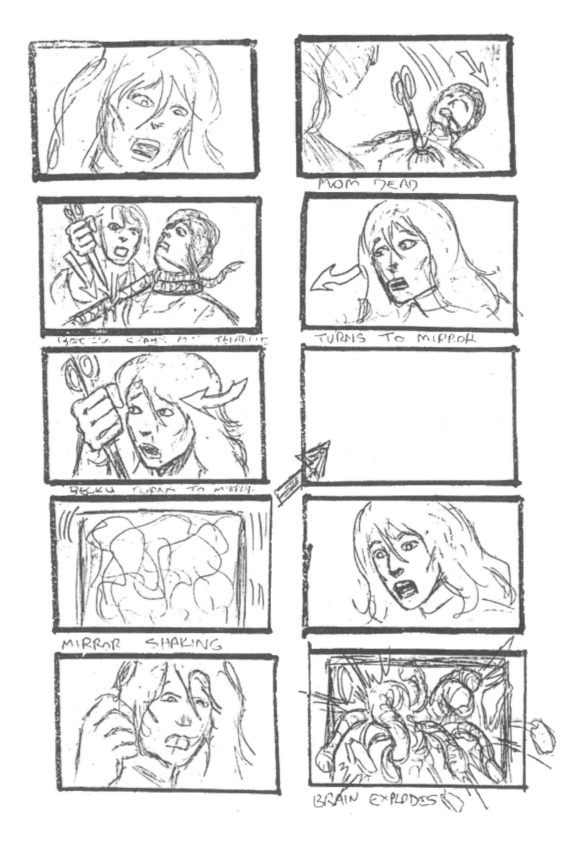

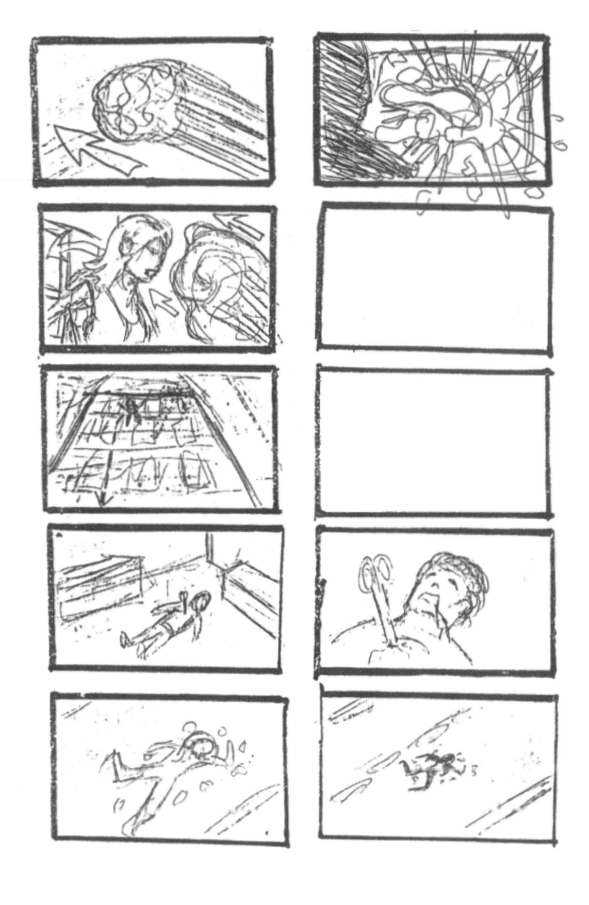

Made in the USA
San Bernardino, CA
17 December 2014